THE ESTATE ACTION INITIATIVE

This book is dedicated to Vilma Esmeralda Pinto.

The Estate Action Initiative

Council housing renewal, management and effectiveness

RICARDO R. PINTO
London School of Economics and Political Science

Avebury

Aldershot · Brookfield USA · Hong Kong · Singapore · Sydney

Published by
Avebury
Ashgate Publishing Limited
Gower House
Croft Road
Aldershot
Hants GU11 3HR
England

Ashgate Publishing Company
Old Post Road
Brookfield
Vermont 05036
USA

British Library Cataloguing in Publication Data

Pinto, Ricardo R.
The Estate Action Initiative:
Council Housing Renewal, Management and Effectiveness
I. Title
354.410086

ISBN 1 85628 358 5

Printed and Bound in Great Britain by
Athenaeum Press Ltd, Newcastle upon Tyne.

Contents

List of maps, figures and tables

Acknowledgements

My thanks are due, first and foremost, to Bob Bennett for being an encouraging and conscientious supervisor throughout the project. I am also grateful to Anne Power and Ron Johnston for their recommendations and comments on the work. Additional votes of thanks go to Chris Board, Jonathan Brooks, Mike Hebbert, Andrew McCoshan and John Sellgren. They may not remember their contribution, but I am grateful to them for providing helpful insights into various aspects of the research. Naturally, I am greatly indebted to the various organizations and individuals who gave generously of their time in order to make the project possible.

I owe a great debt of gratitude to everyone, past and present, in the Geography Postgraduate 'Lab' for providing such a fertile atmosphere for research and a network of support and friendship throughout my studies and subsequently. Thanks also to my proof-readers, David de Silva and Bruce Cannon. It really wouldn't have been the same without your help.

This research project has been undertaken with a grant from the Economic and Social Research Council. Additional financial support has been provided by the University of London's Central Research Fund and the Dudley Stamp Memorial Fund. I am grateful to these organizations for providing the resources which enabled me to conduct the work.

Lastly, thanks to Gisela Menke for putting up with every twist and turn of this project and for her consultant's role as regards converting my cumbersome tables, graphs, figures, maps and much else besides into illustrations which could be understood by the rest of the population. Above all, I will always be grateful to her for constantly reminding me that it is possible to enjoy life *and* write a book - in that order!

Preface

Housing in Britain, and public housing in particular, has undergone a decade of turbulent flux. This book analyzes the developments which have resulted in a changed emphasis and attitude towards council housing, investment patterns and systems, management organizations and forms of ownership. These changes mean that local housing authorities must adapt their policies and seize the new opportunities which present themselves. The discussion in chapter 2 provides the context for the main contribution of the book, which is an assessment of the Department of Environment's Estate Action (EA) initiative. The book argues that EA springs from this new housing context and, therefore, provides a useful framework with which to examine trends in English public housing. It enables the changes and frictions between central and local government to be analyzed, as well as indicating the potential consequences and outcomes of adaptation to the new housing setting.

A series of issues are examined which form the focus of the empirical analysis. Particular attention is placed on the following aspects: the structure of central/local relations arising from implementing the EA initiative, the effects of EA on financial and management effectiveness and EA's housing policy consequences. Chapter 3 discusses the policy context and outlines the methodology to be employed.

The main empirical analysis is presented in five chapters. In chapter 4, interviews with the EA Central team are reported as well as an analysis of documentary material on the background to EA. This discussion allows the origins and objectives of EA to be established from both the government's and the Department of Environment's viewpoints. In chapter 5, the results of a postal survey of all local authorities involved in EA are analyzed in detail. This enables chapter 6 to develop a general assessment of the local authority response to the EA initiative. Chapter 7 presents the responses of EA Central and Department of Environment Regional Offices to the survey findings. Finally, chapter 8 reports on four case-studies which assess EA in the context of specific localities. The analysis attempts to establish EA's success in implementing schemes via a discussion of managerial data, tenant opinions and staff assessments. EA's wider impact on local housing authorities' policies towards public housing is also evaluated and found to be influential.

Chapter 9 synthesizes the main empirical and theoretical findings and assesses the implications of the research for an understanding of the council housing system in general and EA in particular. Issues worth further investigation are also discussed.

List of abbreviations

AC	Audit Commission
AMA	Association of Metropolitan Authorities
BCA	Basic Credit Approval
DoE	Department of Environment
DSS	Department of Social Security
EA	Estate Action
EA HIPs	Estate Action Housing Investment Programme
GLC	Greater London Council
HAs	Housing Associations
HATs	Housing Action Trusts
HCC	Housing Consultative Council
HIPs	Housing Investment Programme
HMSO	Her Majesty's Stationary Office
HRA	Housing Revenue Account
LAs	Local Authorities
LAAs	Local Authority Associations
NFHA	National Federation of Housing Associations
PEP	Priority Estates Project
PESC	Public Expenditure Survey Committee
PSBR	Public Sector Borrowing Requirement
RFC	Rate Fund Contribution
ROs	(Department of Environment) Regional Offices
SCA	Special Credit Approval
TA	Tenants' Association
TC	Tenants' Choice
TMCs	Tenant Management Co-operatives
UHRU	Urban Housing Renewal Unit (Estate Action's former name)
VTs	Voluntary Transfers

Note: PEP normally refers to Politics and Economic Planning or Personal Equity Plans, however, this acronym is now well established in the housing literature in connection with the Priority Estates Project, and is used in this context only.

Part 1
COUNCIL HOUSING MANAGEMENT AND POLICY

1 Introduction

1.1 The subject of the book

Until the late 1970s, the council housing sector in Britain steadily expanded reaching 32% of the total housing stock. This expansion was largely due to a broad post-World War II consensus regarding the necessity of a welfare state in general, and the value of public housing in particular. However, with worsening economic conditions and the steady impact of monetary controls, public housing expenditure came under close scrutiny and eventually became a prime target for cuts. This started with the Labour government in 1975/76 but accelerated after 1979 with the election of a Conservative administration. Since 1974 council housing has declined to 25% of the stock, though clearly, it remains a major public service.

The Thatcher governments were particularly keen to reduce housing expenditure (one of the biggest local government expenditure items) in order to divert these resources to the private sector, bring inflation under control and meet the commitment to 'rolling back the frontiers of the state', leading towards a 'free market' society and economy:

> The monetarist approach was therefore to rely on the private sector for economic growth through the control of the monetary supply, interest rates and the Public Sector Borrowing Requirement. Government expenditure plans reflected this philosophy and substantial reductions were made in the planned expenditure on housing in the belief that private investment would make good the losses and allow housing requirements to be met. (Cooper, 1985, p.11)

In consequence capital investment, revenue subsidies and Housing Benefits were pared back dramatically thus contributing to a build-up of a major backlog of repairs. At the same time, the main political parties had come to accept owner occupation as the 'natural' form of tenure. This fitted smoothly with the Conservatives' policies towards privatization and the creation of a 'property owning democracy'. The stage was, therefore, set for a re-assessment of the role of the state in housing:

> ... during a period in which the welfare state came to be regarded as a barrier to economic recovery, where governments deliberately chose to meet the gap between the resources necessary to finance public expenditure and the revenue actually raised by cutting back on social services and on public housing in particular and when there was a general loss in confidence in state intervention and its desirability was seriously questioned. (Cooper, 1985, p.18)

In such a context, it was inevitable that council housing should experience an unprecedented period of turbulence. Housing has borne the brunt of the cuts in public expenditure in the 1980s with construction of new council units falling to below 8,000 per annum. Combined with the government's 'right to buy' legislation, this sector has experienced both a relative and an absolute decline in size and importance, resulting in a process of 'residualization'. In addition, there have been changes in the characteristics of the people living in council housing and the quality of accommodation available to them. This has resulted in a 'polarization' of the social characteristics of councils housing tenants. Nevertheless, the trends towards residualization and polarization cannot be ascribed solely to the Conservatives as their origins stretch back to the 1960s. They are processes which have merely been accelerated and exacerbated, largely as a result of recent housing policy. Such a focus on the inter-relationship between tenures means that (English, 1987, p.3):

> Attention has been drawn to the increasing coincidence between council housing and what may loosely be called the relatively poor or deprived, and between owner occupation and the non-poor. The argument is basically that, with a low level of new building, inadequate maintenance and the sale of substantial numbers of proportionately better quality houses, the public sector more and more provides poor accommodation for poor households which are unable to achieve the 'normal' tenure of owner occupation.

At the same time, the debate has also moved on from discussion of the effects of council house sales, residualization and polarization, to confront issues of management and ownership of council housing in the mid 1980s and early 1990s (see Clapham and English, 1987). More recently, issues such as housing affordability, mortgage arrears, building society repossession and depreciating capital assets have been the order of the day. The aim of this book is to focus on the management questions by analyzing the change in the housing role played by local authorities in England, particularly in the last decade and secondly, to analyze one of the main initiatives, Estate Action, which has sought to improve the situation.

There can be little doubht that the traditional style of council housing management has had its problems. These stemmed largely from an over-riding concern with the *production* of council units as opposed to the *management* and *maintenance* of the stock: "The almost exclusive reliance on councils as direct landlords caused the scale of council housing to be out of all proportion to the management skills or community needs of the local areas" (Power, 1987b, p.xiv). Council housing undoubtedly provided scope for change and intervention. The vast scale of council housing developments, its inefficiency and the remote style of council housing management (Burbidge *et al.*, 1981) created problems such as long delays for essential repairs, and insensitive and discriminatory allocation policies (see HRG, 1981). According to Cooper (1985, p.113), here it provided the government with the opportunity:

> ... to relieve tenants from the oppression of public sector landlords whose management style could be considered excessively bureaucratic, insensitive, discriminatory and paternalistic. The inefficiency displayed by public authorities in the management of their housing stock certainly provided ground for revision ... The belief that home ownership would improve standards of maintenance, geographical mobility and dwelling choice provided sufficient justification for a change in tenure.

Consequently, criticism of the traditional housing management style formed the justification for the proposals for smaller scale, more efficient and responsive forms of housing management, as well as for alternative landlords. This resulted in a phase of individual privatization under the 'right to buy' policy which has been highly successful, topping the one million mark within a decade. However, the government has also explored other forms of management style and encouraged the development of alternative housing agents such as Co-operatives and Housing Associations. These have received an unprecedented profile as more responsive and efficient, and it was expected that they would eventually take over responsibility for the provision of social housing. Recently, even more radical provisions have been made by the government enabling both the management and the ownership of council blocks or whole estates to be transferred to other landlords such as Housing Associations, Management Trusts, Housing Action Trusts and approved private landlords. This has led to a belief that the government is intent on total 'de-municipalization' for political, ideological and economic reasons.

The majority of these central policies result from government policies regarding monetarism, the welfare state, privatization and efficiency. Many councils have responded to the changed housing context and have begun to restructure their traditional management style, organization and administration. There has been much debate on the merits of decentralization along Neighbourhood Office lines as pioneered in Walsall and Islington (Seabrook, 1984; Hambleton and Hoggett, 1984; 1987); Housing Co-operatives of various sorts as in Islington and Glasgow (Clapham *et al.*, 1987; Clapham, 1989); or Trusts as in Liverpool and Greenwich; and Housing Associations (Maclennan *et al.*, 1989).

These developments have been extensively analyzed and evaluated. However, with the launching of the Priority Estates Project (PEP) in 1979 and The Urban Housing Renewal Unit (later renamed Estate Action) in 1985, central government also started to become involved in this debate in "an increasingly exhortatory if not directive role" (English, 1987, p.11). This role has been increasingly one of central government creating initiatives which attempt to work in partnership with councils in order to improve the situation which currently exists.

This set of issues provides the focus for the book. Both PEP (already well researched and directed essentially at estate based management) and Estate Action in particular, spring from an awareness of the problems confronting many housing authorities and represent a desire to help spread new ideas and practices, as well as promulgating central government policy. The book uses the example of Estate Action in order to evaluate the government's rationale for becoming involved in promoting certain management and ownership forms, the administrative and procedural issues involved and finally, the effect of the initiative.

Apart from its growing significance, there are two main reasons why Estate Action (EA) has been chosen as the focus of the book. First, EA attempts to promote a wide range of management initiatives which appeal to both local authorities and to central government. Hence, it provides an useful example for evaluating the degree to which both authorities and government are serious about experimenting with and developing new housing management styles. Secondly, and as important from the point of view of the book, there has been no major independent research yet conducted on EA, unlike the other initiatives mentioned above. Although a DoE sponsored study has begun at the time of writing (Coopers & Lybrand Deloitte), its focus is very different from that of this book. Given that nothing of an academic nature has been written or published on the EA programme, a series of specific issues are used to focus this investigation:

• *Central-local relations:* EA represents a central policy directed at localities which may not agree or approve of it. It is also directive in that resources can only be obtained and used in government-determined ways. Local government may not agree with the principles of privatization or tenant consultation, but is increasingly drawn into participation through pressures to obtain additional housing resource. How this translates itself in terms of the relationship between EA and local authorities, the balance of power and autonomy are central questions.

• *Procedure/implementation issues:* This issue is important because the implementation of the initiative influences the relationship between EA and local authorities and draws out problems which may result in inefficiencies. Charting these tensions and developments over time reveals a great deal about how government programmes evolve and whether government policy is actually impacting upon authority thinking and practice.

• *Management issues:* central government is highly critical of the 'traditional', centralized council management style and seeks to encourage authorities to experiment, in conjunction with the tenants, with a variety of alternatives including estate management. The extent to which EA has influenced authorities to decentralize their management structures, the tensions that arise from 'new' concepts such as privatization and whether estates are improved as a result, are thus of major concern.

• *Financial issues:* the general housing investment system (the Housing Investment Programme, or HIPs) is seen by central government as being inadequate and failing as regards 'problem' estates. The Estate Action alternative (EA HIPs) squares with, and is a key example of, the government's philosophy of diverting and 'targeting' resources to where they are considered (by central government) to be really needed. This is one of several such financial mechanisms which are much discussed but under-researched. It is important to analyze how authorities have reacted to these, the problems and advantages created and whether a better system results.

• *Housing policy issues:* this aspect relates to the government's insistence that local services be economic, efficient and effective. The question must be addressed as to whether this government initiative has achieved better conditions than the previous situation. Are the EA schemes having a positive impact on the estates? Are the tenants, for whom the service is being provided, satisfied with the results? What have been the wider impacts of the initiative upon housing policy, for example in affecting authorities' attitudes to tenant consultation and difficult-to-let estates? These and other relevant policy issues are also analyzed in this book.

1.2 Plan of the book

The above are the main themes which run throughout the discussion. The book is organized into three sections. Part I reviews the relevant literature, theory and describes the methodology employed in undertaking the research (Chapters 2 and 3). In Part II (Chapters 4 to 8) the main empirical evidence is presented and analyzed. A summary and a synthesis of the main empirical and theoretical conclusions together with the implications for policy are presented in Part III (Chapter 9).

The nature of the subject dictates that the book should begin by establishing the reasons which have created a powerful political stimulus for a shift in emphasis from production of dwellings to a deep concern with management, investment and ownership (Chapter 2). A series of factors are discussed which have given rise to the debate on the alternative to council housing envisaged by the current central administration, namely 'social' housing.

Having established the council housing context Chapter 3 moves on to analyze the policy setting that EA operates in. The rationale for the choice of initiative is expanded on and is followed by a discussion on the EA policy context, the relevant theoretical concepts and the methodology to be employed in the book. The overall hypotheses to be tested and the specific issues to be addressed are outlined.

The empirical analysis of the book (Part II) begins with an evaluation of the reasons behind the formation of the EA initiative, its priorities and its aims so as to pin-point the government's own motives in establishing EA, as well as the objectives of the civil servants charged with designing and running the initiative (Chapter 4). The views of the key agencies involved in its inception are considered. This is followed by a review of EA's published aims which makes use of secondary sources of information and interviews with the civil servants closely involved in generating the initiative (EA Central and their consultants) as well as those charged with implementing it (Regional Officers).

Given the virtual absence of data on EA, the next stage of the analysis uses a postal survey to allow a national perspective on the EA initiative to be developed. An attempt is made to understand how the initiative has been received by local authorities, how they have begun to reacted to it and how the implementation process has evolved. This is achieved through a survey of all authorities participating in the initiative. This was considered to be essential as there has been no independent research data on EA. Chapter 5 analyses this national survey data.

Because of the wide range of issues discussed in Chapter 5, the next chapter seeks to draw out the main themes that arise from the survey results. It also seeks to push the discussion further by investigating the local authorities' belief that EA resources are 'topsliced'; and concludes with an evaluation of the extent of EA's success in achieving each of the stated objectives in its remit. Chapter 6 thus seeks to present a coherent analysis of the operation of the initiative in a national context. It is a discussion based primarily on the local authorities' point of view.

This on its own, is not adequate in bringing out the main issues and tensions which arise out of an initiative which is substantially unlike anything which local housing authorities have been used to until fairly recently. Such a government-inspired scheme forces hard and novel decisions to be made. Frictions arise not only because of the unfamiliar relationships which have to be forged but also because of the perceptions of central control. These administrative and implementation issues are addressed in Chapter 7 through a further set of detailed interviews with the other two crucial actors in the policy community, namely, EA Central staff and the civil servants operating the DoE Regional Offices. Feedback is also sought on the main themes uncovered by the postal survey.

Chapter 8 reviews the results of four case-study schemes selected to provide a spread of regions, initiatives and types of authority. The purpose of the case-studies is to illustrate the detailed issues, processes and problems identified in the previous chapters. The chapter starts with a description of the history and context of each estate and scheme selected and is followed by an analysis of the existing statistical information on the EA procedures and the management statistics on the effectiveness of the four EA schemes. Reference is made to the effects of the schemes using both the assessment of housing officers involved with the developments taking place on the estates and tenant interviews. The second section analyses effectiveness by discussing the main procedural and implementation problems in each locality (as opposed to the national perspective) and is based upon interviews conducted with the key local authority officers involved with EA (such as housing directors and financial programmers). The final section of chapter 8 analyses the effectiveness of the EA scheme in terms of its impact upon various aspects of housing policy. In this way, the case-studies both reflect and amplify the results obtained via the national survey, the Regional Offices and EA Central interviews.

In Part III of the book (chapter 9), the overall conclusions are presented by relating the empirical evidence to the five objectives set above for the book. The chapter synthesizes the empirical and theoretical findings of the book, provides some policy recommendations and concludes with suggestions of potentially fertile avenues for further research on the EA programme.

2 Local authority urban housing management: Past, present and future

2.1 Introduction: A turbulent period for council housing

The growth of council housing (the provision of subsidized accommodation by local authorities) has been a major social achievement. From a position at the turn of the century where 90% of the housing was private rented in nature, today this accounts for roughly 8.5%. By contrast, the public rented sector soared to comprise about 30% of the total housing stock in the mid 1970s (about 5-5.5 million units), and rehoused 300,000 families per annum. The value of this stock has been conservatively estimated at £100bn (Architects' Journal, 1986).

Nevertheless, council housing is no longer regarded as a success. By the mid 1970s, the ambivalence which characterized much of the post-war housing policy was replaced by a view that owner occupation was the natural and normal form of tenure on both sides of the political spectrum. The function of council housing was seen as being to provide a more 'residual' or 'enabling' service for those who were neither able to afford home ownership nor capable of managing their housing on their own. The 1977 Housing Policy Review accepted such an analysis, arguing that the major housing problems had been dealt with and that minor problems were all that needed to be solved (Ball, 1983, p.3). This analysis was intensified and extended by the Conservatives from 1979 onwards to such an extent that 'de-municipalization', or an end to council housing, has become a feasible objective. These changes in attitude have had a profound effect on the local authority housing role, and naturally, the combination of changes in the late 1970s and 1980s has greatly affected the direction and focus of housing policy. Council housing increasingly caters for special needs. There is now a nominal rate of new build, even as the size of the stock is reduced in real terms. Standards of construction have been pared back and the levels of subsidies available have been steadily withdrawn. The ideas of optimal service provision have been shelved and the role of the market has been emphasized. These changes have essentially meant a new era for council housing.

This chapter seeks to analyze the reasons for this dramatic change in attitude towards the provision, management, maintenance and ownership of council housing. It analyses each of the elements which have stimulated and reinforced these changes in housing policy in order to context and explain the background to the development of newer housing management initiatives such as Neighbourhood Offices, Housing Co-operatives and the Priority Estates Project. This leads to a focus on Estate Action, which is the particular initiative which forms the thrust of this book.

2.2 The legacy of system-built and high-rise housing

High rise accommodation, which was widely opposed and rejected in the 1930s and 1940s in favour of suburban estates of cottage houses with gardens, eventually 'came to be seen instead as inevitable and unexceptional' (Dunleavy, 1981, p.2). This was predominantly because of the 'advocacy' of such a policy, in particular, the claims that it would cut completion times, increase productivity, lower costs and so offer hope of easing the burgeoning housing waiting lists and other problems. These proved stronger arguments than those against, which concerned the costs of the policy and the effect on residents of living in high-rise accommodation. These objections were swept aside and the system-built, high-rise housing policy ran its course. Between 1945 and 1975 about 440,000 high-rise flats were built and approximately 3 million people in British cities were displaced and rehoused by the clearance and redevelopment programme.

In fact, in the 1960s, all forms of high-rise were more than twice as expensive per square foot as the three bedroom houses preferred by the general public. In addition: "... over 37 percent more dwellings could have been built at no extra cost [representing a housing gain of 78,000 dwellings at a time of acute housing crisis], while the dwellings provided could have been on average over 30 percent larger than the high flats actually built" (Dunleavy, 1981, p.87). This did not turn out to be a cheaper policy than constructing 'traditional' dwellings.

The vast majority of the British population would prefer to live in a house rather than a flat yet the great majority of the dwellings built in this period were in the form of high-rise flats. The residents themselves have generally tended to be critical of their appearance and sterile environment and arguments exist that this type of local authority accommodation may have unfavourable effects on families with children. Similarly, the elderly are critical of the loneliness and isolation and this type of housing is also said to lead to more anxiety of safety, for example of children, and greater scope for vandalism and crime (see Power, 1987b; Coleman, 1985).

Recently, further issues have arisen which seem to have sealed the fate of this type of public housing - at least in Britain (but see Bulos and Walker, 1987, for a contrast with other European countries). They tended to be oppressively built at high density with a ugly grey finish. The intense communality, the block structure and height, the ubiquitousness of common parts that were neither clearly public nor private and the fact that there was actually too much unused open space in these constructions, all added to the difficulties in many of these estates (Power, 1987b, p.142). Communal parts of the buildings such as lifts, entrances, underground garages and the decks and bridges represented added problems as these were easily damaged or inadequately designed and unable to withstand the wear and tear of so many users. The police generally found them hard to protect, caretakers problematic to maintain, and residents frightening (Hough and Mayhew, 1983).

Structural defects arising from system-building techniques are coming to light, bringing important financial implications. Apart from the issue of structural soundness (e.g. the Ronan Point incident), certain industrial building systems have failed to weather-proof, resulting also in poor soundproofing, as well as in condensation and mould formation (Burbidge *et al.*, 1981). The Association of Metropolitan Authorities' (AMA) study 'Defects in Council Housing' found that over £5bn would have to be spent on the five million system-built dwellings, including the tower blocks built in the 1960s and 1970s in order to reverse the years of decline in public housing maintenance investment and to bring them back into a fit and acceptable state (AMA, 1984). The issue of the level of disrepair in council housing is discussed in greater detail in section 2.3.

These findings suggest that high-rise flats are more unpopular than houses. The social stigmatization resulting in part from inadequate lettings and management policies was also crucial in causing some estates to become unpopular and set in train the cycle of decay, neglect and finally abandonment of dwellings and facilities. Stigmatization eventually became so overwhelming that a number of councils had little choice but to demolish blocks and even whole estates. Liverpool and Glasgow among other councils, have already carried out major demolitions of fairly new housing of this type - housing which has yet to be paid for and which is much needed.

The perceived failure of system-built and high-rise housing and the socio-managerial problems which they give rise to, have been important factors in helping to stimulate a willingness to search for different solutions to the council housing sector. It is here that some of the greatest housing management problems occur, in the so-called 'difficult-to-let' or 'problem' estates, where the design problems are just one element of a predicament which traditional housing management organization, methods and policies have been unable to cope with effectively. Even so, recent work has begun to demonstrate that contrary to normal assumptions in Britain:

> ... far from high rise housing being a physical and social disaster, many of the blocks provided satisfactory accommodation for which there was sustained demand ... It is vital that new and imaginative schemes are tried and advertised, to demonstrate that high rise can, in proper circumstances, be appropriate and decent dwellings.
> (Bulos and Walker, 1987, p.5)

Two major trends highlighted in various works (English, 1982; Clapham and Maclennan 1983; and more recently Forrest and Murie, 1988) also have enormous implications for the housing management task facing local authorities. These are the fact that a huge backlog of disrepair in housing of all tenures is mounting and secondly, the changes in the nature and composition of council tenants themselves have quickened over the last decade. These are discussed in turn.

2.3 The changing nature and condition of the stock

> The maintenance of council houses affects not only the quality of life for the families living in them, but also the value of the public assets involved. Yet, there has been a history of neglect of maintenance of many of the 4.8 million council houses in England and Wales.
> (Audit Commission, 1986c, p.1)

The opening statement of the Audit Commission's report, 'Improving Council Housing Maintenance' was highly critical of the build-up of a backlog of maintenance work which led to the provision of a unsatisfactory service for tenants. The Commission argued that there were too many areas of wastage (e.g. too much work done on an expensive jobbing basis) and called for steps to remedy the backlog of maintenance work as: "The benefits of improved management are likely to be substantial ... as much as £700 million a year." (1986c, p.3).

The Commission's report endorsed the AMA's estimate of £20bn as the cost of dealing with immediate repairs. It was also critical of local authority housing management, such as the unrealistic rents, excessive units, administrative costs and high staffing levels which co-existed with falling numbers of council houses. It recommended that central government release £8bn in accumulated council house sale receipts for housing capital expenditure; that local authorities shed staff; and attract private investment in new partnership building programmes.

There are undoubtedly problems with the maintenance of council property. Authorities are only too aware that this constitutes the biggest single tenant complain, that it serves as a motive for the creation of Tenants' Associations (TAs) and provides a stimulant for tenants to either buy or manage their own dwellings. The National Consumer Council noted that the problem had been exacerbated by the fact that local authorities have traditionally had a *repair* rather than a *maintenance* policy and that inefficiency in local authority operation has meant that the stock has deteriorated (National Consumer Council, 1979). Many local authorities are thus struggling with the basic problem of trying to keep their stock in a wind and water-tight position, let alone ensuring that it meets the needs and aspirations of tenants.

One must, however, be wary of being overly critical of local authorities as factors largely beyond their control have helped accelerate the process of decay and decline. A result of the 'right to buy' legislation is that predominantly the best properties, usually houses with gardens in good locations, are sold, with the consequence that the public sector is increasingly left with the less popular properties. This is exacerbated by the fact that housing sales are occurring at a time when the construction defects of much mass/system-built local authority property of the 1960s and 1970s are coming to the fore, so that many tenants presently live in dwellings which are damp, difficult to heat and may be injurious to health. To these must be added other problems indicated earlier, such as the design and estate layout which often create oppressive and hostile environments. Local authorities are now having to come to terms with the age of some of their stock, particularly that which was built between the wars, much of which is in urgent need of modernization and renovation.

This situation has perversely coincided with an unprecedented squeeze by central government on investment in public housing (an important issue addressed in section 2.6). The reduction in capital spending means that repair and modernization programmes have had to be cut back. There has also been pressure on Housing Revenue Accounts (HRAs) as a result of the reduction in central government subsidy, and a squeeze on Rate Fund Contributions (RFC). This has helped force up rents dramatically which has coincided with high levels of arrears. In effect, all this has meant that *lack of income* has prevented necessary repairs from being carried out by many councils. The combined effects of the council house sales policy, a legacy of an ageing and often structurally unsound stock and central government restrictions on capital expenditure are, not surprisingly, helping to exacerbate the seemingly intractable nature of housing management problems. The AMA's studies (1983; 1984; and 1985) of defects in council housing concluded that the capital cost of reversing the drastic slide in the maintenance of property would total £19 billion:

- £5bn on special repairs to 500,000 non-traditional houses built 1945-55;
- £5bn on 1 million system-built dwellings including tower blocks built in the 1960s and 1970s, and an undisclosed sum to finance demolitions;
- £8bn on 450,000 pre-war traditionally built units at end of 60 year life;
- £1bn on urgent repairs of post-war traditionally built council houses.

The National Federation of Housing Association's (NFHA) influential 'Inquiry in British Housing', which was chaired by the Duke of Edinburgh also concluded that it was necessary to deal with the urgent maintenance problems. It too recommended the immediate release by central government of council house sale funds for local authority capital expenditure and the introduction of a wider based system of rent pooling in order to make £6bn 'available at once' to deal with the most urgent repairs and alterations needed (NFHA, 1985). 'Faith in the City', commissioned by the Archbishop of Canterbury, unlike the government, was not confident about the private sector's ability to take over the local authorities' housing task and concluded: "We can see no alternative to, and recommend an expanded housing programme of new building and improvement financed by public expenditure." (Archbishop of Canterbury's Commission, 1985). More generally it also recommended decentralization of local authority services and a complete overhaul of the system of housing finance, including the cost of mortgage tax relief.

Numerous high-profile reports stressed that council housing had been allowed to fall into a disgraceful condition and advocate rapid change in order to arrest the downward spiral. Although there was not much of a reaction from central government, this unsatisfactory state of affairs acted as a powerful stimulus for innovation and change in terms of management organization and practices which attempt to stabilize and even improve the situation by generating greater efficiency. The development of the new housing management initiatives which begun to emerge in the 1980s both at local and central government level (such as the Priority Estates Project and Estate Action) testify to this.

2.4 Changing socio-economic characteristics of tenants

> Stated simply, there is a closer association between the lowest income groups in the population and the shrinking public housing sector (Forrest and Murie, 1990)

This section discusses what is generally termed the 'residualization' and 'polarization' of the public housing sector. It is now accepted by most housing commentators that the public sector is catering increasingly for the lower income and the most dependent groups in society such as the elderly, the unemployed, one-parent families, long-term sick, low paid and ethnic minorities (Forrest and Murie, 1990; Pinto, 1992a; 1992b). This has profound implications for the local authorities' landlord role, as the proportion of council tenants living in poverty increases and more of them come to rely on various elements of the welfare state. In future, the arrears case of a housing assistant is also likely to be a social security recipient, a frequent user of health services and/or on a case-load of a social worker. Tenants' problems tend to be multidimensional and many agencies may be involved in its solution, thereby necessitating effective co-ordination between the housing department and various council directorates and other agencies such as the DSS (HRG, 1981). The demands of groups with special housing needs such as the elderly and the mentally handicapped are forcing housing managers into contact with other professionals. In other words, housing departments have found themselves drawn into a more social role and: "The increasing portion of society's vulnerable groups who live in the public sector is putting increasing strain on housing management and posing a challenge which traditional methods are unable to meet." (Clapham, 1987a, p.112) These have acted as further stimuli for authorities to develop policies and management initiatives capable of dealing with the situation.

Although the twin problems of a deteriorating stock and the changing social and economic status of tenants affect most of the public sector to some degree, the impact varies from place to place. For example, the 'right to buy' is having a differential geographical impact and is exacerbating tenure differences between areas (Hamnett and Randolph, 1987; Forrest, 1987). Nevertheless: "... the direction of change for all or virtually all local housing authorities is the same, as are the resultant pressures, even if their weight may vary." (Clapham, 1987a, p.112). There is also a geographical dimension to the incidence of the changes within local housing authorities as the problems are concentrated in certain areas or estates. These tend to be the areas with the most unpopular and badly deteriorated housing or 'difficult estates' which, because of the allocation system, are usually inhabited by the most deprived populations (Clapham and Kintrea, 1986; Pinto, 1992b), and which represent 'the residualised part of a residual sector' (Clapham and Maclennan, 1983). They are subject to stigma and alienation from the rest of society.

The breakdown of social order in these areas and the high rates of unemployment, poverty, vandalism and rent arrears suggest a need to alter traditional methods of housing management which are somehow inadequate. It has also brought to the fore the uncertainty and conflicts surrounding the council housing management role and has resulted in its reappraisal and in attempts to change existing council practices through local experiments. However, no consensus has emerged and three different emphases are being pursued. The first stresses the *contractual* nature of the landlord-tenant relationship and seeks to distance housing management from a social role (see HRG, 1981); the second approach seeks to embrace the *social* role more fully (such as Neighbourhood Decentralization); and the last to *devolve* control over housing management to tenants themselves, such as through TMCs (see Clapham, 1987a, pp.114-123, Emphasis Added).

2.5 Housing management: The previously forgotten issue

Council housing, once a privilege, has steadily become housing to be avoided. Commentators contend that the housing management system is:

> ... increasingly centralised, much of it uniform and top-down, and parts of it are in the process of breaking down. Today it is public housing which is often regarded as slum housing; it is local authority housing departments which are frequently seen as inefficient seemingly uncaring landlords of the poor ... we can no longer take for granted the viability of the old housing system, with the old agenda, ideals and methods. (Bonnerjea, 1987)

In order to obtain a firmer understanding of why so much emphasis is now being placed on improved public housing management (as well as alternative landlords) and why traditional practice is so criticized by the government as well as organizations such as the Audit Commission, it is necessary to adopt an historical perspective which analyses the organization and development of housing departments; the main problems facing public housing management in Britain; and finally, the formation of a 'consensus' on the need for new thinking and the re-assessment of public housing management and its structures.

2.5.1 Organization and evolution of housing departments

It is important to note that council housing management is in a unique position in local government in the sense that the Secretary of State and the DoE have virtually "no jurisdiction in regard to the management of the local authorities' housing stock" (Macey, 1982, p.51), except for limited responsibilities under the 1957 and 1980 Acts. There are few enforceable standards and the government plays an advisory role in the running of the local authority housing stock. Central government has not laid down a framework for local government to carry out its duties as a landlord, such as requiring local housing authorities to set up a committee to run its housing stock and appoint housing managers. This compares with the political and legal framework concerning other local services and has led to the argument that it is not the lack of control and decision-making but the lack of a basic frame of operations which makes it difficult for local authorities to operate as good landlords and managers (Power, 1987b). To understand why this is, it is pertinent to review the origins of housing departments.

The first real attempt to chart the history of council housing management was Power's work (1987) which contends that the main reason why attention to housing management *per se* has been neglected, is because authorities became landlords concerned primarily with housing construction and finance. Little attention was spared on the maintenance and running council housing. This is borne out by a detailed analysis of the evolution of local authority housing departments, concentrating on a series of reports on council housing by the Central Housing Advisory Committee (CHAC).

In its reports on the management of council estates (especially 1945; 1953; 1955), CHAC argued that the approach to council management was too piecemeal and disjointed because of the conflicting roles of different professional departments in charge of housing functions. The reports also illustrated that the landlord management structure was remote, badly organized and unconcerned with the wider social dimensions of the slum clearance and rehousing policies being carried out. In the mid 1950s came even greater housing activity due to the twin policies of mass slum clearance and construction. As flats became more fashionable, blocks became dense and waiting lists rose dramatically. Under the intense pressure for housing, allocations became the critical area of housing management and estate level management was sacrificed. Landlord-tenant contact became more limited, arrears were generated and neglected, as were repairs and cleaning.

A further report found that less than 50% of local authorities in its survey had created housing departments and that these were normally only responsible for limited parts of housing management such as lettings and welfare which were based in other departments (CHAC, 1959, p.3). It advocated detailed, unitary, localized management including door-to-door rent collection, local management control of repairs, close co-operation between landlord and tenants, need for management training and even called for tenant and manager involvement in housing design. However, it failed to suggest coherent strategies for local authorities to follow.

The 1960s saw an important swing away from new housing construction in 'green field' sites and back to inner city slum clearance and replacement. A large proportion of those becoming council tenants were from the poorer sections of the working class and the houses they moved into were usually large new high-rise, high-density blocks of flats, many of which were later to become the least desirable of the council housing stock. This period of great dynamism and change was to revolutionize housing management policy and the structure of local authorities, as well as to intensify the problems faced by housing management because of the complex and weak housing management structure (Cullingworth, 1966). Perversely, these arrangements became almost unworkable when all local authorities were reorganized in 1974. Housing departments expanded hugely from an average of 1,400 units per local authority to 14,000 dwellings in 1975 thus making them even more remote to tenants and adding confusion and unwieldy structures into the management organization (Power, 1987b).

The last development came with the Housing Services Advisory Group (HSAG), the body which replaced CHAC. Its report 'Organising a Comprehensive Housing Service' was received as a progressive step towards giving more coherence to fragmented housing management. It prescribed a central housing directorate covering housing policy, development management, private sector matters and advisory issues (HSAG, 1978 and HRG, 1981, p.56). However, the Achilles Heel of what would have been a significant development was the scale of the operation which acted to reinforce the centralised organization of local housing departments (Power, 1987b, p.88):

> The Housing Services Advisory Group was so concerned to advance the unification of housing functions in a single department that it paid no regard at all ... to the urgent need to address the size and scale of the public housing stock, and the economic and management viability of an operational unit of the size it was proposing.

Nevertheless, it did contribute to a search for alternative housing management organizations which were less complex, cumbersome and slow. Thus it was only after management problems became startlingly obvious that the preoccupation with house-building began to dissipate and serious thought began to be given to the management organization and role. The current situation in many local authorities has largely stemmed from this haphazard history and evolution of local authority housing management structures. It has also proved a natural focus for Conservative attention and reform.

2.5.2 The main problems confronting council housing

One of the most thoughtful and comprehensive, though sadly neglected analyses of the problems faced by many council housing departments, was the Housing Research Group's study of four local authorities (HRG, 1981). It is worth listing the immediate housing problems which it identified:

• *General concerns:* variations in the cost of management and maintenance; levels of rent arrears; anti-social behaviour; problem estates; and social and tenure polarization.

• *Difficulties in getting the basic work done:* the cost of keeping rent arrears down; delays and difficulties of re-letting empty council properties; over-stretched and unreliable repairs service; difficulties in the maintenance of communal areas; increasingly bureaucratic housing management; and the increasing but uncertain social role of local housing management.

• *Contradictions within the housing management role:* large scale housing management versus the ability to respond to individual circumstances; allocation to those in need versus minimizing management problems; easier to manage versus cheaper to build; higher expectations but assumed ineffectiveness; and organizational simplicity versus integration.

• *Operational problems in housing management:* uncertainty for staff and tenants about what to achieve and expect; lack of definition about certain types of work; difficulties in supervision; difficulties for staff and tenants in contacting each other; overloading of many housing staff; inappropriate use of staff; lack of routine checking of work done; lack of regular 'feed-up' of information from local to head office; and the lack of co-ordination between housing and other departments and agencies.

• *Weaknesses underlying the practical difficulties faced by authorities and tenants:* ambiguities in the definition of the obligations of councils and tenants and how they should 'normally' operate; lack of standards for monitoring activities and services; confusion over the responsibility for 'unavoidable' social problems; and the lack of control over the quality of services provided by other departments (HRG 1981, pp.148-155).

This analysis of the management problems faced by council housing has been substantiated and expanded more recently by a series of influential papers by Anne Power who argues that the state of council housing has become critical because of scale of construction, provision for the homeless and slum clearance which combine to force upon local authorities conflicting requirements and obscure the growing problems of management. These lie: "... at the root of the crisis and it was inevitable that local authorities would first be overtaken by the scale of their operation and then be prevented by the very scale from responding to the crisis it provoked." (Power, 1987a, p.7), although she later stresses that these issues were by no means sufficient reasons for necessarily forcing local authorities to be bad and inefficient managers (Power, 1988).

The central contention is that while local authorities did achieve many of the post-war housing goals, they were forced into trying to provide for a variety of needs requiring commensurably complex and varied housing management responses. However, given their size, inflexibility, fragmentation and centralised housing management structure, they could not provide flexible and adaptable renting styles and systems, but being the major landlords they were forced into precisely that role. The result was that whole groups were either uncatered for (such as single people) or allocated inappropriate accommodation (such as families with young children in tower blocks). The housing service also had some unusual characteristics compared to other services which compounded the difficulties and inhibited the development of appropriate management organizations. These characteristics were:

• A failure to distinguish between housing *administration* and *service*, which resulted in thorough administrators but poor housing managers.

• *Political control* to a larger degree than in other services resulted in politicians trying to keep rents down (to retain votes), which led to low levels of public stock maintenance. The better off tenants moved to superior accommodation by either exercising their 'right to buy' or by using the transfer system. The more vulnerable households, given their lack of political power, were generally forced to accept poor services in unpopular estates.

• Thirdly, the widespread *belief that housing management was unnecessary*. Council housing provision *per se* was seen as being both sufficient and the solution. Better housing conditions would get rid of the slum problem, hence integrated locally based housing management was considered to be unnecessary. Staff training was almost non-existent; housing management did not offer high professional status; and vital jobs such as repairs and caretaking were reduced and downgraded (Power, 1987a, pp.7-18).

The culmination of all these factors was first officially identified by the DoE's 'An Investigation of Difficult to Let Housing', in terms of poor design, discriminatory allocation procedures, incompetent management, serious lack of demand, high turnover of tenants and general neglect of the worst estates. The investigation concluded that the structure of housing departments was too inflexible, too remote from tenants and too fragmented to cope with the pressures of the then rapidly expanding stock (Burbidge *et al.*, 1981, Vol.1). It confirmed the existence of major housing problems and the seriousness of the state of council housing.

There is evidence in all major cities, and particularly London, that the heavy concentration of public housing, difficulty in letting, the concentration in flats and high levels of deprivation have all had a direct bearing on management performance (see Bonnerjea, 1987; Duncan and Kirby 1983, p.97). But the fact that such a crisis also afflicts the estates in smaller and relatively trouble-free authorities suggests that additional factors also affect both the unpopularity and the problems of the management of certain estates (CES, 1984). These include such factors as poverty, isolation and stigma so that there exists almost everywhere in Britain, some form of unpopular or neglected council housing which ends up being 'hard-to-let', or otherwise known as 'dump' or 'difficult' estates.

There is an appreciable sense of mounting crisis in the most distressed local authorities which has been intensified by the loss of confidence (exemplified by the demolitions taking place and degree of staff turn-over in housing departments), which has resulted from such recent developments as the 'right to buy' legislation, the cuts in public subsidy and the encouragement of alternative housing agents at all costs. More recently, the extension of Compulsory Competitive Tendering to white collar areas such as housing management, has been a significant factor affecting the morale of housing professionals. All the earlier issues can be regarded as further stimuli which were to create an atmosphere extremely conducive to change.

2.5.3 Need for re-assessment and new thinking

To summarize, the 1980s was a period when it became clear that there was an urgent need for re-thinking and re-assessment in the area of local authority housing. Today, housing management is not only dealing with a wider range of stock and tenants than ever before, but for a variety of reasons, the stock is also deteriorating more rapidly and an ever increasing portion of council tenants require some form of special response (as discussed earlier). This is all aggravated by the fact that it is occurring in a period of economic stagnation. Under the impact of a severe economic climate, the staunch commitment to increasing owner occupation (even in late 1992), the continuing decline of the private rented sector (see Figure 2.1 for the tenure changes which are occurring) and severe public expenditure cuts, it can be argued that what it is happening is not merely a short term fluctuation (HRG, 1981, p.35). The fundamental problems are not likely to be reversed in the foreseeable future. The public sector in general, and council housing management in particular, have entered a new phase. There is a growing awareness that a major re-assessment is required and that there is a need to move away from the traditional systems which have been shown to be either unsatisfactory or unworkable. If management is to make a significant contribution to the maintenance of the social and physical conditions of council housing in the 1990s *and* to respond to the challenges set by the new government policies, it must adapt quickly and in ways which meet the real needs of both the tenants and the properties. New and innovative management structures are emerging and developing, but it is also important to stress that there is general agreement that council housing will continue to be important well into the future. The Conservatives, despite their (continuing) over-riding commitment to owner occupation and revitalization of the private renting sector, no longer believe that large numbers of low income households can, or indeed should, buy their homes. Certainly, few dispute that the level of mortgage arrears and repossessions affected disproportionately those with low income and few financial reserves. Additionally, because households go through stages in life requiring temporary rented accommodation, it is imperative that rented housing is provided for many different ages, social groups and incomes (Institute of Housing, 1987).

There now exists a degree of consensus in both academic and political circles that council housing is beset with major problems and that this crisis is not merely a matter of resources and capital expenditure restrictions, but that the scale and size of council management are wrong and that the monopoly local authorities exercise over rented housing should be changed (Griffiths and Holmes, 1985). We have already analyzed the academic literature, but a political awareness of the debate has also emerged. Tenure strategy strongly influences voting behaviour and the two main parties have traditionally had very different interests *vis à vis* council housing, one to protect and preserve it and the other to reduce or eliminate it (Short, 1982). However, with the success of the 'right to buy' legislation, Labour has had to reappraise its council housing policy, which has converged towards that of the current government.

The housing debate is today dominated by questions which challenge many of the basic assumptions underlying the last 70 years of council housing development. Many traditional policies and practices are being questioned, including the very necessity of council housing. The next section thus analyses in detail the factors which have brought to a head the revolution in council housing in the last decade, even though the origins date back to long before 1979 (Malpass, 1990).

The previous discussion has tried to pin-point what is going wrong with council housing and why the management element has been left out of the equation. This section seeks to illustrate some of the crucial elements which have contributed to the current state of what has been described as a 'crisis' in the council housing sector (English, 1982; Audit Commission, 1986a; 1986b). The aim is to demonstrate that the present government has had an explicit vision of how council housing fits into the economic and social priorities of the nation. These issues are analyzed below, together with an account of the legislation enacted by the government in order to meet its objectives.

2.6 A new era for council housing

The Conservatives took office in 1979 seeking to transform the British economy by a return to the values and practices of the free market. From the Budget of 1980, it was clear that Britain had a government for whom improving living standards for families and helping the worst housed to get decent accommodation were not urgent priorities. Rather, inflation was to be brought down at all costs, tax on income was to be reduced, as was the whole scale of the public sector of the economy (Donnison and Ugerson, 1982, pp.160-163).

By the late 1970s the function of council housing was firmly relegated to providing a 'residual' service for those who were neither able to afford owner occupation nor capable of managing their housing on their own. From the Conservatives' ideological stance, housing should be seen as a private commodity which is best provided through the market. The role of the state has effectively changed to cater for the needs of this residual section of the population which cannot fend for itself in the private market. The basic Conservative housing tenets have been seen as being rather straight-forward: owner occupation is the 'natural' tenure; the (mass) housing crisis is over; the private sector can, and should be revived; and the public sector is over subsidized and too generally subsidized (Short, 1982).

This is too simple a characterization. Conservative housing policy has evolved and changed rapidly in the 1980s (see Minford *et al.*, 1987;

Henney, 1985; Coleman, 1988; 1989), but since it is argued that the housing problem has basically been solved and owner occupation is a superior tenure form, it is not surprising, therefore, that council housing in particular has received the brunt of the public expenditure cuts (75% in real terms since 1979), along with attempts to privatize council housing (right to buy) and to transfer it away from local authority ownership (Housing Associations, Tenants' Choice and Housing Action Trusts). Needless to say, such policies have created intense opposition from local government and hostility between central and local government (see Cochrane, 1985; Karn, 1985; Duncan and Goodwin, 1988; and McCoshan and Pinto, 1991).

The rest of this chapter analyses the ways in which central government has influenced council housing since 1979. It is important to bear in mind that, in many ways, these developments represent the extension of trends established under the previous Labour government or even before that (see Malpass, 1990). The difference is that throughout the 1980s, the emphasis has changed and become more extreme so that the aim now seems to be an end to council housing itself. The details are presented below, starting with the important changes to local government housing finance and investment as this is pertinent to the rest of this book (particularly the capital element); before going on to analyze various policies which have affected council housing significantly in the last decade; as well as those which will sculpt the future shape of council housing.

2.6.1 Investment: Financial policies towards council housing

i) The Housing Revenue Account (HRA): Given the Conservatives' commitment to reduce the burden of public expenditure (PSBR), it was inevitable that major changes would occur to public housing finance. A new subsidy system was introduced in Part VI of the Housing Act, 1980 based on the principle of *deficit financing*. Basically this means that the amount of subsidy received by an authority depends upon an evaluation of its annual expenditure on servicing its debt and its management and maintenance (expenditure); and the amount which the authority can be expected to raise from rent and rate fund contributions (income) towards meeting the costs. Local authorities were expected to balance their housing expenditure and shortfalls were to be met from increased rents and/or rates. The Secretary of State was given much greater discretionary powers to determine subsidy levels, which meant that this legislation has been used to reduce the general exchequer subsidies, thus undermining the main mechanisms behind the creation of council housing, such as historic cost financing and rent pooling (Hughes, 1987). In 1980-81 the subsidy was £1,423m. This was reduced in 1990-91 to £510m (see Table 2.1).

Table 2.1: Exchequer subsidies to local authority Housing Revenue Accounts (England & Wales)

Year		£m cash	£m at 1987-8 prices
1979-80	out-turn	1,274	2,237
1980-81	..	1,423	2,106
1981-82	..	906	1,224
1982-83	..	536	674
1983-84	..	280	336
1984-85	..	342	394
1985-86	..	409	444
1986-87	..	534	561
1987-88	est. out-turn	464	473
1988-89	plans	459	422
1989-90	..	490	432
1990-91	..	510	441

Source: Malpass, 1990, Table 7.3, p.141

Table 2.2: Sales and new building by local authorities

Year	All sales	New building
1979	41,665	69,734
1980	81,485	70,824
1981	102,825	49,407
1982	201,880	30,176
1983	145,585	29,823
1984	103,180	29,185
1985	92,295	23,478
1986	88,748	18,532
1987	105,567	16,089
1988	175,736	13,705
1989	109,439	12,201

Source: Housing and Construction Statistics various years; and Local Housing Statistics (1988-1989)

By reducing the level of subsidies the finance system resulted in dramatically increased rent levels throughout the housing authorities. Loughlin argues that the government's objective was to destroy the historic cost financing system by using the subsidy system to push up rents to a level nearer to current market value. Such an objective is confirmed by the fact that: "what is essentially taking place is not a reduction in subsidy but a restructuring of the nature of subsidies" (Loughlin, 1986, p.108). Thus although the housing subsidies fell by £1,000 million between 1981 and 1985, this was totally offset by the growth of income-related rent assistance claimed by council tenants. It is worth noting, however, that because of the increase in rents, the level of council tenant rent arrears significantly increased (Audit Commission, 1984). But, as importantly, a powerful incentive was created for the better-off council tenants to exercise their right to buy which thus reinforced the transformation of the public rented sector into a residual or targeted welfare sector (see Malpass, 1990).

ii) The Capital Account: Until the late 1970s local authorities were largely free to set their own capital programmes on housing expenditure, while central government generally only exercised indirect influence via the operation of the subsidy system. However, increasing pressure on public expenditure, high inflation and interest rates resulted in a perceived need to rationalize public housing investment. The result was an attempt to introduce cash limits to control public expenditure and so a system of annual local authority bids and central government allocation began under the Housing Act, 1974. This culminated in a major review of housing policy, the 1977 Green Paper 'Housing Policy a Consultative Document', which proposed the creation of the Housing Investment Programmes (HIPs). It was sold to authorities as a:

> New form of housing plan, based on a comprehensive assessment of the local housing situation. The main element will be a reasoned capital budget covering the local authority's own capital spending plans - related to its broad housing strategy - for the coming 4 years. On the basis of these plans the government will make capital spending allocations to each authority. Once the allocations are settled, authorities will be free to go ahead with the minimum of intervention by central government. (DoE, 1977, para 9.06)

However, there was another aspect to HIPs of crucial importance which became patently obvious after 1980 under the Conservatives, namely: "... the unprecedented degree of control which central government could henceforth exercise over local authority housing provision" (Aughton, 1986, p.5). Undoubtedly, this was also the intention of the Labour government that introduced it. The control of housing capital expenditure became of crucial importance in Conservative policy, not least because housing accounts for over half the total local authority capital expenditure. Such control was achieved via HIPs and the 1980 Local Government, Planning and Land Act. The HIPs system quickly came to be used as a tool through which government could more easily control a steadily diminishing aggregate housing allocation. The results are clear from Table 2.3.

Since the introduction of HIPs housing expenditure has more than halved in real terms, with the result that local authority housing construction has dramatically declined since 1980 and standards are at an all time low (see Table 2.2 and Figure 2.1 for an understanding of the tenure changes which are occurring). This is the direct result of the fundamental changes to the housing finance system, council sales, subsidy system and the capital controls introduced. The traditional housing finance system had been established on the assumption that there was a housing shortage and that local authorities had an important role to play in dealing with it. Since 1980, a system of public housing finance has been set-up based on a rather different set of assumptions.

There has been a switch in the balance of capital expenditure away from new council building towards the rehabilitation of existing public and private stock. Central government has encouraged local authorities to provide grants for the renovation of private housing up to 90% of the costs (see Hughes, 1987). Also since 1982, authorities were no longer required to conform to detailed controls such as the Parker-Morris space and heating standards and housing cost yardsticks (Merrett, 1979, p.105); and finally, although authorities are awarded borrowing approval *en bloc* for expenditure up to the level approved in their HIPs allocations, the project control system requires the consent of the Secretary of State, for example in the acquisition of land for new house-building programmes.

These diverse elements are part of the conservative housing strategy which enables central government to maintain tight control over capital expenditure, where the private sector is much more likely to be involved with the building work and renovation, and where the strategy closely fits the dominant ideology of promoting owner occupation. On the other hand, the effects of such policies have been felt since the early 1980s implying that such trends have not necessarily originated from the Conservative government's ideological stance. They have undoubtedly been accelerated by recent developments, as an analysis of the HIPs allocations illustrates.

The last decade has witnessed substantial changes to the HIPs system: cuts, moratoriums, encouragements to spend, use of prescribed capital receipts - all of which have undoubtedly resulted in substantial disruption of authorities' strategies and investment programmes (see Gay, 1985). Not surprisingly, councils have consistently over / underspent on the government's HIPs targets. Table 2.3 testifies to the evolution of HIPs into a mechanism designed specifically to be used for short-term financial control over public spending. The planning elements gave way to control.

Table 2.3: Local authority capital investment (in £ milllions)

Year:	HIPs:	Capital Receipts:	EA HIPs:
1978/79	£2432		
1979/80	£2545		
1980/81	£2199		
1981/82	£1786	(40%) £413	
1982/83	£2192	£393	
1983/84	£1801	£684	
1984/85	£1853	£666	
1985/86	£1600	(20%) £325	
1986/87	£1465	£287	£50
1987/88	£1366	£316	£75
1988/89	£1290	£375	£140
1989/90	£920	n.a.	£190

Note: Authorities were only allowed to reinvest a proportion of their capital receipts as from 1981/82; and EA HIP only came into existence in 1986/87.

Sources: Gay, 1985; HM Treasury, 1990; EA Annual Reports

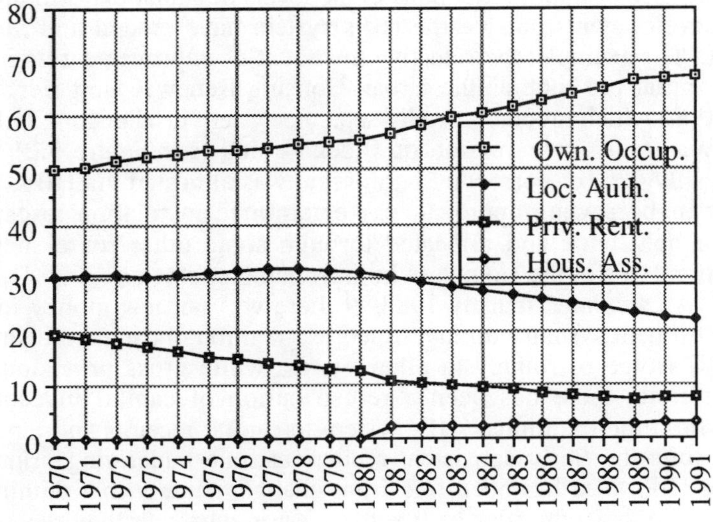

Sources: Local Housing Statistics; Building Societies Association

Figure 2.1: Housing tenure in Great Britain

The HIPs allocations have become progressively less important in housing capital investment patterns and major distortions have become apparent. For example, the capital receipts generated in the shires and the south (bar London) have been very great, thus increasing their share of usable resources relative to the authorities in the northern regions, the metropolitan districts and inner London (Murie and Malpass, 1987, p.114). To the extent that capital receipts now prop-up the public house investment programme, their decline since the late 1980s threatens the housing programme. As the demand for council house purchase by sitting tenants under the 'right to buy' fall off, the main source of receipt will also decline in future. This has led the AMA to argue that the 1988/89 allocation (AMA, mimeo b):

> ... will be funded solely by capital receipts, with no 'new money' being contributed by the HM Treasury ... 1988/89 marks the 10th anniversary of the HIP system and over that time the value of the annual allocation has been reduced by 78.5% in real terms.

These effects will not be too severe in the short run because of the accumulated capital receipts which authorities still hold, but in the long term substantial additional new money will be needed (if receipts continue to fall off) or it will represent a further cut to the capital programme. Consequently, the nature and role of the HIPs system has become somewhat metamorphosed as a reflection of shifts in government policy, not least because of major reductions in the levels of actual expenditure.

Other developments outside the HIPs system have eroded and further debased it. For example, the selective treatment of improvement grants in 1983 and initiatives such as the Urban Housing Renewal Unit (renamed Estate Action) which involve a totally separate system of allocating HIPs is essentially a small scale version of Block Grants (see Figure 3.2). By 1986/87, only 47% of borrowing permission was allocated via HIPs. The remainder of borrowing approval was determined in relation to capital receipts or held back and allocated through some other route such as Estate Action HIPs or the Homeless Initiative among others.

The AMA calculated that by 1988/89 there was no new money in the capital investment system - all investment came through capital receipts or the EA HIPs type of route. In other words, while gross provision has risen over time, there has been a redistribution of capital investment resources from the traditional HIPs system to capital receipts and targeted HIPs. Despite the fairly consistent reductions, one underlying principle behind the HIPs idea has been free from change, namely that within the overall cash limits, authorities be free to invest in whatever they see as the council's priorities. The procedure of withholding HIPs resources and redistributing them through central mechanisms (of which Estate Action is just one) is termed 'topslicing' and is viewed by many as yet another step towards greater centralization of control over housing provision:

> ... within the overall borrowing limit councils have been free to invest in what they see as the local priorities - this, of course, being one of the underlying principles of the housing investment programme idea. Even this, however, is being changed. In 1986/87 the government held back £50 million of loan sanction [for Estate Action] in order to give extra cash to councils which were following its policy of selling council housing estates to private developers. This procedure, called 'top-slicing' is clearly another step towards overall central government control of the housing programme. (Aughton, 1986, p.6)

This is an important issue and there has been much debate as to whether topslicing has indeed taken place or whether the resources available to the Estate Action programme have been 'additional'. This issue is important to EA and to wider public finance and will be discussed more fully in the empirical part of the book.

The relative absence of controls on borrowing before 1977 meant a pattern of investment reflecting local political and professional predilections unaffected by relative needs or any national framework. By the late 1980s. the level of investment bore no relation to local or national estimates of need and the pattern of investment depended on political and professional judgements about the use of creative accounting and capital receipts. Allocations of permission to spend bore little relation to needs but were strongly related to where capital receipts were greatest. The mechanism *did* enable central government to effectively check the total level of housing capital spending (Malpass and Murie, 1987, p.120) in the public sector.

Local authority investment is being channelled towards the renovation of their own stock and improvement grants to private sector owners and, since 1983, these have accounted for two thirds of local authority capital investment and related primarily to purpose-built council stock. Demand for investment has mushroomed in this area not only because of the awareness of the scale of maintenance problems in the stock, but also because of government initiatives such as the Housing Defects Act, the Priority Estates Project and UHRU/Estate Action.

iii) The latest housing finance legislation: It is obvious from the above that the housing finance system was in severe need of reform, a point emphasized in the housing literature (see Hills, 1988; and Gross and Lansley, 1981). The government eventually accepted these arguments and submitted a proposal for reform under the Local Government and Housing Bill 1988/89. However, virtually all the ideas presented in the housing literature have been rejected for, as Malpass (1990, p.163) argues, these ignored the fact that:

> In practice, over the last fifteen or twenty years, governments have shown themselves to be much more interested in short-term feasibility than long-term ideals, and they have been increasingly motivated by the desire to promote the growth of home ownership and to hasten the decline of council housing. The conclusion has to be that tenure neutrality is not the issue [of concern] and home owners are not the stumbling block [to housing finance reform]. The issue is tenure restructuring and the stumbling block is local autonomy.

The result is that instead of fundamental reform of local authority finance, considerations of feasibility have taken precedence and the new régime has come to represent an extension of the 1980 system. This section briefly considers the new developments in public housing finance.

1. The Capital side: SCAs and BCAs: From the government's viewpoint there were several quirks with the previous system, not the least of which were: the difficulties in forecasting capital receipts and in keeping total spending within government expenditure targets; the local authority entitlement to carry forward a proportion of unused capital receipts which produced a 'cascade effect' with distorting consequences for local capital expenditure; and lastly, capital receipts perversely tended to be highest in areas of least need, which did not aid targeting (Malpass, 1990, p.169-70).

Under the new arrangements local authorities receive Basic Credit Approvals (BCAs) plus Special Credit Approvals (SCAs) which set the maximum resources which authorities can obtain through conventional methods (such as borrowing) but the government will now be able to take account of capital receipts in deciding individual allocations, thus aiding targeting of resources. Authorities are now required to use 75% of accumulated capital receipts plus 75% of the receipts for the year in question to finance future investments or redeem outstanding debt, thus mopping-up their reserves. Malpass (1990, p.171) expects that:

> In general, the impact of the new capital controls will vary from place to place, but it is clear that the intention is to give central government much tighter control over local authority expenditure. The application of capital receipts to the redemption of debt will severely constrain capital programmes in many areas, but it will also have the effect of reducing debt charges falling on the housing revenue account. On the other hand, the elimination of the cascade effect will place considerable pressure on rents to support continued expenditure on maintaining and refurbishing existing council stock.

2. The Revenue side: 'Ring-fencing': The objective is to make the whole system simpler, fairer and more effective (DoE, 1988b, p.5-6), hence the attempt to establish a tightly defined or 'ring-fenced' HRA so that authorities will no longer be able to make Rate Fund Contributions

(RFC's) from their surplus HRAs, representing a significant amount of general assistance. There is thus a redefinition of subsidy which collapses housing subsidy, rate support grant and rent rebate subsidy into one HRA subsidy to be paid to authorities. However, this will still reflect DoE assumptions about changes in management and maintenance and rent expenditure thus re-introducing a strong element of central leverage on rent increases. The likely impact of this part has been simply stated:

> The evidence suggests that the 'new regime' for local authority housing finance will deliver what the government wants in the short term: less freedom for local authorities, more council house sales, lower public expenditure, and higher council house rents. But only for a few years. Then they will think of something else. (Malpass, 1990, p.190)

However, it must be stressed that this system was only introduced in the 1990-91 financial year and is thus beyond the scope of this book, except to the extent that it affects the future of the Estate Action initiative and is accordingly discussed in that context. The research was concluded before the details of the new legislation had been finalized.

2.6.2 The alternative to council housing: 'Social' housing?

It has been discussed elsewhere that whereas many local authorities down-played the importance of housing management, concentrating instead on finance and construction, there has now been a marked change in attitude not least because of the problems on many estates as well as because of authorities' seeming inability to adapt their management structures rapidly enough to cope with the changing situation confronting them. The Conservative party has for some time been stressing the value of introducing diversity of tenure and competition in the housing market in general (and council housing in particular) in the belief that this would result in landlords who actually act upon the views of tenants, while also aiding the exclusion of party politics from the management of housing.

The original route chosen by central government was to promote the 'right to buy' where sitting tenants were given the option to buy council properties at discount, thereby obtaining a capital asset. In the intermediary phase the government tried to stimulate the growth of alternative landlords to councils, such as Housing Associations (HAs) and Housing Co-operatives. Recently, however, the government has actually begun to question whether there is a future role for council housing at all, with the result that large-scale, radical initiatives such as Tenants' Choice and Housing Action Trusts have been placed on the statute book. These could potentially spell an end to council housing of any sort.

A government which when elected, had few policies towards housing other than the need to reduce capital/revenue subsidies and increase owner occupation via sale of council property, now appears to be aiming to actually replace council housing with 'social housing' (see Roof, 1990). This would be financed, managed and constructed by a variety of landlords (other than local authorities) including private landlords, trusts of various sorts, housing associations, building societies and housing co-operatives. The final section thus analyses how these substantial changes in attitude have come about and more importantly perhaps, what impacts they are likely to have. This concludes the context for the EA initiative which forms the thrust of the empirical part of the book.

i) The initial phase: Increasing tenant choice

1. Council house sales: Though the sale of council housing was not by any means a new phenomenon (see Holmans, 1987, pp.204-206), the policy proved to be one of the most politically controversial reforms of the 1980 Housing Act. Secure tenants of three years' standing acquired the right to buy the freehold of their house or the long lease of their flat at extremely favourable terms. Although purchase price was based on the market value, the tenant was entitled to a discount on such a value of 33 percent, plus 1 percent for each year by which the tenant's period as a secure tenant exceeds three years, initially up to a maximum discount of 50 percent.

This package of incentives proved very attractive and in the years 1980 to 1983, over 500,000 dwellings representing 10 percent of the public housing stock were sold under the scheme. This led not only to a relative decline but also to an absolute reduction in public sector dwelling numbers, accentuating the process of residualization and polarization (as discussed in section 2.4). Sales peaked in 1982 as pent-up demand was exhausted (Loughlin, 1986, p.101) and in order to maintain the impetus, additional incentives were provided in the Housing and Building Control Act 1984 in the form of a relaxation of residential qualifications and the upping of the maximum discount, whilst also extending the powers of intervention of the Secretary of State. It has been estimated that the number of council properties sold under this legislation has now exceeded 1m (see Table 2.2).

There seem to be several important reasons why the Conservative government went to such lengths to ensure that the 'right to buy' became a success. It has already been indicated that they were committed to increasing owner occupation. Council house sales were thus important for several reasons:

The *political* element relates to the importance of this policy for the Conservatives' electoral strategy since it has proven to be popular and has encouraged traditional Labour voters to vote Conservative. The *economic* element is equally important, given that it links with the rationale of monetarist policy seeking to reduce the size of the public sector and the burden of public expenditure. Housing has received the brunt of public expenditure cuts as discussed elsewhere (see Loughlin, 1986, pp.96-97). Additionally, the discounts have acted as a potent inducement. People would not buy unless the terms were attractive. The discount combined with rising council rents enforced by the deficit finance system, did prove to be a powerful incentive for sitting tenants to purchase their homes.

The *ideological* element focuses on tenure form and was particularly significant. The argument is as follows: a house of your own is inherently good and encourages independence and thrift while a large council housing sector with its large subsidies are both a drain on the nation's resources and an unacceptable extension of state control (Short, 1982, p.64). While this view seriously ignores the extent of public subsidy to owner occupation via mortgage tax relief (see Ginsburgh, 1989), it was not surprising that the sale of council housing took on such a significance within the Conservative party, not least because such house sales seemed to be the most propitious way of maintaining and extending home ownership.

The main concern for the Conservatives was the balance of households in the public and private sectors, with the result that the 'politics of construction rates' has been replaced by the 'politics of tenure forms'. The view that the proportion of households in the private sector is still too small persists (in 1990, 66% of the housing stock was already owner occupied) and, therefore, housing policies have concentrated on privatizing council housing, providing assistance for increasing levels of owner occupation and attempts to regenerate the private rented sector albeit with minimal incentives.

There is little doubt that the 'right to buy' has been spectacularly successful. In a decade, nearly one in six council tenants have bought their homes, the sales being boosted, according to Mason (1989, p.98) by the:

> Government's moves to eliminate blanket subsidies in favour of targeting help on those in need. The existing government and rate-funded subsidies to local authority housing have been steadily reduced, whether intentionally or otherwise making house purchase in the public or private sectors a steadily more attractive option.

Furthermore, the government seems to have no intention of slackening its pace on the owner occupation front. Further policies unveiled in the 1992 Conservative Party Manifesto and subsequently have sought to extend tenants' right to buy, not least by encouraging tenants to 'move out' of the public sector by converting their rents to mortgages. There have also been further shifts of the available public sector investment from councils to non-local government agencies, and more incentives for councils, where tenants do not want to buy, to transfer houses to co-operatives.

As the government tries to push home ownership as far down the line as possible, it is inevitably those on lower incomes which are taking up the option. The Building Societies have already indicated they do not expect (or desire) owner occupation to increase much more. Indeed the number of mortgage payment defaults and repossessions have been increasing rapidly in the last few years creating hardship and demonstrating all too clearly that home ownership is not a housing panacea *per se*. It is perhaps this that has prompted the government to recognize that there will continue to be a need for some sort of 'safety net' to support those that cannot afford to buy (see Glennerster, 1990). This recognition undoubtedly contributed to the next phase of Conservative policy towards housing (see below).

2. *Encouraging the Private Rented Sector and rent (de-)control:* The amount of private rented housing in Britain has undergone a steep decline starting in the early nineteen hundreds, when it accounted for 90% of the total housing stock, to the present day where the relevant figure is closer to 8% (see Doling and Davies, 1984, Table 2.2). But although this has become a marginal tenure and despite the stock's poor physical condition which tends to be older, more unfit and lacking in amenities in comparison to both council and owner occupied housing (DoE, 1982), the sector occupies a crucial position in the housing market. It is very diverse, catering for the very wealthy, pensioners, transients and migrants. Although the great majority of private rented tenants are on low incomes, its importance as a tenure lies in that it offers immediate access, which is particularly important for households which are normally disadvantaged in the housing market, such as single people and childless couples.

This demonstrates both the importance of a thriving private rented sector and why successive governments have attempted to revive it albeit with little success. The present government is no different and is urged onwards by right-wing 'Think Tanks' such as the Institute of Economic Affairs which argue that the British housing market has been in a tangle for generations due mainly to massive state intervention policies which were introduced:

> ... with the best intentions but have led to the worst of outcomes. We find ourselves with too little housing accommodation of the right kind in the right places. Moreover, there is a cost not only in terms of hardship, but in terms of a less efficient economy, a less mobile labour force, and higher unemployment (Minford *et al.*, 1987, p.xi).

Minford *et al.* blame the Rent Acts, the subsidies to council rents, the subsidy to owner occupiers through mortgage tax relief and the system of planning restrictions on land for housing, for aggravating the situation (1987). Measures have been undertaken in an attempt to de-regulate and revitalize the private rented sector via the Housing Act, 1980 which introduced two new tenancies: 'short-hold' tenancy, meaning a fair rent but limited security of tenure (1-3 years) and 'assured' tenancy, meaning security of tenure but market rent. The overall aim of the Act was to stop the decline of the private rented sector by allowing higher rents, a shorter period between rent increases and a reduction in the security of tenure afforded to the tenants (Short, 1982, p.66). In contrast to the 'right to buy', the various measures designed to stimulate the private rented sector have had a negligible impact. Only about 5,000 short-hold tenancies had been created by 1982 (HC Debate 4.4.84 c554W) and most of which were the result of conversion of former regulated tenancies to short-hold ones.

Attempts have so far been unsuccessful yet, there is clearly a need for a sector which provides immediate access to accommodation without need for registration, central allocation and without the necessity for a substantial deposit and intention to remain in the district; as is the case with owner occupation and council housing. This polarization of tenure options has been criticized by the NFHA which makes a strong case for two groups which are in particular need of this form of tenure, namely those who *cannot afford to buy* (the unemployed, those who are too old for mortgages, single parents, those on low/irregular income) and which equally would *not be able to afford to pay high rents* without assistance (via income support or subsidy to reduce rents); and those for whom *owner occupation is inappropriate* including students, those new to an area or temporarily there and current owner occupiers unable to cope with the full costs and responsibilities of ownership due to age, incapacity or poverty. These categories include the bulk of the population at some stage of their lives (NFHA, 1985, pp.24-26).

The government has indicated that it will continue to attempt to create a vigorous and respectable private rented sector, to relax rent controls for tenants and to establish the 'right to rent', but there are considerable doubts as to how significant rent regulation and security of tenure are, compared to the difference in financial assistance to the owner occupied sector. Mortgage tax-relief costs approximately £6bn and capital gains tax exemption on principal residences another £2bn in 1988-89. Not surprisingly, landlords with vacant possession prefer to sell in order to maximize their income. Private landlordism in Britain attracts no tax breaks such as depreciation allowances, tax relief on rental income and capital gains (Ginsburgh, 1989, p.59).

The other method which has been used by central government to revive the sector is the Business Expansion Scheme (BES) announced in the 1988 Budget and enacted in the Finance Act, 1988. Its intention is to offer tax breaks to people with spare resources and willing to put it on risky start-up ventures. However: "renting out a block of flats hardly puts one at the cutting edge of entrepreneurial risk-taking. Many people find the BES assured tenancy schemes distasteful - the equivalent of Rachmanism with a tax break." (Ginsburgh, 1989, p.60, quoting from The Guardian, 15.2.1989, p.16). Although the BES has certainly resulted in extra private rented accommodation, it is far from clear whether all these measures will be successful in reviving commercial landlordism on any scale let alone contain the decline without a major reform of housing finance (The

Guardian, 16.2.1989, p.5; Whitehead and Kleinman, 1986). The private rented sector is currently experiencing a reverse in its fortunes in the early 1990s, but not because of government policies as much as despite them. The increasing levels of mortgage indebtedness, repossessions and rapidly deteriorating house prices have created such a stagnant and unstable housing market that private renting is making a come back as a less risky housing strategy. There is no way of determining whether this will be a durable trend.

ii) The intermediate phase: Alternative agents

1. Housing Associations (HAs): HAs have a long history in Britain but only began to expand rapidly following the creation in 1964 of the Housing Corporation specifically to develop and promote associations; and the Housing Act, 1974 which signified a degree of support from both political parties for this form of tenure, also establishing a generous subsidy (Housing Association Grant of 80-90%) for such schemes. The present government has come to accept the need for an intermediate form of tenure and now sees HAs as the main vehicle for the future construction and management of social housing, even taking over former council property:

> Our new policies put housing associations on centre-stage. We see them as the major providers of new subsidized housing for rent and as possible alternative landlords for dissatisfied council tenants.
> (David Trippier, reported in Voluntary Housing, Feb. 1989)

The government's new-found commitment to the value of this tenure as a potential alternative to council housing is so great that it has even taken the step of re-classifying HAs as belonging to the 'independent' rented sector despite the degree of public subsidy necessary to make them viable. In such a climate HAs have expanded at such a rate, that they are already building more homes (22,200 in 1987/8) than the council sector (15,300) which has seen its capital allocations severely curtailed in the last decade. However HAs remain a small tenure both in terms of number of properties (630,000 versus 4.4m in the council sector) and the overwhelming majority of the 2,000-odd HAs are very small (Housing Corporation Factsheet, 1989).

Associations are non profit-making organizations. They have traditionally housed those in need, but the government was clearly attracted by their specialist nature and the absence of party politics. Additionally, they were lauded as models for housing management, being small, locally based and apparently well-suited to the climate of housing opinion. As 'problem' estates became more widespread, so practitioners became more interested in models of intensive and localized management structures which increased tenant participation. Government was attracted to HAs as an alternative to council housing and lauded them as more efficient landlords. A recent report by the Centre for Housing Research has questioned this assumption (Maclennan *et al.*, 1989, Paragraph 9.4):

> Good management performance and low costs were not the preserve of a single organizational type, and similarly for poor performance and high costs.

This begins to illustrate the government's HA dilemma. While it has clearly come to rely upon this tenure to push forward with its 'intermediate' policies, HAs are not necessarily the most appropriate vehicle for its housing objectives. This will be tested following the introduction of the 1988 Housing Act which has restructured association finance. They are now responsible for setting their own rent levels on all new tenancies; all their new tenants are assured tenants; and since April 1989, the level of grant is fixed at the start of the scheme and will be funded by a mixture of public and private finance. The ratio of public subsidy will vary according to region and type of development but averages at seventy five per cent.

It remains unclear whether HAs will be able to raise the necessary resources from Building Societies, Banks and the City at favourable terms because these financial institutions know little about them and they are not helped by their small and fragmented nature. A number of HAs have already merged or build consortia in order to raise the necessary private capital. Additionally, rent levels are expected to rise (as they are currently doing even though still subject to Fair Rents). While Housing Benefit may insulate the unemployed, it does little for those on low income and will begin to affect the others as Housing Benefit is restructured and further eroded.

Consequently, it is likely that the HAs 'advantages' (of being small scale and in receipt of generous finance) will change as the latest legislation forces them to merge and become more commercially minded. The likely expansion of the sector will, in all probability, be modest and their main route for fast growth lies in the government's encouragement for them to offer themselves as alternative landlords to local authorities under the Tenants Choice (see 2.6.3iii below). However, HAs have not shown themselves to be overly keen on the idea and remain concerned that the new financial régime may push up rents and undermine their traditional role of housing those in need.

While relationships with local authorities have not always been smooth, the two have worked together in providing new homes. The government's proposals for Tenants Choice threatens such links. This has placed HAs in an invidious situation between meeting tenants' needs, central government policies and long term relationships with local authorities. The NFHA has responded by stating that it will not support transfers unless there is a majority ballot vote, the authority is not opposed to the proposal and adequate resources will be available to deal with the necessary repairs (HA Weekly, 20.1.89, 'Tenants Choice and Housing Associations'). Another side-effect of the Housing Act, 1988 has been to encourage voluntary transfers by local authorities of their housing stock to HAs. There are good reasons for doing so as this would protect their stock from predatory landlords, ensure their ability to meet their homelessness requirements and enable such housing to be freed from the capital and revenue constraints operating on the council housing sector.

This cautious reaction by the HAs has not gone unnoticed by the government or its supporters who have made it clear that unless HAs become more pro-active, the Government will seek other agents more willing to promote its policy of diversification of tenure (David Trippier, Minister at the DoE, reported in Voluntary Housing, February 1989; and Coleman, 1989). There are already those who argue that HAs should not be the only choice and that: "In putting so much emphasis on housing associations, the Government may be refloating Local Authority housing under a new flag of convenience but on the old sea of public money" (Coleman, 1988, pp.40-41). Nevertheless it would be very optimistic to expect HAs to rapidly obtain a much larger share of housing tenure than its current 3%. In the meantime, local authorities will continue to be constrained from providing much new housing for general needs while their waiting lists and homelessness continue to expand, as well as from spending sufficient amounts on repair and maintenance. The government has instead sought to encourage authorities to turn their decimated capital investment programmes into their existing stock via the PEP and EA programmes.

2. Priority Estates Project (PEP) and Estate Action (EA): The DoE established PEP in 1979 in an effort to develop a model for integrated estate based housing management. PEP brought about major organizational changes (radically different from the centralised local authority housing structure), in which all functions are organized within a locally based team and where control and decision-making is vested in the local project manager. Political and central management control is only exercised over broad areas of policy resources and monitoring as opposed to day-to-day decision making (see DoE, 1987c).

Many local authorities have since experimented with the initiative. Local offices ought to control of four basic management functions: repairs and communal maintenance; tenant liaison; rent control; and lettings as this would offer a more manageable scale of operation, an integrated service, direct dealing between the residents and housing workers, scope for initiative and decision making and power to deliver. Many housing estates were in a desperate situation so: "there was a willingness to relax normal procedures and bureaucratic ties with the centre." (Power, 1987a, p.29)

It has been argued that such an initiative could transform housing estates. A survey was conducted in 1984 of 20 local estate management schemes, three of which were PEP estates. It suggested that estate based management did result in impressive improvements in landlord/tenant relations; protected investment in such estates; responded to tenants priorities; local management of repairs, rents and lettings was popular, efficient and cost effective; rent arrears were contained; local care-taking and autonomy was important; the local housing office acting together with the police and residents were essential in reducing crime and social abuse; that such projects were 'affordable' and brought about substantial cash savings." (Power, 1987b, p.239-240; 1984).

Nonetheless, PEP is no panacea and there are severe limitations to the estate based approach. It requires intensive input and outside support; it is an impermanent one-off intervention (model) with DoE consultants for a limited period of time; it has no legal or financial framework; it is hard to disentangle the local organization from the centre (i.e. the council); and it is based on insecure finance (requiring cuts and reorganization at the centre). Estate budgets can be used creatively and innovatively but they are also potentially a tool for increased inequality and disadvantage where they are used to force poor estates to pay for the whole structure of costs (Bonnerjea, 1987, p.37). A further limitation is that it is aimed almost exclusively at management. Its objective is to make the worst estates more viable housing communities with better services by changing the bureaucracy. However, this does not change wider housing policy, choice and opportunity; whereas the socio-economic problems are deep-set and cannot be resolved simply by changing the style of housing management. Nevertheless, because of its achievements, PEP has served as a model for other authorities and housing initiatives to build on.

The government's second major venture in trying to encourage changes in management as well as ownership, is through the Estate Action initiative which can be seen as an evolution of PEP. This is the subject of this book and is analyzed thoroughly in subsequent chapters. Suffice to say at this stage that Estate Action was set-up to encourage authorities to try to improve their most difficult estates through the use of alternative management styles and forms of ownership, with an element of 'targeted' DoE financial support.

iii) The more radical phase: De-municipalization? The latest phase was signalled by the Housing Bill, 1987 which proposed markedly different changes to solve the problems facing council housing. As Mason argues, the: "Conservative housing policy has developed through what appear to have been a series of uncoordinated responses to unrelated events ... it is only recent policy initiatives that appear deliberately intended to bring an end to municipal housing." (1989, p.98)

Three reasons appear to have influenced this changed attitude: first, "the dramatic and unexpected success of council house sales, with its side-effect of reducing the potentially damaging electoral impact of adopting radical policies; secondly, central government's growing lack of confidence in local government; and the increasing use [by councils] of their housing stock as a weapon in the party political battlefield" (Mason, 1989, p.98). Regardless of the reasons why central government has chosen to press for an end to council housing, there can be no denying the powerful nature of the instruments enabling the transfer of the housing stock out of council control. Two significant proposals have been carried into law with minor modifications, namely Tenants' Choice (TC) and Housing Action Trusts (HATs). A third method of privatizing large portions of council housing exists via the Voluntary Transfer (VT) of blocks, estates or even the entire stock to other landlords or private developers.

1. Voluntary Transfers (VT): This power was first initiated under the 1986 Housing and Planning Act and the 1988 Housing Act elaborated on how councils can dispose of some or all of their housing stock. Under VT, no requirement is made of local authorities to consult the tenants affected (other than offering alternative accommodation), although the Secretary of State must be satisfied that the tenants support the developments. Most councils interested in pursuing this option have used the balloting arrangements for TC as a means of presenting evidence of tenant support. This voting system is highly controversial because at least 50% of all those balloted have to vote 'No' to stop a transfer since abstention is effectively counted as a 'Yes' vote.

This technical problem has acted as a hindrance for many authorities who have gone as far as to consider and implement this option. The crucial difficulty is that when VT goes ahead, tenants who voted 'No' or abstained will also be obliged to transfer to the new landlord (unlike the TC mechanism - see below). In spite of these concerns, three authorities have so far transferred their entire stock to newly-created Housing Associations because of two key advantages: firstly, the government's financial restrictions have starved them of resources. Though VT authorities can circumvent centrally determined capital borrowing restrictions for new construction or refurbishment of the existing stock. Secondly, voluntary transfer to Housing Associations is regarded in some quarters as a mechanism for both retaining and even expanding the supply of rented social housing. These two issues may persuade many other councils that limited scope presently exists for the expansion of social housing under their own control and that VT may be a better option, especially if selective transfers of stock can be achieved which also meet tenants' aspirations. VTs are likely to be of small but growing importance in the future.

2. Tenants' Choice (TC): Introduced in Part IV of the Housing Act 1988, this piece of legislation extends the rights and choices given to council tenants in 1980 through the Tenants' Charter and the 'right to buy'. Potentially the most powerful instrument available under the Act, tenants individually (in houses) or collectively (in flats) can choose to transfer their existing homes to another landlord. Independent landlords must be approved by the Housing Corporation as 'appropriate' (viable and competent) social landlords before they may take over council housing stock. The choice is determined via a voting system whereby non-voters are assumed to be in favour of transfer, possibly because the Government may have anticipated lack of interest from tenants.

The government's immediate aim via TC is to give more choice to council tenants who either do not wish or cannot exercise their 'right to buy'; and to expose councils to competition which might result in a better standard of services. For their part, local authorities are primarily opposed to the policy because of their desire to retain their housing stock. They worry that 'ring-fencing' may have been designed to force up rents and to encourage tenants to opt out of council control either exercise their 'right to buy' or through TC.

Nevertheless various factor may inhibit tenants from making widespread use of TC. Unlike the 'right to buy', there are no potential cash benefits to the tenants - only the likelihood of steeper rents imposed by relatively inexperienced landlords. It is not surprising that tenants have not been keen to transfer, not least because as Glennerster *et al.* argue, this choice is largely non-existent. There are in fact few capable (or willing) landlords to pick from. Additional problems arise from the fact that an individual's choice can run against a neighbour's; most residents are likely to vote for the *status quo*; and because ownership confers power that ensures landlords' rights rather than tenant choice (1989, p.22). The measure seems to be more about taking stock out of council control than about presenting choices to tenants, but public housing will continue to be privatized as local authorities, central government, private developers and housing associations seek a transfer of ownership, subject to the tenants' veto. It seems unlikely, however, that TC will progress at the rate that the government may have anticipated. Other inhibiting factors include the fact that:

> A number of surveys have found majorities of tenants expressing a desire to remain with their councils. Evidence also suggests that many councils are making efforts to meet the needs of their tenants, seeking their tenants' views and improving services. If this is the case, the Act may be seen as having acted as a successful catalyst. (Rao, 1990, p.9)

3. Housing Action Trusts (HATs): Sections 65-92 of the 1988 Housing Act contain strong powers enabling Trusts appointed by the Government to take over large patches of the 'worst' council housing, renovate them (with £125m set aside for the programme over three years) and transfer them to alternative private landlords. The objectives of HATs are to: take over council housing within the designated area; repair, modernize and improve the stock; improve the living conditions and general environment of the area; and secure diversity of tenure.

An analogy can be drawn with Urban Development Corporations (such as the London Docklands Development Corporation) as the Trusts will take over estates for five years without any obligations or accountability to the local populace. This is justified by the government by appealing to the fact that the size of the areas concerned and the magnitude of the problems have been beyond the capacity of authorities to handle. The government maintains that housing authorities will be relieved of their most difficult housing stock which will enable them to concentrate their efforts and resources on the remaining stock.

Because of the mounting public concern and lobbying about the lack of provision for a tenant ballot on whether they want a HAT to be imposed in their estate or not, following a late amendment by the House of Lords, the Act now includes the right for tenants to vote against the HATs and for designation to be conditional upon a 'Yes' vote. The irony is that while HATs are in principle for the benefit of the residents, the tenants themselves campaigned vociferously for the de-designation of their estates. Their main concerns are that there will be fewer homes following demolitions and refurbishment, that homes will be sold to developers who will try to attract higher income households and that homes will be re-let at unaffordable rents. They also remain worried about other factors such as changes to the conditions of tenure, the 'right to buy' and other tenants' rights.

Indeed the reaction has been such that as the HATs campaign has progressed, it has become clear that the Government not only badly misjudged the costs involved, but also the climate of tenant opinion, their degree of activity, organizational abilities and unwillingness to transfer out of council ownership. Plans for all six sites originally earmarked for HATs (Lambeth, Leeds, Sandwell, Southwark, Sunderland and Tower Hamlets) have either been dropped or rejected by the tenants.

That is not to say that the idea is now bankrupt. Tenants in Hull have voted for the creation of the first HAT and Labour-run Liverpool City Council has endorsed the concept by asking the DoE to examine the possibility of setting up a HAT in its area (The Ind, 3.4.1991, p.2). Also, the Government may simply choose to transfer the HATs resources to other councils which may be more willing to entertain stock transfers, resulting in further privatization of municipal housing. On the positive side, however, councils are now fully aware that the survival of social housing rests on their hands. It is to be hoped that this will encourage local authorities to provide an even more responsive and effective housing service to tenants.

To summarize this section, the government has been concerned over time to move away from any reliance on local authorities to provide social housing. This links up with their monetary, ideological and political policies but has taken time to evolve to its natural conclusion. The government has come up with a plethora of initiatives aimed at increasing tenant choice of tenure, however, all of them seem to be aimed at actually reducing the size and power of council housing. In no circumstances do councils have the opportunity to actually increase their housing stock, even if community charge/council tax payers were willing to accept it.

However, the dismantling of council housing is not necessarily going according to plan. The 'right to buy' has been extremely successful but will increasingly involve tenants in the poorer properties, locations and increasingly flats. The Housing Associations will not be able to expand as quickly as the government might have hoped and are unwilling either to increase their rents rapidly or take-over estates from unco-operative councils. HATs have been a decided flop thus far, TC has been limited and tenants remain nervous about private landlordism, particularly where the prospect of rising rents is extremely likely as a consequence. Lastly, VTs of stock have been few, nevertheless, there are no grounds for complacency. Local authorities' best line of defence must be in attempting to improve their housing service, to be responsive to tenants and to actually involve them in the decision-making process. However, even this may not be enough in the long term if they are financially constrained from responding to tenant wishes. In the meantime, the housing situation is set to deteriorate further.

2.7 Conclusions

This chapter has been concerned to set the context and demonstrate the reasons why the last decade has been so turbulent for housing authorities. The council housing role has been redefined in the 1980s and for a variety of reasons, the concern has shifted perceptibly from an emphasis on 'the numbers game' to a commitment to the provision of a service to the client. Crucial within this is the realization that, in providing a good quality housing service, management must be at the forefront. This has resulted in a variety of attempts to develop new, more effective ways of owning and managing public housing.

This is a message which many authorities are already aware of and actively pursuing. However, it is also something which government, through PEP and Estate Action in particular, has sought to disseminate. With the emphasis on management go other messages relating to efficient use of resources, tenant consultation and also ownership by other organizations and landlords. It is for these reasons that EA has been chosen as a key example to analyze in order to determine the effects of this commitment to a new style of council housing management. The next chapter introduces Estate Action in greater detail and locates it within its policy context, describes the main issues which the book seeks to examine and then concentrates on describing the methodology to be employed in carrying out the empirical work.

3 Policy context and methodology

3.1 Introduction

The previous chapter illustrated the difficulties arising as a result of a complex set of factors: emphasis on owner occupation, the 'right to buy' and other powerful anti-council housing devices, resource squeeze, rising rents, deterioration of housing stock and a transformation in the socio-economic characteristics of the tenants. In such a context, *local* authority housing has come under severe criticism from the political as well as the academic front, much of which has concentrated on authorities' traditionally centralized management structures and remote procedures which seem unable to respond quickly and effectively to the needs of their clients. This has prompted local authorities to become generally more open to initiatives which place the tenant at the forefront while also introducing more effective housing management structures (Clapham *et al.*, 1987). Examples are co-operatives (LHU, 1987b), decentralized organizations such as neighbourhood offices (Hambleton and Hoggett, 1984; Seabrook, 1984), and a variety of other initiatives (LHU, 1987a).

This state of affairs has also presented difficulties for *central* government policy. On the one hand there is a belief that council housing is badly managed, that scarce resources should be diverted towards resuscitating the private rented sector, that a new 'social' housing sector should be generated which includes housing associations and co-operatives and lastly that owner occupation remains the best tenure form. On the other hand, there is an obvious and proven need for greater public expenditure directed towards the housing sector. The symptoms are there for all to see after decades of neglect (see chapter 2). However, the government remains committed to its policy that public expenditure should be tightly controlled and that home ownership should continue to be stimulated. In an attempt to overcome this dilemma, its response has been to develop several new strategies:

i) *Privatization* through three main agents: volume builders, building societies and home owners. The housing problem is seen as being the inadequate resources and the government's aim has been to supplement and/or substitute state spending with private funds, thereby also generating further opportunities for owner occupation through disposal, renovation and re-sale of former council property (Brindley and Stoker, 1988).

ii) A second government response has been to reinforce and commend the work of the *Priority Estates Project* (PEP) which, as we have seen, is based on a decentralized management structure, but which has tended to emphasize the management problems rather than the physical problems, and thus does not require a large injection of new financial resources (Cantle, 1986, p.80). The PEP approach is selective and concentrates both staff and financial resources into small areas together with assistance from the police, social services and additional resources from the Urban Development Grant (see Power, 1984; 1988).

iii) The last strategy, *Estate Action*, combines the previous two elements whilst also making an increasing proportion of housing capital investment resources (EA HIPs) available to local authorities. Estate Action (EA) gives improvement allocations to councils in return for a commitment to improve their management of estates and decentralize. It also encourages local authority involvement with the private sector in order to renovate estates. EA's remit, as stated when it was launched by Sir George Young in June 1985, is as follows:

- To identify authorities and estates where new initiatives can be pursued;
- To develop new or relatively untried solutions to the problems facing these [run-down] estates, including transfers of ownership and/or management to management trusts, involving tenants, or to tenants' co-operatives;
- To encourage authorities to adopt, where appropriate, one or more of a range of existing disposal solutions such as:
  - i) sales of tenanted estates to private trusts or developers;
  - ii) sales of empty property to developers for refurbishment or sale/rent;
- To encourage authorities to improve the management and maintenance of their own estates by establishing local autonomous estate based management schemes on PEP lines;
- To advise ministers of the need for new machinery, incentives or legislative change to promote the full range of solutions; and
- To provide a report on progress by the end of June 1986 (DoE, 1985a).

The EA Unit has been in existence since 1985, yet unlike the other two strategies and in spite of its increasing importance to housing authorities (a number of which now receive over half of their housing investment allocation via EA HIPs), there has been virtually no research conducted on the government's intentions or to assess its contribution and its effectiveness - except for the DoE approved Coppers & Lybrand Deloitte project which remains to be published. It is, therefore, upon EA that the rest of the book focuses. The next sections will add detail to the initiative, analyze relevant concepts which impinge upon an understanding of the initiative and describe the methodology to be employed in evaluation. The evidence is presented in subsequent chapters.

3.2 Policy context and nexus of research

Estate Action (originally called UHRU - the Urban Housing Renewal Unit), attributes crucial importance to certain issues and was originally targeted only on 'problem' estates (see chapter 6 for EA's methodology in selecting estates). The archetypal UHRU/EA solution 'package' would include the following:

> The key ingredients are a responsive, comprehensive and *effective local management* ... including the development of tenant management cooperatives to encourage the *fullest possible tenant involvement* ... we encourage local authorities to *involve the private sector* in the upgrading process, both to generate additional resources and to widen the tenure mix. (DoE, 1986, p.6, Emphasis Added)

Whenever such opportunities existed, EA would also encourage the disposal of empty dwellings and in the case of tenanted dwellings, the Unit would explore the scope of disposal to trusts or co-ops (DoE, 1986). EA was thus intended to benefit local authorities whilst also fulfilling central government policy. We have discussed that since 1980, local authorities had seen their HIPs allocations reduced sharply while capital receipts became increasingly the normal method of capital allocation (see chapter 2). A key element was thus that EA would appeal to authorities by enabling more capital resources to be targeted (through EA HIPs) to run-down council estates. The programme was also intended to encourage local authorities to continue experimenting with various 'new' management options which, as discussed above, many were already showing signs of being interested in. Authorities could bid for EA HIPs (as opposed to the normal annual capital allocation or HIPs), but this had to be accompanied by DoE defined 'new or relatively untried' management options such as employment initiatives and estate based management.

The EA initiative had much appeal for central government. Research at the DoE had identified the scale and nature of problems in certain council estates (DoE, 1978; Burbidge *et al.*, 1981). Also, the government's policy of selling the most desirable property through the 'right to buy' legislation, the difficulties of growing unemployment up to the mid 1980s and the widening of the distribution of income, all exacerbated the problems on run-down estates. The government was probably very aware of these problems even if it could not acknowledge them (Glennerster, 1990). Through EA, the government could be portrayed as responding to the management and maintenance situation in the most problematic sector of council housing where local authorities were seen to have failed. At the same time it created another avenue for privatization and diversification of the council housing stock through various disposal solutions.

In terms of government's monetarist policy towards public expenditure, while the DoE gained control of which schemes proposed by authorities were acceptable, central government did not actually provide any additional resources via grants. The rapidly escalating EA HIPs (£50m; £75m; £140m; £190m; and £280m), was merely borrowing approval given to authorities (if their bids conformed to EA criteria) on top of the HIPs annual capital allocation which authorities then had to borrow from private sources in the usual way. The amount of EA HIPs was decided on an annual basis according to a government decision of what extra resources the country could afford and it had to be allocated and spent within the financial year. Controversy has raged as to whether EA HIPs resources are 'additional' as implied by the Treasury or merely 'topsliced' (or withdrawn) from the annual HIPs allocation and redistributed to authorities through EA (this is discussed in Chapter 6). A further point to note is the fact that EA HIPs is one of several financial 'targeting' mechanisms being employed by the DoE (see Figure 3.2) but which are totally unresearched. It is hoped that the issues and lessons learned from an evaluation of the EA initiative may be of use for the other ones.

From the discussion above it will be evident that the EA system involves several different agents. The *Treasury* decides the EA HIPs allocation annually and requires that such resources be spent within the financial year. *EA Central* (based in Marsham Street) formulates policy, oversees and co-ordinates the whole process and makes final decisions on bids submitted by authorities for schemes to be funded with EA HIPs. Nine *DoE Regional Offices* and the *Merseyside Task Force,* prioritize their authorities' bids for schemes seeking to utilize EA resource, liaise with local authority officers and monitor schemes. The *Local authorities* (through various departments including housing, finance and architects) consult tenants, generate bids, erect and implement successful schemes. The council *tenants* themselves and the *Tenants' Associations* are expected to be fully involved and consulted and finally, the *DLOs or contractors* actually undertake the work. Additionally the private sector may be involved in partnerships to renovate properties or authorities may contact their associations in an effort to influence the operation of the programme. These interactions are fully illustrated in the Figure 3.1. There are two stages in the application process (Forms A and B) requiring increasingly detailed information; a Quarterly Financial (C) and an Annual Assessment Form (D). This gives an indication of the degree of co-ordination, complexity and cost involved in generating EA proposals. Even if bids conform to EA criteria and receive support, the allocation must be spent before the end of the financial year or the allocation reverts back to the Treasury.

The following section seeks to develop the discussion by analyzing the various concepts which seem valuable to such a system of interactions between central, regional and local government.

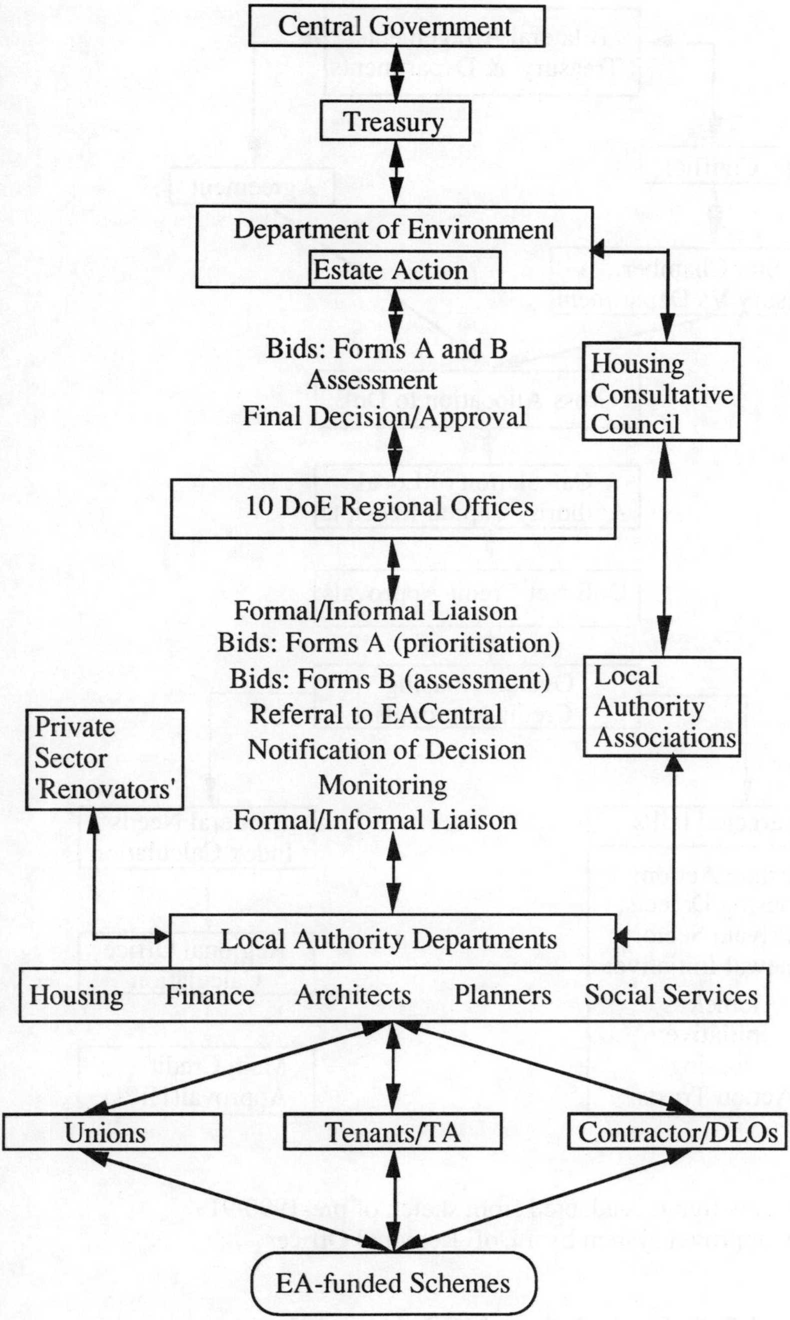

Figure 3.1: EA agents and the policy context

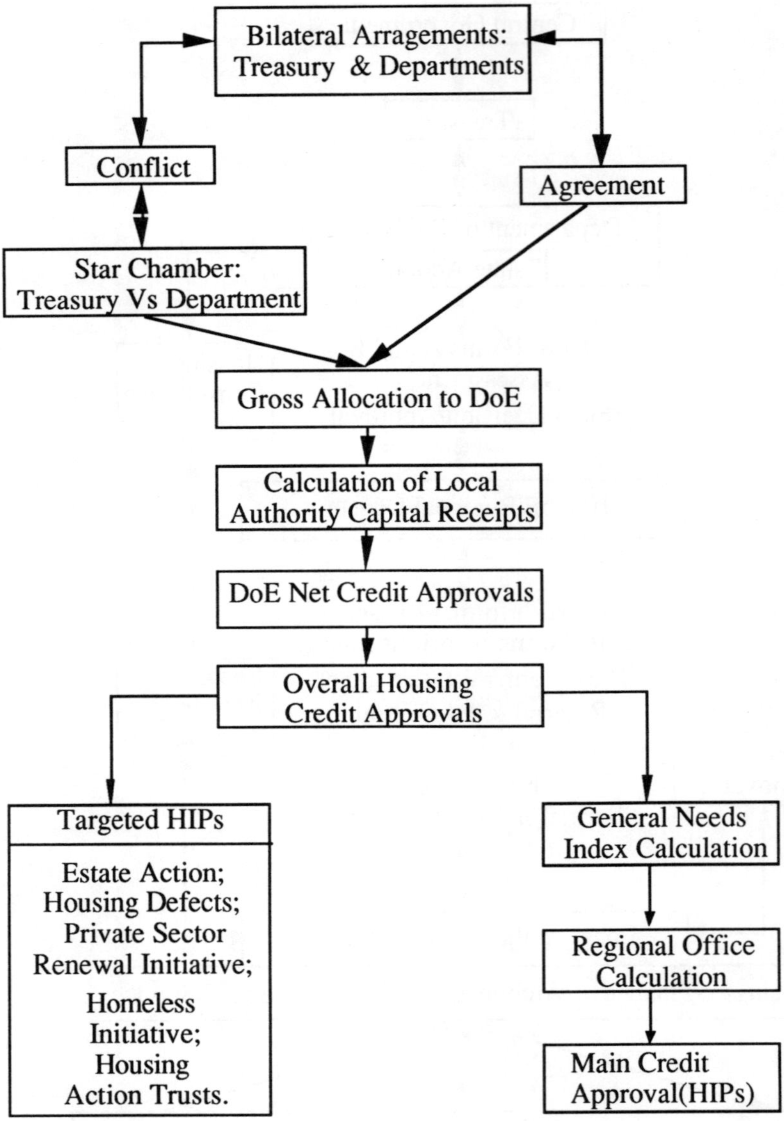

Note: This figure is adapted from sketch of pre-1990/91 credit approval system by a DoE Regional Officer

Figure 3.2: DoE calculation of HIPs / targeted resources

3.3 The conceptual issues: Central-local relations

Stripped to its core, the main issues of concern from a conceptual stance relate to the nature of the *relation* and *interaction* of the various agencies and organizations that form part of the EA initiative. It is the operation of these organizations which, therefore, determine EA's success or otherwise in achieving its goals. In this case the key actors are considered to be the EA Central team based at Marsham Street, the Regional Offices of the Department of Environment (DoE), the local authorities (and the various departments involved in generating and implementing EA schemes) and the tenants and their representative Associations. This pre-determines the nature of 'relevant' conceptual frameworks which enables us to make sense of the complex interactions and relationships between the various agencies which eventually give rise to EA schemes.

Most perspectives on central-local relations start from the position that there has been a steady process of centralization of power away from the locality in most local services. It is held that this has been occurring for the last 20-odd years but that it has greatly accelerated in the last decade under the Conservative government and that this process of centralization of local autonomy is well exemplified by an analysis of the developments in council housing (Rao, 1990, p.4):

> Historically, in centre-local tensions over the proper role and functions of local government, housing has always been particularly sensitive. It has been a focus of conflict since 1979. In the last decade the development of housing legislation and the use of legislative powers by central government to control local government housing activities have reflected the crisis in the relationship between the two.

It is argued that the government has employed three principal strategies:

- Housing finance has been centralized (developments in capital and revenue finance)
- Alternative housing agencies have been encouraged (such as Housing Associations and Tenant Co-operatives, which are non-elected and can be more easily controlled by the centre)
- Increased central compulsion (exemplified by the 'right to buy' and HATs). For a fuller discussion on the centre-local issues and housing, readers are referred to Karn (1985); Duncan and Goodwin (1988); and Pinto (1991b). There are several key models which may be employed to conceptualize these developments. These are analyzed below.

3.3.1 The traditional view: Agent or partner

Until the mid 1970s, the conventional wisdom limited discussion solely to the relationship between central departments and local authorities whilst maintaining that this relationship took two different forms. Under the 'agency' model, local authorities implemented national policies under the supervision of central departments. In the 'partnership' model, both were seen as co-equal in the relationship. There was thus a tendency to view central government as both homogeneous and monolithic and it was assumed that the relationship had shifted from partnership to agency primarily due to the financial dependence of local authorities upon central government. This process was criticized as undermining local autonomy.

This orthodoxy was challenged in the mid 1970s because of the accumulation of a number of findings which could not be incorporated into the existing framework (for a detailed critique see Rhodes, 1981, chapter 2). Research into policy areas where central and local government were in conflict demonstrated the problems faced by the centre in obtaining compliance as well as the capacity of local authorities to resist central control and maintain their own policy objectives. Growing evidence of the key role played by professionals in policy-making, various linkages between central and local government and the centre's limited ability to achieve detailed policy control also contributed to the dissatisfaction with the limitations of the orthodox framework culminating in the establishment of the Social Science Research Council's research initiative on central-local relations in 1978. This research was also inspired by an awareness of the changing pattern of service allocation responsibilities; the increasing size of local authority expenditure on public services despite coinciding with the onset of a period of recession; and the increasing politicization of local authorities, as reflected in the changing attitudes towards local policy-making held by central government, political parties and the public (Houlihan, 1988, pp.9-11).

3.3.2 The dual state thesis

This concept proceeds on the basis that the state in the modern society cannot be analyzed as a single cohesive entity. The scale and scope of state activity in all developed nations has expanded dramatically in the Twentieth Century. It has assumed an increasing range and degree of responsibilities and has become organizationally more complex. The state apparatus has fragmented into different branches, elected (eg. local government) and non-elected (eg. civil servants, boards etc), all responsible for implementing many aspects of social policy. This is what enables tensions and conflicts to arise, themselves exacerbated by internal differences within each branch.

Conflicts within the state may thus occur both horizontally, between different branches of state apparatus, and vertically, between different levels within each branch (Saunders, 1984, p.23). This suggests that analyses which rest either on a reduction of local government to central state or on a reduction of local political struggles to class categories, should be rejected. Since these involve different functions, modes of interest mediation and different ideological priorities, local political processes must be analyzed by means of theories and categories which are distinct from those which are applicable to processes at the national level, hence the rationale for developing a dualistic theory of British politics (Saunders, 1984).

Rather, the state has two main functions: social investment and social consumption. State intervention at central level relates primarily to the politics of production and proceeds through a policy process of corporatist mediation functioning primarily in the interest of capital (e.g. via investment in physical infrastructure). At the local state level, however, activity is geared primarily towards the social consumption aspects of state provision, which are consumed individually by the population as a whole or by sections of it (eg. health care and housing provision). Such policies are developed through competitive political activity at local level and address themselves at issues of social rights and needs.

The interests at the centre are primarily those of production (industrial and financial capital) whereas at the local level interests cut across class lines and are formed on the basis of specific and locally based consumption classes (e.g. council tenants). There exist tensions between the two functions because increases in social consumption via, for example, increased taxation may have negative effects on private profitability. This may result in a 'rationality problem', and a 'legitimation crisis', as state intervention and a belief in the needs and rights of individuals conflict with private property and the market principle.

These two political processes can be distinguished along four main dimensions (Table 3.1). The organizational dimension is the most fruitful of these bearing in mind the particular issues to be addressed in the thesis, however, this is only briefly discussed since this part of the theory borrows heavily from Rhodes' work (see below). Saunders basically accepts Rhodes' argument that government organizations at the central and local levels relate to each other; that these form part of a wider environment which includes other organizations; and that dominant groups must mobilize their power resources (constitutional, financial etc) to achieve their objectives. This means that local authorities are neither agents of the centre nor partners with the centre, but are rather *loci* of power which is mobilized in relation to power exerted by the central authority (Rhodes, 1981, p.24).

The Dual State Theory has stimulated a great deal of debate and criticism by Marxist as well as non-Marxist writers (such as Duncan and Goodwin, 1982; Rhodes, 1988; Dunleavy, 1984; Flynn, 1986). Saunders himself has acknowledged the degree of criticism as being wide-ranging, identifying and responding to some common critiques such as that: the elements cannot or should not be separated; the book is ethnocentric and ahistorical; and problems of empirical application (1986).

The following quotation by Duncan and Goodwin (1988, p.35) is indicative of the reaction and leads the discussion neatly to an analysis of the structuralist contribution to the debate:

> This work has been of vital importance in highlighting the specificity of the local level, and in arguing for a conceptualisation of the local state that is based primarily on its 'uniqueness' and on its separation from the centre ... but for us the approach is still fraught with problems.

3.3.3 Uneven social development

Despite Saunders' criticism of class-based theories, a major contribution to the debate has come from Marxist geographers who have grappled with the inadequacy of the concept of the unitary state. The starting point of this argument is that local service variation is a crucial determinant of central-local tension. Turning to public housing, the consequence of this argument is that there is also variability in housing production, distribution and consumption and that:

> In all this, variations over time and space are argued to be particularly important. As such, 'states' and 'localities' (not 'state' and 'locality') are key themes ... a central objective is the search for an explanation of the causal processes at work determining housing provision, accounting for state activity (or the lack of it) and producing different outcomes in different localities. (Dickens *et al.*, 1985, p.xi)

Like the Dual State Theory, Dickens *et al.* also start from a position that there is no such thing as the unitary state. It is thus necessary to look at localities and local states as well as central government. To understand the process of housing provision one must analyze not only state policy regarding consumption but also production and participation or protest at the local level. Duncan and Goodwin contend that policy autonomy is inherent in the very idea of local government but that other studies have generally been too based on quantifiable variables, political factors and have 'lacked any conceptional framework which could link government and external social relations' (1988, p.xv).

Their argument is that national variations in the housing situation conceal huge sub-national variations and since it is in the local authorities that decisions are taken over housing provision, these have to be analyzed. The focus of attention is the balance between capital and labour - 'the varying strength of labour might provide a key in explaining variations in housing provision both nationally and locally.' (Dickens *et al.*, 1988, p.8)

According to this view civil society allows three sorts of practices: the social relations of circulation, reproduction and social intervention. Examples of what these comprise include housing tenure, housing as a vital element for the domestic economy and voluntary organizations such as tenants' associations, community groups and political parties which seek to intervene in housing production, circulation and consumption. There are also other features of civil society which are important: firstly, it is highly differentiated by generation, gender, ethnicity, religion and spatially, and secondly, while it is essential to capitalism's existence, 'this plethora of social practices is partly, and to a varying degree, independent of capitalist production - it may even threaten the latter' (p.13).

The *operation* of civil society in conjunction with its *interaction* with state institutions is of crucial importance. This is where the 'local state' fits in because apart from providing local administration, state institutions must manage, respond to and transcend local class relations and other local social relations since civil society is unevenly developed and, therefore, spatially differentiated. Dickens *et al.* (p.17) place particular stress on one dimension of civil society, namely the spatial or locality:

> It is unrealistic to suppose that local variations have no local effects, and they might be important in understanding local housing conflict for instance. But more serious than this, national level analysis in isolation could miss specifically local mechanisms, local social processes, which help produce social change in particular places.

So the argument is that uneven social development and local states are linked both because space can affect social processes and because social processes themselves are uneven. A local social process refers to something active and specific to localities (but not necessarily unique to them) rather than local deviations to national level processes such as local action, local consciousness, local culture, local history and such like. A national process is not merely the average of a mass of local ones, but should apply to all areas in practice. A 'locality' demonstrates not only a degree of variation - it refers to a socially defined unit distinguished by active and specific local differences in causal process.

These arguments have been illustrated by analyzing three housing actions (homelessness and squatting; private property rights and legal action; and rent increases and collective action - Dickens *et al.*, 1985) and this analysis is then extended by Duncan and Goodwin (1988) to cover a larger spectrum of issues under the headings of centralization of policy, centralization of finance and rate-capping and abolition. The conclusions are that local social relations and the nature of local state institutions are of critical importance in influencing the nature and focus of the housing action, mainly because of the inability of local state institutions to adequate respond to, and meet, local demands. Also, local social relations are significant in generating a collective form of action and each example must be understood as something with a complex pre-history and with wider implications for housing consumers and the shape of housing consumption

To sum up these subtle and complex arguments, it is worthwhile quoting the proponents at length (Dickens *et al.,* 1985, p.234):

> ... conceptually more important than state institutions, which are in themselves empty and without power, are the social relations of a particular state. These social relations are, in turn, an expression of the social forces in a society at a particular time and in a specific economic, social, political and ideological context ... This suggests that what the state does over the housing question hinges on the struggle in and around a particular state ... The housing question itself will vary over time and space according to changes in state power and activity, state social relations, and ultimately the wider balance of social forces. Housing consumption is a central component of the housing question and also a very problematic process. Ultimately it dissolves into issues of power and access and control of scarce resources ... Such issues often, by their nature, involve tensions and conflict.

At the end of the book we return to discuss the value of this concept, based on the experience of the EA initiative. The next section deals with the notion of Sub-Central Government which became the dominant paradigm in the central-local government debate of the 1980s and early 1990s.

3.3.4 Sub-central government

Rhodes has been at the forefront of the resurgence of research into central-local relations in Britain (1981) and in 'Beyond Westminster and Whitehall', he presents a re-conceptualization of the study of Sub-Central Government (1988). The meso-level of analysis is of particular relevance, the basic argument being that there are a large number of governmental and political organizations at the sub-central level of government with a range of relationships and that the concept of 'policy networks' is useful in ordering the plethora of links and searching for regularities in the relationships. This model of inter-governmental relations is presented and an attempt is made to demonstrate the relevance of the concept to an analysis of the EA initiative.

i) Organizations and agencies (micro level): The contention is that the behaviour of individuals or organizations is not merely a product of their environment and that they can influence their environment in varying degrees. The micro level of analysis involves exploring relationships within and between these, and the 'power dependence' framework analyses relations between central government and local authorities - it emphasizes the game-like nature of the links, the resources of participants and the rules of the game, strategies and appreciative systems conditioning their exchange. Such a framework is argued to be applicable to intra- and inter-network relations (see Rhodes, 1988, pp. 87-94).

Central-local relations resemble a 'game' with both participants jostling for advantage, deploying the *resources* (financial, hierarchical, constitutional-legal, political and informational) at their disposal to maximize influence over outcomes and trying to avoid becoming dependent upon the other. An organization's resources must be deployed effectively in order to realize the potential for power based on the rules of the game and the choice of strategies. The *rules of the game* are those which set the limits within which discretionary behaviour can take place; and the *strategies* (eg. bargaining, incorporation, confrontation, persuasion, and incentives) are:

> ... the means for imposing upon other organizations an organization's preferences concerning the time of, conditions for, and the extent of the exchange of resources. An organization which effectively deploys its resources will maximize its scope for additional manoeuvre (or discretion) and be able to choose amongst the various courses of action and inaction. (1988, p. 43)

Table 3.2 classifies the various individual actors and agencies operating at the level of the Sub-Central Government while at the same time adapting it for the purposes of EA, thus demonstrating that these meso/micro-level issues can be 'applied' to an analysis of the Estate Action initiative.

ii) Policy networks (meso level): Policy networks are defined as a 'complex of organizations connected to each other by resource dependencies and distinguished from other ... complexes by breaks in the structure of resource dependencies' (Benson, 1982, p.148). Rhodes uses the concept, noting that it is possible to distinguish a variety of policy network in Britain, such as professionalized communities. The main policy network of relevance here are the 'Policy Communities' which are characterized by stability of relationships, restrictive memberships, high degrees of vertical interdependence based on shared service delivery responsibilities and insulation from other networks (as well as from the public and parliament to some extent). Such a description closely fits the Estate Action initiative (see Figure 3.2), for if one analyses the various agencies involved in EA, these clearly form part of a policy network. Professions are important (such as civil servants, housing and architects) as are inter-governmental networks in the shape of LAAs. It is interaction within the policy network which is of crucial explanatory value.

Since the centre controls resources and has many strategies available (such as legislation and coercion), policy networks are not necessarily a constraint on central government and can be manipulated in the government's interest. The relationship is *asymmetric*. Additionally, the centre has a *multiplicity of interests* and policy networks may be based on a department or a section of a department, each with a distinctive style where the relationships are shaped by the 'departmental philosophy' (Rhodes, 1988, p.82). This diversity is matched by the *range of interests* within central government. The 'guardians' (Treasury) seek to restrain expenditure while 'advocates' comprise such service spending departments and policy networks which have a direct involvement with the services of Sub-Central Government, as well as those which have no such involvement. The DoE, being responsible for local government acts both as 'guardian' in the negotiations about local government grant and as 'advocate' for the services over which it has responsibility - this omits the particular interests associated with a specific policy initiative. So to the range of policy networks, it is necessary to add a parallel and profuse range of interests. Central level interests relating to Estate Action may be described thus:

Treasury==>Ministers/StarChamber==>DoE==>Housing==>Estate Action

The analysis of policy networks presupposes that they have a key impact on policies but Rhodes recognizes that policy is both a dependent and

Table 3.1: The four dimensions of the dual state thesis

Dimension	Class Politics	Sector politics	Tension
Organisation	Central	Local	Centralised direction versus local self-determination
Functional	Production	Consumption	Economic versus social priorities
Political	Corporate	Competitive	Rational planning versus democratic accountability
Ideological	Profit	Need	Private property rights versus citizenship rights

Source: Saunders, 1984

Table 3.2: Estate Action: Organizations and actors

Organisations	Actors
1)The 'centre'	[Westminster and Whitehall]
Central departments	[Treasury; DoE: Estate Action]
2) a) Territorial ministries	[n.a. EA applies only to England]
b) Intermediate institutions	[DoE Regional Offices]
c) Non-department bodies	[n.a./peripheral eg. NFHA, HC]
d) Local government	[81 EA local authorities]
e) Sub-central political organisations	
i) Political parties	[Labour; Conservative; Alliance]
ii) Interest groups	[private renovators; LAAs; TAs]
iii) Professions	[civil servants; housing staff etc]

Source: After Rhodes, 1988, p.88, Table 2.4

independent variable and that the analysis of policy networks cannot be limited to an analysis of process - it must encompass policy content which is conditioned by the *two-party system*. Ministers are both heads of bureaucracies at the heart of policy networks and leaders of majority parties. Policy networks have not supplanted party political channels of communication and influence whose effects are all pervasive. He suggests that if policy networks are closed, the party is one of the means of prizing them open and the fluctuating relationship between the two is central to understanding the sources of inertia and innovation in the policy process: "SCG became the locus of conflicts rooted in multiple social cleavages, and the politicization of local government began to pervade central-local relations. (Rhodes, 1988, p.84)

The consequences (of the politicization of local government) includes the revival of municipal socialism (the new urban left); rejection of local government's 'responsibility ethic' in favour of the politics of confrontation; and the militancy of unions reacting to 'cuts' in public expenditure, privatization and limitation of union power among other things. Policy networks *can*, therefore, act to constrain the government's ability to respond to the changes in Sub-Central Government:

> The very existence of policy networks caused certain policy-making processes and outcomes. A product of the welfare state, they had a vested interest in, and helped to fuel, its continued expansion. In an era of economic decline, they resisted political pressure for cuts: a bulwark of inertia ... Total expenditure continued to rise ... [and] only housing of the major welfare services experienced a 'cut' in expenditure in real terms. (Rhodes, 1988, p.85)

The contention is, therefore, that the various policy networks are characteristic of Sub-Central Government and exploring this variety involves examining the relationships within networks, the process of exchange and the rules and strategies governing resource transactions.

3.3.5 The housing policy community

The discussion so far has not been applied specifically to the housing context. Houlihan explores the characteristics and complexity of the relationship between central and local government as it has developed in housing policy, focusing on the main linkages between the various levels of government such as the professions, agencies and consultative bodies and their impact; and the relationship in terms of the problems of policy implementation:

> Only by combining analysis at these ... levels [of individual actors within organizations, the organizations themselves, and the wider social structure] can an adequate theory and understanding of the relationship between central and local government be provided which takes sufficient account of the complexity and ambiguity in the relationship. (Houlihan, 1988, p.56)

He highlights certain inadequacies in the Rhodes model, in particular the fact that while a focus on resource dependencies is an important first step in the analysis of the policy sector which aids understanding of the linkages that bind members together (and thus explaining particular network configurations), the framework seems unable to go beyond this. The way forward is to use an approach which focuses on the *linkages* through which resource dependency relations are mediated and articulated. This has the advantage of drawing attention to the processes which characterize the pattern of exchange and the way in which relationships are structured and managed.

Few communities have discrete boundaries so the aim is to understand the community through an analysis of the background and roles of the main members. The *formal* roles are those publicly adhered to while the *informal* ones are those roles acquired and developed primarily as a result of intra-organizational and inter-organizational relations within the network. Such roles include integration (important as complexity increases and involves the integration of organizations into a community), leadership (setting of public goals, organizing the community and controlling entry), resource acquisition (a prime need which includes finance and clients and legitimacy: both at individual organizations and at community level) and bridging (linking the policy community to the wider social structure). Community survival and effectiveness are dependent on the fulfillment of the four roles; and behaviour of members will be influenced by a variety of factors such as organizational/survival interests, interest groups, resource dependency relations and links to sources of power outside the community (Houlihan, 1988, p.88). Within this policy community, certain sources of ideological influence (political parties, professions, non-state voluntary and private organizations and other contiguous policy communities) are identified, as are seven linkages in the policy community (see Figure 3.3). The network of EA-related organizations (Figure 3.2) can be considered as a policy network which fits neatly into Houlihan's conception of the housing policy community.

1) Bureaucratic: for example the 1980 Housing Act specifying rules, regulations and defining the rights and duties of the organizations. However: "Although bureaucratic linkages are basic to central control over much of local authority housing policy they are difficult and expensive to sustain ... As a result there is a strong incentive to develop other linkages" (1988, p.78), such as the use of experts to make technical judgements.

2) Technical linkages: this refers to the increasing use of Policy Planning Systems, such as HIPs, which operate at the centre-local interface. There was originally a strong emphasis on comprehensiveness of problem analysis and search for solutions, forward projection of costs and policies, priority setting and performance reviews but these are now used as a weapon in local authorities' bids for resources (Houlihan, 1983; 1984). Policy Planning Systems involve an acceptance of the significance of data,

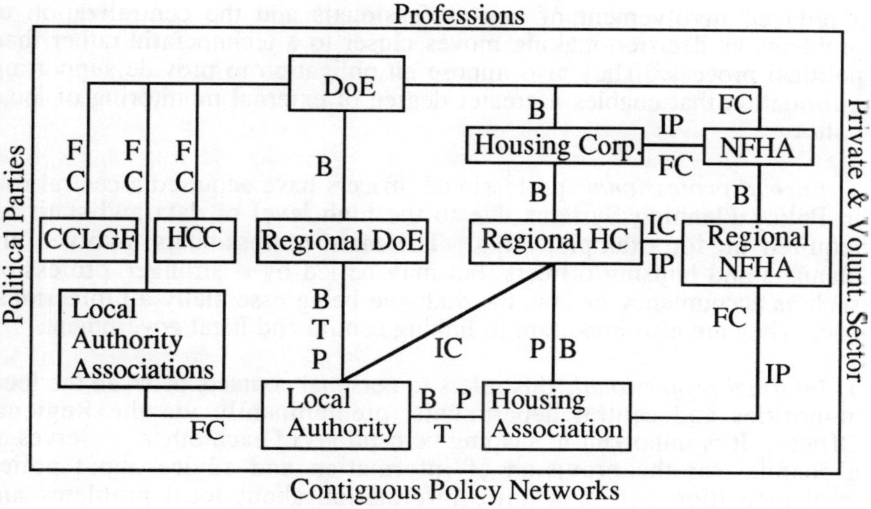

Key: Form of Relationship		Basis of Relationship	Character of Relationship
B	Bureaucratic	Convention, legislation	Relatively clearly defined; predictable; regular; frequent
T	Technical	Shared expertise and ideology	Continuous, narrowly based
P	Formal Professional	Requirements of plan	Periodic; cyclical; often strong financial element
IP	Informal Professional	Shared interests and problems	Irregular; Frequent
IC	Informal Consultative	Information tansmission	Irregular; infrequent; often strongly political
FC	Formal Consultative	Information exchange	Regular; often overtly political
—	Party Political	Broad consensus ideology	Infrequent; not always consensual

Source: Houlihan, 1988, Table 4.2 and Figure 4.1

Figure 3.3: The national housing policy community and the nature of the links

a reduced involvement of non-professionals and the centralization of problems as decision-making moves closer to a technocratic rather than political process. They also impose an obligation to provide supporting information that enables a greater degree of external monitoring of local policy.

3) Formal professional: professional officers have acquired a central role in Policy Planning Systems due to the high level of data and statistics required in, for example, HIPs. The main professionals involved are planners and housing officers, but may be led by a 'stronger' profession such as accountancy or law, the dialogue being essentially a professional one. They are also important in linking central and local government.

4) Informal professional: this refers to personal contacts between the local authorities and central departments, predominantly via the Regional Offices. It is important in shaping perceptions of each other. It serves as a channel for the provision of information and advice about policy implementation and to acquire information about local problems and successes. It operates at two main levels of contact i) middle management of the local authority and concerns interpretation of rules and regulations and ii) at senior or chief officer level and concerns discussion of problems of mutual interest. Regional Offices (ROs) are keen to maintain personal contact as it softens their image and they get to meet the implementing officers of, for example, Estate Action or the HIPs programmes.

5) Informal consultative and 6) Formal consultative: there are various degrees of formality ranging from the six monthly or quarterly meetings of the Housing Consultative Council (HCC) and the Consultative Council on Local Government Finance (CCLGF), to the periodic meetings between local authorities and regional officials. The least formal are the common meetings organized by Regional Officers to promote policies involving authorities in their region. More formal are the Local Authority Associations (LAAs) which maintain regular contact with DoE ministers on a wide range of issues. The most formal is the CCLGF, which like the HCC meetings, has declined in importance but has managed to survive because both parties see the meetings as a valuable forum for information exchange, where policy priorities can be expressed, local authority responses monitored and matters of policy interpretation and implementation pursued.

7) Party political: such links include those which operate through the national organization of the parties and, secondly, those that involve Ministers and LAA representatives. Both major parties have opportunities for the representation of the interest of their councils and councilors, but these links have received little attention. As for the LAAs, despite their privileged access based on party connections the central problem remains whether they really do result in greater influence (Houlihan, 1988, pp.75-85), nevertheless, these constitute the final linkage in the range available within the central-local network.

3.3.6 Summary of ideas

This section has been concerned with trying to provide a conceptual backcloth to inform the thesis. It has involved analyzing the various concepts which impinge upon the initiative under discussion: the traditional conceptualization of 'central-local relations' swinging from a 'partner' role for local government to an 'agent' status; as well as the view of the centre as homogeneous and monolithic has been criticized. The Dual State Thesis points out crucial flaws in such literature in general, and the state theory literature in particular, namely that it is incorrect to diagnose the local state as a mere extension/agent of the central state. This line of argument has also been pursued within the structuralist framework by Dickens *et al.* who also believe that it is not sufficient to analyze housing policy at the national level. Their contention is that local social relations and the nature of local state institutions are of crucial importance and that the human world of action is temporal, spatial and located in unique circumstances which give a specific action its character.

The Dual State Thesis argues that the analysis must be split into the production processes (a function of the centre) and the consumption processes (a function of the local state) and both of these are further differentiated according to the political, structural, ideological and organizational dimensions. The latter is particularly useful as a framework or background for the book but the relevant parts are mainly derived from Rhodes' concept of the Sub-Central Government which, like Saunders, argues that there is no such thing as an unitary state. It is made up of a multiplicity of organizations where even central government is split into departments and sub-departments, below which is the sub-central government. An argument is presented as to why this framework is relevant and why the concept of 'policy communities' may be pertinent to research on the Estate Action programme, but that the links between the various actors and agencies within policy communities are not adequately articulated.

The work and perspectives of Houlihan adds to Rhodes' conceptualization of 'policy communities' and transforms them back to the issue of public housing in Britain. This approach is used as the main set of concepts relevant for the interpretation of the empirical findings of the thesis. The intention is to return to these conceptual issues in the final chapter of the thesis. The rest of this chapter discusses the methodology employed in conducting the empirical work.

3.4 Methodological issues

Having introduced EA, its explicit objectives and its policy environment, it is now possible to move on to define the aims and methods used in the thesis. There is an extremely problematic and changing situation facing local housing authorities (Chapter 2) and there have been a variety of initiatives to try to improve the management and maintenance of these areas which have concentrated on 'difficult' estates (such as Housing Associations, Tenant Management Co-operatives, Trusts, HATs, neighbourhood offices, PEP etc). Each of these, however, either involve local authorities solely (except PEP) or are aimed at a specific method, style or organization of management. EA is different. It intimately involves both authorities and government, encourages a variety of innovative management styles and ownership forms and places tenants at the forefront of proposals. EA also involves central government resources and local authority investment whilst encouraging a third dimension, namely private sector involvement and funding.

It is, therefore, an initiative which is a useful surrogate for evaluating much central government housing policy, as well as how authorities are responding to the new pressures and opportunities being presented to them. Naturally, this book does not hope to provide enlightenment on all areas of government housing policy. Rather, it seeks to identify the interactions necessary in establishing EA-funded schemes; how its objectives were established; how authorities have reacted; the effects on local housing programmes, priorities and policies; what tensions and difficulties arise in meeting the challenges facing council housing by using the initiative; and lastly what lessons can be learnt and applied as a result of the research. In line with the main objectives of the book discussed in chapter 1, the rest of the work is translated into the following format:

- origins and formation of the EA initiative, its appeal to central government and the civil service (DoE); and the reaction of its policy community (Chapter 4);
- operation and implementation process involved (Chapters 5, 6, 7)
- advantages and disadvantages resulting from such a policy (Chs 5, 6, 7)
- the outcomes/effectiveness (Chapters 6 and 8)
- synthesis of the main conclusions and theoretical implications (Ch 9)

To this end, and given the specific environment within which the EA initiative operates, it is important at this stage to describe the methodology employed to enable the rest of the book to concentrate purely on the evidence itself. It is clear from the discussion above that EA is a relatively novel subject area which operates at three main levels: central (EA/Treasury/Cabinet); regional (DoE Regional Offices); and local (housing authorities in England). An approach was thus necessary which could provide substantial first-hand information on the complex interactions at these levels. In the end it was decided that it would be appropriate to use both intensive and extensive explanatory tools.

Given the paucity of data, a national survey which could incorporate all the authorities participating in EA was essential to elucidate general patterns and issues. However, questionnaires lack the depth and explanatory power which is provided by employing interview techniques and these are, therefore, used primarily to pursue the more important issues brought out by the survey analysis. Semi-structured interviews are employed within the case-studies and it also proved to be the most appropriate technique to conduct the research at the regional and central levels. The fact that there are relatively few DoE Regional Offices (10); EA Central officials; and case-studies (four), made such a strategy feasible as well as allowing for depth and complimentarity. There were several stages in the research and there is thus a balance of extensive and intensive methodologies throughout the analysis which 'feed-off' one another, thus generating a large body of original material which, it is hoped, yields high explanatory power. The sequence of the research is now described briefly:

- unstructured interviews with local and central agencies, housing researchers, academics and professional staff. These were intended to amplify the knowledge obtained via the literature review or the published information, to the actual operation of the EA initiative. This formed the basis of the next structured stages;
- a national questionnaire survey;
- semi-structured interviews with the ROs;
- semi-structured interviews with central agents including consultants; and
- case-studies comprising semi-structured interviews in four localities.

3.4.1 The preliminary stages

The first stage consisted of reading all the existing public information which relates to EA (Annual Reports, DoE Circulars, press cuttings and PEP Guides - see DoE, 1987c), however, the only method of obtaining an authoritative understanding of the initiative was to interview informed individuals at all levels. Accordingly a series of visits and interviews were conducted to discuss the initiative with the Central team, DoE consultants, DoE Regional officers charged with liaising with local authorities, local authority associations and representatives, housing professionals and researchers, as well as the local authorities themselves by approaching the housing officers co-ordinating the EA schemes (see Table 3.3). This enabled a comprehensive picture to be built up of the situation since 1985 and the main issues were identified for inclusion in the national questionnaire.

Table 3.3: Authorities visited/interviewed at survey stage

Brent	Newham	Birmingham	Middlesbrough
Greenwich	Southwark	Bolton	Gateshead
Hamsmith & Ful	Tower Hamlets	Dudley	Salford
Kensington & Chel	Wandsworth	Knowsley	Sandwell
Islington	Westminster	Langbourgh	Sheffield
Lewisham		Leicester	Wirral

3.4.2 A national questionnaire survey

It was considered necessary to approach local authorities directly with an original survey in order to investigate the extent to which local authorities were interacting with EA, gauge the range of innovative management initiatives being investigated and implemented and to examine the nature of the relationship between EA and local authorities. Given the rapidly evolving nature of this initiative, it was imperative to capture aggregate data for all the authorities so as to evaluate its success and generalize on its evolution and achievements. There were several stages:

i) Piloting the survey: 'Piloting' was considered to be essential to ensure that the survey draft was logical and representative of the relationship with EA and the situation as it exists; to assess whether all the objectives of the survey would be obtained; discuss issues of presentation; and to eliminate any remaining ambiguities and superfluous questions. Various methods were utilized. The respondents' opinion was that the survey was sensible with some minor modification of categories for conciseness and clarity. All authorities insisted that the high degree of structuring in the survey was the best approach to adopt as it made the survey quicker to complete, provided consistency of response and reduced ambiguity, however, they insisted that authorities should have the opportunity to express themselves if their experience deviated from the 'normal' situation. An 'other' category was thus added to all the appropriate questions, together with space for comments.

The type of information requested was primarily of a subjective nature (requesting opinions rather than 'hard' data) for important reasons. Firstly, many of the developments in the EA initiative seemed to be informal in nature, therefore, authorities' perceptions were valuable. There was also a trade-off between the level of detail, the type of information requested, the time necessary to respond and the resulting response-rate. It was decided that a structured approach would work best in this particular case with an opportunity for authorities to rank the importance of their responses. Most importantly, the thrust of the survey as an EA evaluation exercise was in any case, subjective in nature. More detailed output measures were also sought when appropriate. For example, 'hard' data was sought on capital and revenue costs to authorities in implementing such schemes and the number of staff involved.

Based on this process, a set of issues were selected for inclusion in the survey. Because of the lack of alternative data and research on EA, the issues selected came mainly from the preliminary unstructured interviews conducted with 10 local authorities participating in the EA initiative. It was, therefore, likely that the issues addressed in the survey would reflect the concerns and priorities of those interviewed at the time. This means that with hindsight, the advantages listed in the survey could have been more extensive, however, because of the lack of alternative information at the time, the survey reflected the knowledge and experience that was available. In an attempt to 'balance' the survey, the 'pilot' was also sent to a DoE Regional Office and the comments and suggestions were also incorporated.

ii) Circulation of survey: The final survey (see Pinto, 1992d, Appendix 1 for a copy of the survey) was then mailed to all Housing Directors concerned requesting for the survey to be passed on to the appropriate officer co-ordinating their involvement with EA, as it proved difficult to identify these individuals in advance. While there were 87 authorities which had been involved with EA and which had been successful in receiving EA HIPs (between 1985 and 1989), the survey was actually circulated to a total of 81 authorities because six authorities had only received EA funding for Homeless Initiatives. This is an issue with which this book was only peripherally concerned (as opposed to the management style and ownership forms) and it was decided that these authorities could be excluded without unduly damaging the thrust of the survey or the analysis.

iii) Response-rates: A 50% response-rate was achieved in the first round. This was not considered satisfactory given a population of 81 authorities, so substantial effort was devoted in 'chasing-up' the large number of authorities which had indicated the intention of completing the survey but which had not done so by the dead-line. This was a period of critical importance, for it allowed time to continue the process of visiting and interviewing authorities in order to gain an understanding of changing circumstances to the EA set-up; different authorities' approaches; their experiences and schemes; as well as augmenting the response rate and thus adding to its quality. The visits facilitated the identification of potential case-studies. This stage enhanced both the analysis and the interpretation of the data. A protracted time period was the compromise made to obtain a 75% response-rate (61 authorities). This level of response was regarded as essential in order to be able to generalize with a high degree of confidence from a relatively small population.

iii) Statistical analysis: A decision was made at the outset of the empirical analysis that statistical significance testing could not be employed on the various tables to be presented. This decision was based on a number of key criteria: the sample size is small (61 authorities) from a population which is also small (81 possible EA authorities); the population itself is highly non-random in selection; and the key dimensions of comparison were expected to stand out clearly from inspection of cross-tabulated results. The use of descriptive tabulations derives from the chosen methodology of intensive study of the national sample, complimented by case-studies and 'triangulation' using EA officers and council tenants.

3.4.3 The semi-structured interviews

An attempt was made to obtain information on various EA, RO, and LA issues which were added to and/or developed from the national survey. Such a method had the advantage of facilitating the creation of a greater level of detail and explanation as well as enabling 'triangulation' of information to take place. Interviews were thus the appropriate tool and in particular, semi-structured interviews which introduced a flexibility for additional information and explanatory factors to be discussed and incorporated. In this manner data were introduced with which to compare and enhance the survey information, thus creating the potential for greater explanatory power for the analysis. An attempt was made to keep interviewees within 'relevant' areas although they had free rein to discuss issues, their causality and to introduce related factors which they considered to be relevant.

i) Interviewing DoE regional officials: The Regional Offices (ROs) have a central role in facilitating the implementation of the EA project. It was thus important to identify this role, the functions performed and the nature of the interaction with authorities. The author initially contacted all 10 ROs to ascertain which were willing to co-operate (see Map 1). This was done in order to obtain first hand information of their involvement with the EA initiative and its implementation, but EA Central expressed misgivings about the idea, stressing that these were busy government offices but accepting that it could not prevent the research if the ROs were willing to be interviewed. In the end, five ROs were selected partly with EA's objections in mind, but mainly because the ROs approached were the most influential on the basis of the number of authorities bidding for EA resources. These five ROs contained 62 out of the 81 authorities. It might have been interesting to have investigated the other ROs, however, two of the ROs had no EA schemes and to have interviewed more ROs would have been repetitive.

Personnel from five ROs were interviewed (RO1-RO5). Two interviews were conducted in RO1. RO1a refers to an unstructured interview which corresponds to a discussion at the early stages of the research when an attempt was made to obtain feedback on the issues being addressed in the survey, as well as to gain an understanding of the operation of the Regional Offices prior to the preparation of the more detailed and precise semi-structured interviews (RO1b - see Pinto, 1992d).

ii) The 'Central' interviews: EA is a relatively recent initiative which has grown significantly in importance. The only feasible way to develop an understanding of the scheme, its origins and operation was to interview the main actors charged with deciding its priorities, objectives and generating its organizational, financial and administrative system. A variety of key EA-related (current and former) founding members of the initiative were interviewed so as to obtain a 'rounded' perspective (EA1 - EA 5/6). A variety of issues were discussed which broadly related to EA's origins, its present state and future development. A schedule of topics for the semi-structured interviews was the technique employed, the advantage being that it was flexible enough to provide scope for discussion and the pursuit of relevant topics, while also enabling aggregation of issues as the basic questions were structured in a compatible manner.

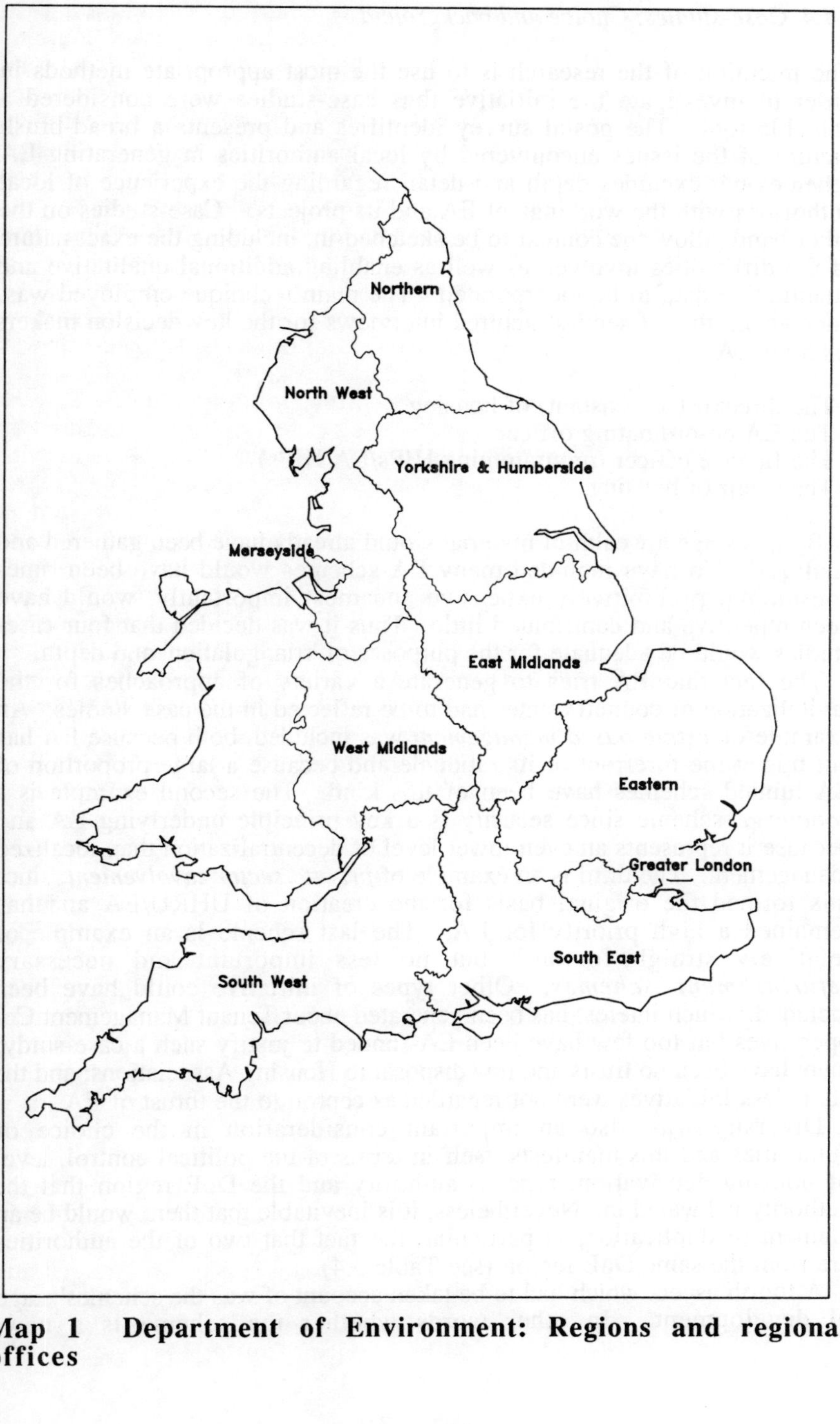

Map 1 Department of Environment: Regions and regional offices

3.4.4 Case-studies: Choice and background

The intention of the research is to use the most appropriate methods in order to investigate the initiative thus case-studies were considered a valuable tool. The postal survey identifies and presents a broad-brush picture of the issues encountered by local authorities in generating EA schemes but excludes depth and detail regarding the experience of local authorities with the workings of EA and its projects. Case-studies on the other hand, allow the context to be sketched-in, including the exact nature of the difficulties involved as well as enabling additional qualitative and quantitative data to be incorporated. The main technique employed was, once again, that of semi-structured interviews for the key decision makers *vis à vis* EA:

- The director (or assistant) of housing
- The EA co-ordinating officer
- The finance officer (programming HIPs/EA HIPs)
- The Chair of housing.

By this stage a wealth of material would already have been gathered and analyzed. To have included many EA schemes would have been time-consuming, prohibitively expensive and most importantly, would have been repetitive and contributed little. Thus it was decided that four case-studies would be adequate for the purposes of 'triangulation' and depth.

The fact that EA tries to generate a variety of approaches for the revitalization of council estates had to be reflected in the case-studies. An example of *estate based management* was included, both because EA has put this at the forefront of its rationale and because a large proportion of EA-funded schemes have been of this kind. The second example is a *concierge* scheme since security is a key principle underlying EA and because it represents an even lower level of decentralization than localized management. The third is an example of *private sector involvement* since this formed the original basis for the creation of UHRU/EA and has remained a high priority for EA. The last scheme is an example of relatively straight-forward, but no less important and necessary *refurbishment schemes*. Other types of initiative could have been included. Much interest has been generated about Tenant Management Co-operatives but too few have been EA-funded to justify such a case-study; there have been no trusts and few disposal to Housing Associations; and the Homeless Initiatives were not regarded as central to the thrust of EA.

Diversity was also an important consideration in the choice of authorities and this manifests itself in terms of the political control, level of housing deprivation, type of authority and the DoE region that the authority is located in. Nevertheless, it is inevitable that there would be an element of duplication, in particular, the fact that two of the authorities are from the same DoE region (see Table 3.4).

A fourth aspect which had to be taken account of was the schemes' stage of development. In other words whether the scheme is a new, continuation or an 'old' scheme which no longer receives EA funding. Although the original intention was to examine a new scheme about to start in the 1989/90 financial year (before); then again six months later (during); and once more twelve months later (after), this proved to be impractical because there would not have been insufficient time for the effects of the scheme to have worked themselves through sufficiently to enable evaluation of impact. The schemes chosen were thus either subject to continuation funding (so as to analyze how this translates itself in terms of the planning, spending and efficiency and effectiveness of the schemes) or completed schemes, all dating from 1986/87. The reason for this is quite important since it can justifiably be argued that results take a long time to filter through and that any evaluation of the effectiveness of EA schemes would be inadequate if it did not consider this.

The choice of case-studies has been made with these factors in mind. It is natural that the case-studies should be biased towards the most deprived authorities (with a housing deprivation or 'Z-score' of 1) which also tend to be predominantly Labour-controlled. Although information exists on the types of initiative funded by EA, this is extremely rudimentary, offering little in the way of description upon which to base a rational explanation for the choice of case-studies. Consequently the author was forced to base choice upon personal knowledge and experience obtained via first-hand visits to over twenty authorities (see Table 3.3). The case-studies were chosen with the criteria described above in mind (Table 3.4).

Table 3.4: The case-studies: Background information

LA	Scheme Type	Auth Type	DoE Region	Politics	Z-Score
LA1	Concierge	Distr. Council	E. Midlands	Labour	1 (Worst)
LA2	Private Sector	Metr. District	North West	Labour	1
LA3	Refurbishment	Outer London	London	SDP/Lib	1
LA4	Est. Based Mmt	Distr. Council	North West	Conserv	3

3.4.5 Investigating tenants' opinions

In obtain an indication of the schemes' effectiveness, it is important to consider the opinions of the customer, in this case the council tenants. Pinto (1992d) has looked into this issue by canvassing tenant opinion regarding the extent to which the block or estate has improved (in terms of its image, environment, comfort and safety, and level of managerial support) as a result of the EA schemes. The focus was on a 'before/after' approach, which has both advantages and disadvantages. In this book we will not discuss the findings in detail, except as indicative of the general effects of EA-funded schemes so as to enhance the other measures of EA's impact. Readers a referred to Pinto (1992d, Appendices 4 and 7) for the methodology and findings of the tenant survey.

3.5 Conclusions

This chapter has reviewed the stimulants giving rise to the EA initiative, namely the government's moves towards privatization and the creation of the Priority Estates Project; EA's objectives which are quite variable in nature; and the complex policy environment within which EA operates, highlighting the EA Central, DoE Regional Office and local authority structure. This led to an introduction of the most relevant concepts which relate to the operation of these central-local organizations. The 'Agent/Partnership' model, the 'Dual State Thesis', the 'Uneven Social Development' and the 'Sub-Central Government' frameworks were all discussed. All have elements which would seem to touch upon the operation of the EA initiative, however, it is left to the last chapter to discuss their relevance in the light of the intervening research findings.

This chapter also translated the aims of the book (stated in chapter 1) into an appropriate methodology which involves the interplay of various research techniques - a postal survey, semi-structured interviews and case-study work. Each method will highlight and emphasize different aspects which will result, it is hoped, in a through analysis of the EA initiative. It was also useful to discuss the methodology at this stage so that the subsequent chapters could be freed to concentrate on the evidence without frequent methodological interruptions.

Part 2
THE EMPIRICAL EVIDENCE

4 The policy background: Origins, formation and initial reactions

4.1 Introduction

The initiative that was launched in 1985 contained a mixed set of criteria. On the one hand, EA was to facilitate and help fund the creation of housing co-operatives, trusts and private sector involvement - all designed, it could be said, to encourage the continued contraction of the council housing sector. Yet, it was also to encourage authorities to improve their management structures, tenant consultation procedures and to help improve their estate security and environment (see chapter 3 for EA's remit). In other words, measures to counteract the management difficulties faced by housing authorities (chapter 2) and thus improve the circumstances for many council tenants.

This chapter seeks to analyze how and why the EA initiative took this shape. Since there were neither debates in parliament nor any published information on the process which led to the inauguration of the initiative, the methodology used in this chapter has been to contact key individuals involved in the build-up and creation of the EA scheme in order to obtain a first-hand understanding of its origins and formulation. The last part of the chapter also analyses the local authorities', (local Authority Associations (LAAs) and housing commentators' initial reactions to the EA Unit when it was launched. The sources of information used in this chapter are primarily derived from a set of semi-structured interviews conducted mainly with EA Central staff, although some supporting evidence comes from the DoE Regional Officials interviewed. The methodology was explained in detail in the latter part of chapter 3.

4.2 The civil servants' priorities: Managerial issues

The government's conception of the future role of council housing has been discussed together with the fact that it has now been relegated to a 'enabling' role and that local authorities are generally regarded as bureaucratic, inefficient and uncaring landlords. When the key civil servants behind the formation of the EA initiative were interviewed about its origins, influences and which models fed into it, they all stressed that it was the managerial issues (rather than political considerations) which were paramount - as management was then a key DoE interest. This was not a spontaneous initiative. Rather it was the culmination of a series of DoE studies and three main antecedents may be identified.

4.2.1 The DoE's investigation of 'difficult to let' housing

The origins of the EA initiative go back to the mid 1970s, to Mike Burbidge and the Social Research Division (DoE) which: "... produced reports on what was then called 'difficult to let' housing [Burbidge *et al.*, 1981] ... With the ageing of the public housing stock, a message was going out that whereas councils had traditionally found it very easy to let their properties, a lot of it was becoming difficult-to-let and manage. Suddenly, there were large chunks of property where boarding-up was taking place and even demolitions in extreme cases" (EA 2).

These three volumes (Burbidge *et al.*, 1981) served to highlight the fact that the management of estates was a key issue behind many of the problems in these areas: "At the time, the emphasis and blame was placed on the planners, architects and developers for building 'non-traditional' housing which nobody wanted to live in. After the research, however, it became clear that this was also happening in the traditional type of low density housing such as the cottage estates and that this was because of the design of these estates, their locations, their lack of physical infrastructure and, more importantly, the fact that management had not been taken on board. For example, repairs were not being dealt with and there was a lack of management presence on the ground" (EA 2).

Clearly a variety of factors interacted to create 'difficult to let' estates and it was at this point that the DoE's housing management advisory group: "... set-up seminars around the country with local authorities, carefully discussing the findings of the research on 'difficult-to-let' estates. We found that local authorities themselves had begun to understand the issues and started to change their management emphasis. Some authorities were actively experimenting with different methods of managing their properties and the DoE's Housing Advisory Group began to publish 'good practice' reports on these." (EA 2)

The report 'An investigation of difficult to let housing' was thus important for several reasons: it represented the first official recognition of the existence the difficulties; it was thorough in its analysis of the causes of the problems; and it recommended various alternatives which combined with the issues discussed below (4.2 ii) to produce the PEP and the EA initiatives.

4.2.2 Tenant and town hall

The research reports undertaken under Burbidge's supervision served to highlight the weakness of the management presence on the ground. This was added to by: "A further study by Lesley Andrews, who spent over a year examining the situation in these difficult estates from the bottom-up [participant observation]. She came-up with a list of policy recommendations which were to prove influential to the formation of PEP" (EA 1) and also, by implication to EA's development:

• *Housing management functions:* area housing management teams should control lettings (the key to good management practice), repairs (carried out by a small team of on-site tradesmen), be involved in the design brief of new projects, arrears control, public relations with residents and the administration of transfer requests and other administrative matters.

• *The organization of housing management:* management functions should be carried out by area teams, decentralized to convenient locations, with each manager responsible for all the management and administrative functions listed above. In Andrews' view: "There is no reason why this devolution of powers should not be accompanied by the allocation of a budget for the area" (1979, p.273). The report also maintained that 'the style of management should be participatory rather than bureaucratic', personal initiatives ought to be encouraged and council policy goals should be clearly stated to residents and staff alike.

• *Housing management roles:* all management officers' briefs should be extended. Housing management assistants should be encouraged to develop a wider working knowledge of their patch which would aid decisions on lettings and public relations work. The role of resident caretakers should be re-evaluated.

• *Staff training/staffing requirements:* "If the service is to be effective it is essential that officers with the appropriate educational background and personal resources for the development of management skills are attracted and retained" (p.275). Basic training should be given in communication skills such as interview techniques, public speaking, letter writing and even a staff training officer. Attention should also be given to attracting women to the service (with suitable training and working hours) as female residents and the elderly of both sexes prefer to deal with women on sensitive issues. These were all issues which had not been tackled to any great extent.

• *Housing management and estate residents:* the area team officers should be accessible to the residents. Convenient locations and flexible hours are desirable, as are receptionists to handle all visitors, calls and arrange interviews with staff members: "Perhaps more importantly, contact between officers and residents in all types of situations need to be informed by altered attitudes. These must be based on mutual respect ... There should be more on-going contact with officers giving unsolicited information using not only meetings but posters, local newspapers or area office newsletters. At the same time expectations should not be raised unless the prospects for meeting them are real, and shortcomings in the services offered should be honestly admitted." (p. 276).

The recommendations were quite revolutionary and via three PEP consultants, the DoE undertook to attempt to raise authorities' awareness of the value of intensifying the management presence on certain estates. This was the next phase of DoE involvement.

4.2.3 The Priority Estates Project (PEP)

In (EA 2)'s view the next crucial step which 'gave the whole thing impetus', was the idea of PEP which became a key initiative pursued by the DoE, primarily to encourage a greater and more local management presence on the estates: "At this juncture the department decided that the way forward, was to set-up pilot projects to 'pump-prime' the process by demonstrating how to achieve better management." (EA 2), and it was at this point that Ann Power came in: "She was the engine that took it over in astute ways" (EA 2). (EA 1) notes that: "She brought useful experience from her work in setting-up co-operatives in Islington and from her research in the USA where she was looking at far worse estates than in Britain. She is the one who dressed-up the skeleton of the idea, such as generating more local employment such as caretakers, localized budgets etc (EA 1)".

(EA 2) adds that: "A number of authorities were experimenting with a variety of initiatives. These were studied and reports were produced periodically [by the DoE's Housing Advisory Group] to encourage authorities to go on experimenting and innovating. Having successfully engineered and planted the idea, PEP sold itself with DoE funds and the number of such initiatives began to spread" (EA 2). To sum up, one of the key tenets behind the EA initiative is that of encouraging better, more efficient and local management structures. This concern with the management aspect has its origins in a number of DoE reports which had previously highlighted this as a crucial, but missing element in the most problematic portions of council housing. EA's managerial emphasis was thus the culmination of this research, experience and interest. According to those interviewed, the EA initiative was built upon the DoE experience and it was natural that this should greatly influence the final form of the initiative and that local management should end up with a high profile.

4.3 The government's objectives: Housing policy

The civil servants acknowledge that: "Even by this date [1985], the Conservative government had failed to establish a major policy for social housing. In terms of its arguments for the diversification of tenure, the only issue was the 'right to buy' and improvement grants for the private sector" (EA 2). The implication is that in certain respects, the thinking behind the origins of EA and the EA initiative itself served to focus and extend central government housing policy. This section discusses in what ways the initiative may have contributed to the development of the Conservative housing policy.

4.3.1 'Badly managed, inefficient and bureaucratic'

By default EA's starting point was a critique of established management practices since it was, after all, an initiative set up to encourage authorities to innovate and experiment with new management and ownership structures, such as locally-based management and repair offices, disposal and TMCs. EA can thus be seen as a central government initiative to demonstrate to local authorities how they could improve their management practices. According to a DoE Regional Officer involved in implementing the EA initiative: "The overriding objective was to tackle the problems of run-down and difficult-to-let estates by a variety of means. Management was seen as the basis upon which success was either secured or not. It is true that the 'hub of the wheel' is estate based management because if the estate is badly managed, it is likely to go into decline once again. Therefore, the emphasis is on effective management and decentralization, ideally with repair depots and decentralized budgets too." (RO 5). The initiative was designed to force local authorities to the adequacy of their own management arrangements. The government's motive was either to further undermine council housing by pointing to its problematic management or to genuinely force authorities to consider their clients' needs more seriously... or both.

4.3.2 Politically sensitive issues

In terms of the political origins of EA: "It was reported after the election, that Mrs Thatcher wanted to 'do something' about the inner cities - to provide a more public face and to concentrate on those areas which existing programmes were not reaching. This came back to the civil service which also recognised that there were pockets of bad housing other than in inner cities" (EA 3). A further factor mentioned by both (EA 2) and (EA 3) relates to the succession of riots in 1981. These were of significance to EA insofar as: "It spurred the government to explore other ways and means of dealing with the situation in estates [and inner cities], such as the Merseyside Task Force and a variety of other schemes, such as the Brixton initiatives and the Inner City Projects" (EA 2).

It would make sense for the government to attempt to concentrate resources into those areas which could be considered as the potential 'flash-points'. These would naturally be the run-down council estates with their high concentrations of unemployed, ethnic mixes and poor and sterile environments. Indeed, it had been widely reported that riots had originated in certain estates, such as Broadwater Farm in October 1985 (see Lord Gifford, 1986; 1989). This situation would undoubtedly have acted to make the government more willing to consider approving the EA scheme. A DoE Regional Officer was blunt about EA's motives: "The origins of UHRU were essentially political. There was a desire by politicians for something to be done about the inner city ... or to be seen to be doing something" (RO 1b).

This motive was to impact directly on the form that EA took: "Ideas were being desperately searched within the department, which could bring work to people in such estates, as well as to improve the estate itself and its management ... the idea being that there was always going to be a number of people with skills and energies in these areas - what was needed was to harness these. Community Refurbishment Schemes (CRS) were thus born using Inner Cities and Urban Programme cash. The Merseyside Task Force worked successfully with a number of authorities ... [this] constituted another strand to the origins of EA" (EA 2). The employment issue has now expanded to become the key EA focus in 1990/91.

The same individual notes also that: "Ministers were constantly worried about the media and the reports of 'no go' estates, arson, crime and so on; and the Home Office was also greatly concerned about crime, vandalism and the design and layout of estates" (EA 2). All these concerns were to give rise to other EA criteria such as its emphasis on security measures and the employment of Alice Coleman to look into estate designs and layouts (DoE News Release No.612) with a budget of £50m.

4.3.3 Reforming the HIPs mechanism and targeting resources

According to a key member behind the formation of EA, a novel though not unexpected aspect of the initiative was that: "There was within the DoE a keen interest in the operation of the HIPs system. Originally, borrowing approval had been issued on the basis of seven distinct categories. There had been several battles with local authorities and their associations who had the attitude that the DoE should give them the allocation and let them 'get on with it'. This led to a reduction of categories to four, then three and eventually the DoE gave in altogether in 1981, when there was a single HIPs block of allocation" (EA 2).

However, an important issue for the DoE was: "... whether the cash was going to the right places and whether councils were spending the HIPs allocation on a variety of things, but too little on their own stock. There was a concern that the block system was not getting the parts which it should reach. According to the HIPs returns, the high incidence of voids and arrears all indicated that some of the worst problems were not being tackled" (EA 2). It would be reasonable to assume, therefore, that it was the notion of 'targeting' public resources to where they were most needed that was probably behind this concern. Indeed, one of EA's central tenets was to be its ability to focus resources onto specific spatial areas which the DoE considered to be the neglected and in most need, namely the public housing estates (see chapter 3 for the method of selection).

As discussed above, central government was concerned that authorities were not investing public resources where they thought these ought to be properly directed. Given its emphasis on targeting resources to where they were most needed and its concern with 'value for money' exercises, EA fitted perfectly the Conservative government's *penchant* for demonstrating to councils how to achieve economy, effectiveness and efficiency in the delivery of local services.

The fact that this was and remains a crucial issue behind the EA initiative is voiced by a leading EA Central member: "In a sense EA HIPs does go against the trend for reduced public expenditure on council housing, but not in another. The government is very keen on 'targeting' resources to specific things, so as to ensure value for money ... EA is entirely consistent with those objectives and indeed, the issue of targeting resources, is the basis of our arguments with the Treasury for finance" (EA 4). A founding member of EA leaves no doubt of the importance placed on this aspect by the government: "EA was all about targeting authorities and resources. Initially it invited 69 authorities to submit bids. It then became open for all authorities, since it was argued that even resource-rich authorities have their problem estates. With the employment initiative, EA is about to narrow once again into funding fewer but larger schemes in the future" [see chapters 7 and 8 for more details] (EA 5/6). The attempt to target resources was clearly a fundamental component behind the formation of the project.

4.3.4 Pressures for additional public finance

Certain pressures operated upon the Treasury to force it to allow local authorities to borrow additional housing investment resources (as implied by EA HIPs). It was discussed elsewhere that several studies have evaluated the state of disrepair of the housing stock in England and Wales and that they estimate that it would cost £20bn to correct this in the case of council housing (see Balchin (1989) for recent estimates of £50bn-£70bn) and that this is deteriorating at a rate of £1bn per annum.

The evidence of serious under-investment and disrepair has acted to compel the Treasury to rescind its strong aversion to increasing public housing investment, which has seen capital allocations to the council sector reduced by 75% in real terms since the late 1970s. The last impetus for financial relaxation and change was probably provided by the DoE study (published some time later in 1987) on the state of the housing stock, which largely supported the other studies in its estimates of investment needed. It was a significant factor in the origins of EA. This is confirmed by a leading EA Central member: "The philosophy was that something had to be done on the ground - some initiative was needed to alleviate the situation ... The other factor that was important was the DoE stock condition survey, indicating the degree of disrepair of council property" (EA 3). This is backed-up by the Regional Officers: "In 1985, there was a stock condition survey, the purpose of which was to provide ammunition for the PESC. It tried to find out if there really was a housing problem and its extent, in order to present it to the Treasury. It was a double-edged sword. While it provided evidence for PESC, it also provided ammunition for the critics, such as the AMA" (RO 5).

The above quotation would almost imply that the DoE undertook the study specifically to use as leverage against a reticent Treasury. EA HIPs may thus also be seen as a Treasury concession in recognition that the rising tide of council housing disrepair had to be alleviated. This represented a significant shift in both Conservative government and Treasury attitude to the public housing sector, even though this additional resource was to be directed only to the most run-down public housing. The question must be asked as to the extent to which the EA initiative is merely symbolic in seeking to tackle this particular problem given that the amount of EA HIPs, although increasing, is insignificant compared to the figure generally agreed as the minimum necessary. This paltry sum (relative to the level of disrepair) may have reflected the degree to which the Treasury hoped that the private sector would, in due course, become more involved in the renovation of these estates and 'lever-in' the additional resources necessary to upgrade them (see chapter 3). These issues are explored subsequently.

4.3.5 Privatization, diversification of tenure and transfers of stock

There can be little doubt that the government has sought to use the EA initiative to maintain the council housing privatization impetus. A key DoE civil servant states, regarding the motives behind the creation of EA and the terms of EA's remit as far as politicians were concerned, that the rough 'pecking order' of priority is as follows:

> 1: Ministers were sold on the idea that if estates could not be let, there had to be other alternatives - the most obvious one being disposal to willing private sector enterprises; 2: Encourage the formation of co-operatives because of the diversification of tenure element; 3: Development of estate based management; and 4: The continued development of the employment /CRS initiatives. (EA 2)

The centrality of the privatization issue in the origins of EA is not in question: "As far as fulfilling central government policy towards housing, there are three important emphases within EA: firstly, an attempt to involve the private sector in order to break-up monolithic estates; secondly, to enhance the 'right to buy' policy since people are clearly not going to buy unless the estates are improved; and thirdly, in order to bring certain council properties back into use" (RO 1b). Such a view is backed by another Regional Official: "The government's housing policy, it is to reduce the role of local authorities to mere 'enablers', hence all the legislation such as 'Pick a Landlord' and HATs so as to get rid of problem council housing altogether. This aim is not undermined by EA." (RO 5)

It is not surprising that when the initiative was launched, its objectives were rather mixed and included attracting private investment; transfers of ownership / management to trusts, tenants' co-operatives, Housing Associations etc; sale of estates to private trusts or developers; sale of empty property to developers for refurbishment for sale or rent (DoE, 1986). The preceding sections of this chapter have sought to pull out the reasons why this should be the case.

4.4 Putting together the idea and the team

As a result of the various issues discussed: "Around 1983/4 ideas were put together within the Department about how to tackle the worst 20% of council estates or so. The period of policy formation for EA was, therefore, very long ... It was probably at this point that the two strands came together, namely what the DoE team of civil servants were working on and what ministers were particularly concerned about" (EA 2). This is a direct reference to the union of the two key strands within EA (management and sales/disposal), reflecting the preoccupations of the two actors involved in designing EA (civil servants / government).

Two former EA members closely involved in the first few years of the initiative add: "There is no doubt that EA first emphasized private sector involvement as the key aspect of the initiative. The ministry then had to backtrack and to state that the other options were equally valid for support and it was at this point that estate based management came more into its own" (EA 5/6). It seems that: "Even Sir George Young appeared to have been somewhat frustrated by the slow progress of the privatization element and the Central team had to explain that the demand was simply not there, wrong locations etc" (EA 5/6). This is further indication that the politicians very much saw the initiative as being about continuing with their policies for diversification of tenure, as opposed to the civil servants who seem to have initiated it largely for different reasons, primarily with a concern for the management of estates.

It is thus interesting to note that the emphasis on the private sector and sales was created with strategic reasons in mind by the civil servants, principally for the benefit of the politicians: "The private involvement and diversification of tenure elements were added primarily in order to make the package attractive to the politicians" (EA 1). The key civil servants behind the formulation of the details of EA had other priorities: "They were particularly keen on the estate based management element, having been persuaded of its value by the PEP experiments" (EA 1).

It was almost inevitable that the final EA programme would ended up as a compromise: "Because of the way the civil service operates, the practicalities are that it is the people operating in the field which had to sell the idea and emphasis to the under-secretary, who in turn had the task of translating this into a package which he could sell to both the Minister and the Treasury. Above this, the permanent secretary had to convince the cabinet and right at the very top, the Prime Minister herself had to be assured of its value." (EA 2) In order to get through all these hurdles an attractive package had to be designed, hence the assortment of EA criteria.

4.5 Convincing the Cabinet and the Treasury

A discussion on the precise reasons why such a proposal was supported in the end is valuable precisely because, as a Central officer reflects: "At the time, the government line was very much in favour of cutting public expenditure whereas EA was clearly a form of additional public housing expenditure" (EA 2). In terms of persuading both the Treasury and the Cabinet of the value of the initiative, it transpires that the argument used by the DoE/ Ministers/ Consultants, was that investment in public estates would be beneficial in several respects:

- These were areas of high unemployment and other socio-economic deprivation;
- If these estates were not dealt with, "they would have a cancerous effect on other estates, including some private estates", and also that: "There were pockets of public estates which had become owner occupied. If these estates were allowed to continue to deteriorate, the government's emphasis on owner occupation would have a hollow ring" (EA 2);
- The conditions on the estates were often so bad that other government departments [eg the Home Office] were also involved in spending public money, such as in the form of unemployment benefit and crime prevention measures;
- The EA initiative would have some effect in increasing privatization of property as well as encouraging developers to use land to build housing for sale or rent;
- Then there was: "The 'value for money' argument where the cost of replacing housing demolished on shitty estates would cost X amount, whereas the cost of keeping them going for another few decades would be Y" (EA 2); and lastly

- The fact that: "A large number of bodies such as the Audit Commission had made estimates of the vast sums required for public housing. All of this acted as pressure on the Treasury to comply" (EA 2), although at the end of the day, he himself recognizes that the resource available is marginal compared to what might be spent estimating *en passant*, that it represents about 0.05% of the amount needed in 20 years. Nevertheless, the fact that: "... the PM was very taken with the EA initiative" (EA 2) was helpful, not least because whereas most initiatives of this sort last little more than two or three years, EA is receiving increasingly more EA HIPs and would seem to still rank high in the minds of ministers and the Treasury.

4.6 Sir George Young's advisory group

It has become standard procedure for ministers to set these up: "... both for comfort and as a 'sounding board' for new ideas, as opposed to being totally reliant on civil servants. They are designed to operate between the ministers and the civil servants" (EA 2). Given the nature of the advisory group (consisting of Tom Baron, Chairman of Christian Salveson, Tim Melville-Ross, general manager of Nationwide Building Society, Harry Simpson former GLC housing director and Herbert Walden, general manager of the Heart of England Building Society), one would have expected it to have been highly influential in pushing for disposal and privatization (if they considered it to be feasible), however, this does not seem to have been the case and the group's role was somewhat tenuous.

Despite the background and vested interests that many of these people may have had: "There was nothing in concrete terms which the Advisory Group did. They observed the progress of Estate Action, such as how many authorities and which types of scheme [to target] but they were not around long enough to steer it in any direction". These people (in particular Walden and Simpson) were: "... all genuinely concerned about the social housing problem but their ability to influence anything was limited by time and in the end they only met three times" (EA 2).

In actual fact the civil servants designing the EA framework received *support* for the emphasis on estate based management: "The advisory group had little influence on the initiative. They just discussed the agenda set by the civil servants such as the criteria to be established. The one aspect where the advisory unit contributed, was in that Tom Baron believed that if the initiative was to be successful, it would have to be in some way innovative or novel and that this role was fulfilled by the estate based management criterion" (EA 1). This worked in favour of the civil servants who were in any case keen to make this the primary focus of the initiative.

4.7 The launch and the initial reactions

In June 1985 Sir George Young launched the initiative, indicating the policy thoughts, targeting 69 authorities and asking them to put together ideas for EA support and organize visits to the estates (see chapter 3 for its remit). It is worth stressing the point that: "There was no consultation with local authorities or their associations in the setting up of the initiative. Neither was there consultation with the Regional Offices" (EA 1). This officer acknowledges the possibility that the initiative and its procedures might have been more refined if authorities and associations had been involved in developing them. EA did travel to numerous authorities to inform them of the initiative and what they hoped to achieve under it, however, this does not comprise consultation in the true sense of the word.

This then is the history of the origins of the initiative, its formulation and its launching. EA created a stir within the local authority housing policy community. (EA 2) agrees with (EA 1) that there was a lack of consultation with other important agents which EA would have to work with and that this may have been partly to blame for the hostile reception to the initiative (EA 2):

> I suspect that there was no discussion. It was thrust upon them [local authorities]. This would explain their initial reaction to the initiative because as a result they greeted EA as a privateer's party designed to lead to the selling of all blocks; brought-up the issue about 'topslicing'; and saw it as further extension of controls over local authorities.

Expanding on the issue: "As far as the authorities and their associations were concerned, the reaction to the launch of EA was of privatization under another guise" (EA 2). The interviewees estimate that this reaction was true of at least half of the authorities initially targeted. The LAAs were also critical of the initiative's objectives which were seen to be heavily skewed in favour of disposal of the council housing stock: "We have been very suspicious of the privatization element of Estate Action ever since a gaffe by Kenneth Baker regarding its true motive, namely that of priming estates for sales and privatization" (AMA interview, 6.4.89). It was also criticized: "All authorities are opposed in principle to 'topslicing' resources since we believe in local authority discretion", and "Estate Action is a gimmick for the DoE to get press coverage. We are very cynical about such an initiative" (AMA interview, 6.4.89).

Reactions were so severe that certain authorities even vowed never to become involved with the initiative because of the principles involved: "What non-compliant authorities fear most and indeed Environment Secretary Patrick Jenkin has confirmed, is that the HIPs allocations will be adjusted to provide funds to councils willing to take on joint public/ private sector ventures" (PSLG, 1985, p.8). The notion of voluntary disposal of parts, or even whole estates, was novel and uncontemplated, and the reaction was suitably vociferous. While the EA Unit was welcomed for example by the National Consumer Council, Building Societies Association and the House Builders' Federation, the Chairman of the AMA is reported to have said that the Unit was merely: "designed to give a superficial impression that the Government is doing something about Britain's inner city decay when in fact it is doing nothing." (John Donnelly quoted in PSLG, July 1985, p.8)

This is a theme picked up by the newspapers under such headings as 'Cheap answer to £19bn problem', stressing that (Guardian, 8.8.86, p.6):

> Until the financial resources are available to deal with the backlog of repairs, the housing waiting lists, the homeless and the poorly housed, such initiatives have to be set in a context of increasing housing distress and its accompanying social and economic ills.

But the press has, in general, emphasized the fact that the initiative was created primarily with privatization in mind: 'Putting up the privatization sign' (Guardian, 23.11.1985, p.29); 'For sale: run-down estate, in need of some modernisation, few mod cons. No reasonable offer refused' (Guardian, 7.6.1986, p.29); and 'MPs to fuel council estate sales boom' (Guardian, 24 April 1986), all stressing that: "Refurbishment for sale by means of a partnership with private developers has become the official remedy for public sector ills" (Hardcastle, 1986, pp.40-41). However, there remain difficulties (Times, 17.06.1986, p.68), not least because:

> Government policy appears to be somewhat confused. It wants the private sector to adopt the dominant role in inner city building and renewal as local authority resources are reduced, but does not realise that such a policy means giving positive help, as well as encouragement, to the private developers and builders. It ... effectively asks them to do it with one hand tied behind their backs because of planning, land and resource constraints.

Despite the importance of the initiative, the rather muted reaction of the academic community to the launching of EA relates to two aspects. Firstly, it has been critical of the nature of the financial system, namely 'topslicing' (Murie and Malpass, 1987; and Aughton, 1986). Secondly, it has also been critical of the inadequate nature of the resources being provided. Balchin (1989, p.224) argues that:

> ... local authorities (Labour as well as Tory) have been forced to sell-off their estates to property companies for refurbishment and re-sale - 20 000 unit being lost to the public sector in this way, 1982-5. To ensure that local authorities would not be slow in disposing of their estates, the Department of the Environment set up the Urban Housing Renewal Unit (UHRU) in 1985.

However, reference to the initiative has been restricted to this level of analysis. There has been no thorough examination of the EA initiative and its effects years after its launch, despite the fact that it has now allocated in the region of £1bn of capital approvals. It is this gap which this book aims to plug, starting with a nationwide analysis of its operation.

4.8 A description of the EA initiative

The EA initiative has now been in existence for five years. The following discussion is an attempt to describe the local authorities that have participated in the initiative, the number of schemes and levels of resources allocated by EA to the various DoE regions and authorities, the composition of council stock housing and the levels of housing deprivation confronting the participating authorities. The discussion will refer to Maps 2 - 8 and Tables 4.1 - 4.3 contain details on structure of housing stock, housing deprivation, number of EA schemes and total expenditure per local authority / EA scheme. The details of the operation and impact of the initiative are the subject of the empirical analyses in chapters 5 to 8.

4.8.1 Authorities targeted by EA

Map 2 provide a picture of the spread of authorities which have been successful in bidding for EA resources. At the start of its life the Urban Housing Renewal Unit targeted 69 authorities which, based on HIPs return information, were considered to have the greatest housing problems. It did not prove to be possible to obtain a list of these authorities from EA Central. While the willingness existed to release the information, they were unable to trace the original list of authorities. Map 2 shows the 69 authorities that received EA support in the first year, a further 21 different authorities in the second, 20 in the third and a further 20 in the fourth. Between 1986 and 1990, EA funded 130 local authorities with very different housing characteristics (see Maps 3 and 4).

While a list of the authorities which were originally targeted by EA would have enabled Map 2 to pick out the authorities which had refused to participate with EA, one can still point out the authorities which experience great housing deprivation (based on Z-Scores) and yet did not participate in EA until the third or fourth year. If this is taken as a crude surrogate for reluctance and/or unwillingness to participate (for reasons discussed in the previous section), then a list can be compiled of such authorities (see Table 4.1). Hackney, Liverpool and St Helens are noteworthy for their hesitation given the high degree of deprivation in these authorities - or they may simply have been unsuccessful in obtaining EA resources.

Table 4.1: Reluctant participants, year and housing Z-score

4th year:		**3rd year:**		Derwentside	1.82
St Helens	4.23	Hackney	8.23	Blackpool	1.47
Southampton	1.58	Liverpool	4.23	Enfield	0.71
Barnet	0.86	Stoke Trent	2.52	Easington	0.50
The Wrekin	0.26	Brighton	2.49	Sefton	0.01

Source: Estate Action Database

Table 4.2: Authorities with housing need but no EA funding

England	Lincoln (1.69)	Blaenan Gwent (3.27)
Barking & Daghm (1.27)	N. Bedfordshire (2.37)	Cardiff (1.42)
Bournemouth (1.28)	Oxford (2.47)	Cynon Valley (2.90)
Corby (1.67)	Penwith (1.72)	Dwyfor (1.30)
Ealing (4.28)	Portsmouth (1.22)	Islwyn (1.43)
Grt Grimsby (1.08)	Reading (1.50)	Llanelli (1.55)
Grt Yarmouth (1.03)	Scunthorpe (2.08)	Merthyr Tydfil (3.34)
Hastings (2.20)	**Wales**	Rhymmen Vall. (1.87)
Hove (2.20)	Afan (1.93)	Rhondda (4.67)
Kerrier (1.57)	Arfon (2.58)	Swansea (1.19)

Source: DoE Z-Scores and Estate Action Database; data in ( ) are Z-scores

Table 4.3: Key indicators of authorities involved with EA

Authority and Total EA HIPs		Authority and No. of schemes		Authority and High Z-scores		Authority and Low Z-scores	
Rochdale	18.9	Tower Hamts	26	Hackney	8.6	Eastleigh	-4.3
Tower Hamts	18.5	Newham	19	Newham	8.1	East Herts.	-4.0
Sheffield	17.7	Knowsley	15	Lambeth	7.2	Tewkesbury	-3.9
Greenwich	14.2	Hull	15	Ham'smith	7.0	Woking	-3.3
Salford	13.6	Hartlepool	15	Tower Hamts	6.9	Waverley	-3.2
Newham	13.5	Birmingham	14	Haringey	6.6	Lewes	-3.1
Manchester	10.7	Bolton	13	Brent	6.3	Spelthorne	-2.8
Coventry	10.4	Sheffield	13	Islington	6.2	Woodspring	-2.7
Wigan	10.3	Bradford	12	Wandsworth	6.1	Guidford	-2.7
Walsall	10.2	Wirral	12	Camden	5.6	Lichfield	-2.6

Source: Estate Action Database (Note: Total EA HIPs is in £m)

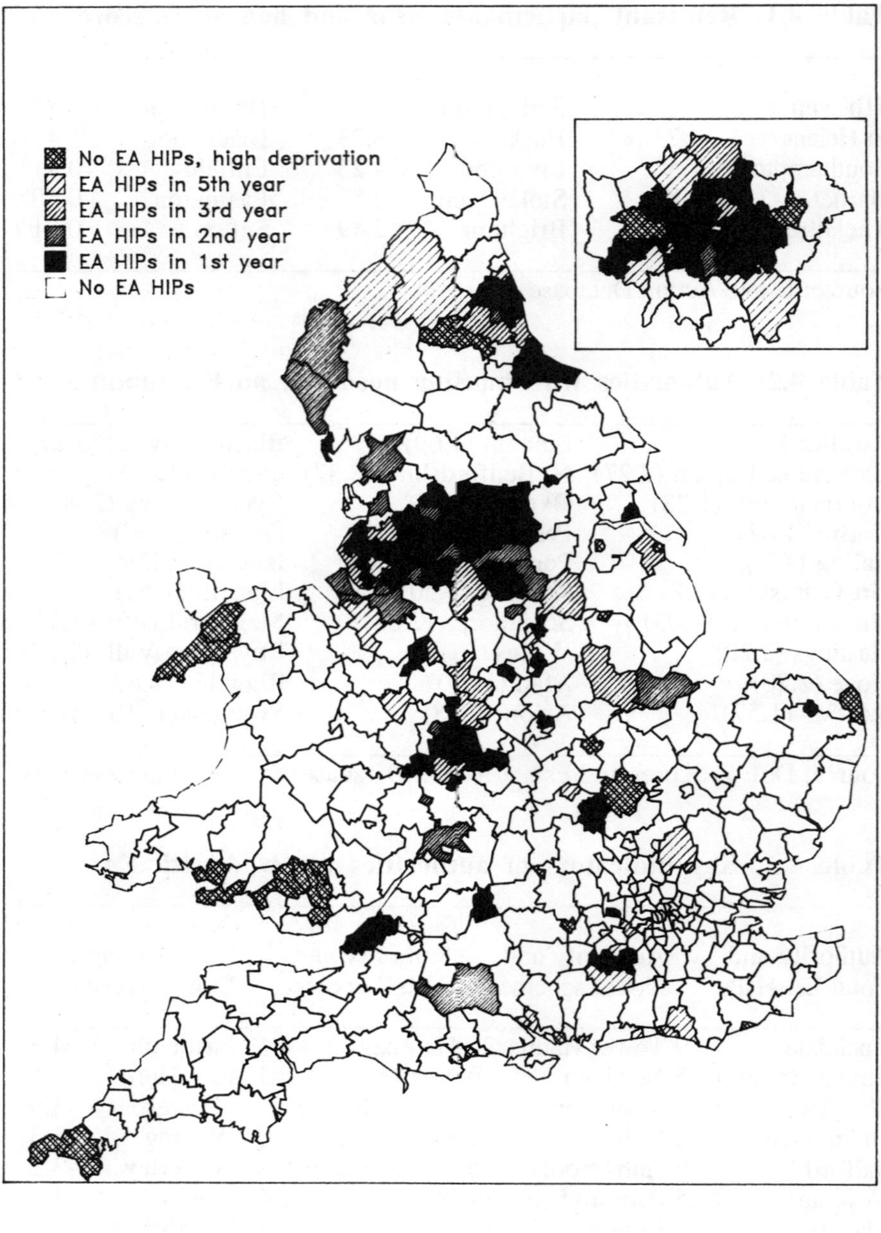

Map 2 Local authorities targeted by Estate Action (1986-1990)

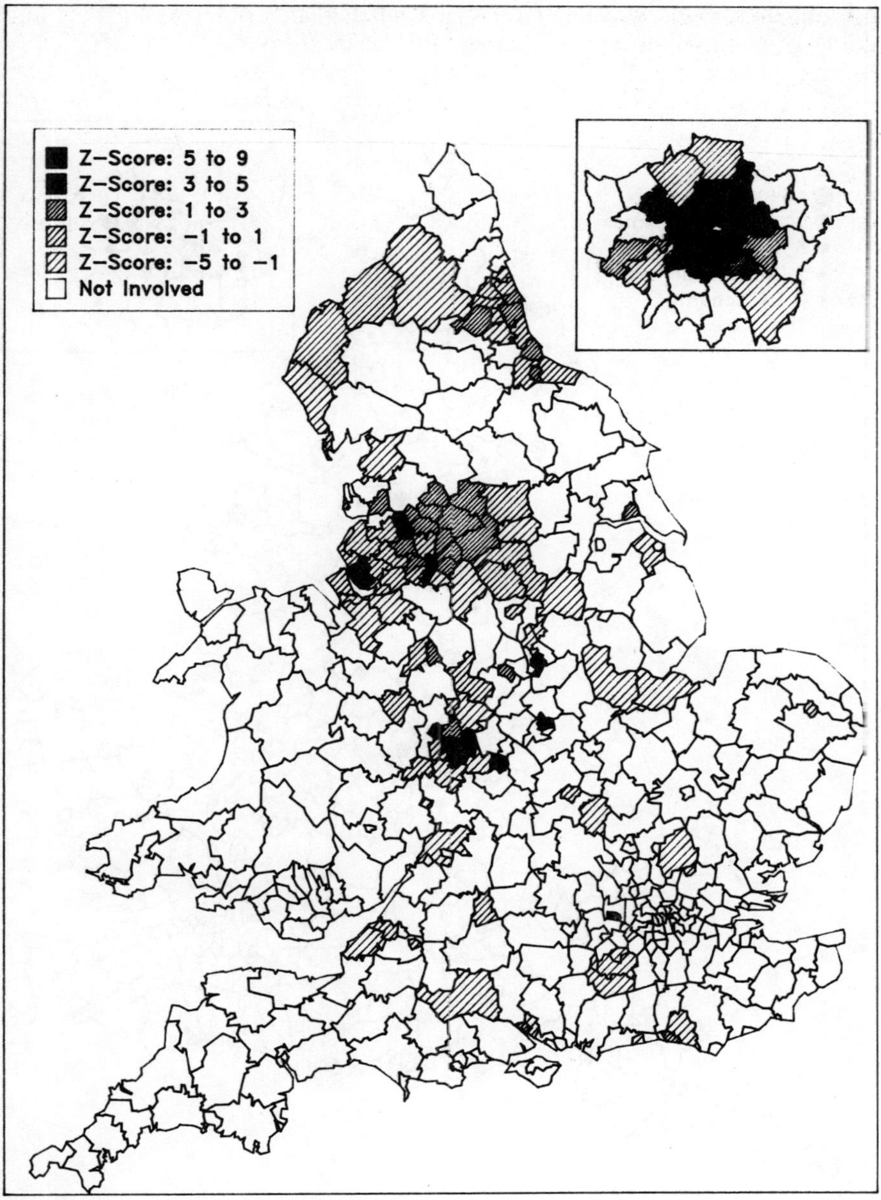

Map 3 Level of housing deprivation in the targeted authorities

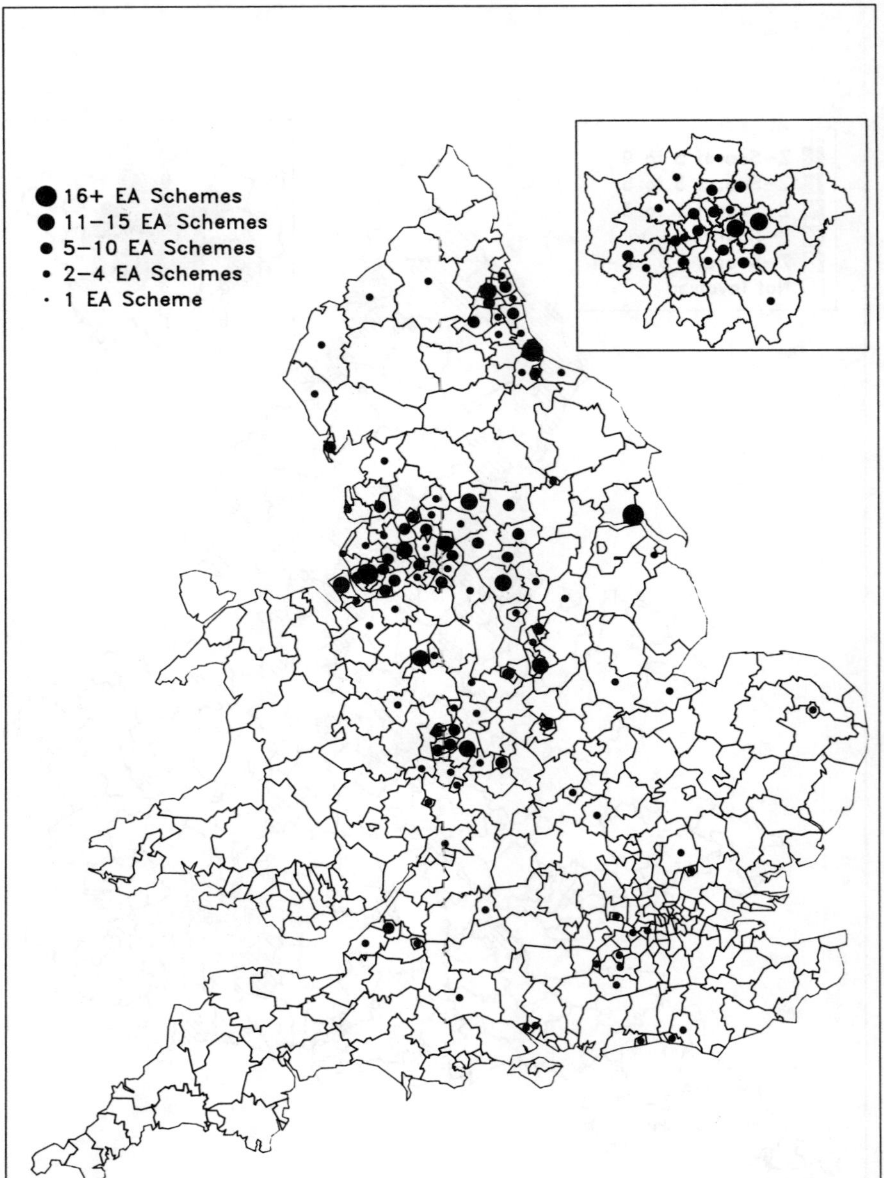

Map 4 Number of EA schemes per local authority (1986-1990)

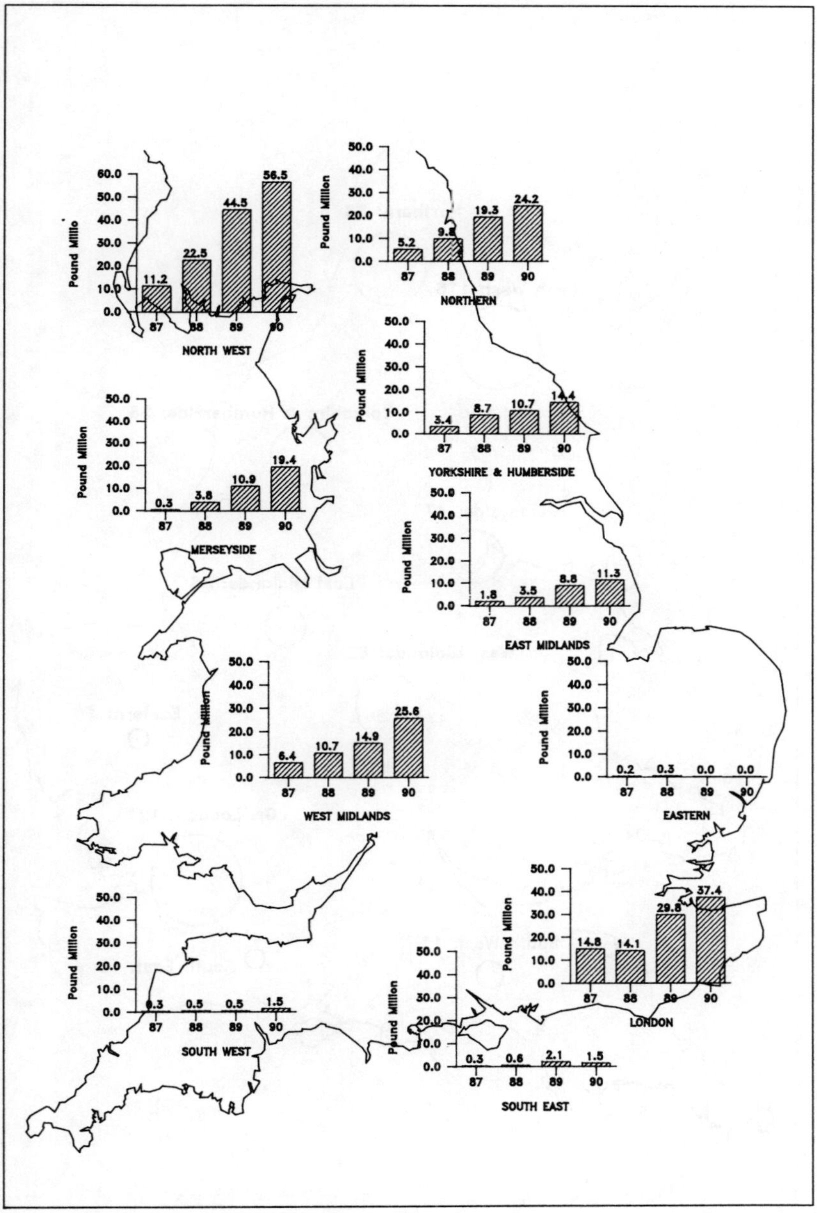

Map 5 EA HIPs: Regional allocations (1986-1990)

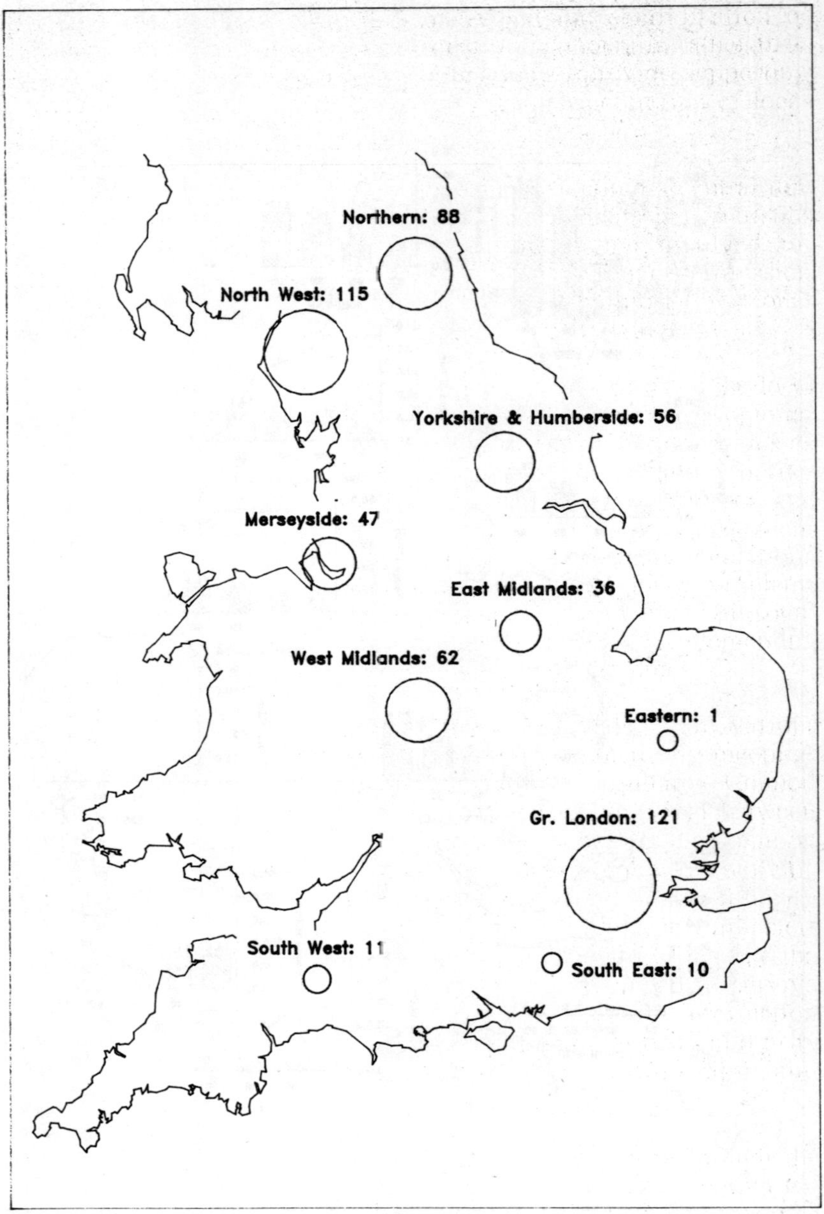

Map 6 Total amount of EA HIPs per DoE region (1986-1990)

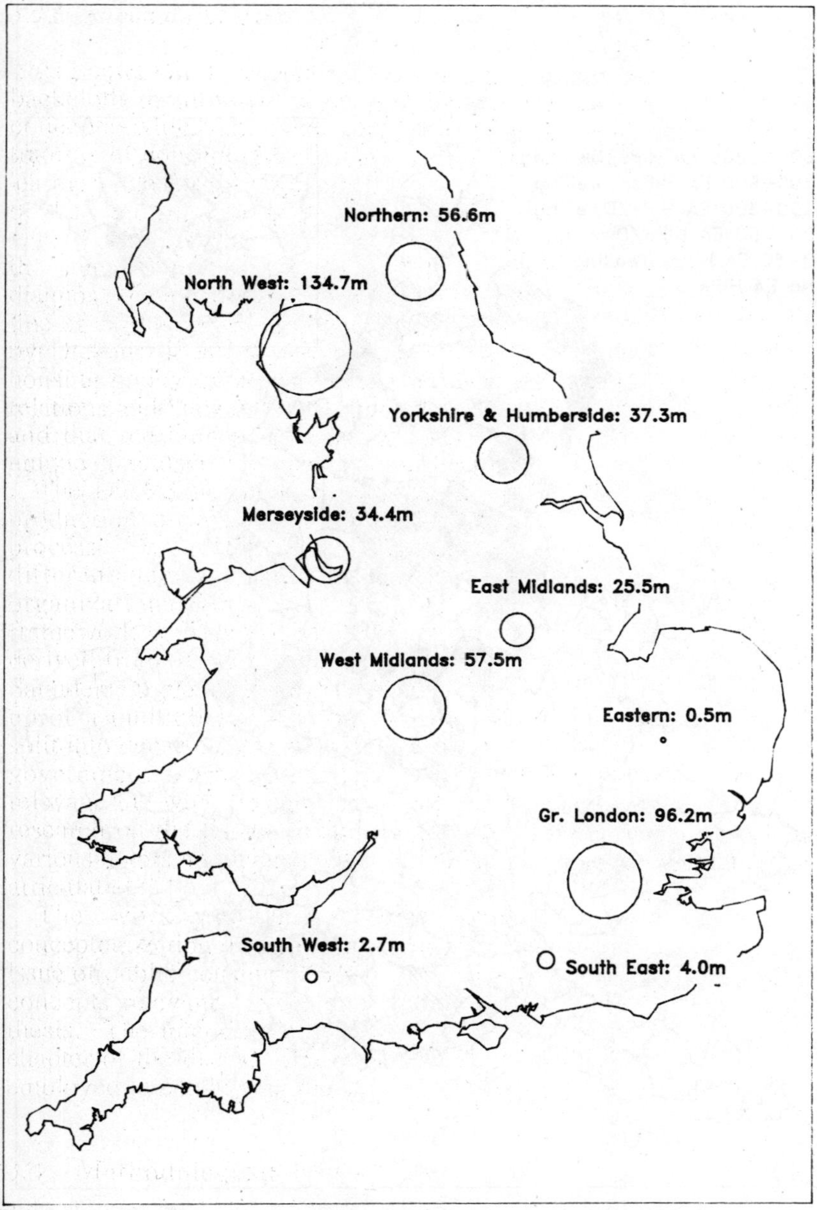

Map 7 Total EA HIPs allocation per DoE region (1986-1990)

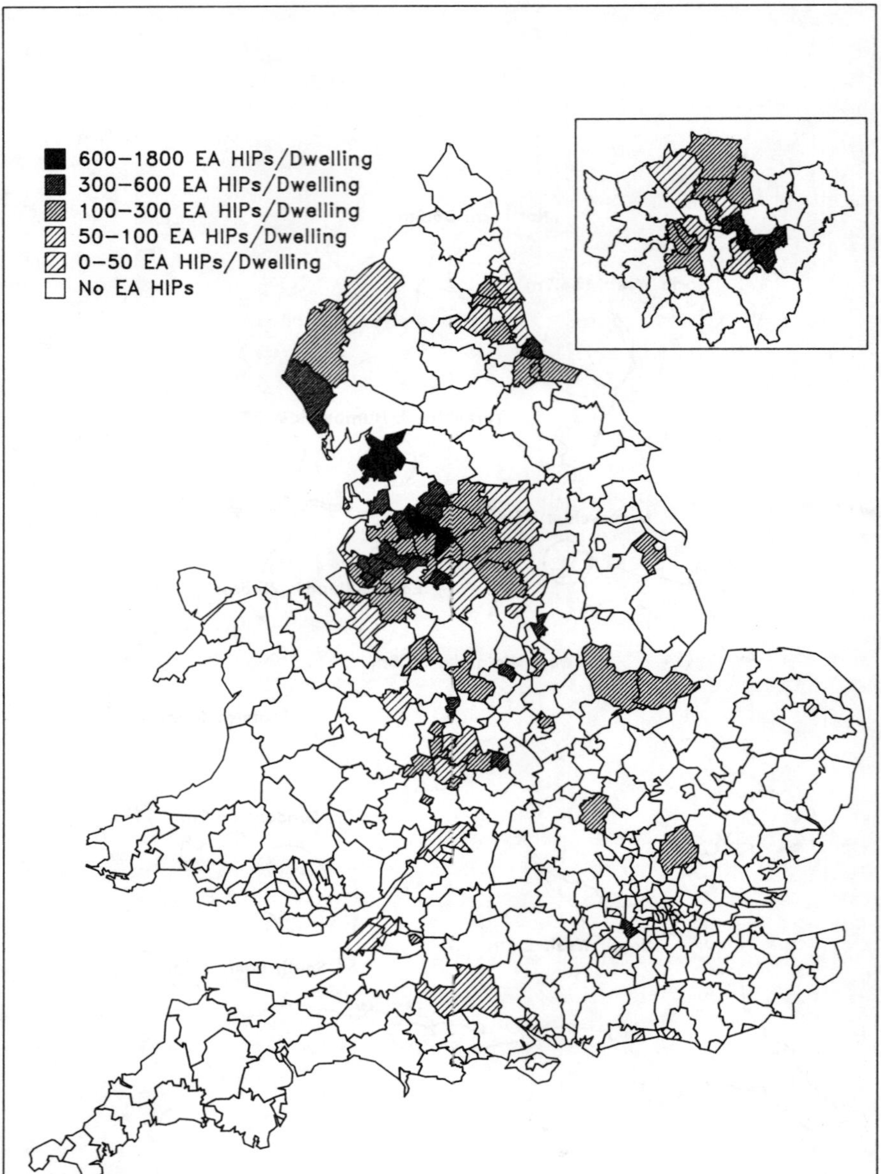

Map 8 EA HIPs expenditure per dwelling (1986-1990)

Map 2 enables a further important point to be drawn out. A number of authorities (28) face high housing deprivation levels but have not obtained EA support (see Table 4.2). The table lists only those authorities which have housing deprivation levels greater than one, in other words, authorities which have been deemed by the DoE to be in definite need of additional investment. The reasons why they have not obtained EA HIPs resources are two fold: they may have decided not to bid for EA support and/or the bids submitted for EA funding may have been unsuccessful. Table 4.2 probably contains a mixture of both cases. Another important factor to point out at this stage, is the fact that severe housing deprivation is by no means confined to England and there is little doubt that South Wales would also benefit from EA-type initiatives. However, the EA initiative is only concerned with England at this point in time.

4.8.2 Composition housing deprivation

Map 3 extends the discussion by analyzing the level of housing deprivation experienced in the authorities which have received EA funding. The highest levels and the greatest concentration of housing deprivation occurs in the London Region. Other intense clusters of housing deprivation are to be found in the North West, Merseyside, Northern and Yorkshire and Humberside regions. By contrast, the remaining regions actually have a preponderance of authorities exhibiting below average levels of housing deprivation ranging from -1 to -5 (these are identified in Pinto, 1992d).

4.8.3 Number of EA schemes per authority

Map 4 presents a simple analysis of the authorities which have been successful in setting up EA schemes. The circles increase in size proportionately with the number of schemes funded by EA. The most successful authorities can be identified from Table 4.3. Although the Table demonstrates that it is the London authorities which have the greatest housing need (in terms of Z-Score), only Tower Hamlets, Greenwich and Newham have had EA success commensurate with their housing requirements. At the other extreme, many authorities which in principle do not have much housing need have obtained EA support (see Table 4.3 for the level of funding obtained). 19 authorities in all have obtained EA resources and yet have Z-Scores of below -2.0. Later chapters will discuss why, after the first year, EA changed its focus from being entirely targeted at the authorities with the greatest housing need.

4.8.4 Distribution of EA resource allocation and schemes

The next map (5) again uses the data provided by the EA team in order to illustrate the way in which EA HIPs resources have been distributed across the 10 DoE Regions for each of the financial years from 1986 to 1990.

Clearly the North West, Northern and London regions have been exceptionally successful in obtaining EA resources. This is also reflected in the symbol map (6) and the number of schemes per region (Map 7). The data presented in Maps 6 and 7 are not unexpected given the distribution of authorities which have obtained EA resources (Map 2) and their degree of housing deprivation (Map 3).

A last point to note comes out of Map 8 which illustrates the level of EA HIPs expenditure per participating authority. By comparing Maps 3 and 8, it is clear that rarely do the authorities with the highest levels of housing deprivation receive the highest levels of EA HIPs expenditure per local authority housing unit. Some councils such as Hyndburn (£1,596p/u), Rossendale (£1,158p/u) and Lancaster (£1,092p/u) have done exceedingly well out of the EA programme in comparison to their levels of Z-Score or housing deprivation (2.27, 2.07 and -1.11 respectively). This brief introductory description to the EA initiative, the participating authorities and regions set the context for the empirical chapters to follow.

4.9 Conclusions

The EA initiative is interesting because it is widely seen as a measure designed to 'fuel sales of council estates', to improve the state of (dis)repair of much public housing *and* of centralizing financial control and decision-making over council housing. At the same time, it can also be regarded as a measure to improve the provision of the housing service via the encouragement of various models of housing management, the efficient targeting of scarce resources to where they are most needed and pushing for the introduction of even greater levels of tenant consultation.

In looking at EA's origins, the previous sections have shown that EA represents, in a real sense and for different reasons, an attempt to achieve all these things. It has been demonstrated that EA has arisen out of a mixture of real concerns for the way council housing was operating, as well as out of efforts to push forward with central government housing objectives which had, until that point, been largely confined to extending the 'right to buy' as far as possible. It can be argued, therefore, that the initiation of EA marks a watershed in Conservative thinking on public housing, as it becomes much more imaginative and daring.

At the same time it can be argued that the EA programme marks a realization on the part of central government of the inadequacy of a housing policy which concentrated solely on increasing home ownership and the reduction of public sector investment. EA represents one of the first Thatcherite housing initiatives which actually offered (from the Treasury's point of view) additional expenditure rather than cut-backs in local authority housing investment. Ironically, the housing policy community and the academic commentators concentrated their critique almost entirely upon the privatization element of the initiative and the fact that the EA resources were 'topsliced'. The other elements of the programme's remit were largely ignored.

This chapter has also presented an introductory description of the authorities which have been supported by the EA initiative, their housing characteristics and the levels of expenditure per participating authority. Indicators have been given as to the identity of authorities which may have been reluctant to become involved with EA and it has been stressed that the EA programme still has not reached all the most deprived housing authorities (especially in Wales although the analysis did not include Scotland). Finally, the analysis went up to the regional scale in order to discuss the level of expenditure and the number of schemes per DoE region which have been supported by the EA programme for the years 1986 through to 1990.

5 The local authority perspective

5.1 Introduction

This chapter presents a comprehensive analysis of an unique survey comprising all the local authorities involved with Estate Action (EA), conducted in order to provide detailed information on its background and interaction with local authorities. The survey analyses the reasons why authorities become concerned with EA and the type of schemes which are implemented as a result. It also considers the administrative procedures which govern this central/local government interaction, its advantages, disadvantages, as well as the degree to which the resulting schemes are achieving success in renovating the run-down estates that EA was formed to deal with.

The postal survey was designed, piloted and circulated in August 1988 and a response-rate of 75%, or 61 authorities, was obtained (see chapter 3 for a full methodological discussion). The descriptive analysis is divided into six parts as follows:

- Analysis of the control variables
- General background information
- Estate Action administrative procedures
- Tenant participation and evaluation
- Counterfactual information - What if EA did not exist?
- Evaluation of EA schemes

Each part is analyzed separately and closely follows the structure of the postal survey (see Pinto, 1992d, Appendix 1). Since no research exists on the EA initiative, the emphasis of this chapter is to contribute via an in-depth analysis of the operation of the initiative. The approach adopted means that the analysis is both detailed and disparate in nature, therefore, part of Chapter 6 is devoted to condensing and summarizing the most salient findings of the survey.

Five main variables were chosen to provide additional context and background to the analysis. These variables were used primarily for cross-tabulation purposes and a chief motive for use was also to detect any biases in sample response:

i) Department of Environment regions: There may well be regional differences in the way EA operates, possibly reflecting workloads which vary considerably between Regional Offices, different socio-economic contexts as well as other factors. In order to analyze these possible effects, DoE Regions / Regional Offices are used as an element to cross-tabulate other variables with. There are nine official DoE Regions. The Merseyside Task Force deals with the EA initiative in exactly the same way as the other Regional Offices and is not treated separately here, making it ten (see Map 1 and Table 5.1). However, two regions are excluded from subsequent analysis: the SE because there were no responses and the SW because the one response made cross-tabulation meaningless.

Table 5.1: Response-rate cross-tabulated with DoE regions / Regional Offices

Region	Number of Authorities	Response-rate	
		Number	Percent
London	15	10	66
Yorkshire & Humbs	9	6	66
Merseyside	5	4	80
Northern	9	8	88
North Western	22	16	72
West Midlands	11	8	72
East Midlands	6	5	83
Eastern	3	3	100
South Western	1	1	100

Source: DoE, 1987a; Local Authority Survey

ii) Housing deprivation (Z-scores): This strata variable (Table 5.2) was chosen because the level of deprivation might conceivably influence certain issues dealt with in the body of the questionnaire, such as the degree of authority involvement with EA and whether the Unit is seen by authorities as being beneficial. In an attempt to draw out such relationships, the level of housing deprivation is analyzed using the DoE's established index of housing deprivation (Z-scores), which has been used in numerous housing studies such as the Audit Commission's (1986a).

Table 5.2: Response-rate cross-tabulated with housing deprivation (Z-scores)

Housing Deprivation	Number of Authorities	Response-rate	
		Number	Percent
High level deprivation	35	24	68
Mid level deprivation	19	17	89
Low level deprivation	27	20	74

Source: Audit Commission, 1986b; Local Authority Survey

iii) Political control of authority: It is possible that the nature of local political control and the policies being pursued may influence authorities' responses to EA; how fully they co-operated with it; their perception of the way it operates and so on. As a result the authorities were categorized into four different groups according to political control as set out in the Municipal Year Book (Table 5.3), but since there were only two responses in the 'Other' category, this was omitted from the cross-tabulations.

Table 5.3: Response-rate cross-tabulated with political control

Political Control	Number of Authorities	Response-rate	
		Number	Percent
Conservative Party	11	9	81
Labour Party	63	46	74
SDP/Liberal Party	4	4	100
Other ('hung')	3	2	66

Source: Municipal Yearbook 1986/87; Local Authority Survey

iv) Authority type: This variable is included because it is conceivable that attitude and response to EA may vary according to the type of authority. The overall response-rate for Outer London authorities was somewhat lower than average. This is a reflection of the fact that these particular housing officers felt that they were more hard-pressed than elsewhere and consequently were unable to return the questionnaire. The definition of the type of authority was obtained from the Municipal Year Book and the authorities then split into four groups (see Table 5.4) in order to simplify the analysis.

Table 5.4: Response-rate cross-tabulated with authority type

Type of Authority	Number of Authorities	Response-rate	
		Number	Percent
Inner London	5	4	80
Outer London	10	6	60
Metropolitan Districts	33	23	69
District Councils	33	28	84

Source: Municipal Yearbook, 1986/87; Local Authority Survey

5.2 General background information

i) Who did the authority appointed to liaise with and co-ordinate EA bids?

17% An EA team
19% An EA co-ordinating officer
45% An officer with *ad hoc* EA responsibilities
36% Other factors (eg PEP officers; and estate working parties)
Missing Cases = 8 (13.1%)

Note: The authorities could tick more than one option throughout most of the questionnaire as appropriate to their particular authority and context, hence figures do not total 100%.

EA has been in existence for several years but despite its rapidly increasing resources, the majority of authorities did not consider it important enough to create posts specifically (or even primarily) aimed at bringing in additional resources to the authority. The results imply that in the majority of cases, EA tasks were allocated and incorporated among the existing housing staff. This is surprising given that this is one of the few options available to authorities to augment their HIPs allocations, thus circumventing capital restrictions. However, the workload generated by EA may not be sufficient to justify a position/team exclusively for EA bids which is probably why its responsibility is often shared between the existing staff (in 45.3% of the cases). The fact that the initiative operates on a year to year basis may also discourage the creation of such posts.

ii) What were the authorities' main reasons for being concerned with EA between 1986/87 and 1988/89 (see Table 5.5)?

1. *EA HIPs is a rapidly increasing and much needed resource:* By far the main reason for authorities' interest in EA is because it is regarded as an extra source of income. As discussed elsewhere (chapter 2), the main font for council capital investment has traditionally been via the Housing

Investment Programme, but since the early 1980s this has been consistently and deliberately run down, and it was predictable that authorities should soon come to appreciate the value of EA HIPs to their housing programmes. The main point to note, therefore, is that this has also been consistently registered as the factor that authorities ranked as being of the highest importance (regularly obtaining the top overall ranking of 1 - Table 5.5).

2. The authority wanted to try out *Decentralization / estate based management:* Authorities also expressed a good deal of interest in this aspect. In recent years, many authorities have been searching for ways of improving the management and maintenance of their housing stock (discussed in Chapter 2). This frequently means some sort of decentralization since EA stresses that its central theme is that schemes should, as a matter of course, consist of plans to improve estate based management. Additionally, if councils are themselves committed to this form of housing management organization, it is natural that they should seek to use EA resources rather than their own HIPs allocations.

44% of the authorities were interested in this option offered by EA (1986/87), and this increased to 52% at the height of the decentralization debate before registering a slight decrease in interest to 50% in 1988/89. Therefore, attempts at using EA to promote decentralization in authorities has remained at consistently high levels throughout the period covered by the survey. This reflects the discussion in chapter 2 regarding many authorities' willingness to promote new housing management initiatives.

3. *Innovative management structures:* Authorities also seem to have been fairly receptive to promotion of different management structures and 38% of the respondents indicate that this was one of the main reasons for their involvement with EA. This is increasingly becoming a priority - it was registered primarily in Ranks 3 and 4 (see Table 5.5). The concern and willingness of many authorities to break the previous mould of management style and organization is expressed in these figures which show a 12% increase in interest in this aspect from 1986/87 to 1987/88 and a further 3.4% increase in 1988/89. There has been a consistent desire to use EA in order to promote innovative management structures.

4. *Other things:* Promotion of 'other' initiatives has declined rapidly in the three years but includes: 'security measures'; 'to supplement the HIPs borrowing approval' / 'play ball with the government'; and 'to undertake environmental works, refurbishment, remodelling, upgrading of estates'.

5. *Employment initiatives:* The creation of employment opportunities by using under-utilized resources within council estates has only recently began to be articulated and promoted (see McArthur and McGregor, 1989; Pinto, 1991c; 1992b). It is debatable whether local authorities are undertaking these primarily because of EA promotion, nevertheless, even in 1986/87 this issue was of greater concern to authorities than was

Table 5.5 Authorities' main reasons for being involved with EA

The authority wanted to try:	Year	Very Important ◄► Not Important: Rank 1 (%)	Rank 2 (%)	Rank 3 (%)	Rank 4 (%)	Not Imp. (%)	Overall Rank
1. EA HIP is rapidly increasing and a much needed resource	1986/7	44.9	4.1	8.2	22.4	20.4	1
	1987/8	52.5	5.1	3.4	18.6	20.3	1
	1988/9	47.4	10.5	3.5	17.5	21.1	1
2. Estate based management / Decentralization	1986/7	4.0	16.0	6.0	18.0	56.0	2
	1987/8	5.0	15.0	10.3	21.7	48.0	2
	1988/9	10.3	10.3	10.3	19.1	50.0	3
3. Innovative management styles	1986/7	4.0	4.0	20.0	10.0	62.0	3
	1987/8	5.0	13.3	16.7	15.0	50.0	3
	1988/9	3.4	15.5	13.8	20.7	46.6	2
4. Other things (such as security & environmental)	1986/7	8.0	6.0	4.0	12.0	70.0	4
	1987/8	1.7	8.3	1.7	10.0	78.3	4
	1988/9	0.0	5.2	1.7	13.8	79.3	5
5. Employment initiatives	1986/7	0.0	8.0	0.0	6.0	86.0	5
	1987/8	0.0	0.0	8.3	11.7	80.0	5
	1988/9	1.7	0.0	8.6	13.8	75.9	4
6. Diversification of tenure	1986/7	4.0	2.0	0.0	8.0	86.0	5
	1987/8	5.0	1.7	0.0	10.0	83.3	6
	1988/9	3.4	0.0	3.4	13.8	79.4	6
7. Homeless initiatives	1986/7	2.0	6.4	2.0	0.0	89.6	7
	1987/8	1.7	6.8	1.7	3.4	86.4	9
	1988/9	1.8	5.3	3.5	1.8	87.6	9
8. Concierge schemes	1986/7	2.0	2.0	2.0	2.0	92.0	8
	1987/8	1.7	5.0	1.7	8.3	83.4	6
	1988/9	5.2	5.2	6.9	3.4	79.4	6
9. Private sector disposals	1986/7	0.0	2.0	2.0	2.0	94.0	9
	1987/8	3.4	3.4	1.7	6.8	84.7	8
	1988/9	1.8	1.8	1.8	8.8	85.8	8

Note: Overall Rank is determined on the basis of the 'Not Important' answers. In 1986/7, only 20.4% of the authorities considered the fact that 'EA HIPs is rapidly increasing' to be 'Not Important'. This therefore receives the top Rank. Source: Local Authority Survey; Missing Cases = 11; 1; 3

promotion of private sector involvement. Employment initiatives have been given increasing consideration and priority by local authorities (from 14% to 24.1% over three years), nevertheless, many do not place this as their top priority - it is their fifth overall priority. This may be changing because EA has now thrown all its weight into all-out promotion of the 'enterprise initiative' for reasons discussed in later chapters.

6. *Diversification of tenure:* While authorities were greatly concerned with and interested in, decentralization and innovative management structures, diversification of tenure was not such a great priority for them. The scores registered started from a low level (14%) and peaked at 20.6% by 1988/89. This increase may indicate that continuing EA promotion of diversification of tenure has begun to bear fruit and that sooner or later, central government will have an impact upon local authority policy and practice even if the councils may be opposed to it in principle.

7. *Homeless initiatives:* This is not a key local authority concern, nevertheless, a number of such initiatives were accepted and funded by EA, whose remit did not in fact mention this option. Chapter 6 analyses this issue in greater detail where it is argued that this type of initiative is used as a 'safety-valve' by EA when it is in danger of underallocating its resources.

8. *Concierge initiatives,* namely staffed receptions at the entrance of tower-blocks: It was only in 1987/88 that EA formally took concierges into their criteria and began promoting them, although some authorities (e.g. Brent) were already pursuing these. The fact that local authority interest in concierges increases demonstrably thereafter, must reflect the combination of increasing authority awareness of this initiative as well as EA promotion. By 1988/89, 20.6% were actively looking to implement concierges. The overall ranks are indicative of these developments (8th and 6th).

9. *Private sector involvement and disposals:* During the exploratory interviews (see Table 3.3), authorities indicated that they were not at all concerned to either dispose their stock to the private sector or involve it in any way so as to renovate run-down estates in partnership. Despite EA's initial emphasis on this issue, in actual fact very few of the schemes turned out to be of this type. There is a feeling among housing officers that EA quickly realized that it was pushing the private sector aspect too hard and too quickly for authorities' liking in 1986/87.

Interest in using EA resources in this way started from very low levels (6%), probably because partnership with the private sector was a relatively novel concept for most authorities at the time and/or because it was something which certain authorities fundamentally opposed. However, by 1987/88, some authorities do seem to have become convinced of the virtue of this EA policy (15.3%) but the proportion remained quite low and interest decayed to 14.2% in 1988/89. While EA may have had some success in changing authorities' interests in certain aspects, the results also imply that if authorities are determined (and their housing problems are not acute), they may be able to refrain from pursuing paths not in accord with their own policies.

iii) What did authorities perceive EA to be primarily concerned with / stressing? (see Table 5.6)

This section examines what local authority officers *perceive* EA to have been stressing in the three years concerned. The official EA view is that its criteria have not changed since EA was inaugurated, however, in the preliminary interviews authorities suggested otherwise, expressing uncertainty, lack of confidence and confusion about the changes in EA practice. This question was posed to examine these issues.

1. *Estate based management / decentralization:* The overwhelming majority of authorities felt that this is what EA placed greatest emphasis on over the three years. This is reflected partly in the authorities' own priorities (Rank 1) and is mirrored in the bids made by authorities, as well as by the actual schemes that got under way. It is worth noting the sharp increase in statistics for Rank 1 over the three years (from 11.1% to 42.1%), indicating a substantial elevation of this criteria as far as EA promotion is concerned. This ties in well with the previous discussion (in chapter 4), that private sector involvement and disposal was initially seen as being *the* focus of EA. Since authorities reacted half-heartedly to this idea, the emphasis began to shift to estate based management thereafter.

2. *Security and environmental works:* EA has emphasized the fact that comprehensive renovation involves as much the security and environmental aspect as the capital investment and actual management of the initiatives. However, the authorities experience is that EA blows 'hot and cold' for this initiative because although support remains at fairly high levels, it does fluctuate. Nevertheless, judging from the overall ranks received, it remains one of EA's central tenets.

3. *Private sector disposals / involvement:* This issue has been contentious from the beginning. Several prominent authorities (such as Liverpool City Council) initially refused to participate in the scheme and despite the fact that the original name of the initiative was changed (from the Urban Housing Renewal Unit to Estate Action), the stigma has not been dislodged for many councils. Few local authorities were greatly interested in private sector disposal (Table 5.5), which may explain EA's shift in focus to estate management but the results also demonstrate that, far from the issue of private sector involvement dying away, not only has it been retained, but the amount of emphasis placed on this initiative has actually increased (3rd to 2nd). It may not have had much success but that is not to say that this option has been abandoned and it remains to be seen how much and for how long authorities can resist this option, especially as the alternative sources of council housing investment continue to dry up.

Table 5.6 What authorities perceive EA to be emphasizing

The authority wanted to try:	Year	Rank 1 (%) Very Important	Rank 2 (%)	Rank 3 (%)	Rank 4 (%)	Not Imp. (%) Not Important	Overall Rank
1. Estate based management / Decentralization	1986/7	11.1	46.7	15.6	20.0	6.3	1
	1987/8	43.6	16.4	12.7	20.0	7.3	1
	1988/9	42.1	17.5	10.5	25.8	4.2	1
2. Security & Environmental Works	1986/7	6.7	31.1	17.8	13.3	31.1	2
	1987/8	7.3	23.6	18.2	23.6	27.3	2
	1988/9	3.5	10.5	15.8	31.6	38.6	3
3. Private Sector Disposals	1986/7	15.6	11.1	4.4	20.0	48.9	3
	1987/8	18.2	18.2	16.4	10.9	36.3	3
	1988/9	15.8	23.6	14.0	14.0	29.9	2
4. Innovative management styles	1986/7	0.0	4.4	13.3	24.4	57.9	4
	1987/8	1.8	7.3	12.7	23.6	54.6	4
	1988/9	3.5	7.0	12.3	26.3	50.9	5
5. Diversification of tenure	1986/7	6.5	8.7	13.0	13.0	58.8	5
	1987/8	7.3	12.7	7.3	18.2	54.5	5
	1988/9	10.5	17.5	19.3	8.8	43.9	4
6. Concierge schemes	1986/7	2.2	0.0	4.4	5.1	86.7	6
	1987/8	0.0	1.8	7.3	10.9	80.0	7
	1988/9	15.8	1.8	1.8	15.8	64.8	6
7. Employment initiatives	1986/7	0.0	2.2	6.7	4.4	86.7	6
	1987/8	0.0	1.8	5.5	10.9	81.8	8
	1988/9	1.8	3.5	1.8	15.8	66.6	7
8. Homeless initiatives	1986/7	0.0	2.2	4.4	5.1	88.3	8
	1987/8	0.0	0.0	3.6	18.2	78.2	6
	1988/9	1.8	0.0	1.8	28.1	68.4	8
9. Other things	1986/7	0.0	2.2	2.0	2.2	93.3	9
	1987/8	1.8	0.0	0.0	1.8	96.4	9
	1988/9	3.5	0.0	0.0	1.8	94.7	9

Note: Overall Rank is determined on the basis of the 'Not Important' answers. In 1986/7, only 6.3% of the authorities considered the fact that 'EA is keen to promote decentralisation' to be 'Not Important'. This therefore receives the top Rank. Source: Local Authority Survey; Missing Cases = 13; 4; 2

4. *Innovative management structures:* These statistics were unexpected insofar as EA was formed to encourage local authorities to develop new ways of managing their property. Quite clearly, the majority of officers did not perceive this to be particularly stressed by EA. The highest scores registered were Rank 4, indicating that while authorities note an enthusiasm for this aspect of EA's remit, it was nevertheless of middling priority. A consistent pattern of increasing importance being placed on this type of initiative by EA (42.1%, 45.5% and 49.1%) is emerging but in terms of overall rank, it declines to fifth place.

5. *Diversification of tenure:* The change of emphasis over time is also true of diversification of tenure. In 1986/87 it was perceived by housing officers as being only fairly important (as far as EA is concerned) but was stressed more heavily in subsequent years. This may have occurred because many reasons, but the fact that EA has met little success in promoting this element may signify an attempt to redress the balance in the third year. EA may also have felt that authorities had had two years to get used to these ideas and that they ought to begin reacting a bit more positively to the option of mixing their tenure patterns, hence the reason why it becomes more 'forceful'.

6. *Concierge schemes:* Little was known about these prior to 1987/88 and EA must be given the credit for publicizing them more fully via a report circulated to all authorities (Skilton, 1988). The majority of authorities do not feel that this is being stressed very much by EA (see Table 5.6), and concierges were ranked 6th, 7th and 6th. EA's main priorities in allocating its resources clearly lie elsewhere.

7. *Employment initiatives:* EA seems to have placed increasingly more importance on the generation of employment opportunities. CRSs were promoted from the start, nevertheless, employment initiatives only became more visible during the 1988/89 round of bids, when there was quite a large increase in the proportion of authorities who felt that this was being particularly emphasized. This aspect remained fairly peripheral and EA has not paid much more than lip-service to this. However, things are set to change markedly in the 1990/91 round, with 'employment' initiatives becoming the key element behind the EA initiative. Questions must be asked about why this has now become the number one priority for EA and chapter 4 provided some answers as do chapters 7 and 8.

8. *Homeless initiatives:* Not only did authorities themselves not register a great deal of support for promoting homeless initiatives (Table 5.5), but they did not perceive EA to be stressing this initiative very much either (Table 5.6). Nevertheless, the perceived emphasis placed on this type of initiative by EA has continued to increase rather rapidly (in terms of the total score rather than overall rank), despite the lack of matching local authority enthusiasm. In fact, one would have expected this to have abandoned in 1988/89 when a new DoE initiative was announced specially to generate initiatives for the homeless (but see chapter 6).

9. *'Other' factors:* Few of these are mentioned but include 'tenant consultation', 'comprehensive improvement', 'arrest of sink effect on estates'; and 're-establishment of the social balance'. This implies that EA tends to stick closely to its agenda (in terms of what it agrees to fund) and is not prepared to deviate very much. Alternatively, it may reflect that authorities do not feel confident enough to risk submitting 'non-conforming' bids. If the latter is the case, it must be questioned whether EA can really help authorities to innovate.

5.3 Administrative procedures

i) Referring to the time period between submission and approval dates, do you consider that there was an undue delay in general?

No 26%
Yes 74%
Missing cases = 3 (5%)

Note: The preliminary interviews indicated that virtually every single authority approached felt that the EA team seemed to take a long time to process the bids. Nevertheless, with the benefit of hindsight, the phrase 'undue delay' may be interpreted as being 'loaded'.

A high degree of consensus existed among local authorities that an unacceptably high proportion of bids for EA support were delayed by the EA Unit's administrative procedures. Authorities have a tight schedule of one financial year within which to prepare initial bids (Form A); send these to the Regional Officials for processing; prepare tenders and Form B for final approval; before having to actually spend the allocation in the time available (see Figure 3.1). Given that so many authorities (74.1%) contend that they experience delays on the part of EA, the present situation is clearly unsatisfactory. The consequence of such a problem is discussed more fully below and in Chapter 6.

Cross-tabulating the authorities experiencing 'undue delays' with DoE Regions indicates which of the regions were particularly bad in processing applications (Table 5.7). This procedure illustrates that the West Midlands, Northern and Yorkshire & Humberside regions are particularly slow at processing forms, while the East Midlands is much better than average at keeping delays to a minimum. No firm reasons for this can be postulated, but it would appear that the perceived delays do not simply reflect the number of authorities per Regional Office.

Cross-tabulating the same variable with political control indicates that the delays occur irrespective of the political composition of the authorities, although Labour-controlled authorities indicate that they experienced the most delay (Table 5.8). Lastly, cross-tabulation with type of authority identifies that the most acute problems lie especially in the Inner London and Metropolitan authorities (Table 5.9). EA would be well advised to look particularly into the operation of these Regional Offices in order to identify exactly what is wrong since together, these authorities make up a high proportion of the total number of authorities involved with EA.

Table 5.7: Undue delay cross-tabulated with DoE region

Region	Number of Authorities	Response-rate	
		Number	Percent
London	10	7	70
Yorkshire & Humbs	6	5	83
Merseyside	4	3	75
Northern	7	6	85
North Western	15	11	73
West Midlands	7	6	85
East Midlands	5	2	40
Eastern	3	2	66

Missing Cases=4; Source: Local Authority Survey

Table 5.8: Undue delay cross-tabulated with political control

Political Control	Number of Authorities	Response-rate	
		Number	Percent
Conservative Party	8	5	62
Labour Party	46	35	76
SDP/Liberal Party	3	2	66

Missing Cases=4; Source: Local Authority Survey

Table 5.9: Undue delay cross-tabulated with authority type

Type of Authority	Number of Authorities	Response-rate	
		Number	Percent
Inner London	4	4	100
Outer London	6	3	50
Metropolitan Districts	21	19	90
District Councils	27	17	63

Missing Cases=3; Source: Local Authority Survey

ii) What were the main reasons why this delay occurred in so many of the schemes/authorities?

71%	Administrative delays on the part of EA
54%	The time required by local authorities in working up the bids
51%	The lack of an adequate timetable for EA bids
51%	Bids being invited too late and with unreasonable deadlines
37%	Lack of clarity about EA criteria
24%	Changing EA criteria and the need for authorities to resubmit
2%	Other reasons
	Missing Cases = 20 (32.8%)

The responses indicate that local authorities feel that EA's administrative arrangements are primarily to blame for the current situation (70.7%). The present system with its two bidding stages (A & B bib forms) requiring detailed information may be part of the problem. Further cross-tabulation analyses reveal that the authorities which complained most about EA administrative delays were in the Merseyside (66.7%) and London (50%) regions. If EA wishes to review its administrative structure, it would do well to start with these.

It is not a surprise that local authorities would try to accuse others for the delays to schemes, however, they were also self-critical. 53.7% of the respondents acknowledged that the delays were partly because of the time needed by themselves in forming EA bids. It remains unclear whether this is in fact, because of local authority delays, incompetence and general inefficiency or whether this resulted because of the level of detail and type of information required in EA forms, the inadequate timetable, or both. The present administrative, timetabling and organizational arrangements begin to appear flawed.

Fifty one per cent contended that an inadequate timetable has been formulated for bidding, consultation and spend to be achieved and that bids were invited too late by EA and with unreasonable deadlines. These issues also surfaced in the preliminary interviews conducted. Many authorities apparently made representations to the DoE that the timetabling did not complement very well their HIPs rolling capital programme, thus causing difficulties. These issues are discussed in greater detail in chapter 6 but when cross-tabulated, authorities of all types and in all regions indicated that they considered this to be a problem. The timetabling arrangements are seen as a general problem across virtually all authorities.

The last two reasons cited for the 'undue delay' relate to EA criteria. 36.6% indicate that EA criteria lack clarity. This is perhaps both a cause and/or effect of the fact that 24.4% of authorities also felt that EA criteria kept changing (resulting in a need for authorities to resubmit their Forms A and B) thus contributing to delays. Several other reasons have been put forward to explain why this occurs - these are detailed in chapter 6. It seems realistic to assume at this stage that most of these can be improved upon, starting with a need for EA to rethink its timetabling and administrative organization.

iii) The survey tried to probe deeper into the consequences of the fact that so many authorities experienced delays by asking them to: *'Pin-point the precise aspects which were adversely affected by EA administrative procedures and inadequate timetable.'*

51%	The authority's rolling capital programme
87%	Whether all the EA allocation was spent in the financial year
87%	The timetabling of schemes [when started/finished]
13%	Other factors
	Missing Cases = 7 (12%)

The survey results suggest that the situation is far from satisfactory. Authorities are directed to plan their housing strategy three years in advance under the HIPs system, however, if they are successful in their EA bids, it may necessitate substantial rearrangement and reorganization of the authorities' housing investment programme in order to cater for and accommodate the additional approved spending. This disjunction is what results in programming difficulties with the rolling capital programmes in 50.9% of the cases. Given the uncertainties and delays already discussed, it is not surprising that 87% of the authorities also indicate that the system affects whether all the EA allocation is spent in the financial year. Adverse consequences (such as tenant complaints and increased costs) resulting from late starts and/or completion of schemes (87%) is analyzed in later chapters.

According to the 'other' category, the administration and timetable adversely affect 'the tenant consultation process and meeting tenants' wishes which are not in accord with EA policies'; 'delay and undermined tenant confidence' were mentioned; and lastly, 'DoE year by year basis of controlling capital programmes is a hindrance ... it is rather an artificial distortion in our three year programme.'

iv) Did your authority manage to spend the allocation within the financial year or not, and why this was the case?

No	39%
Yes	61%
	Missing Cases = 2 (3%)

Not surprisingly, a high proportion of authorities (39%) did *not* manage to spend all their EA allocations in the specified time. It might be argued that this is as high as most local authorities' success with mainstream HIPs, however, all the comments and arguments presented by the EA co-ordinating officers suggest otherwise. Therefore, it is worthwhile probing deeper into the situation in order to try to gain a better understanding by cross-tabulating the yes/no answers with relevant strata variables (Table 5.10). Most authorities (61%) achieved spend but in three regions (East Midlands, London and Yorkshire and Humberside), over half of their authorities did not manage it. This level of underspend does not merit complacency. This situation is at best inefficient. At worst, it is unforgivable when council housing is so desperately under-funded. Of course in a wider context, the same could be said of the existing levels of arrears, voids, disrepair and so on.

Table 5.10: Underspend cross-tabulated with DoE region

Region	Number of Authorities	Response-rate	
		Number	Percent
London	9	5	55
Yorkshire & Humbs	6	3	50
Merseyside	4	1	25
Northern	7	2	28
North Western	16	5	31
West Midlands	8	3	37
East Midlands	5	3	60
Eastern	3	1	33

Missing Cases=3; Source: Local Authority Survey

The major problem in spending the EA allocation arises primarily in Inner London, though Metropolitan districts and Outer London also suffer from this problem to a considerable extent (Table 5.11).

Table 5.11: Underspend cross-tabulated with authority type

Type of Authority	Number of Authorities	Response-rate	
		Number	Percent
Inner London	4	3	75
Outer London	5	2	40
Metropolitan Districts	23	10	45
District Councils	28	8	28

Missing Cases=2; Source: Local Authority Survey

Another point to note is that the higher the level of deprivation, the higher the percentage of authorities not achieving spend (Table 5.12). Increasing local authority reliance upon capital receipts favours the authorities in south England (except for London) with the greatest sales, and those authorities with the least housing deprivation (see Malpass and Murie, 1987). It appears that this imperfect situation is compounded for those who benefit least from the current HIPs system because they are also the ones who are primarily underutilizing their EA resources.

Table 5.12: Underspend cross-tabulated with housing deprivation

Housing Deprivation	Number of Authorities	Response-rate	
		Number	Percent
High level deprivation	24	11	45
Mid level deprivation	16	6	37
Low level deprivation	19	6	31

Missing Cases=2; Source: Local Authority Survey

The attention now turns to those authorities that did achieve spend:

61% Did manage to spend all their EA allocation because:
52% The EA set-up was well timed and effectively co-ordinated
54% Other reasons
Missing Cases = 26 (43%)

While 87% of all authorities feel that the present system causes them problems in terms of whether all the allocation is spent within the financial year, nevertheless, 61% did manage to overcome this difficulty. What this has meant in terms of corner-cutting and shoddy workmanship in order to achieve spend can only be guessed at.

Authorities in the West Midland, East Midlands and Eastern regions in particular, did concur that the EA set-up was well timed and effectively co-ordinated, but only 51.1% of them stated that they achieved spend because EA involvement was 'well timed and effectively co-ordinated'. 54.3% of them indicated that they managed to achieve spend because of reasons *other* than EA. The following quotations give a good indication of the reasons why: 'because of an effective response from all council sections involved, mobilizing resources quickly and anticipating approval'; design work undertaken 'at risk' until the allocation is confirmed; 'flexibility by the DoE and creativity by the LA'; and 'making realistic bids that are well developed and capable of being implemented'. None mention that this was because of EA and its flexibility, but to some extend this is to be expected given the level of centre-local tension which exists between EA Central and the authorities. We turn next to those that did not achieve spend:

39% Did not manage to spend all their EA allocation because:
Missing Cases = 2 (3.3%)
63% Inefficiencies and delays by EA in getting out approval
46% Inefficiencies and delays on the part of local authorities
42% Inefficiencies and delays on the part of contractors
21% Other reasons
Missing Cases = 37 (60.7%)

Thirty nine of the authorities underspent but unfortunately there is no way of estimating how much resource is lost this way. All the responding authorities in the East Midlands and the Northern Region indicated that the blame was theirs while all the others accepted little blame themselves for underspend. Underspend was cross-tabulated with regions resulting in the following areas which experience this problem acutely: Yorkshire and Humberside (100%), Northern (100%), East Midlands (100%) and the North West (80%). No single party control or politics is particularly significant. Local authorities again accept much of the blame themselves and inefficiency on their part (45.8%), however, the greater portion of the blame is nailed firmly to EA's mast, as can be seen above (62.5%).

Problems with contractors failing to deliver on their contract/tender promises is the other main reason for underspend. Unfortunately there is no indication of whether this was mainly the Direct Labour Offices' (DLO's) fault or the outside contractors' as this information was not requested. The reason for underspend seems to be spread evenly among the main agents involved but 20.8% of the authorities also named 'other' reasons, which is a large enough figure to merit further analysis. Such reasons include: 'Late notification [by the DoE] of allocation'; 'normal delays in going out to tender and contractor starting'; 'unrealistic timetable'; and the 'lack of flexibility in the allocation system'.

v) 'What normally happens if your authority cannot spend the allocation in the year?'

5%	Penalized with no EA funds the following year
45%	Renegotiated the allocation with EA the following year
53%	Allowed to spend the allocation on other schemes
13%	Other factors
	Missing Cases = 23 (38%)

A small percentage of respondents (5.3%) perceived that if they underspend, they lose out on EA HIPs the following year. This seems to somewhat extreme and if this is not the case, a letter to authorities clarifying the situation would not be amiss (one of the responding authorities is based in London and another in the West Midlands). This illustrates the mixed signals which authorities complain they are receiving from different Regional Offices (ROs) about the EA aims and criteria.

The impression from the survey and the initial interviews with local authorities is that in the great majority of cases, the Regional Officials do their best to facilitate smooth implementation of schemes. When final approval is actually given, the responsibility for schemes is passed on to the ROs and 44.7% of the authorities indicated that they were able to come to some sort of arrangement with the ROs although the exact repercussions of the arrangements remain unclear at this stage.

When in danger of underspending, authorities have (in the main) received some sort of unofficial EA/DoE 'approval' to spend the resources on any other project on the understanding that the EA schemes would be completed the following year from mainstream HIPs or capital receipts (52.6%), perhaps because scheme readiness was the main hold up. This is an eminently reasonable policy in that it matters not which resources are used to complete the schemes, as long as they are undertaken. This is especially the case if it there is a risk that those schemes may be lost, in part because of the DoE itself. This informal sanction occurred in *all types* of authority as well as in *all DoE regions*. This does show a degree of flexibility and responsiveness on the part of EA Central.

'Other' consequences mentioned include: 'We have to make up the difference the following year'; 'unspent HIPs is lost'; 'reallocation of funds across EA projects in the same year'; and 'negotiate the best arrangements in the circumstances'.

vi) If approval arrives late, which factors were affected?

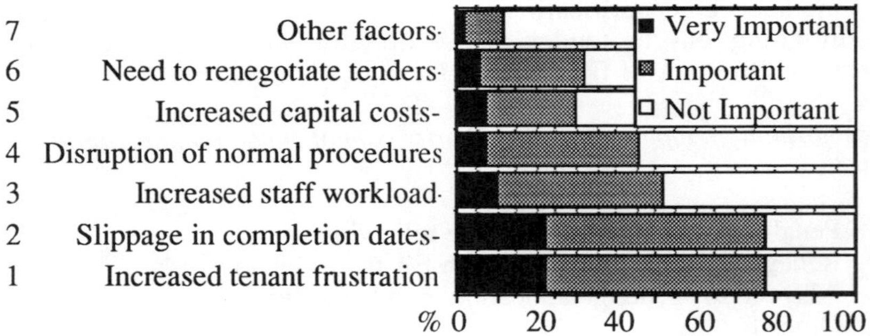

Missing Cases = 11 (18%)

1. *Increased tenant frustration:* 78% noted that this occurs. This is partly the effect of the next category (2), namely the slippage in completion dates of schemes. There is normally a time gap between bid submission and receipt of final approval which is prolonged by administrative delays over and above the normal ones. It must be remembered, however, that some tenant frustration probably pre-existed the EA bids. The next chapter links tenant frustration and delays to argue that the flawed EA timetable is at the base of these problems.

2. *Slippage in completion dates of schemes:* That 78% of authorities also experience some degree of slippage must be cause for concern. The EA administration would perhaps benefit from looking through the results of these survey analysis chapters for clues about why and where this is occurring, how it manifests itself, as well as what could and should be improved.

3. *Increased staff workload and duplication of work:* This arises partly from the fact that for most officers (52%), EA work is only an *ad hoc* part of their job description, which means that EA work is thus seen by staff as 'additional' workload. Undoubtedly the consultation, planning and co-ordination required to pull an EA scheme together; as well as to find the information necessary for Form A and Form B is an intricate and complex job. This is not at all aided by the lack of computerization in authorities and delays the which as seen earlier, beset EA procedures leading, for example, to the renegotiation of tender documents. Interviewees at the preliminary research stage stress that duplication of work arises primarily when criteria and weight placed on certain EA criteria change (see sections viii and xi).

4. *Disruption to normal planning procedures:* The fact that 46% of the respondents were of this opinion is yet another reference to the fact that the one year timetable for scheme completion is inadequate. This makes planning and co-ordination that much more complex. Chapter 7 probes into why this is the case.

5. *Increased capital costs to schemes* (30%): If tenders lapse (see below), for example, as a result of EA approval arriving late, its likely that the prices of materials and other capital costs will have increased. Authorities normally (though not always) only go into Form B stage once the tender costs have been established. If this is the case, barring gross delays and inefficiencies by authorities whose interest is to go to tender as quickly as possible, these problems must be the result of EA delays. A factor which cannot be controlled for, of course, is the weather.

6. *The need to renegotiate tenders:* Preparation of tenders is a long process involving costs for authorities in terms of staff time spent in preparation of such complex and detailed documents. These are then submitted to EA for final approval yet 32% of responding authorities indicated that they had to renegotiate their tenders when final DoE approval arrives late. This is an extraordinarily high figure and blame is seen to rest upon EA. Potential consequences include increased costs and tenant complaints. Waste is clearly endemic if EA final approval arrives late.

7. *Other factors:* There were few of these (11%) but include: 'Loss of credibility [in] Estate Action'; and 'inadequate time for tenant consultation', which is an issue which will be discussed in more detail subsequently.

vii) Continuation funding is the only way that authorities can get medium term support for schemes. It is of crucial importance to the larger and/or phased schemes and a substantial proportion of the total annual EA HIPs is committed this way:

76%	Always secured continuation funding from EA
36%	Obtained more than two years' funding for their schemes
13%	Were given some form of guarantee from EA
52%	Stated that this system of capital allocation caused problems
	Missing Cases = 9 (15%)

Since the Treasury allocates the finite amount of EA HIPs on an annual basis, authorities rarely gain the total allocation necessary to upgrade whole estates in one go. They are, therefore, forced to phase the renovation of large projects and to juggle with substantial sums in stages, in the hope of maximizing their EA HIPs allocations in subsequent years. The point to note is that EA is hampered by the fact that by law, it cannot guarantee funding for anything with a timescale longer than one year. Continuation funding thus becomes essential in circumventing this clause. To its credit EA has realized that authorities require a longer period to complete large projects. Via the notion of agreeing *in principle* to continuation funding, EA acknowledges that schemes may take longer than one year and that (should it still be around the following year), a certain amount of resources will be committed for that particular scheme. Thus it is an informal system where no guarantees are actually given, yet *half* of EA's total annual resources are committed in this manner.

For obvious reasons, it is important to get an indication of whether EA always meets these *informal* obligations. This has occurred in 75.5% of the cases. In other words, a quarter of the respondents at some stage did not get the 'promised' funding, which must have implications for both tenants and authorities. Cross-tabulation of this variable with DoE regions shows that revocation of EA 'promises' to fund future phases occurred in all DoE regions except the East Midlands, where the continuation funding commitments were always met. This does not promote the confidence and trust which is essential to the initiative and by no means aids forward planning or value for money.

EA initially stated that it would fund schemes for a maximum of two years. However, 35.8% of the respondents stated that this had been exceeded in their case, adding impetus to the local authority suspicion that EA bends its rules at will, however, this is perhaps a recognition that for many local authority proposals, even two years is inadequate. Cross-tabulation of this variable indicates that all DoE regions allocate funds in excess of two years so perhaps it is almost inevitable that this rule would be changed sooner or later, as happened in the 1990/91 round.

Thirteen per cent of the authorities were also under the impression that EA did guarantee their continuation funding. This is surprising (though useful in avoiding problems of uncertainty in capital programming) in that this is illegal from the point of view of EA's constitution. Few authorities received such 'guarantees' and these were in the Yorkshire and Humberside and the West Midlands regions.

Fifty two per cent of the responding authorities indicated that the continuation funding system caused problems. With no guarantees of further funding, authorities must find resources from their own HIPs or capital receipts to 'cover' the scheme in the eventuality that EA support does not materialize. This seems to be a wise precaution since as discussed earlier, about a quarter of the authorities in this survey have been denied such allocations. The point, however, is that resources are finite and should be fully invested instead of being held back just in case EA decides to renounce its commitments - formal or otherwise. A considerable amount of financial juggling occurs before such schemes are allowed through by councilors who want to be satisfied that schemes are sustainable. Authorities of all types, regions and political backgrounds experience problems although the Labour controlled authorities were more critical of this aspect.

The last part of this question prompts authorities to express what types of problems were caused by the system of continuation funding. The scale of response underlines the seriousness of the issue. Some problems arose primarily out of the delays and inefficiency of the EA administration in processing bids and typical comments include: 'Delay in accepting tenders, programming work and involving the tenants'; 'Level of allocation is not known until very late - finance from authorities' own HIPs has to be secured as a back-up'; and the 'requirement for council resources to be reserved at an unknown rate to support EA', since EA now expects authorities to contribute a proportion of the capital costs from their own HIPs.

Others point to the incompatibility between EA's timetabling and those of optimal contractual work: 'one year funding and contractual commitments were in conflict'; and there were related criticisms regarding the financial timetable itself: 'Difficulty in having to work up schemes with sufficient tenant consultation, prepare detailed designs, go out to tender and complete the works to spend the allocation in one financial year'; and 'Need for advanced tenant involvement and increasing information prior to approval and allocation and no commitment by EA'.

Many other comments concerned specifically the uncertainty surrounding the issue of continuation funding: 'lack of certainty that resources will be available to complete the scheme'; 'Uncertainty and the need to phase projects in order to maximize EA support'; and 'Not known if continuation funding will allow further phases to be undertaken'. Programming EA continuation funding is extremely frustrating to work with and to accommodate within the local capital programme.

viii) 'What exactly will or will not be approved'. EA will not necessarily meet all the elements that together make up a bid if it is believed that parts of schemes should be funded out of authorities' mainstream HIPs allocation:

69% What was funded did vary within and/or between years
36% Know exactly what EA will not approve
Missing Cases = 11 (18%)

The fact that 69.4% felt that there were changes in what is funded by EA from year to year (as well as within years), is confirmation of the pervasive feeling among officers that criteria change according to whether EA is about to underallocate its resources or not, a point developed in Chapter 6. For example, sometimes (and in some regions) roofs, windows and kitchens are included and sometimes not. This undermines confidence in EA and adds to the feeling of shifting 'goal posts'. The perception that the elements approved varied is strongest in London (100%) and Merseyside (100%), where all the responding authorities felt this to be the case; and in the West Midlands (80%) to a lesser degree (Table 5.13).

Table 5.13: Annual variations in funding cross-tabulated with DoE region

Region	Number of Authorities	Response-rate	
		Number	Percent
London	8	8	100
Yorkshire & Humbs	4	2	50
Merseyside	3	3	100
Northern	8	5	62
North Western	14	9	64
West Midlands	5	4	80
East Midlands	3	2	66
Eastern	3	1	33

Missing Cases=13; Source: Local Authority Survey

As a consequence of this uncertainty, only 36% of all respondents knew exactly what EA *will* approve. These are damaging figures but in theory, relatively simple to remedy by simply issuing a letter to authorities setting out precisely what will be approved under EA. This is standard DoE practice and there is no reason why it cannot be used in the case of EA unless this uncertainty does act as an useful tool for EA. It does nothing for DoE/local authority relations or for value for money.

The survey also prompted authorities to 'indicate, based on their experience, which elements EA will not approve'. Views are generally critical: 'There seems to be a continual change in emphasis which causes some confusion', but one view was almost supportive: 'It funds different types of work - depends on the package of works'. Based on past experience across the country, EA does not seem to be willing to do much for the inside of dwellings (often the tenants' chief priority) such as internal improvements, modernization and repairs. It will no longer fund refurbishment of kitchens and bathrooms. EA seems to be willing to support are insulation, heating and windows, however, there is contention over these as certain authorities list them as items that EA will not fund in their schemes. Other aspects excluded are scaffolding, structural repairs, re-roofing, vandalism, revenue costs and community facilities. This list serves only as a rough guide because as illustrated elsewhere, there are frequently differences between and even within regions.

ix) How closely do local authorities and EA monitor their schemes:

93% Authorities monitor their EA-funded schemes
Missing Cases = 2 (3%)

The fact that virtually all authorities monitor these schemes reflects a growing trend amongst both local authorities and central government. This is now regarded as essential in order for decision-makers to get some idea of problems and difficulties as they arise. Through EA, many authorities are also experimenting with different management organizations or ownership forms, which means that they need to have facts and figures so as to evaluate the success of schemes and the extent to which they can be generalized across the authority. Such a high degree of monitoring also reflects the need for authorities to scrutinise spending in order to be able to fill in the EA assessment forms (C and D).

The main forms of scrutiny were via project control and capital spending monitoring but also included working groups, programme targets and even housing management targets such as void and arrears levels, though this was rare. EA monitoring included:

71% Asking for all the annual scheme assessment forms
89% Asking for all the quarterly scheme assessment forms
50% Sending officers to inspect the scheme during/after work
4% Sending officers to audit spending on schemes
13% Other
Missing Cases = 5 (8%)

EA obviously keeps close watch on developments in authorities via the quarterly (89.4%) and annual assessment (71.4%) forms. These are primarily concerned with the financial aspects but which also includes environmental and socio-economic issues, in order to find if there has been any sort of improvements on the estates. With this degree of monitoring, there is little need to inspect schemes (50%) and even less point in auditing records (3.6%). What matters is that the schemes are erected and operational within a reasonable time period. The other forms of EA monitoring included occasional and/or yearly authority visits, regular meetings with DoE staff and EA observers. EA is keen on photographic surveys (12.5% - 'before' and 'after' the works/schemes are completed), the best of which invariably end up in its colourful and up-beat Annual Reports.

x) The chief advantages of working to improve 'problem' estates via EA:

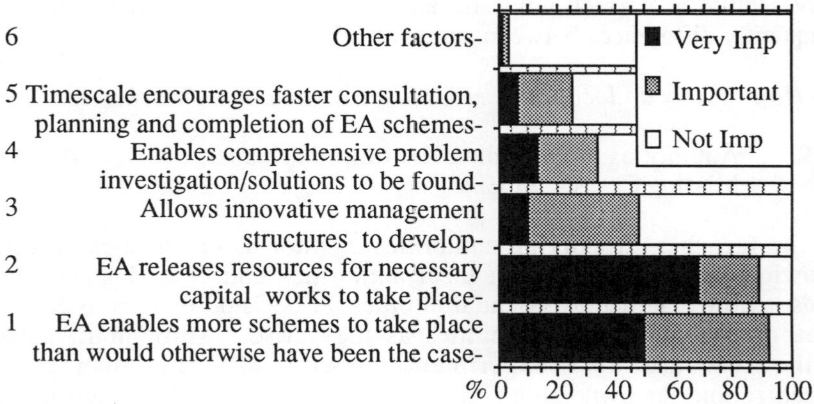

Missing Cases = 1 (2%) Source: Local Authority Survey

1. *EA enables more schemes to take place than would otherwise have been the case:* This fits with the results presented in Table 5.5 which indicate unambiguously that the primary reason for authorities being involved with EA is the issue of funding. Housing legislation has squeezed both capital and revenue subsidies and there is a feeling that any source of 'extra' funds must be seized. Consequently EA can be seen as having enabled more schemes to be set up by 91.7% of the respondents. This is an important finding for obvious reasons.

2. *EA releases resources which enable necessary capital works to take place* (88.3%)*:* Authorities again stress that their prime intention via EA has been to obtain additional funds. This leads one to question whether EA is just doing what councils would have been doing themselves if these additional (EA) resources were available to them via an enhanced HIPs system or through some other method. Enabling more schemes to take

advantages of working through EA. This is particularly important to SDP/Liberal (75.0%) and Labour (73.9%) controlled authorities. The order of its importance declines in relation to the type of authority. This illustrates in broad terms which authorities are most likely to be dependent upon EA resources (Table 5.14).

Table 5.14: Resources cross-tabulated with authority type

Type of Authority	Number of Authorities	Response-rate	
		Number	Percent
Inner London	4	4	100
Outer London	6	6	100
Metropolitan Districts	23	22	95
District Councils	27	21	77

Missing Cases=1; Source: Local Authority Survey

3. *EA allows innovative management structures and schemes to develop which would otherwise not have occurred:* To EA's credit, 47.5% of the authorities do feel that there are real advantages to be gained from the existence of such an organization - what is left unclear is what percentage of authorities would have engaged in these anyway, if they had the resources to undertake such schemes themselves. There is much evidence to suggest that authorities are primarily using EA for their own benefit and to fulfil their own priorities, nevertheless, this is deemed to be one of the advantages of working to improve 'problem' estates through EA mediation.

4. *EA enables comprehensive problem investigation to occur and thus comprehensive solutions to develop:* Only 33.9% of the authorities were greatly impressed with this potential advantage, among other things because the one year financial timescale forces the pace a bit too much to be very effective. The key point to emerge was that rushed developments may mean lower quality schemes.

5. *Its timescale encourages accelerated consultation, planning and completion of schemes:* Few authorities saw great virtue in this aspect (25.4%), possibly because accelerated consultation, planning and completion of schemes does not necessarily result in better planned and higher quality projects. In fact, most authorities may feel this to be a disadvantage or as not working very well in practice, especially in relation to tenant consultation.

6. Authorities mentioned few *'other' advantages* (3.4%) but comments include: 'Many EA objectives coincide with council policy'; 'No advantages - no more applications'; and on the positive side, 'Estate based repair teams are being recommended.'

xi) The chief disadvantages to working with EA and its procedures:

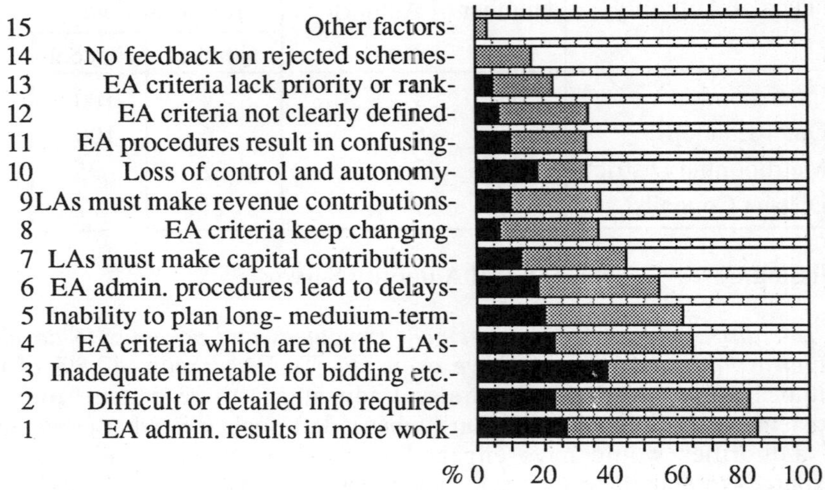

Missing Cases = 1 (2%); Source: Local Authority Survey

1. *EA administration resulting in more work for staff:* It is not surprising that this is seen to be one of the greatest disadvantages (83.4%). Staff have to be aware of developments in EA and literally 'keep their ears to the ground' in order to keep abreast of EA's more subtle twists and turns, such as what it is particularly keen to embrace at different points in time. Officers indicate that it takes much effort to keep tabs on these formal and informal developments and that there is a considerable amount of paperwork involved with this initiative. Cross-tabulating this variable with DoE Regions indicates that authorities in all regions and all political persuasions note this as a problem and, as in most issues regarding the initiative, a large degree of consensus pervades. The fact that many of these officers only spend a proportion of their time on EA adds to the perception that such involvement constitutes extra work.

2. *Difficult and time consuming nature of information required by EA* (81.6%): In their view not only are there numerous EA forms, but these are also substantial, complex and time-consuming to compile. Additionally, the information required is rarely easily available to authorities, assuming that it exist at all. Form A comprises of 34 sections

(4 pages); Form B over 100 questions (8 pages); Quarterly assessment Forms (4 pages); and an Annual scheme evaluation report (2 pages). Housing officers are greatly concerned with this part of EA.

Cross-tabulation against the strata variables reveals unanimity amongst all types of authority. This is a very real problem, but one which cannot easily be solved, especially if EA is keen to maintain the degree of control over schemes which it currently exerts through all the paper work. Whether these are necessary is another issue (see chapter 7), but the above two factors were by far the most important disadvantages to officers.

3. *Inadequate timetable for bidding, acceptance and allocation of EA HIPs:* As previously discussed, over three quarters of authorities feel that there was an 'undue' delay between submission and final acceptance of bids by EA, resulting in side-effects such as the under-using of the potential allocation available to council housing and that many of these difficulties could be traced to EA's timetable. This aspect is again stressed by authorities, where 70% of them felt this to be one of the primary disadvantages to EA. There is a good case for starting the whole EA bidding procedure long before the start of the financial year concerned so that authorities have a full year in which to spend that allocation as effectively as possible, without having to worry about submitting bids within EA deadlines. Bids should be approved early enough so that authorities can still spend their allocations in a financial year which is rapidly coming to a close. Criticism of the timetable is not specific to certain regions or authorities. It is all-pervasive and is one of the aspects analyzed in greater detail in subsequent chapters.

4. *EA criteria which are not the authority's:* A substantial proportion (65%) recorded strong reactions to the fact the relationship meant working with criteria which are not always the councils', with the implication that their *autonomy* would thus be undermined. This is true to the extent that what one can bid for and what EA expects is pre-determined and, therefore, authorities must conform to these if they hope to get any funding at all. However, EA does not in any way force authorities to become involved and there is the valid argument that within the umbrella initiative that is EA, authorities have a great deal of flexibility to bid for elements which do not infringe their own policies and priorities. If there is a willingness to exploit this, the opportunities to do so exist. Quotations to this effect from preliminary interviews include the following: "All EA schemes are what we would have done anyway, but we are lucky that we've decentralized as this is highly regarded by EA".

Table 5.15 shows that the more socialist the nature of council control, the greater the perception that EA did undermine local authority autonomy and/or that this was a disadvantage to working with EA. It is important to note that 44.4% of the responding conservative-controlled authorities also perceived this to be the cases.

Table 5.15: Other criteria versus political control

Political Control	Number of Authorities	Response-rate	
		Number	Percent
Conservative Party	9	4	44
Labour Party	46	33	71
SDP/Liberal Party	4	2	50

Missing Cases=2; Source: Local Authority Survey

5. *Inability to plan for the medium or long term in EA schemes:* This pervasive (61.7%) criticism refers yet again to the fact that EA can legally fund schemes for only one financial year, though special arrangements are available for schemes spanning two or more years. Approximately a third of authorities have received EA funding over a longer period, probably because EA has come to appreciate that a limitation of two years' funding is inadequate for major capital projects but a major criticism of the set-up remains that it impairs forward planning to the degree that is considered appropriate by authorities. Bids may be phased but there is no certainty that these will be honoured since EA itself survives on an annual basis.

6. *EA administration procedures resulting in delays to schemes:* 55% responded that this was a major disadvantage for reasons which have been discussed earlier, but it should be added that a major problem internal to the EA bureaucracy, seems to be the fact that the division of responsibility between EA Central and the Regional Offices is blurred. The bids are sent by authorities to the ROs and these are then shuttled back and forth until the decision is finally made (see Figure 3.1). Cross-tabulation of these responses with authority type (Table 5.16) reveals that this is a problem for all excepting District Councils, which perhaps reflects the fact that they tend to have fewer housing problems and submit fewer bids for EA support. This is an area which needs to be more scrupulously analyzed by EA and there are indications in subsequent chapters that a much greater degree of decentralization is now occurring.

Table 5.16: Administrative delays versus authority type

Type of Authority	Number of Authorities	Response-rate	
		Number	Percent
Inner London	4	3	75
Outer London	6	4	66
Metropolitan Districts	23	15	65
District Councils	27	11	40

Missing Cases=1; Source: Local Authority Survey

7. *Need for authorities to make capital contributions to schemes:* For the first years of EA's existence all allocations were met from the EA HIPs. One of the more significant changes, however, has been the insistence by EA that authorities should contribute a proportion of the capital costs (currently 50%) from their own HIPs. 45% of the responding authorities are very critical of this development. Others refuse to contribute, arguing that EA does not actually pay for anything - it merely enables authorities to borrow an additional amount for their housing investment. They have been prepared to string along and use EA to their advantage, but if the amount received from EA does not cover the full costs of the schemes, their keenness to participate begins to ebb, particularly if it is seen as yet another mechanism of reducing local authority autonomy over housing. Cross-tabulation with 'political control' reveals that opinion is unanimous that this is a major disadvantage. In terms of authority type, district councils were the least concerned about this issue, possibly because of the amount of capital receipts which they have accumulated in recent years.

8. *EA criteria which keep changing:* The notion of changing criteria (36.7%) has already been touched upon and there is little doubt that it does cause numerous dilemmas for authorities: confusion, extra costs and delays remain a problem but there is no reason why this should remain the case indefinitely with EA. Further cross-tabulation shows that the authorities which suffer most from 'fluctuating criteria' are the ones within the Northern and the London regions.

9. *Need for authorities to make revenue contributions to schemes (38.4%):* EA has consistently declined to meet any of the increased revenue costs associated with the initiatives which it helps to create, despite the fact that it is supposed to encourage authorities to innovate and to demonstrate the benefits of new ways of organizing their stock and management. Similar government initiatives such as PEP, do make provision for revenue costs to be met at least temporarily. Thus, for example, via the Urban Programme, the DoE meets 75% of the costs and can, therefore, reasonably expect to approve such schemes. Authorities are highly critical of the fact that through EA, not only does the DoE *not* meet any of the costs involved in the schemes (other than issuing authorizations for additional borrowing approvals), at the same time it also gets to *approve all* the schemes. Nevertheless, surprisingly few authorities have seen this as a disadvantage to working with EA and its procedures. This must reflect the stringent financial climate that local authorities operate in.

Cross-tabulation with the strata variables (Table 5.17) suggests a confused and contradictory response which indicates that authorities do not seem to be certain about whether the additional revenue cost involved is good or bad. Perhaps this is because not all schemes incur additional revenue costs, although it is the Inner London boroughs which are particularly concerned about this.

Table 5.17: Revenue contribution cross-tabulated with authority type

Type of Authority	Number of Authorities	Response-rate	
		Number	Percent
Inner London	4	3	75
Outer London	6	1	16
Metropolitan Districts	23	6	26
District Councils	27	13	48

Missing Cases=1; Source: Local Authority Survey

10. *Loss of control, autonomy and democracy over housing:* Despite the initial local authority rhetoric regarding this initiative and the early speculation and criticism (refer to chapter 4), only 33.3% of respondents see this aspect as being a primary disadvantage to working with EA. It is not surprising that their attitudes have metamorphosed. As mentioned previously, EA has become such a umbrella organization that it can be argued that authorities wishing to gain supplementary resources should be able to find elements within EA without greatly compromising their own policies. The charge of reduced autonomy is thus somewhat defused. Secondly, as authorities are keen to point out, EA has had difficulties in allocating all of the resources potentially available to it. This situation presents an advantage to authorities which will disappear (or reverse) as more authorities bid for EA resources in future. It must be said that nobody forces authorities to liaise with EA - though it entails compromises, they enter into the partnership fully aware of the possibility.

11. *EA administrative procedures resulting in confusion for staff:* This is another disadvantage cited by 33.4% of the respondents. The issue of changing criteria and 'moving goal posts' has been discussed. That officers dealing with EA should be confused to some degree is regrettable but almost inevitable for reasons already discussed. This point will be elaborated on in the next chapter.

12. *EA criteria which are not clearly defined:* This was considered to be a disadvantage for 33.4%, an extremely large proportion for something which ought to be taken for granted. But should it? Every Annual Report lists the familiar aims (plus what has been added) under such headings as 'Private Sector Involvement', Estate Based Management' and 'Employment Initiatives' but clearly, if there is uncertainty and confusion, these standard slogans cannot mean the same thing to each officer in every authority. Most importantly, does it mean the same thing in the same way to EA Central (and for the various Regional Offices, for that matter) as it does to those who are bidding under those headings?

Perhaps EA ought to place greater emphasis on compiling brief guidelines and reports on what exactly it means by these phrases and slogans, together with examples of models and variations. This could help to clear up the criticism. After all, if officers do not have a clear idea of what they should be aiming for, they are unlikely to be successful in their bids, resulting in both delays and costs due to abortive work, not to mention further mistrust. Neither is the problem confined to a single Regional Office. The degree of confusion is evenly spread, peaking in the London and Northern Regions (Table 5.18).

Table 5.18: Changing criteria cross-tabulated with DoE regions

Region	Number of Authorities	Response-rate	
		Number	Percent
London	10	5	50
Yorkshire & Humbs	6	3	50
Merseyside	4	0	0
Northern	8	5	62
North Western	15	5	33
West Midlands	8	2	25
East Midlands	5	2	40
Eastern	3	1	33

Missing Cases=2; Source: Local Authority Survey

13. *EA criteria lacking prioritization or ranking:* 23.3% consider it problematic that EA has made no attempt to attach any sort of prioritization to its lengthening criteria. Can and does EA treat all these initiatives/bids with impartiality and with the same degree of importance? If so, and more importantly if not, then authorities must be supplied with this information to use as a basis for more rational decision-making *vis à vis* EA and their bids. We have seen (Tables 5.5 and 5.6) that what local authorities perceive EA to be emphasizing varies so much (both annually and by region) that as things stand, the initiative means different things to different individuals/authorities. This needs to be clarified.

14. *Lack of feedback on why schemes are rejected:* A small but important 16.7% of respondents felt this to be a disadvantage. There can be no good reasons for not informing authorities of the exact reasons why their bids have been rejected. This should be a simple aspect to rectify and would certainly clear confusion and improve authorities' confidence in the initiative, while also helping with future applications. Cross-tabulation indicates that the lack of feedback from the DoE is principally a problem in the Northern, London and West Midlands regions.

15. *Other comments (3.3%):* The include: 'Allocations are 'top-sliced' and so there is now even less scope for successful traditional HIPs bids'; and '[EA] causes a great deal of extra work for staff since exactly the same schemes would be prepared if we were given the resources in HIPs'.

5.4 Tenant participation and evaluation

i) Has the involvement with EA resulted in greater tenant consultation, participation and input into schemes than would otherwise have been the case in the authority?

Yes 31%
No 69%
Missing Cases = 0

This is a vital EA element which explicitly recognizes the fact that in the past, many schemes have been implemented without tenant involvement and have turned out to be unworkable. 31.1% of the respondents did feel that EA involvement had led to increased tenant consultation in their authorities. This is undoubtedly an indication of success, but it is worth noting that given EA's commitment to and heavy emphasis on this objective, perhaps a larger degree of success might be expected. Also, when asked to specify in what ways this greater degree of consultation had been achieved, the majority indicated that this had *not* occurred primarily through their involvement in generating EA schemes *per se*. EA's influence begins to be questionable.

The survey probed into how the relationship with EA may have resulted in greater consultation. The responses related principally to PEP involvement, tenant forums and to some extent EA itself. Most of the other factors related to the tenants in some way: 'Tenants forums established as part of the decentralization package'; and 'Strong Residents Association formed. Regular consultation meetings'. Only one authority praised EA directly: '[Our authority] has not had a significant record of tenant involvement. EA guidance has made the Department more conscious of the need to consult'. Thus,, even in these 31.1%, the main reasons why greater tenant consultation has occurred, relate mainly to reasons beyond EA itself.

When this variable is cross-tabulated with DoE regions, it is the authorities in the Eastern and East Midlands regions which have benefited most by improving their tenant consultation, while authorities in the London region benefited least. It was generally the district councils and the ones with the least deprivation which indicated improvements in their tenant consultation as a result of EA involvement.

In fact, 68.9% of authorities felt that involvement with EA had *not* necessarily led to a greater degree of consultation. This is because:

63%	Authority/officers are satisfied with existing levels of consultation
35%	Fear raising tenants' expectations but unable to guarantee schemes
30%	Authorities are expected to plan, consult, cost and submit schemes too quickly and too late to allow for full and effective consultation under EA's timetabling arrangements
5%	Costs incurred by the authority in preparing bids while there is no guarantee that they will be approved by the EA administration
20%	Other factors (Missing Cases = 21 (34%))

Most (63.4%) stated that this was because authorities/officers are satisfied with existing levels of consultation. This response would suggest that authorities seem to have reacted positively to the general criticism about bureaucracy, paternalism and not involving their tenants sufficiently, and many councils have responded by taking consultation more seriously by laying down consultation procedures. The survey results suggest that by the mid 1980s, this objective would appear to have been fulfilled independently of any government initiative. This may or may not be true. Certainly it could be argued that greater consultation is occurring precisely because of the EA initiative's insistence that this is a pre-requisite for financial support (see chapter 9). Nevertheless it was the SDP/Liberal and Labour-controlled councils which have maintained the same levels of consultation, mainly because they argue, they were satisfied with the pre-existing arrangements. It is primarily Conservative authorities which have benefited in terms of introducing this element into their authorities as a result of EA (Table 5.19).

Table 5.19: Satisfactory tenant consultation cross-tabulated with political control

Political Control	Number of Authorities	Response-rate	
		Number	Percent
Conservative Party	4	2	50
Labour Party	34	22	64
SDP/Liberal Party	2	2	100

Missing Cases=21; Source: Local Authority Survey

Of great concern is the possibility that *less* consultation may actually result from EA involvement. Suspicion of such a perverse side-effect arises from the fact that 35% of authorities noted their fear that they may raise tenants' expectations yet be unable to guarantee delivery of the schemes. Under EA's procedural arrangements authorities must go through all the motions of designing, planning and costing a scheme, as well as involving the public at all stages of the process. However, there is always the danger that schemes will not be approved and so no additional resources will be forthcoming. A tenant backlash is the likely consequence mentioned by some councils and the danger is that even those committed to full and meaningful consultation may only involve tenants once EA approval to spend has been obtained and the details of the scheme set.

Further points arise from the fear of Regional Office underallocation or local authority underspend, both of which are analyzed more fully in chapter 6. We have discussed the problems experienced with the EA administration leading to delays in approval and that speed is of the essence if all councils are to spend their EA allocations within the financial year. A side-effect of this is that councils may be tempted to scale-down or even sacrifice tenant consultation; if they are to both get the resource and spend it (30%). The justification may be that resources and schemes are better than full consultation but no scheme to show for it.

Several 'other' reasons (20%) were identified in the survey as to why greater tenant consultation did not occur in these authorities. These include the following reasons, none of which are unexpected: 'Our local authority already committed to increasing tenant consultation before EA [was formed]'; 'Tenant consultation happens anyway, and is being improved'; and lastly, the 'Cramped timetable and scheme length makes effective consultation harder'.

ii) Which forms of consultation actually took place in your authority and at what stage of the process did this occur?

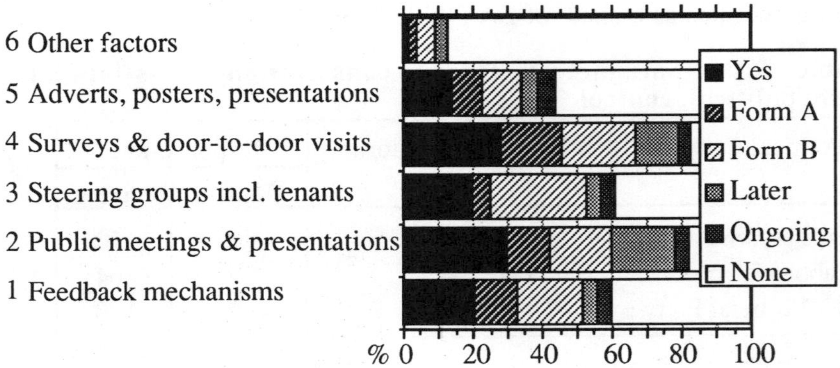

Missing Cases = 4 (7%); Source: Local Authority Survey
Note: The 'Yes' category includes only those authorities that indicated that this form of consultation had occurred, though not when it had occurred.

1. *Feedback mechanisms in order to incorporate tenant input* and (3) *Steering groups composed of tenants, officers and architects:* 59.6% of responding authorities stated that they had some form of mechanism for incorporating tenant input and feedback. An equal proportion had formed steering groups for their schemes. These are advanced forms of consultation and if it is true that 60% of the authorities undertake these, then it is encouraging to note that such a high proportion of authorities consider these to be important.

2. *Public meetings and presentations:* These are particularly useful for discussing scheme proposals and ironing out details and are very common forms of tenant involvement (80.7%). This, as most methods of consultation, is especially useful if it is on-going but the evidence is that this is the case only with a small percentage of EA schemes.

4. *Questionnaire surveys and/or door-to-door visits:* The evidence indicates that the main form of consultation for EA schemes is questionnaire surveys and/or door-to-door visits (82.5%). These are presumably used to identify the issues and areas of concern which form the basis of the actual schemes submitted to the DoE. In actual fact, things do not quite work that way as discussed below.

5. *Adverts, posters and presentations* (43.9%): These are designed primarily to draw tenants' attention to the fact that changes are planned for their estate. This is a smaller figure than expected and is probably a manifestation of the fact that if authorities are to consult, plan, design, bid and spend their allocation within a year, they may well have to skip the 'frills' and concentrate on 'true' consultation such as meetings and steering groups.

6. *Other forms of consultation* (12.3%): These include: 'Tenant Management Board and Tenants' Associations'; 'Small group meetings and Tenants' Association meetings'; and 'Weekly tenant surgeries' but overall, it would appear that authorities *are* concerned and committed to tenant consultation and that the EA schemes do achieve high levels of consultation but that, as described earlier, in the majority of cases (68.9%), such levels are *no different* to those of schemes normally funded by the authorities. EA is thus failing in the strict sense since part of its purpose is to promote greater and more meaningful tenant consultation. At the same time, the very fact that this is known to be a major objective may compel authorities to ensure high consultation levels in EA schemes.

The issue is more complicated. A closer analysis of the 'quality' of consultation reveals a somewhat disappointing scenario. If we accept that consultation should occur *before* the schemes are decided (for otherwise they would be mere rubber-stamping exercises) and that they should preferably be on-going, it is no overstatement to argue that EA is failing badly and that this is a feature *inherent* to the way that it operates as currently organized. The argument here is that only a *small* proportion of authorities actually consult with their tenants at Form A stage. Rather this occurred mainly at Form B, namely when the costings and other details of the schemes are already known in broad terms and presented to EA for final approval and funding. The suspicion must be that this proportion would be even larger if the 'Yes' category could be unravelled. This surely, is a contradiction to a key EA principle, but this is a consistent pattern for all the various forms of consultation.

Most of the consultation actually takes place between the time that EA approves the initial bid (and invites authorities to work up the scheme in greater detail) and the time that this (Form B) is submitted for final approval. This makes sense for authorities. They obtain an indication of whether their applications are likely to succeed, tenants' expectations are not raised until authorities are fairly certain of receiving the allocation and staff time is not wasted on organizing consultation, designing the project, drawing up the tenders and other fine details. But in a very real sense, this process works against optimum tenant consultation and involvement. This important issue is also analyzed in great detail in subsequent chapters.

iii) To what extent has tenant consultation resulted in change to EA schemes?

Little Change	66%
Substantial Change	18%
Sub-Total	84%
No change	4%
Not Known	13%

Missing Cases = 5 (8%)

If change resulting from consultation is desirable (since tenants are presumed to be in the best position to decide what is needed and how that should be provided), then the statistics show a healthy element of change (84%) which clashes slightly the housing officers' responses to the previous question. However, only a relatively small part of this total change was substantial (17.9%). Perhaps the reason for this is that the housing officers have guessed rightly what tenants wanted done on their estates (and so the bids required little change), but if this is the case, why then all the fuss about placing greater emphasis on tenant consultation?

The more likely explanation for the small amount of substantial change is a direct consequence of the fact that authorities are put in a position where the bulk of the consultation process must be conducted and incorporated within the period when EA asks the authority to work up the schemes in greater detail and the point when Form B is tendered to the DoE. This would suggest that the reason why most authorities make little change may be firstly, because of a combination of insufficient time for adequate consultation and for collecting and incorporating those suggestions, and secondly, because those recommendations do not square with the original conception of the scheme as set out at Form A stage. A third factor is perhaps, because the scheme was exactly what was needed or wanted by the tenants with few exceptions; or lastly, because tenants did not have many ideas or suggestions, in which case it is quite natural that there should be limited change in the majority of schemes. The first two options seem more probable.

The degree of change to schemes cross-tabulated with the level of housing deprivation (Table 5.20) demonstrates that it is *not* the most deprived authorities which experience the greatest degree of tenant feedback which is subsequently incorporated into schemes. Nevertheless, the levels of tenant involvement seem to be fairly high.

Table 5.20: Change to schemes cross-tabulated with housing deprivation

Housing Deprivation	Number of Authorities	Response-rate	
		Number	Percent
High level deprivation	23	11	78
Mid level deprivation	15	11	86
Low level deprivation	18	16	88

Missing Cases=5; Source: Local Authority Survey

iv) How were the approved schemes primarily chosen?

10% They were suggested by the EA team
62% Consultation between the authority and the EA team
50% Consultation between the authority and the tenants
7% Formation of a project group for each EA scheme
13% Other factors
Missing Cases = 1 (2%)

These results confirm that EA *can* have a direct impact upon authorities. For 10% of the authorities, the main reason why their schemes were chosen was because they were suggested or recommended by the EA team. One assumes that local authorities went through with them because the suggestions were relevant and beneficial to the area or estate. Cross-tabulation with DoE regions reveals that it is only in Merseyside that any number of authorities (66.7%) are influenced by EA, but the small number of authorities in this category (3) makes the statistic deceptive.

The majority of schemes were primarily chosen as a result of consultation between the authorities and EA (61.7%), which seems to imply that tenant consultation and involvement was *not* the primary consideration of a great many cases, but is not altogether surprising that this occurs under the present arrangements. Authorities must bid for schemes which conform to EA criteria (thereby possibly clashing with the intention to help authorities to innovate) and everything must be done within the financial year. Additionally, a crucial reason for success in bidding for EA HIPs quoted by many of those interviewed, was a very informal one - the authority's relationship with their DoE Regional Office and the quality of the officers thereof. That schemes should come to primarily reflect EA/LA considerations is almost inevitable.

Half of the respondents did reveal that the approved schemes were chosen primarily as a result of consultation between themselves and their tenants. The discrepancy in numbers arises as usual because authorities were free to tick more than one category. However, in this case the categories are mutually exclusive, in the sense that the primary reason for choosing a scheme cannot be because of EA suggestions as well as being primarily because or EA/authority consultation and/or primarily because of authority/tenant consultation. Officers seem to have been collectively ambiguous in their answers. What is clear is that few authorities formed steering project groups (6.7%). Part of the reason may be uncertainty about funding and the short timescale. In fact, the 'other' category was more important (13.3%) and the primary reasons why schemes were chosen included: 'Schemes which met EA criteria but main HIPs resources were insufficient to fund'; and 'Developed by local manager/housing officers and chosen due to known problems'. One even indicated that a scheme was chosen 'Following appointment of consultants'.

v) Indicate whether the authority will be bidding for additional EA allocation in the future:

No 5%
Missing Cases = 1 (2%) They would not participate in future because:

33% Negative experience with EA/the failure of previous schemes
33% The resulting increased revenue costs to the authority
34% Authorities are expected to make capital contributions to schemes
67% Other reasons
Missing Cases = 58 (95%)

Only a small number of authorities (3) stated that they would *not* participate in the EA programme. Negative experiences with EA and the lack of scheme success were mentioned, as was the increase in revenue cost incurred as a result of EA schemes not being subsidized or supported. Authorities are left to cope with increased cost themselves unlike other government initiatives such as the Urban Programme schemes. Another factor in this decision relates to EA's decree that as from 1988/89, authorities would be expected to make a contribution to the capital costs from their own HIPs allocation. This appears to be an offence to certain authorities given that they already have to 'jump through so many DoE hoops already'. The 'other' reasons for cutting the links with EA include the 'Proposed changes in spending capital receipts' and the 'Lack of DoE appreciation of the housing needs of the area'. The overwhelming majority (95% -Missing Cases = 1 (2%)) of councilors are committed to continuing their relationship and involvement with EA:

40% Positive experience with EA and the success of previous schemes
81% EA represents vital and increasing resources
53% Lack of choice since EA's resources are essential to the authority
7% Other factors
Missing Cases = 4 (7%)

Initially the situation reflects well upon EA. Forty per cent concurred that they have had positive experiences with EA and/or the fact that their EA schemes were succeeding (though we will shortly see that they attribute this success primarily to themselves and their tenants, not to EA). However, the 'other' reasons mentioned would indicate that the majority of authorities will continue to bid not so much because of EA, but rather *in spite* of it.

80.7% will continue their involvement but only because EA represents vital and increasing resources. Such an attitude has remained consistent throughout the period covered by the survey and there can be little doubt that authorities aim to use EA for their own ends as far as possible. Equally, over half of all authorities (52.6%) admitted that they were involved with EA through lack of choice, since the resources available to EA were considered to be essential to their authorities. What clearly emerges here is that authorities will continue to be involved but not always for the 'right' reasons. Local authorities are still *using* EA to their advantage as amply demonstrated throughout the survey but at the same time, EA's power is probably increasing in relation to the authorities. As more authorities become involved and the number of bids submitted to EA increase, EA may well be in a position of being able to 'pick and choose' schemes in the future.

A few authorities quoted 'other' factors but financial aspects remained uppermost: 'HIPs is rapidly falling; EA is increasing'; 'Due to decreasing HIPs allocations'; and the 'Need to fund local management projects'. In other words all were in it for the resource and one even implied that their authority had become dependent on EA: 'Need to complete future phases of existing schemes'.

5.5 What if EA HIPs had not been available?

This part of the survey poses certain counterfactual questions in order to gain an understanding of what authorities would have done if they did not have to rely on EA HIPs as much as the majority currently do (as we have seen in previous sections).

i) With regard to the EA schemes which have been implemented in the authority, how high a priority would they have been given if EA HIPs had not been available?

41%	In the process of being implemented anyway from main HIPs
73%	Under discussion for future implementation
10%	Low priority
7%	Not previously considered
3%	Other reason
	Missing Cases = 2 (3%)

This question serves as a surrogate for the degree to which authorities have had to *compromise* in order to obtain additional resource and whether EA is indeed working as force for innovation (if these types of schemes had not been given high priority previously). The first factor suggests that EA has not been a great force for change. 40.7% planned to construct such schemes from their own resources. Presumably, having found out about the EA programme and realizing that their plans fell within its wide criteria, they did what any responsible organization would have - they used EA funding instead.

Normally though, not only did authorities know about the initiatives sponsored by EA but they were actually under discussing for future implementation (72.9%). These were probably being left to the future because they were unable to come up with the necessary finance. By virtue of its resources (and 'fitting' bids), EA has enabled more schemes to proceed beyond the drawing board - schemes which would otherwise not taken place for years. This may explain why, despite the low levels of tenant consultation and little change to proposals, the great majority of schemes are still evaluated as being substantially improved; as well as why authorities (largely) have not seen EA as greatly undermining their autonomy. The majority are clearly bidding only for those initiatives which they had planned to undertake in the future and which are, therefore, likely to be in accord with council priorities and policies. This lends further support to the argument that if authorities are prepared to engage in EA, they can find the opportunities without too much compromise, but see (ii) below. Many authorities planned to implement these EA schemes at some stage and cross-tabulation with the Regional Offices reveals that the great majority have not deviated much from what they had intended to implement, with the exception of the authorities in the West Midlands (see Table 5.21).

Table 5.21: Implementation cross-tabulated with regions

Region	Number of Authorities	Response-rate	
		Number	Percent
London	10	7	70
Yorkshire & Humbs	6	4	66
Merseyside	4	4	100
Northern	7	7	100
North Western	15	10	66
West Midlands	8	3	37
East Midlands	5	5	100
Eastern	3	3	100

Missing Cases=3; Source: Local Authority Survey

Ten per cent of responding authorities indicated that the schemes which had been implemented had only been given low priority previously and that 6.8% had not been considered at all. These may be interpreted either as evidence that EA is not achieving its objectives (since so few authorities are actually undertaking things which they did not consider before and that EA has had very little effect on the authorities' deliberations) or conversely, that with its financial clout, EA is slowly beginning to become more influential and even forceful in attempting to fulfil its aims and that authorities are beginning to toe the line. On a less sinister note, this may simply reflect the greater number of options being placed in front of local authorities.

A few indicated 'other' positive elements to EA: 'Varies - some would have gone ahead anyway, others would not'; 'Work would have begun, however it may not have been as comprehensive as EA funding has allowed'; and 'Decentralization to local management offices would have been difficult'. These reinforce the view that more schemes have taken place than would otherwise have been the case and illustrates that EA is achieving one of its aims - it has enabled resources to be directed to difficult-to-let estates.

ii) Would you have used the EA HIPs any differently, if it had been available to use as your authority saw fit?

16%	In a different area or estate
23%	In a different scheme or way
48%	More effectively in general
23%	More effectively in each of the EA schemes
11%	Other factors
	Missing Cases = 17 (28%)

The first two factors are good indicators that certain authorities *are* having to compromise to a certain extent in order to secure EA allocations. That is surely what must be deduced if 15.9% of the authorities argue that they would actually have used the resources in different areas/estates and a further 22.7% would have used those resources in different schemes/ways if they were not 'tied'. The conclusion must be that it is not always the localities which officers perceive as having the greatest need that end up with the schemes and resources. To the extent that the housing officers are the ones best able to decide what is needed and where, this must be seen as a serious concern. Worse still, when the first factor is cross-tabulated with housing deprivation, Table 5.22 illustrates that it is the most deprived authorities which indicate that they would have invested in different areas or estates if they had the choice (all of which were Labour-controlled). This is a serious issue which should be further investigated.

Table 5.22: Different area or estate cross-tabulated with housing deprivation

Housing Deprivation	Number of Authorities	Response-rate	
		Number	Percent
High level deprivation	17	3	17
Mid level deprivation	14	2	14
Low level deprivation	13	2	15

Missing Cases=17; Source: Local Authority Survey

The following two factors indicate further reasons to confirm the suspicion that inefficiencies arise from the EA structure. 47.7% of the authorities felt that they could and would have used those resources more effectively in general if they did not have to cope with the EA administration and if these resources were available for them to use as they wished (see Table 5.23). A further 27.7% also argued that they could have used it more effectively in each of the particular schemes. These are serious findings given the government's 'value for money' drive.

Table 5.23: Generally more effective cross-tabulated with housing deprivation

Housing Deprivation	Number of Authorities	Response-rate	
		Number	Percent
High level deprivation	17	9	52
Mid level deprivation	14	6	42
Low level deprivation	13	6	46

Missing Cases=17; Source: Local Authority Survey

'Other' factors indicated (11.4%) were that the EA HIPs allocation would have been used: 'In exactly the same way, just cutting out all the new bureaucracy', and that if left to its own devices, these: 'Resources would have been spread more widely (political reasons) and therefore effectiveness *may* have been reduced'. This represents more peripheral support for EA. But for a government concerned with economy, effectiveness and efficiency in public affairs, this evidence justifies further consideration and research. A strong case may be made from the evidence presented above for reform in certain crucial aspects of EA. These are summarized and discussed in greater detail in the next chapter. As mentioned elsewhere, there is evidence of changes for the better, however, the situation could further improve.

iii) Do you consider that your authority's needs, priorities (and thus autonomy) have, therefore, been compromised in order to obtain EA HIPs?

Little compromise	56%
Substantial compromise	25%
No compromise	13%
Not known	6%

Missing Cases = 13 (21%)

There can be no more clear-cut evidence of the fact that EA can and does exert considerable influence upon authorities. 81.3% of authorities felt that their authorities' needs and priorities had been compromised at least to some extent. Only 12.5% gave a clear signal that they had not been compromised in any way due to their involvement with EA. The rest (6.3%) abstained from registering any view. When cross-tabulated with politics, it was mainly Labour-controlled authorities which indicated that they had been compromised and only Labour councils indicated that they had been substantially compromised.

iv) Do you expect that as time progresses and as capital expenditure constraints tighten up in future, that your bids and schemes will come to reflect EA's objectives and priorities more and more?

No	0%
Yes	67%
Not Known	33%

Missing Cases = 3 (5%)

The results are conclusive. Not a single authority indicated that it did not expect this to be the case. Thirty three per cent avoided the issue by saying that they did not know, but every other responding authority indicated that they did expect EA's influence to increase in the future. Cross-tabulation shows that authorities in all regions agreed and there was also little variation with political control. A survey quotation was particularly barbed: 'EA is a process of centralization ... it is also bureaucracy gone mad ... [Nevertheless, the authority] spends a lot of effort on EA - local authorities just cannot afford not to go in for it ... it is worthwhile chasing after despite the confusion, delays and frustrations'. For many authorities EA allocations can top 50% of their annual HIPs allocation in a successful year. In other words, EA HIPs has become absolutely crucial for many authorities. Their dependence on EA is beyond doubt (except where they also have large capital receipts) and the scope for greater assertiveness by EA must grow progressively.

5.6 Evaluation of EA schemes: Preliminary findings

The last section of the questionnaire addresses the degree to which the estates have improved following the completion of these EA schemes. All the evidence presented comes from the national survey.

i) Would you say that the situation in your estate(s) has improved?

No	2%
Little	31%
Substantially	67%

Missing Cases = 12 (20%)

Little need be said here, except to note that according to officer evaluations, the EA-funded schemes appear to be working remarkably well. If the great majority of the estates (67.3%) have indeed shown substantial improvements, as indicated, or general improvement (98%), then it would seem to imply that EA is doing its job and that this DoE initiative does justify its increasing annual budgets despite many of the critical issues discussed earlier. The results suggest that targeting resources along DoE-prescribed lines does work. Effectiveness of policy is an issue which is developed in chapter 8.

ii) What were the primary reasons for this perceived or actual improvement?

98%	The authority and the efforts of its officers
57%	The [efforts of the] tenants themselves
39%	[The efforts and] intervention by EA and its team
10%	Other reasons
	Missing Cases = 12 (20%)

Authorities naturally consider themselves and their efforts to be the key to these developments (98%). It would have been surprising if it were otherwise, since it is the officers that decide which estates need changes, the form of these changes, bid via EA, build the scheme and staff it. EA's contribution in this sense, is not much more than as an 'enabler' since it holds the purse strings. This notion of authorities using EA as a facilitator has been consistent throughout the analysis, as has been the conclusion that even in this role, there are clearly problems and efficiencies which operate in its procedures and administration, and there are certainly grounds for recommending improvements.

The second main reason for the success achieved by these schemes was accorded to the tenants themselves and their input and efforts (57.1%). The main means by which tenants would have contributed to the success of the schemes would be, firstly, through the consultation process, and the previous section has analyzed this issue fully, and secondly, by their reaction to the changes and efforts to work with local councils in order to make their homes and environments better places to live in.

Last comes EA itself. While it has been described as an enabler, its role in theory is much larger than that. It seeks to promote a number of initiatives yet, it would appear from the data that authorities bid overwhelmingly for those elements which suit them and their priorities. EA is also supposed to advise authorities on what they consider as the best ways of improving and managing their stock, based on the experience of other authorities across the nation. This is a demanding role, nevertheless, EA does seem to have met with a degree of success. 38.3% of respondents felt this to be the case. This should be neither ignored or under-rated.

Ten per cent ticked the 'other' reasons option: 'Substantial improvement - appears to be because of capital expenditure', 'Physical improvement of environment and property', and 'Decentralization policy and consultation mechanisms set up to discuss issues with representatives on the estates'. There is a glaring omission in the possible categories, namely joint tenant/council/EA co-operation. The fact that only two indicated that this was the primary reason for the improvements is indicative of the fact that despite the rhetoric, the true relationship in this initiative is principally between EA Central, the Regional Offices and the local authorities.

iii) A preliminary indication of the improvement on the estates

It must be stressed that there are weaknesses with these data as few authorities completed the questionnaire adequately enough to be included in the analysis. While 61 authorities responded to the survey, the data from 40 authorities (constituting 53 schemes) have been incorporated into this section, representing a 65.5% overall response-rate. The objective of the exercise is to obtain an useful indication of the degree of success met by the EA-funded schemes which have already been implemented.

Table 5.24 summarizes the main findings of an evaluation of impact. Based on the housing management indices chosen, the statistics imply a very pronounced improvement in the management situation of the great majority of the schemes funded by EA. Transfer requests have decreased in 44% of the estates, the average time taken to re-let property has also declined (in 57% of the cases), as has the number of dwellings still classified as 'difficult-to-let' (57%). Similarly positive results are evident as concerns the level of vacant dwellings (57%) the incidence of crime(62%) and vandalism and graffiti (63%).

While it is recognised that these improvements cannot be separated from wider developments in the authorities concerned, nevertheless, these findings suggest that 'targeting' EA HIP is having a measurably beneficial effect (see Pinto, forthcoming), which is the objective as far as the EA schemes and the tenants are concerned. It is important to bear this fact in mind when reading the rest of the book, although this must be counterbalanced by the fact that these figures are not very robust and are based in part on the subjective assessments of EA co-ordinating officers. Nevertheless, it is encouraging to note that there would appear to be very positive results accruing from EA schemes and chapter 8 builds upon this analysis by evaluating the effectiveness in four case-studies located in different settings.

It is relevant to note at this juncture that further analysis has been carried out from the postal survey but that for reasons of space and simplicity, this information and the accompanying statistical tables have not been included here (those who are interested are referred to Appendix 6 of Pinto, 1992d).

Table 5.24: Evaluation of EA schemes: Management statistics

Management Indicators:	Increased %	Decreased %	No change %	Not Known %	Valid Cases
Outstanding transfer requests	18	44	22	16	45
Average time to re-let the dwellings	5	57	28	10	42
No. dwellings (still) difficult-to-let	0	58	26	16	38
Current tenants with rent arrears	19	57	18	6	47
Management costs per dwelling	56	0	7	37	27
Vacant dwellings	15	57	22	6	47
Incidence of crime	2	62	30	6	52
Incidence of vandalism & graffitti	2	63	29	6	52

Source: Local Authority Survey

5.7 Conclusions

This chapter has presented an overview of the survey's findings, faithfully following the structure of the questionnaire. This was considered to be necessary primarily because by nature, this sort of approach was essential if the analysis was not to lose coherence and flow. The general drift of the findings indicate that local authorities feel that EA's operation is far from optimal although EA does appear to have achieved positive impacts on the locality.

There is some divergence in what local authorities wish to use EA HIPs resources for. Local authorities are above all attracted by the fact that EA is an increasing source of housing finance and by the opportunity to further decentralize their management structures. While they have come to perceive EA to be about encouraging new management styles, they are wary of the fact that EA's second highest priority seems to be that of further privatization of council housing.

The administrative procedures are generally felt to be cumbersome which, combined with the problematic timetable, creates pressures towards the end of the financial year, possibly resulting in wasted resources and a host of other difficulties such as in coordination, renegotiation of tender agreements and confusion. The merits and disadvantages of the EA initiative were analyzed before turning to the issue of tenant consultation. Only 31% felt that involvement with EA resulted in a greater level of tenant consultation and many felt that the quality of consultation was actually jeopardized. Local authorities also argue that most of the schemes which have been funded would have been implemented from mainstream HIPs anyway or were under discussion for future implementation, which suggests that EA results in a lot of 'dead-weight' schemes as far as the DoE is concerned. The overwhelming majority of authorities also expected EA's influence to increase with time.

Lastly the preliminary evaluation of the impact of the EA initiative using aggregate data suggests substantial (positive) impacts on the estates in 67% of the responding authorities on the basis of a number of management criteria such as the reduction in the number of requests for transfer, the remaining number of dwellings classed as 'difficult-to-let' or void and the incidence of crime and vandalism.

6 The local authorities' view: A summary and evaluation of Estate Action

6.1 Introduction

This chapter has several objectives. At one level it seeks to build upon the previous chapters by bringing together the main points from the analysis of the survey results. The chapter summarizes a wealth of material from which further details have been published in Pinto (1990 and 1991a). Another aim is to discuss additional factors which are important to the initiative but which have not been touched upon, for example, the 'topslicing' of resources and the extent to which EA is fulfilling its remit. The final purpose is to assess why the problems discussed in the previous chapter arise and begin to analyze the role of the other key agencies involved in the implementation of EA schemes, namely the Department of Environment's Regional Offices (ROs) and the EA Central team. This chapter is thus an important precursor to the next two (chapters 7 and 8) which respectively deal with implementation and effectiveness.

6.2 Local authority interaction with EA: A summary

In terms of the detailed operation of the EA initiative, it is obvious from the survey (Chapter 5) that the overwhelming local authority opinion is that EA is not operating effectively and that it is primarily EA's administrative and operational procedures which work to inhibit smooth and effective co-operation and co-ordination with authorities. This results in underused EA HIPs resources and possibly also compromises the quality of the schemes themselves. There are several inter-related issues which arise from a detailed analysis of the interaction between EA Central, the ROs and local authorities in attempting to renovate and better manage run-down council estates using the EA approach. This section goes further than chapter 5 by both summarizing the main problems and postulating possible solutions.

6.2.1 Deficient timetabling arrangements

According to the survey results one of the primary factors which undermine smooth interaction in implementing EA, is that its timetable is not well geared to the one which local authorities must operate to, particularly with respect to capital programming. The importance of this issue was underlined in the survey by the fact that 69.5% of the respondents noted that one of the chief disadvantages of working with EA was the 'inadequate nature of the timetable for bidding, acceptance and allocation of EA HIPs', which they argue to be more problematic than the normal HIPs system. 51% of the authorities stated that the main reason why they experienced unreasonable delays between the time they submitted Forms A and B, and the time they finally received official approval, was because of the lack of an adequate timetable for bids. A further 51.2% also stressed the difficulty by contending that EA invited authorities to bid too late in the financial year and imposed unreasonable deadlines. An example illustrates the difficulty. In the 1987/88 round, London authorities were invited to submit bids on the 16th February 1987. Final approval arrived between July and November and the resources had to be spent by April of the following calender year. Such a timetable inevitably creates very tight deadlines particularly on large, complex and costly schemes.

It may be suggested that the bids should be processed much earlier so that the total approved allocation is known to authorities at the *start* of the financial year in question, thus enabling the resources and schemes to be more optimally planned and programmed. This is an issue which was taken up by the AMA in a letter to William Waldegrave (the then Minister for Housing and Planning, mimeo), whose response confirmed the findings of the survey:

> I note what you say about the timetable ... and I agree that we should do what we can to improve it ... we have brought forward the bidding round for next year and our aim is to accelerate it even further for the following round so that bids are received in the preceding summer.

Although a few authorities have indicated that the timetable has improved for the 1988/89 round, the situation is still far from adequate. Even if the financial round is started earlier EA still has to allocate substantially more resources each year (see Table 6.1). In other words, any marginal improvements may be erased by the increased demands placed upon the EA machinery. This results in the danger that either EA will underallocate or local authorities will underspend what few resources are being made available to attempt to solve the situation, in what is frequently the worst of the council stock. These issues are considered in detail below (6.2v).

Table 6.1: EA visits, schemes and distribution of resources

No. of authorities visited by EA	86/7	87/8	88/9	89/90	90/91	91/92
No. of authorities visited by EA	145	175	na	na	na	na
Schemes in progress	138	202	320	320	225	340
New schemes started	138	117	190	150	120	120
Of which involving priv. finance	18	22	25	45	38	60
No. of dwellings being treated *	60	87	160	150	105	160
Disposals to priv. sect. excl. RTB*	3.4	3.2	4.0	4.2	2.5	3.5
Total EA HIPs per annum (£m)	50	75	140	190	190	320
Estates with tenant partip. in manag.	3	7	8	30	10	30
Distribution of EA resources (in percentages):						
Security measures	30	19	23	20	na	na
Env. improvement/remodeling	25	19	30	22	na	na
Heating/Insulation/Anti-conden.	25	24	18	23	na	na
Management related facilities	10	10	6	4	na	na
Homeless initiatives	10	7	na	na	na	na
Refurbishment	na	19	23	31	na	na
Total	100	100	100	100	na	na

Source: Various EA Annual Reports; * Figures in thousands

Table 6.2: Nature of consultation and stage when this occurred

Stage	A	B	C	D	E	E
Yes	20%	30%	22%	28%	14%	2%
Form A	5%	12%	12%	18%	9%	2%
Form B	27%	18%	19%	21%	11%	5%
Later	4%	18%	4%	12%	5%	4%
On-going	4%	4%	4%	4%	5%	0%
Total	60%	82%	61%	83%	44%	13%
No	40%	18%	39%	17%	56%	87%

Missing Cases = 4 (7%); Source: Local Authority Survey
Note: 'Yes' includes those that indicated that consultation had occurred but not when and how; a) Feedback mechanisms in order to incorporate tenant input; b) Public meetings and presentations; c) Steering groups comprising tenants, officers, architects etc; d) Questionnaire surveys and/or door-to-door visits; e) Adverts, posters and presentations; f) Other forms of

6.2.2 Problematic administrative procedures

The survey results indicate that the administrative arrangements involving several different agents described earlier (chapter 3), create major difficulties for local authorities. 74% of responding authorities felt that they experienced an 'unreasonable delay between the period they submitted EA bids and received final approval'. Cross-tabulation of those which experienced delays by individual DoE regions indicate that this was a widespread perception throughout all the regions, though it was particularly acute in the West Midlands, Yorkshire and Humberside, and Northern Regions (see Table 5.7).

In 71% of the cases the main reason for the delays experienced was argued by the authorities to be the time it took EA to process bids. This problem was exacerbated by the fact there are never guarantees that bids which are time-consuming and expensive to generate will actually be approved by the DoE until final notification is given, yet considerable staff time and other costs are involved in the preparation of both forms (A and B); all of which is abortive if EA rejects these at any stage. Given the scarce nature of such capital resources, the EA budget is heavily overbid, therefore, there will always be a number of authorities with good bids which will be rejected. In consequence, the investment in generating bids will be squandered unless authorities undertake the scheme from their own HIPs allocations or capital receipts and very few believe themselves to be in a position to do so. This is especially true of large-scale schemes where the authorities' own HIPs allocations will be insufficient.

There have been suggestions, therefore, that this process should be replaced by a one stage mechanism with officers being called upon on an *ad hoc* basis to provide further information, thereby greatly reducing the delays which exist. These problems have been acknowledged by EA which has indicated that the two-stage process should be eliminated (LHU, mimeo). This has not yet occurred but there are good reasons for believing that it could ease the administrative delays which currently have important negative consequences, such as delaying the opening date of EA-funded schemes (for 77.9% of authorities); and resulting in increased tenant frustration for a further 77.9%. For 87%, this delay was important in determining whether they managed to spend all their allocations as well as adversely affecting the housing rolling capital programme in 50.9% of the cases. The analysis of the local authority survey responses suggest that the negative consequences and repercussions of the EA administrative problems can be substantial for they do not seem to be very compatible with authorities' own procedures.

6.2.3 Changing EA criteria or emphasis

With regard to the initial interviews carried out by the author with housing officers, a source of frequent complaint relates to EA criteria of what is permissible for authorities to bid for through EA. In other words, there is measurable uncertainty about criteria whose emphasis is argued to be continually changing (as indicated in their responses in Figure 6.1) so that authorities ended up feeling uncertain about which initiatives are being emphasized by EA from year to year. This is reflected in two phrases which were repeated frequently during interviews, namely that EA is all about the 'flavour of the month' and that 'the goal posts keep being moved.'

In consequence, 36.7% of authorities in the national survey blamed the processing delays upon the fact that EA criteria keep changing and on the need to re-submit bids (also resulting in increased cost to authorities). 31% considered that the criteria were ill-defined and a further 23.8% that the criteria were problematic because they lacked any ranking or prioritization. The uncertainty was even greater with regard to elements which EA will *not* fund as part of an estate's package of solutions. 69% of authorities replied that EA's policy of not funding certain elements which did not meet their criteria, actually varied over time; and a mere 36% actually knew exactly what EA would *not* fund.

When prompted as to why this uncertainty existed, officers argued that this was partly related to whether EA was about to underallocate its resources to authorities and, therefore, needed to off-load any remaining EA HIPs quickly (before the end of the year) to avoid embarrassment. Whatever the real explanation, the simple fact remains that there can be no basis to bid for EA resources and schemes if there is any doubt regarding what is (or is not) acceptable to EA and such a situation can only encourage waste and inefficiency. Ministerial Guide-lines have now been issued so perhaps EA itself is aware of the confusion which certain authorities operate in. It is too soon to evaluate whether the guide-lines have achieved their purpose in spelling out in detail what will and will not be considered under EA and in what circumstances.

6.2.4 Adequacy of tenant consultation

From the outset EA put tenant consultation at the forefront of its agenda as a crucial element underlying the 'themes' it tries to encourage. The evidence is that in this respect, EA has not been too successful and that the very nature of its operation compromises its ability to fulfil this objective.

Sixty nine per cent of all authorities indicated that involvement with EA had *not* resulted in 'greater tenant consultation, participation and input into schemes than would otherwise have been the case in their authorities'. This is argued to be primarily because most authorities (63.4%) were satisfied with the existing consultation levels although 30% argued that greater consultation with tenants had not come about because they were expected to 'plan, consult and submit bids too quickly and too late for full and effective tenant consultation to occur'. The argument in chapter 5 suggested that authorities may actually be underplaying the extent of EA's influence with respect to tenant consultation, however, this is again a reference to the timetabling arrangements and the fact that it makes it difficult for authorities to consult effectively, design and plan the scheme, programme the capital allocation and spend it all within one year. Procedural delays did not help the situation.

A further 35% indicated that involvement with EA had not necessarily resulted in greater consultation because they feared raising tenants' expectations, while not being in a position to guarantee delivery of proposals. Success depends entirely upon whether the bids fit EA criteria for that particular year and whether they 'make the cut' and thus form part of the group of approved bids in that particular DoE region. These factors all seem to jeopardize effective tenant consultation. This view is confirmed in Table 6.2.

Consultation took place mainly through questionnaire surveys (82%) and public meetings (83%). The main point to note, however, is the extremely small proportion of authorities that consult tenants at Form A stage when the overall bid and its costings are outlined. It is only at Form B stage that tenants are normally consulted. This seems contradictory *vis à vis* the aim of effective tenant consultation since by this stage, the broad outline of the EA scheme has been decided and the flexibility for tenant input significantly reduced.

From the authorities' view-point, this makes sense since tenants' expectations are not raised until *after* the authority has obtained confirmation that the scheme has a good chance of being successful. However, by this time (Form B), as previously indicated, authorities are having to move rapidly if they are to spend their allocations. It is also worth noting the very low level of on-going consultation. Given that EA took it upon itself to make consultation of primary importance in its schemes, according to the evidence supplied by local authorities, it appears that this is not being fully achieved, partly because of authorities' uncertainty about committing staff time and technical resources as well as raising tenants' expectations when there is a real possibility that bids may be rejected by EA (but see the concluding chapter).

There is thus a case for EA *underwriting* both the technical cost of scheme preparation and the tenant consultation exercises, especially if the bids are rejected. This would be costly but at the very least it would create a great deal of goodwill in authorities which are already financially pressed. This is important as it leads to other desirable developments which are essential for smooth and effective implementation of an initiative which depends upon four crucial levels: EA Central, the ROs, and the authorities and tenants.

6.2.5 Underusing housing resources

Apart from the issue of topslicing (see 6.3 below) and those relating to the adequacy of a system of capital allocations based on a single year timetable, the survey illustrates another significant problem. EA is found to be a problematic and inefficient method of allocating authorizations for capital work yet this is a system which is not only increasingly used by central government (for example in the Private Sector Renewal and the Homeless Initiatives - see Figure 3.2), but also one which is undermining and replacing the HIPs system (Malpass and Murie, 1987). Apart from the difficulties already highlighted, the EA HIPs capital allocation system is problematic in two other respects. It can be underallocated or it can be underspent. Both result in a further loss of housing investment at a time when it is important to improve the management and maintenance situation in certain sectors of council housing and to use whatever is available as efficiently as possible.

Underallocation: The annual EA HIPs is divided amongst the 10 Regional Offices to be allocated to their authorities but as has been demonstrated the timetabling arrangement is somewhat problematic and authorities and their representatives have argued that this has resulted in the EA HIPs not being entirely allocated to the authorities. The AMA estimates that in 1986/87, EA may have underallocated by as much as £10m (out of £50m) and that this also occurred the following year (AMA, mimeo a). If this is the case, then the EA system may result in serious losses of potential capital resources which are already contracting rapidly. The DoE denies this. In reply, Waldegrave states: 'The whole of the £75 million [for 1987/88] is committed. And last year approvals totaling some £52 million were given.' (Waldegrave, mimeo) The EA Annual Reports also indicate that the allocations have been fully committed.

Local authorities have countered this argument by stating that the delays experienced indicate that bids cannot be processed quickly enough. Even if EA is becoming more efficient, the rapid increase of its total allocation may nullify such progress that occurs. Additionally the confusion over EA criteria concerning what will (and will not) be funded also reflects the fact that at certain times of the year, EA is desperate to allocate quickly and almost irrespective of the type of package or scheme. This could also help explain why, despite an almost total lack of interest by local authorities in using EA HIPs to generate Homeless Initiatives (see Table 5.5), 10% and 7% respectively of the total EA HIPs allocation went on these initiatives for 1986/87 and 1987/88; while the proportion was only 10% and 10% for the key element underpinning EA, namely estate based management (Table 6.1).

The problem of underallocation and the need to find simple schemes that can both be processed and enable resources to be spent quickly (eg. Homeless Initiatives), may explain these figures. Certain authorities have been extremely successful at obtaining EA funding because they have learned to hold such bids 'on the shelf' for later in the financial year, when the ROs requests schemes which can be processed and spent quickly. This may occur either because the region has had difficulty in allocating its share or because it has been able to secure additional EA HIPs from other regions. Thus the DoE ROs can lose their allocation to one another if they are in danger of underallocating their proportion and there is, therefore, competition between *authorities* as well as between *regions* for EA funding.

Underspend:

> The normal sequence of events is a) visit by EA Unit b) letter inviting submissions of Form A c) Approval in principle to schemes d) Local authority working up schemes, tenant consultation, detailed designs, costings, committee approvals, out for tender, submission of Form B e) Further allocation of EA funding. By this time its usually well towards Nov\Dec\Jan of the financial year with spend having to be achieved by the following March. (Quotation from Postal Survey)

In such a context it is authorities themselves which end up either underspending or not using resources in the most effective manner possible. While 87% of the authorities stated that EA administration and timetabling adversely affect whether all the allocation is spent in the financial year nevertheless, 61% of them did manage to spend it all. The point to note, however, is that only 51.5% stated that this was because 'the EA set-up was well timed and effectively coordinated'. 54% made it clear that they only managed to do so by undertaking work 'at risk' until the allocation was confirmed or by making bids which are capable of being implemented.

A substantial proportion (39%) did underspend although the actual extent was not quantified partly so as not to adversely affect the survey response rate. This financial mechanism thus appears to be an inefficient method of distributing capital allocations. Authorities argue that there is a great deal of waste when bids are aborted or rejected. Even on successful bids, underspend may result and other repercussions for the quality and cost of schemes can be envisaged (but see chapter 8). The next two sections deal with related issues. A brief examination is made of the notion of topslicing but the bulk of the chapter is devoted to an exposition of the extent to which EA is fulfilling its official objectives.

6.3 EA funding: Additional or topsliced?

This is an issue which reared itself throughout the preliminary interview and survey stages of the research. From the outset local authorities were wary of EA, primarily because many initially saw EA as yet another method resulting in the centralization of decision-making and financial control of council housing (Chapter 3). It is accordingly worth briefly commenting on the issue in order to draw together the evidence for the contention that 'topslicing' takes place, not least because it is a mechanism which is increasingly employed by the DoE for its special schemes.

Only one officer interviewed during the survey preparation stage (preliminary/trawling interviews) believed that EA HIPs represented truly extra capital resources (additional to the annual HIPs allocations), as implied in the Chancellor's Autumn Statement: "*Extra* resources are being provided for the renovation of the local authority housing stock through the Urban Housing Renewal Unit" (Hansard, 1986, Emphasis Added). Rather the majority of authorities believed that it was topsliced from the rapidly dwindling annual HIPs allocations, centralized and then re-allocated to authorities. The point to note is that the resources are then re-allocated on DoE terms and conditions rather then being 'unspecified' allocations for authorities to use as they see fit (as under the HIPs system). In unstructured terms, some support exists for the widespread belief among authorities and their representatives such as the AMA and the LHU (Interviews), that EA HIPs resources are topsliced.

Table 2.3 indicates that HIPs capital allocations have contracted so much in recent years that EA's allocation could easily have been transferred from HIPs to EA HIPs without anyone knowing for certain. This is naturally rather a simplistic argument, but corroborating evidence comes from an EA Annual Report (DoE, 1986, p.7):

> Depending on local needs and circumstances, UHRU is able to orchestrate a range of public sector inputs to its package solutions. Most significantly, the Unit has access to Housing Investment Programme (HIP) resources of £50m in 1986/87 to help.

This quotation undoubtedly implies an element of topslicing. The government White Paper on Public Expenditure for the same year was more explicit: "Out of the total HIP allocations to local authorities for 1986-87, a special allocation will be reserved for projects identified by UHRU" (H.M. Treasury, 1986). Some authorities interviewed indicate that even the Regional Officers responsible for helping implement the initiative no longer insist that EA HIPs is totally separate from HIPs. Some ROs even refer to the resources as being topsliced. Despite the references to this financial aspect, however, little 'hard' information exists upon which to conclude on this issue with any degree of certainty, which is precisely why the debate continues.

6.4 The objectives and achievements

We have discussed elsewhere EA's remit (chapter 3). EA has employed three principal strategies. Firstly, it has re-routed capital resources for improvement and it has 'targeted' these upon the most problem-prone sections of the housing stock of authorities willing to become involved. Its resources have increased rapidly (from £50m to £270m in 1990/91 - see Table 6.2) and have come to figure prominently in a substantial number of authorities' capital programmes. EA has also attempted to introduce new methods of managing and disposing of this type of council stock and its aims have not remained static since its inception - it has diversified and now includes the use of concierges (see Skilton, 1988) and employment generating / enterprise initiatives (DoE, 1988a). The balance of schemes and resources is illustrated in Table 6.1.

Having discussed the administrative and implementation characteristics, it is important to attempt an evaluation of the initiative in broad terms, not least because EA was launched back in July 1985. Therefore, this section seeks not to comment on the quality and success of the EA initiatives themselves (see chapter 8) but rather to evaluate EA's success (in broad terms) in achieving its stated remit by making use the limited official data that exist. Each element of the remit is discussed in turn.

i) Identify authorities and estates where new initiatives can be pursued

In 1985/86 EA identified 69 such authorities using the relatively simple criterion of local authority Housing Investment Programme (HIPs) bid returns which 'appeared to have the most severe problems' (DoE, 1986, p.3). Over time the selection criteria become more refined. In theory, only estates with poor layouts and designs, lacking defensible space (DoE, 1987a, p.2) and demonstrating management problems would be eligible to apply for EA resources (see Table 6.3).

Table 6.3: Eligibility criteria for EA funding

Criteria	National Averages (England 1986)
Higher than average vacancies	2.5%
High rent arrears	£46 per tenancy
High tenant turnover	9.8%
Other evidence of tenant dissatisfaction (eg. low take-up of 'right to buy')	
Other measures of social malaise [eg. litter, vandalism and graffiti]	

Source: Form A Applications Guidance Notes, 1988/9

Authorities have indicated in preliminary interviews and the survey results, that as far as they were concerned, the most worthwhile EA feature was that resources were set aside *specifically* for authorities with the most difficult stock and management problems. There was some candid agreement that run-down estates had been ignored to some extent (demonstrating the failure of the general HIPs allocation to meet priority needs) and that there was, therefore, a rationale for 'targeting' resources on this particular element of council stock and management, if not necessarily through the particular financial mechanism that now exists.

Over time though the spatial focus seems to have changed and become diffused as more and more authorities have been invited by EA to participate and submit bids for its resources (see Table 6.1). The reasons why this has occurred has not been set out officially but *all* authorities are now eligible to apply for EA resources. This would imply that the issue of targeting resources upon the most needy authorities and estates has to some extent been toned down, prompting some authorities to argue in preliminary interviews that EA has now lost its most legitimate *raison d'etre.* Strictly speaking, however, EA has fulfilled this element of its remit and indeed, there are indications that with its new emphasis on fewer and larger 'enterprise' or employment initiatives, the focus may be narrowing once more - perhaps to the opposite extreme.

ii) Provide a progress report by the end of June 1986 and iii) To advise ministers of the need for new machinery, incentives or legislative change to promote the full range of solutions

There is now an established tradition of publishing Annual Reports on EA activities so that the public has some understanding of how the resources are being used in broad terms but there is little or no basis to evaluate whether EA has been successful in achieving the third part of its remit. The only connection that EA may have had with legislative changes is possibly with the newly designated Housing Action Trusts (HATs), where some commentators have highlighted the fact that all the estates which were originally proposed for HATs designation had either received EA funding or had been the subject of a bid (LHU, Interview 8. Feb. 1989). This means that the DoE had a substantial amount of detailed information on these estates - more than enough to select prime candidates for HATs designation.

Although the HATs concept originates from different sources (Henney, 1985), nevertheless, council housing officers have maintained that EA has required too much information in the application procedure, not all of which is relevant to the bids being made. There is, therefore, an issue as to whether the information gathered by EA has been used for another purpose. Secondly, of course, there is also the view that these estates have been primed for sale by extensive investment through the EA programme (Grant, 1988). A key former member of the EA team has indicated to the author that this information has been used in determining HATs (see also chapter 7) even though, as it has turned out, six out of seven HATs estates have so far been either de-selected or voted down by tenants (Guardian, 6.10.90). There seems to be little else that EA has directly contributed to although they have collaborated with the Priority Estates Project team in setting up Estate Management Boards (see Zipfel, 1989).

iv) Encourage authorities to dispose of their stock

As discussed in chapter 4 this was originally a prime political motive behind the creation of EA. Greater detail of what is meant by 'disposal' is set out in a letter to Chief Executives elaborating upon the reasons why EA encourages authorities to look to the private sector to help them tackle the problems of their run-down estates. The benefits include resources in addition to local authority HIPs and EA HIPs; the fact that diversity and new forms of tenure help create a new atmosphere and ease management difficulties; and empty properties could be brought quickly back into profitability. Consequently EA would encourage three types of scheme: disposal of empty blocks/parts of estates for refurbishment and onward sale; for refurbishment and onward renting; and disposal of tenanted properties to new landlord bodies, such as trusts or ownership co-operatives (EA letter, 30.9.1987). EA has tried hard to promote diversification of tenure via this method:

> Last year [the] Council made three EA bids: two were successful. Both included the disposal of properties to either a private developer or Housing Association. The one that was not successful did not!" (Authority in the Northern Region)

According to the EA's Annual Reports, a number of authorities seem to have become convinced of the value to them and their tenants of off-loading some of their stock to the private sector. In 1986/87 20 schemes (14% of the total) were for onward sale or to develop unused land. This increased to 24 and 34 schemes in the following two years (forming respectively 12% and 18% of all the EA HIPs funded schemes).

This must be a reflection of the fact that authorities are placing increasingly more emphasis on involving the private sector, this being one of the key EA tenets. The national survey tried to obtain information about various aspects of EA's remit with special emphasis on the variety of management initiatives which it tries to promote. The results were aggregated and ranked in Tables 5.5 and 5.6 (Rank 1 = highest priority and Rank 9 = lowest). This procedure illustrates some interesting trends derived from responses to the questions: 'Indicate your authority's main reasons for being concerned with EA'; and secondly, 'Indicate what *you* think has been stressed by EA'. As discussed in chapter 5, it proved necessary to ask housing officers the latter question because EA has not acknowledged that its criteria/emphases have changed, whereas local officers interviewed were suggesting a different situation. The overall ranks were used and incorporated into Figure 6.1, thus providing information which is pertinent to the discussion to follow.

It is interesting to compare side by side what authorities are mainly concerned with as opposed to what they perceive EA to be interested in, in order to see if there are great similarities or differences - in other words, we attempt to compare the responses in Table 5.5 with those of Table 5.6. The result is that in every single case there is a disparity in intention between the two, which is crucial in understanding the findings discussed in the rest of the chapter. The immediate point which arises from Figure 6.1 below, is the fact that authorities' interests hardly ever coincide with those of EA, particularly in the case of private sector disposal; but more importantly, the priorities attached (even to compatible interests) is always different. This is not surprising but it does illustrate very well the reason why the two camps frequently seem to be at 'loggerheads' with each other, particularly in the first few years of EA's operation. The discussion to follow draws upon these results to develop the analysis on EA's remit.

Figure 6.1 illustrates that a growing percentage of authorities perceive that EA places major and increasing importance on private sector disposal in the renovation of estates, since this has been elevated to EA's second most important element (Rank 2). There is a sharp clash of interest here as it is ranked very low in terms of local authority priority (9th, 8th and 8th respectively). Nevertheless 18% of the total number of schemes funded by EA were of this sort. This suggests that over time, EA has been able to persuade authorities of the value of such schemes and/or that many authorities are so desperate to obtain additional capital resources to supplement their dwindling basic HIPs, that they are prepared to even contemplate this option which was decried with such contempt back in June 1985.

v) To encourage authorities to improve the management and maintenance of their own estates by establishing local autonomous estate based management schemes on Priority Estates Project lines

More or less from the start EA put management at the forefront by stating its determination to follow the PEP model of local management:

> Estate Action will only support schemes where the existing assets, the existing investments and tenants interests will be safeguarded by adequate arrangements for housing management and repairs. Some form of on-site management presence is virtually always desirable; and on many estates ... this would be on the lines developed by the priority estates project ... Where estates have become run down, it is unlikely that a continuation of the present management and repair arrangement will prove acceptable in a bid for Estate Action resources. (DoE News Release, 17 Feb. 1988, p.2)

Figure 6.1 shows that authorities believe that EA was genuinely seeking to promote decentralized management but unlike private sector disposal, this is an aspect of the EA remit that was very much in accord with authorities' own intentions. It is not surprising that many EA schemes turned out to be of this type according to Annual Report figures

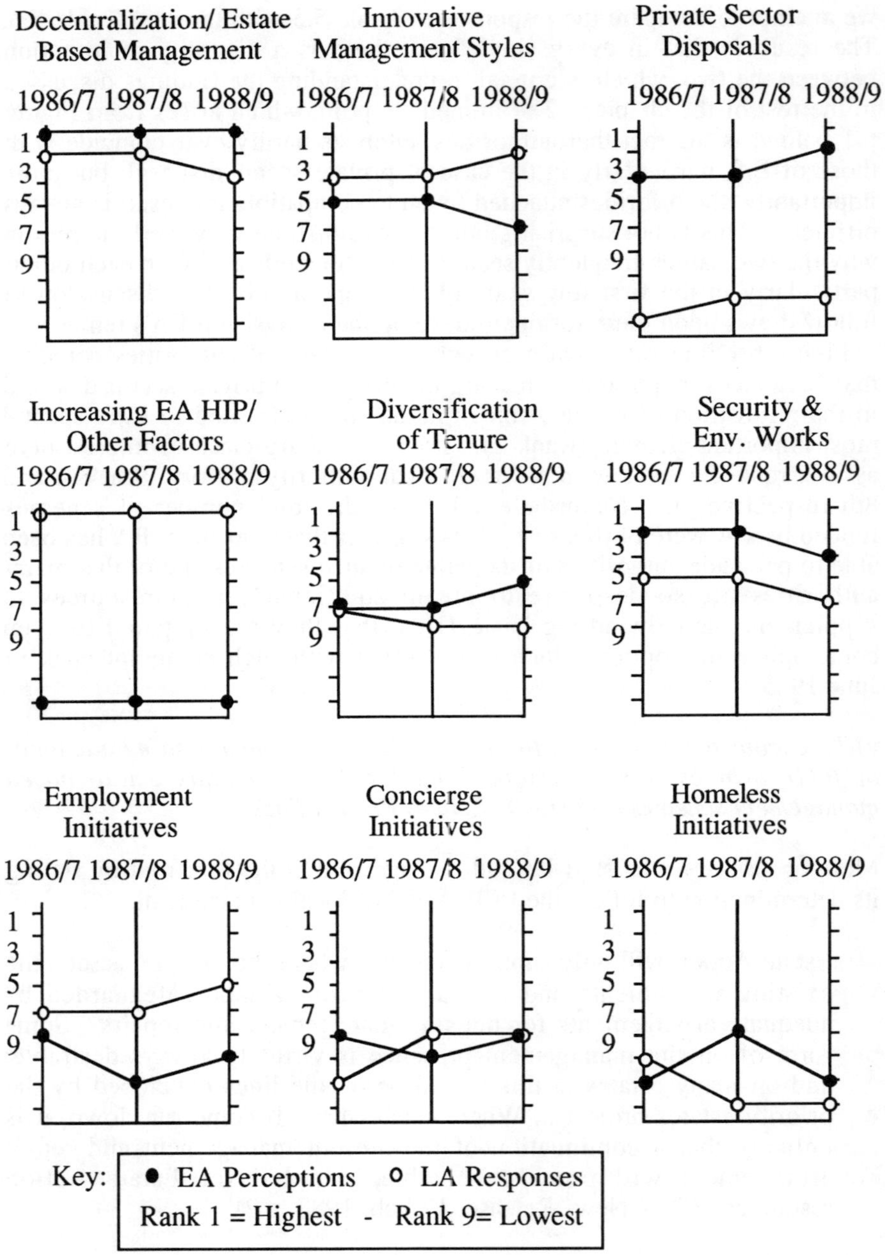

Source: Local Authority Survey (based upon Tables 5.5 and 5.6)

Figure 6.1: Overall/aggregate ranks of survey scores

(Table 6.1). In the three years concerned, respectively 40%; 57% and 57% of the new EA schemes either introduced or strengthened estate management (DoE, 1986; 1988a).

Plainly, this is one aspect where EA has been very successful in terms of the *number* of schemes funded although it is recognised that this is a very crude measure of success. It is argued by most authorities that this occurred primarily because this part of the remit mirrors closely what they as authorities, were looking to develop in their estates anyway; as well as reflecting a general trend for authorities to decentralize and experiment with localized management. Support for this contention comes from the fact that this has consistently ranked highly (the 2nd and 3rd most important factor) in authorities' motives for being involved with EA - after increasing EA HIPs.

vi) The last element of the remit is, *'To develop new or relatively untried solutions to the problems facing these estates, including transfers of ownership and/or management to management trusts, involving tenants, or to tenants' co-operatives'*, which also include concierges, homeless initiatives, security and environmental measures, affordable heat, employment initiatives and refurbishment:

Using official as well as survey data it is possible to assess whether EA has been fulfilling this element of its remit. The wording places the main emphasis upon developing *new* or *relatively untried* solutions so the crucial issues are whether it is new/relatively untried and how many have been implemented. Success, degree of replication in the rest of the stock and effectiveness can only be evaluated via the detailed case studies undertaken at a later stage (chapter 8).

1. Transfer of ownership/management to Trusts or Housing Associations: These are another facet of the disposal solution which EA is keen to promote but authorities have been unwilling to pursue this option in improving their more problematic estates. Although the Thamesmead and the Stockbridge Village Trusts have been featured as models of what EA is prepared to fund, no Trusts have actually been generated with EA support, advice or funding. While some disposal of council land and housing has occurred, the numbers involved by no means correlate with the degree of priority attached to this by the DoE. The available data indicate that no Housing Associations were formed under EA auspices in the three years covered by the survey and very few since, as far as the author is aware.

2. Transfer of ownership/management to Tenant Management Co-operatives (TMCs): EA is keen to promote these even though they are by no means new. TMCs has been in vogue for some time without their full potential being exploited. The new legislation (Housing Act, 1988) has created a climate more conducive to change and authorities themselves are now paying much closer attention to this particular initiative. Islington and Glasgow for example, were actively investigating these and illustrating their potential benefits long before EA was established. While these co-operatives are used nationally as models for other authorities, the same cannot be said of EA-funded TMCs. As with other 'themes' it seeks to encourage, there is a feeling among authorities that EA has not introduced anything new. To quote housing officers interviewed, the prevailing attitude is that it merely 'jumps on the band-wagon' and takes-up the latest 'flavour of the month' where the original ideas and developments originate from authorities themselves. Nevertheless, this represents another laudable attempt by the EA Unit to spread 'good practice'.

TMCs are not new and neither has EA been the catalyst for experimentation with them. While EA may claim credit for funding five co-ops in the first two years (no data is available for these in the third), Cloverhall (Rochdale) for example, had already been created and had received help from PEP with EA merely providing resources in support of re-roofing, insulation, internal modernization and anti-condensation measures. In the case of Langridge Crescent (Middlesbrough), the authority had decided to create a TMC independently and only became involved with EA when it realized that it could get EA to fund the necessary refurbishment (Interview by Author). Despite some common interest in generating this type initiative (Figure 6.1 - diversification of tenure), disappointingly few TMCs have actually been implemented under EA. The most likely reason must be because TMCs are a long-term prospect which requires careful planning, tenant training and meticulousness over organizational, lettings and financial aspects. EA's operational timescale must conflict with that required in forming viable TMCs.

3. Security works/Concierge schemes: A large proportion of EA's budget has gone on schemes involving security works on estates or setting-up concierges (30%, 19% and 23% respectively - see Table 6.1). This is rightly seen as an important element in revitalizing estates and EA has consequently promoted entry-phone schemes and improved security measures such as doors, fencing and better lighting. However, only those schemes under the heading of 'defensible space' and the concierge schemes could be considered as being relatively untried.

It is worth noting that the South Kilburn concierge scheme in Brent featured in the 1986/87 Annual Report, was not an EA scheme. Given the benefits that can potentially accrue to such tower blocks, a number of authorities were anxious to experiment with this initiative. EA became impressed with concierges and has attempted to promote them via for example, sponsoring a report on the creation and benefits of concierges (Skilton, 1988). In 1986/87 seven concierge schemes were formed, increasing rapidly to twenty the following year (no data are available for the last). In the context of EA's remit this *was* a relatively untried solution and one which EA must be given credit for stimulating and encouraging. In terms of the other initiatives taking place under the heading of security, these are on the whole, rather mundane initiatives which authorities maintain would have happened in the course of maintenance if they had the resources to so do. Whether this is true remains an open question.

Figure 6.1 illustrates yet again the discrepancy between what authorities seek to generate through the initiative, and what EA itself seems keen on promoting (as far as housing officers can tell). There is an increase in the priority accorded to concierges over time (as reflected also in the numbers). There is a corresponding increase in the perceived EA ranking, indicating that the EA Unit has become more interested in approving and funding such schemes. If the data are anything to go by, the implication is that the number of concierges supported will remain static in future.

4. Homeless initiatives: The EA homeless initiative was launched in August 1986 for 14 London boroughs with the worst problems but then extended to all EA authorities in October. Its aim was to bring vacant council properties back into use for the benefit of the homeless and involved works which could be substantially completed in that financial year (DoE, 1987a, p.9). Twenty nine schemes were supported in 1986/87, using 10% of all EA resources (and 7% the following year; no data for 1988/89). It is interesting to speculate on why this initiative was introduced by EA. While the numbers of homeless people have been rising in recent years, such initiatives were neither new nor relatively untried. Neither were they primarily management-oriented, as is the case in most EA themes.

Authorities themselves have apparently not been particularly interested in using EA HIPs to promote this type of initiative either (ranked 9th and lowest in terms of local authorities' relative priorities in Figure 6.1). At the same time, EA's perceived interest in promoting homeless schemes has remained fairly strong (ranking 8th, 6th and 8th) even though a special Homeless Initiative, separate from EA but using the same system of targeted capital allocation (see Figure 3.3) was created by the Minister for Housing in 1987. Surprisingly, authorities still feel that this element was still being stressed by EA when they expected it to have died away. An explanation for this has arisen (through the initial interview process) which is not altogether related to EA's remit or the 'themes' it tries to develop, but rather to the perception that EA has in the past, had trouble allocating its resources within the timetable available. Homeless Initiatives may, therefore, offer a 'safety valve' by which any unallocated EA resources which are in danger of being unused can be processed very quickly through the machinery and spent as a last resort to avoid DoE embarrassment, both in front of local authorities (for not being able to allocate everything) and the Treasury (for its inefficiency).

Supporting evidence for this contention comes from housing officers who argue that they have learned to hold schemes 'on the shelf' towards the end of the financial year when EA begins to look for schemes which do not require much scrutiny and which allow resources to be spent quickly so as to beat the end of year deadline. Additional evidence for this comes from the 1986/87 Annual Report itself, where it is made clear that this initiative was only launched late in the financial year (perhaps implying the existence of an unallocated sum) and then extended to all authorities in October. One of the stated criteria for the selection of such initiatives was that it should involve: "... works which could be substantially completed in the 1986/87 financial year" (DoE, 1987a, p.9).

5. Environmental works (and building face-lifts): Fifty nine schemes involving layout, landscaping, clearing rubbish and tidying up were funded by EA in 1986/87. In the following two years, environmental schemes were of two sorts: 68 and 106 of the schemes respectively included environmental improvements, whereas 49 and 119 of the schemes involved improvements to the exterior of dwellings. Given the nature of such schemes, they take a large proportion of EA resources (Table 6.1).

There is no doubt that these are important elements in renovating 'difficult estates' but once again, the general impression obtained from housing officers is that their authorities were either doing these themselves or capable of doing so if they had resources. In other words, action is occurring through EA both because it releases resources and provides targets for authorities to follow. Although this may have little to do with EA showing authorities what is more effective or things which they had not considered before, it is still a positive outcome. In terms of estate layout, much discussion was generated by Alice Coleman's work (1985) and it appears that this is to be given a higher profile in the EA 'themes'. Professor Coleman has been commissioned to develop (in partnership with local authorities) experimental solutions for poorly designed estates. Additional resources to the tune of £50m have been promised by the DoE for these models.

6. Adequate and affordable heating: This is another element that only became clear in 1987 after the second Annual Report was published. It states that: "Efficient and affordable heating was quickly identified in year one as another Estate Action priority" (DoE, 1987a, p.8). However, when authorities were prompted in the survey to identify the main reasons for their involvement with EA, this aspect hardly figured at all as one of their priorities for using EA HIPs resources. Nevertheless a substantial number of these initiatives, including insulating and condensation works, have received support from EA (25, 49 and 93 schemes) to provide affordable heating.

7. Community Refurbishment Schemes (CRS)/Employment initiatives: CRS combines Urban Programme and Employment Training resources to enable local unemployed people to work to improve the environment of run-down estates. Such work often includes enclosing gardens, general landscaping, clean-ups and minor works lasting a maximum of two years. These were originally pioneered in Merseyside but EA has helped to extend them elsewhere. Thirty CRS/employment initiatives have been set up thus far and although this does not involve EA HIPs *per se*, these schemes normally complement other EA measures (such as the introduction of estate based management), as part of the overall strategy to revitalize the estate. This issue was not widely advocated and promoted in the past and EA has played a part in extending awareness and debate through regional conferences on the topic. This type of initiative has recently taken a much greater emphasis under the heading of 'enterprise initiatives' and as EA's new focus, it will inevitably receive a higher profile in future. Subsequent chapters also explore why this important new-found focus has come about and the success such schemes are likely to meet.

6.5 Conclusions

The discussion illustrates that there are difficulties with the EA HIPs method of targeting and allocating capital resources for schemes in accord with its priorities. The authorities question whether these are indeed additional resources and mistrust EA's privatization objectives. Many councils use EA HIPs primarily as it is one of the few legitimate ways of supplementing their own HIPs allocations, provided it does not compromise their policies. Consequently EA's main advantages are seen by local authorities as being that it has enabled more schemes to occur than would otherwise have been the case and that it has released resources which enable necessary capital works to take place. Authorities argue that this would have occurred more efficiently and at less cost (given also the size of the EA bureaucracy) if the topslicing mechanism did not exist (see chapter 5).

EA's main role to date has been to provide funds which local authorities have used to set-up schemes which they wanted to but lacked resources for. EA has been most successful where its objectives have coincided with local authorities' own housing priorities (in promoting estate based management, concierges and employment initiatives in particular). It has had some success in enabling authorities to dispose of surplus land and stock in conjunction with the private sector.

In terms of the actual procedure, operation, timetabling and other details which relate to the nature and quality of the necessary interaction between EA and local authorities, several issues have emerged which undermine the success of the government's initiative. Not the least of these is the inadequate timetabling arrangements. From this arise most of the other difficulties discussed, such as flawed tenant consultation and the degree of underutilized housing investment resource. Nevertheless, the EA programme is fairly new and it remains to be seen what the long term repercussions of the problems identified by the survey will be. One of the few things which seems certain is that as capital resources continue to dry-up and the recent changes in housing legislation bite deeper, EA's ability to be more forceful in achieving its more controversial policies is likely to increase.

The next two chapters analyze the key elements of a scheme of this nature. Chapter 7 deals respectively with the EA Central and Regional Officer views of the initiative; and chapter 8 brings to a close the empirical part of the book with some detailed case-studies of EA schemes in different settings and localities, in order to assess effectiveness.

7 Implementation: DoE Regional Offices and Central team interviews

7.1 Introduction

As discussed in earlier chapters, this book represents an attempt to unravel the operation and impact of the EA initiative. Chapter 4 analyzed the political and managerial origins of the scheme; in chapter 5 it was necessary to obtain a broader understanding of the characteristics of the initiative, hence the postal survey; and chapter 6 summarized the key issues to come out of the survey and the local authorities' general view of the EA initiative.

The discussion in chapter 3 revealed that EA operates within a complex policy environment which involves at the DoE level, both the EA Central team and also the 9 DoE Regional Offices (10 when the Merseyside Task Force in included) charged with implementing EA. The operation of these two organizations is clearly central to the aims of the book, not least those of analyzing the implementation, financial effectiveness and central-local relations within EA. Consequently it would have been inadequate to have left the discussion at the local authority level (via the survey) and then progressed straight into a micro analysis via the case-studies (chapter 8).

Therefore the aim of this chapter is progressively to build upon previous work by presenting the views of the other two key agencies involved in the implementation of this central government initiative. Firstly, some context is provided based on a brief resumé of what is generally accepted to be the regional role of the DoE. The discussion then moves on to present the opinions, based on semi-structured interviews, of members of five Regional Offices (ROs) regarding the EA initiative. It is important to remember that EA represents only one element of a larger DoE housing role. The methodological discussion in the latter part of chapter 3 has explained why it was considered to be sufficient to interview five of the Regional Offices, not least because the ones chosen contain the great majority of participating authorities, EA schemes and EA HIPs resources allocated (see Maps 5-7).

The discussion concludes with an analysis of the role and evolution of EA Central. The crucial relationships between EA Central and the Regional Offices and the corresponding relationship with local authorities are also analyzed so as to enable the analysis to handle all the key organizations within EA's policy community and to fulfil the aims of the book.

7.2 Between the centre and the locality: The literature

It is useful to begin the discussion by setting in context the EA, RO and local authority relationship prior to progressing to an actual discussion of the issues raised via the semi-structured interviews. The DoE has a large regional presence in a complex administrative mosaic which is heterogeneous in nature within and between departments, and serves the managerial and service implementation interests of Whitehall. Therefore, according to Rhodes (1988, p.163-164) they are a:

> resource of the centre, embedded in multiple linkages, but with limited resources of their own which enable them to mediate between the centre and locality. The degree of discretion varies within and between departments over time ... [They] are neither bureaucratic agents nor decentralised bodies.

There is broad agreement regarding what constitutes the DoE ROs' role in England. Young (1982) sees them as comprising the following:

- *Formal executive responsibilities:* including much administrative work to implement national policy and following annual procedures such as the HIPs allocation round;

- *Whitehall's co-ordinator in the region:* giving the collective reaction of all government departments at regional level to other government agencies;

- *Active promotion of government policies:* vitally important to central government, since it is local authorities which are responsible for implementing many nationally determined policies. The ROs also have a promotional role, such as explaining the details of inner city policies;

- *'Mothership':* ROs aim to fill gaps by encouraging authorities to develop particular policies eg. to take-up/ apply for certain grants; and direct expert advice is provided;

- *Arbitrator:* For example, the ROs sometimes find themselves having to act as arbitrator between two authorities with conflicting ideas;

- *Directly influencing local policy-making:* this has increased over time, such as in regard to structure plans where the DoE's influence is normally felt from the beginning of the process of preparation and continues through subsequent negotiations until the plan is given final approval;

- *Assisting local authorities in the lobbying process:* local authority lobbying takes three main forms i) contact between officers and the chairmen of service committees, and civil servants and ministers of central departments (with local MPs also getting involved) ii) lobbying by a third party where appeals are made to Chambers of Commerce Economic Planning Councils, LAAs and so on, to intercede on behalf of local authorities and lastly, iii) they use the ROs to press central government since ROs play 'a classic middleman role having loyalties to the centre while developing loyalties to the region' (1982, p.89). This is a useful 'ear at court' and ROs appear to present an impartial view in convincing the centre; and

- *The 'eyes and ears' of Whitehall:* departments need detailed information about how policies are being implemented at the sharp end since they themselves are far removed. Their function is to: "provide confidential, accurate feedback to the centre so that policy can, if necessary, be amended to make it more effective." (1982, p.90)

The discussion is further developed within the inter-organizational framework with the argument that: "it cannot be simply assumed that regional offices and their parent departments can be treated as a single entity" (Houlihan, 1984, p.402). Houlihan too stresses the 'middle' role of ROs, pointing to Hambleton's study illustrating the crucial interpretative function of ROs in relation to inner city and housing policy (Hambleton, 1983) and notes the domination of the regional state by professional and bureaucratic interests. He identifies seven major 'linkages between central and local government' (see chapter 3 and Figure 3.3 for a discussion of these links and their mode of operation).

Houlihan argues that: "... the region is not simply a passive recipient of information, a task which the headquarters could easily fulfil, rather it is involved in checking the veracity of information, identifying new information requirements and evaluating the information supplied." (1984, p.410). The pattern of linkages that operate through the ROs is extensive and evolutionary, with the centre in a position to choose from a range of opportunities for intervention in the local housing policy area. Thus the ROs have an important mediating role in central-local relations generally and a crucial role in facilitating and improving the implementation of government policy, such as the EA initiative (see concluding chapter).

7.3 DoE Regional Office interviews

This section identifies the role of the Regional Offices (ROs) and the functions they perform, before going on to discuss its interaction with local authorities in implementing the EA initiative and the resultant schemes. Officials from a spread of five of the most influential Regional Offices were interviewed in order to obtain first hand information of their involvement with the EA initiative and their importance to its implementation. Several key aspects arising from the survey were raised via semi-structured interviews so as to gain a detailed understanding of the difficulties faced by the ROs in implementing EA. The methodological elements are discussed in Chapter 3 and each regional office(r) is referred to in the following convention: RO 1a; RO 1b (same office, different interviews and officers); RO 2; RO 3; RO 4; and RO 5. The results reveal that the ROs and the local authorities are greatly dependent upon each other in fulfilling their EA aims.

7.3.1 Central-local relations: The administrative relationship

It is important to understand that the EA element is only one of a large number of functions performed by the housing section of the ROs. These functions are to: "Execute policies coming from Head Quarters [Marsham Street]; allocate a large amount of resources to the authorities in that particular region; and perform all the housing case-work namely, to deal with any matter arising from government policy *vis à vis* authorities" (RO 1a). It is within this context that the ROs operate even though: "These functions and the degree of control and autonomy have changed over time." (RO 1a). These developments and the reasons for them are discussed below.

i) The past: In the first year of EA's operation RO involvement was minimal with the Central team distributing all the information, receiving the bids, processing these and monitoring schemes: "1985/86 was the campaigning year for EA and so only certain authorities - in particular urban authorities - were invited to submit bids for EA funding" (RO 3). However, it was speedily appreciated that the Central team could not cope with the volume of work, not least because it is a small directorate and, as a result, the pressure mounted to upgrade the ROs role.

The ROs see their role as one of liaison with local authorities in order to implement government policy, in this case the EA initiative and they now deal directly with authorities, giving them advice and interpreting policy for them: "We are EA's mouth-piece on the ground. Local authorities 'sound us out' on their proposals and we give them advice based on our interpretation of what is likely to find favour" (RO 2). In effect, therefore, the RO involvement begins during or even before the time authorities are preparing their initial bids (or Form As).

When Form A is received by the ROs: "These are prioritized in terms of the 'quality' or 'innovativeness' of the schemes proposed. In principle, priority is determined by the number of EA criteria which are fulfilled in the bid and these are then ranked into a list which is sent to EA Central" (RO 1a). Each region's EA HIPs allocation is then dependent on the *quality* of the list of bids submitted, not on the basis of other traditional criteria such as HIPs patterns or the General Needs Index. The result is that certain regions can receive twice as much (as a proportion) under EA HIPs as under the ordinary HIPs system, the reason being: "... because of the quality of our schemes and the fact that our authorities are now prepared to embrace EA and are geared-up for it" (RO 3).

The prioritized list is sent to EA Central which then determines which schemes to accept for the second stage (see Figure 3.1). The ROs were *not* certain of the exact nature of the selection procedures but an informed guess was that this was done on the 'Star Chamber' principle, whereby the Central team is convened to discuss the merits of each scheme proposal. The members of this team includes each region's EA contact; professional staff (eg. architects and quantity surveyors); and the leading EA staff. Based on these decisions, the ROs then receive a list of the schemes to 'work-up', and thus obtain: "A rough idea of how much will be available to us. This regional slice is then split into two amounts: resources which are ear-marked for *continuation* funding and resources to be allocated to *new* schemes" (RO 2, Emphasis Added). Authorities are notified about which schemes to proceed with and: "ROs and LAs must then work in tandem although in practice, most LAs finalize schemes and issue tenders independently" (RO 1a), and then submit the more detailed Form Bs. There is apparently no deadline by which this Form has to be completed but: "local authorities are perfectly aware that it is in their own interests to fill it in and send it back A.S.A.P." (RO 2), as they will have more time to complete schemes.

In the previous system, the Central team would then make the final decision as to whether or not to fund these schemes and ROs would send out an official letter of notification to the successful authorities Thereafter local authorities were free to let the contract and perform the work in the time available. The ROs subsequently monitored the progress of the schemes, primarily via the Quarterly Assessment Forms (C) and Annual Assessment forms (D). At the time RO discretion and control was admittedly minimal. Since then, as a result of criticism by individual local authorities, the Housing Consultative Council (HCC, mimeo), the ROs and the fact that EA Central was feeling the pressure of the administrative workload, the ROs' autonomy has been increased appreciably.

ii) The present: Progress has been made. Within approximately the same procedure, ROs can now argue against verdicts made by EA Central: "We can counter EA decisions. There may be argument over the merits of certain schemes or they may need more information because for example, authorities have submitted over-optimistic bids" (RO 2). As a result a '*central reserve fund*' was devised for bids which are delayed but which are of good quality. Additionally ROs are now allowed to *over-programme* their regional slice of EA HIPs by 15%. This is possible because no firm commitments are made to authorities until final approval is notified (after the Form B). A further development is that: "In the course of the year, schemes drop out and we can replace them without necessarily going through the whole procedure again" (RO 3), which is clearly important in minimizing the delays identified in the postal survey.

The situation has become more flexible: "In the past we had no real control. Every scheme had to be sent back to EA. Since then, they have devolved a great deal of financial authority to the ROs. We have total control over on-going [continuation] schemes. In terms of new schemes it is now the Regional Controller who makes the final decisions, although we also submit copies [of Form Bs] to EA. They have 10 days to suggest changes and recommendations. If they don't, we can go ahead and issue final approval ourselves" (RO 3). The EA/RO relationship has recently undergone further changes which in theory, should result in improvements to the operation and the processing of bids, thus helping to allay some local authority concerns.

iii) The future: EA is currently undergoing a marked change in emphasis (1990/91). It has announced that:

> Estate Action's effort and resources would be focused in future ... the Department would seek in particular to promote proposals which encapsulated the widest range of features of the sort that Estate Action has been developing in schemes to date. (DoE, 1989, p.14)

This has been taken to mean (among ROs), that there will be fewer and larger schemes and there are fears that this will mean that the financial powers and administration devolved as a result of poor co-ordination in the past, will be re-centralized. Such a perception was echoed in all ROs, although there is measurable vagueness and uncertainty about the future (even as late as January 1990). There is also unease about the fact that there will be fewer but larger schemes, with two officers commenting that EA: "... seems to have 'peaked' and its allocation is going to be reduced in future" (RO 3). It is equally conceivable that the opposite may happen with greater powers being devolved to ROs for the bulk of EA work.

7.3.2 Nature of the LA / RO / EA relationship

i) ROs and EA: All the officers interviewed stress that they know each other and get on well, 'we are all civil servants working together' and sometimes have conferences to discuss EA but that problems remain. First, although EA HIP has increased, staffing levels are 'not great' and have not kept pace. Second: "Inevitably, people on the rim believe that the centre imposes ridiculous timetables - we have a wide number of responsibilities other than EA" (RO 4), and last: "There were tensions two years ago ... There were many appeals by ROs which resulted in delays. They [EA] are still the paymasters and issue the regional allocations but their role is now largely quality control, co-ordination and dissemination of good practice ... We still have problems but we have good relations and we are all committed to the initiative." (RO 5). One officer indicated that there are 'rumours' of even greater devolvement and decentralization in the 1990/91 financial round, when all regions will have their own pool or resources to deal with as they see fit, but also pointed out that what is being rumoured rarely turns out to be the case in reality (RO 1b).

ii) ROs and ROs: All five ROs indicated that there was little contact with each other: "The only formal contact is at Regional Controller level. This takes place every two months and deals with such issues as new policy initiatives, further devolvement of EA activity and changes in procedure" (RO 1b). This seems a pity because they could well learn from each others' methods for example, of dealing with EA projects so as to streamline current procedures. Two regions intimated that they had learned much from one another's experiences and that co-ordination had improved as a result.

iii) ROs and LAs: The general feeling is that the quality of their interaction with the local authorities is mixed but that it 'has improved'. Tensions arise because: 'The regional allocation is never large enough' and 'They do not always want to do what the ROs advise them', but all the ROs agree that: "There has been a substantial change in attitude in the last couple of years. Local authorities now understand how to play the game and also there are substantial sums at stake whereas mainstream HIPs have shrunk" (RO 4). Another officer put it more prosaically: "Even the most 'dyed in the wool' Labour local authorities realize the way local government finance is going and that they have to 'bite the bullet' and 'play the game'." (RO 3)

A perspective which links well with the literature discussed earlier, was that: "I hope that ROs are seen as a buffer between them and the central department, that we act as their 'friend in court' and that whatever their grievances, we can listen to them and take it back [to EA]" (RO 1b). All insisted that they had begun to work more constructively with authorities, with fewer tensions and more frequent contact.

iv) The importance of the ROs: The ROs were unanimous about the value of their contribution to the efficient implementation of the EA initiative: "EA would not have been so successful [otherwise] ... We clarify EA criteria, give advice and so on. Civil servants are needed to twist arms and badger local authorities to make sure they do these schemes. It would not have been possible without the ROs (RO 2)". In a similar vein: "It wouldn't have been so successful because local authorities look upon us as their representatives and expect us to work for them." (RO 1b), the inference being that the interaction would have been different if the authorities were dealing directly with EA Central.

They also believe that: "It is vital to have lots of contact with local authorities, build relationships, get to know the people, the area, its problems and housing stock" (RO 2), and on an even more positive note: "We have taken to EA with gusto - it is something which we have to offer to local authorities ... We derive much job satisfaction from knowing that we are part of the developments. We make sure that their proposals are presented in the right way and that we emphasize any novel features in the proposal that might otherwise be overlooked" (RO 4). The ROs clearly see themselves as being rather essential to the implementation process.

v) The importance of the Central team: The Central team's role is also judged by the ROs to have been vital: "EA has been important. For example, they have advanced the timetabling cycle, produced manuals to help local authorities and taken steps to devolve power to the ROs" (RO 2). Another argues that the devolution which has occurred: "... has been the result of pressure from ROs for EA to do so ... and there have been slight improvements in the timetable. They are also a useful source of advice and information. Their visits are invaluable and we get to see the problem on a national scale, instead of the narrow regional focus" (RO 4).

They acknowledge that although the timetable has helpfully been 'brought forward', so-doing also means that: "Estate Action work now comes in at our busiest period" (RO 1b), namely when the HIPs forms are being assessed. A number of ROs added that the EA part of their role takes: "... a disproportionate amount of our time [roughly estimated at 20%] given the amount of borrowing approval involved and the immense input required in terms of staff time" (RO 1b). To this can be added the fact that no extra staff have been employed by the DoE, although this has been alleviated by the fact that there is now less work for the ROs because some of their responsibilities have been transferred to the Housing Corporation. Naturally enough some feel that perhaps: "The ROs could have more autonomy to make decisions without EA. EA could maintain a smaller team at the centre to formulate and decide on policy and good practice, but would not be needed otherwise ... this would work much better" (RO 2). This leads the discussion to an analysis of the main issues arising from the survey (discussed in chapter 5; summarized in chapter 6). Feedback was sought from the ROs so as to incorporate their perspectives.

7.3.3 Implementation: Issues arising from the survey

i) Timetabling arrangements: All regions bar one (RO 1b), acknowledged that the timetable is a problem: "Delays and lateness were the main difficulties ... implementation would improve if there was a little more flexibility with tenders but the real issue is about having enough time" (RO 4), hence the proposal that: "We need a continuing rolling programme over three years instead of the one year timetable" (RO 2). Officers were adamant that the situation is being rectified by bringing the timetable forward: "The problem is becoming better although we accept that it will never go away" (RO 3), mainly: "... because of the one year rule" (RO 1a). Typical comments were that: "EA Central itself must bid for their resources on an annual basis. This is the reality of government finance now and EA was a relatively new scheme which needed time. Local authorities have now managed to gear themselves to it" (RO 2); and that: "... the problem arose partly because EA grew very quickly and it formulated procedures as it went along. In part, we did not understand the administrative issues such as how long it takes to devise a scheme and the long lead times" (RO 4). As has been discussed, EA did not see fit to consult with either ROs or the authorities when it was designing its operational procedures (see chapter 4).

The one dissenting opinion was that the perceived problems with the timetabling were 'hard to believe' because: "EA HIPs has become part of the capital programming mentality and our authorities are already thinking about the next round of bids without waiting for us to send them a letter of invitation to participate" (RO 1b). It is ironic that such a statement comes from the region which by general agreement amongst those interviewed, is one of the worst performing ROs.

ii) Bureaucratic procedures: There was an awareness that: "... perhaps we are slightly over-bureaucratic" (RO 2), and that "Form A is a problem. There is insufficient information and context with which to judge schemes and Form B requires too much too late" (RO 5). Continuing with the procedural vein: "We have wondered ourselves why it is necessary to have all the information in Form B. Not all of it is used in the evaluation of schemes. A lot of the EA procedures have evolved over the years There is an argument for starting from scratch again and to question what is really relevant" (RO 4). On the other hand there was also the opinion that: "Local authorities gripe too much about the procedures. The forms are not that difficult to complete ... the main problem for them really is the fact that they must commit staff resources when there is no guarantee of anything. Perhaps EA should underwrite these costs." (RO 2)

iii) Changing criteria: All ROs reject local authority claims that criteria have changed in any way, pointing to the fact that these have been spelled out in the Annual Reports and that Ministerial Guide-lines had recently been issued. The author suggested that *confusion* may have arisen because of perceived changes in *emphasis*. Reasons why this should occur include: "It is not a perception ... Each year there is a new theme. They [EA] retain certain aspects such as innovation, disposal and so on, but they have refined what they expect. Next year it is the 'enterprise' issue and even further tenant involvement in estate management. EA retains the basic objectives but the emphasis definitely changes ... after all, what was innovative four years ago is no longer so now" (RO 2). In contrast: "At first the money was there and EA was not as discerning but with more authorities submitting bids which fulfil more EA criteria, we are no longer approving those bids that used to be accepted in the past. This could be part of the explanation" (RO 1b) for the reason why authorities complain of shifting EA criteria. Expectations of what constitutes good quality bids change. It was also suggested that: "While a lot of local authority criticism of EA and the ROs may be justified, part of that is the resentment felt because they have to go through these hoops ... We talk to our authorities a lot. If they are not getting things right and wasting valuable time and resources, its because they decide to take 'flyers' ... Bids often represent what councilors want rather than conforming to EA criteria" (RO 2). This is likely when there are local politicians with local mandates.

The following quotation highlights the difference of opinion between the ROs and the local authorities: "There are misunderstandings. We feel that we have said everything about EA. They have obviously not heard us, perhaps because they are more in tune with the physical improvements than the management issues. EA has deliberately not been 'hard and fast' about what it will not fund. I would have thought that this worked in local authorities' favour in the long term - perhaps it doesn't" (RO 4). In general, the opinion is that the emphasis does change although there remains contention over whether this is justified or not.

iv) Tenant consultation: All the ROs showed awareness of the dilemma confronting authorities in this respect (previously discussed in chapters 5 and 6): "It is fair to suggest that most authorities only actually involve tenants at Form B stage, when they get an indication of whether their bids are likely to succeed ... Tenant consultation is the greatest problem for local authorities. They are reluctant to consult until they have a good idea of what is to be done and the amount they are likely to get. Its a 'chicken and egg' situation. Additionally, tenant consultation can also be protracted and result in failure to deliver schemes" (RO 2).

Another officer was defensive about the issue: "It is not our fault. The reason why tenant consultation is not full, is because local authorities themselves are afraid that they will not get EA funding. It is they that get bashed about by their tenants, not us" (RO 3). A further comment was that: "It [the timetable] is undoubtedly too tight ... but it is not an insurmountable problem. Local authorities ought to know which schemes and estates they want and start low-key consultations for the next round" (RO 1b) in advance. A suggestion was that the EA Unit should underwrite the costs of tenant consultation, thus enabling this to be more effective: "It might be costly but it would undoubtedly create a great deal of goodwill in local authorities instead of the rhetoric [about generating full and effective tenant consultation]" (RO 2), an argument similar to the one presented in chapter 6. None of the ROs queried the survey results that tenant consultation does not occur as expected. Discussion revolved only around why this occurred and how to improve it.

7.3.4 Financial aspects

i) (Under)Allocation of funds: Four of the ROs insist that: "There are no great difficulties in allocating the resources available" (RO 3) to their authorities. This was primarily because of the numerous bids received (see Table 5.26) and the fact that ROs can now over-programme (namely, approve more schemes in principle than they have resources for) and thus have additional schemes to replace the ones that 'slip'. One even comments that: "In fact, we've scored our allocation and even more. We were able to overprogramme our regional allocation by 50%" (RO 4), which clearly means that one or more of the ROs must have under-performed and lost resources. Clues about their identity can be gained from the survey results, where London must be a candidate (see cross-tabulations in Tables 5.10 and 5.13). This RO stresses that: "All bureaucratic procedures take time", and that: "There are unique problems ... we have taken care of this [underallocation] by massively over-programming in London" (RO 1b). Over-programming in this region was 25% compared to 10%-15% in other regions but despite the optimism, the region still appears to underperform.

ROs were perfectly aware of the potential side-effects of procedural delays for authorities, commenting that: "I'm sure it does cause authorities difficulties if ROs allocate late in the financial year" (RO 5), in part because: "We do ask for a lot of information ... there is always a great deal of work involved regardless of the size of the scheme. This imposes quite a lot of burden upon local authorities which are thus over-stretched" (RO 4). Other reasons for the fact that delays are persistent were commented upon: "The same applies to the ROs [ie. being over-stretched]. The EA work has mushroomed and there have undoubtedly been delays. Some delay is justified for example, when we need more information while others are less justified, such as loss of staff and retraining resulting in delays" (RO 4).

That underallocation can and does occur and that EA HIPs is transferred to other ROs is beyond doubt. The ROs monitor the financial situation via the Quarterly Assessment Forms (C) and in principle, are able to step-in when authorities: "... are about to hit problems. Around November/ December we have to decide whether we [as a region] can utilize all the EA HIPs or not and around January/February we make a decision about whether to send it back" (RO 3). All the underallocation is pooled into the Central Reserve Fund: "This is then reallocated to those ROs which can make use of it and *can* spend it in time, but this is a rushed affair' (RO 3).

One regional official candidly revealed that: "Our RO took that step last year [ie. return some of their EA HIPs allocation]. We have to pass it around from time to time but it was because of unusual problems and we generally use what we get. Everyone guards their pot jealously" (RO 3). This leads to an analysis of the degree of pressure bearing upon ROs to allocate quickly to their *own* authorities. They are unanimous in their responses. The typical view is: "No doubt about it. We fight for what we get and see that it is used. This may well affect whether the best schemes are picked, but we play the game according to the rules" (RO 3). One explicitly indicated that there was a bit of 'horse-trading' at the margins, namely that: "... a scheme may not necessarily take place according to the original bid" (RO 1b).

They were quick to point out that there is no attempt to deliberately obtain resources from other regions but that they did try to process their bids as quickly as possible: "We aim to do so by September/October and we've been able to do very well from other regions, particularly London which has problems" (RO 5). According to Regional Officers' common knowledge, this has become a regular occurrence in the London region. The London civil servants note with annoyance that they were not authorized to invite their authorities to submit late bids to take advantage of pooled/underallocated resources at the end of the financial year, unlike the other regions. This is not surprising given the reputation it has acquired with EA Central and the other ROs. The conclusion is that underallocation occurs in most regions (some being much worse than others) and that authorities located in these may lose out, but equally, underallocation may reflect inexperience or inefficiency on the part of local authorities in submitting correct bids to their ROs.

ii) Underspending resources: All ROs acknowledge that underspending *may* have occurred in their authorities but did not accept blame themselves: "There are reasons which are not necessarily because of us. These include the fact that they [authorities] tell us that they can cope with spending 'X' amount, they submit bids late and they may simply be looking for a scapegoat" (RO 1b). Continuing with this vein, another indicated that they could process bids in 4-6 weeks and that if it took longer, it was because authorities did not provide the necessary information. Additional delaying factors include discrepancies in data, tenant consultation and negotiation which is expensive and time-consuming and the fact that authorities expect an immediate response and can't: "accept that ROs can not just tick forms and send them back" (RO 2). There was also a feeling that there was degree of 'ritual noise' by local authorities (RO 4).

The experience regarding underspending differed: "... Our Regional Office has had problems and delays are common. Our procedures did not tie-in very well with local authorities' own programming and we were allocating EA HIPs very late in the financial year. But we have changed our procedures ... We would like to think that we are improving all the time but local authorities are even more bureaucratic than we are!" (RO 3). Another was even more forthcoming: "I have sympathy with local authorities. We have argued [to EA] that a system dependent upon an initial bid [Form A] just to give the green light and then upon a fuller form [Form B] with all the details just creates too much pressure and delay in the system ... Much better to have a more detailed form at the start, thus providing a context to the scheme which has been subject to discussion and consultation. Form B could then be a lot less detailed and critical, resulting in fewer problems and delays" (RO 5).

The other issue was the fact that there are two timetables at work. The DoE/EA finds out what resources will be available in October. However, HIPs are only known in December, on the basis of which, local authorities reconstruct their capital programme. They must guess both what amount to put aside to meet the 50% contribution from mainstream HIPs which EA expects, *and* how much staff resource to set aside for the preparation of EA bids. However, by the time the final decision arrives, capital programmes have been determined and may well require re-programming: "This is in addition to all the procedural problems from the way EA has organized its approval systems. It is not possible to bring the timetable any further forward." (RO 3)

On the positive side the interviews confirmed the survey's findings that *informal* arrangements did exist for authorities in danger of underspending their EA allocations (see chapter 5). These would be renegotiated the following year (in the case of Urban Programme-funded schemes), although it was more common for authorities to be allowed to spend the EA borrowing approval on other schemes across the authority, since EA HIPs is non scheme-specific: "If they hit snags, we allow them to use EA HIPs as they see fit but when it comes to re-negotiating continuation funding, we calculate that they have spent as set out in advance ... so local authorities must meet the shortfall in resources for EA schemes from their mainstream HIPs or capital receipts the following year. This still happens. There is no way of preventing it" (RO 3).

The ROs argue that even EA Central accepts this as inevitable: "... the building trade fluctuates wildly and even the best planned programmes hit snags, such as lack of supply of [construction] material" (RO 3). EA and the ROs are not too concerned because: "Local authorities know that we do not have any legal sanction over their allocations and they have the genuine power of virement anyway ... Sometimes they consult us, but we are not worried about when the scheme is completed - as long as it gets done" (RO 4). Problems arise only if there is successive underspend since there is only 10% virement on capital programmes (RO 2).

As to what happens to underspending authorities, four ROs insisted that they did not penalize authorities with fewer resources - except in terms of a 'credibility factor': "If authorities underspend continually, we *may* not be convinced that they can spend large amounts in a short period" (RO 2 -

Emphasis Added). In other words, bids may be prioritized in terms of their quality but decisions are also made on the basis of other professional considerations. A fifth officer was more assertive, indicating that there were no penalties "... unless the local authority was performing appallingly, in which case this would affect it in the future" (RO 1b), which is in itself a form of *a priori* discrimination which goes beyond the 'quality' of the bids.

iii) Targeting and the new financial régime: In terms of opinions regarding whether EA funds are 'topsliced' or 'additional' (see debate in chapter 6), the balance of personal opinion among the ROs was for the former. A civil servant simply stated that: "Our ministers do not take that view [of topslicing]" (RO 1b). Others were willing to discuss the issue: "The resources would not be there if EA wasn't around to attract additional finance ... [and] it is simplistic to conclude that merely because mainstream HIPs are being reduced and EA HIPs is increasing, that it is topsliced" (RO 2). Alternatively three ROs confided unofficially that they believed that it was indeed topsliced: "I agree entirely that EA HIPs is topsliced. EA HIPs constitutes the biggest slice although there are other such initiatives such as the Homeless Initiative" (RO 3), which is a direct reference to the other forms of DoE targeted resources (see Figure 3.3). Nevertheless such a financial system was felt to be justified: "EA HIPs has altered the distribution of resources. More has probably gone to difficult-to-let estates, as intended by the targeting exercise ... If you trying to get local management, employment initiatives and diversification of tenure, you need a specific system for it to work." (RO 4)

The ROs strongly rejected the notion that local authority autonomy may have been undermined as a result of their involvement with EA: "Targeting is still more effective than not targeting and local authorities still have all the discretion in the world to decide whether to participate or not" (RO 2). Another quotation was: "That is what authorities not getting it [EA HIPs] would say! It is unfair to them, but we are addressing a particular need" (RO 3); and that: "In the medium term, EA probably enhances local authorities. Better-managed estates produce more contented tenants who will not exercise their 'right to buy' or opt out [of council housing]" (RO 4). It remains difficult to decide what are the long term consequences of involvement in the EA project, but an interesting comment was recorded: "I don't think EA does that [reduce local autonomy and increase control over public housing], but it is part of wider moves towards local authorities. EA is just one tool to allow resources to go to certain areas but the end result is still the same - it still leads to interference with council housing" (RO 1a).

There is agreement among all ROs that the much-vented local authority contention that a much better system of capital allocations would be an enhanced HIPs system with 'strings' attached (namely, forcing authorities to spend a certain amount of resources on their 'problem estates' and on certain types of scheme as in EA), is *redundant* given the changes in housing finance introduced in April 1990: "Part of the difficulty has been to make such resources go where they are needed. This had not happened before and EA HIPs is more equitable because of this ... We still do not know how the EA part of things will work [in future]. Things are being left very late and we could face an embarrassment. At this time last year [June], we would have sent out the HIPs forms" (RO 5).

This uncertainty about the impending changes to EA was shared by *all* ROs. The only thing which is certain is that EA will focus on 'flagship' schemes in future and that: "Ministers like to be associated with good schemes. They have got accustomed to doing visits and receiving some kudos out of it. Therefore EA will continue to be some sort of supplementary pot but I can not see the system making much difference in terms of the effectiveness of the capital allocation system" (RO 3). This was a view shared by another region: "The new financial régime will not affect the problem [of underallocation/spend]. Nothing much will change under the new system because it is being altered other reasons" (RO 1b). The general opinion is that the prospects are not good as regards improvements in EA's financial deficiencies as a result of the new financial proposals introduced in April 1990.

7.3.5 Centre-local issues and degree of EA scheme success

Opinion is diverse regarding central government's true motives in creating the EA initiative and its reasons for awarding EA more resources. At one extreme it can be seen as: "... either a way of central government imposing control over local authorities or as attacking a problem. We can see tremendous improvements in the estates. I do not think that its emphasis is the former" (RO 3). But there are also rather different views of what EA is about: "It is very much a means of extending central government control over local authorities ... they want tenants to be more involved and to give power to the tenants in relation to local authorities. EA is a means to an end" (RO 1a). A supporting comment along similar lines is that: "EA does *not* legitimate council housing. By making tenants more aware of what they can do and by helping them extend their control over housing, the next logical step is for tenants to want to take-over their housing themselves [and to opt out]. EA is totally compatible with the thrust of government housing policy" (RO 2 - Original Emphasis).

However most ROs tread the middle line: "It [EA] has gained resources because it has proved its merit and shown results; there is clearly a demand for the initiative; and local authorities have come forward with proposals which have been imaginative and workable. EA has thus been able to petitioning for more funds and done a good job" (RO 2). What they are certain about is that: "Everything depends upon the enthusiasm with which local authorities have taken up EA" (RO 4). Most ROs also agree with local authority suspicions that EA does result in increased central control or alternatively, that the motive is to place the tenant at the forefront while also helping authorities.

Regarding the future of EA, three ROs were convinced that EA will be around for 'at least one more year' and secondly, that it will probably become less of a major programme: "We can see it lasting another 3 to 4 years but its expansion is slowing down and government policy is to shift local authorities from housing provision to an 'enabling' role. Therefore EA will not last long. It all depends on the success of the enterprise issue and how the new financial régime performs" (RO 2), and that: "A few years ago, housing was a hot debate but this seems to have been replaced by concern with the environment" (RO 1b). In this, the ROs have been mistaken. The 1992 Conservative Party election manifesto has awarded the EA initiative still further resources and responsibilities, not least HATs.

To the extent that there has not been any evaluative study of the impact of the initiative and of its success, it is interesting to note that there is an all-pervasive feeling amongst ROs that the initiative is having a very positive impact on the ground: "EA will be[come] less of a major programme and more of a flagship type of scheme which is a terrible pity because the message of EA has spread out and some of the estates have been outstanding successes. They have changed the atmosphere on the estates and local authorities are thinking differently about estate management, upkeep and other solutions." (RO 5). Similarly: "EA has been successful. It has confronted a problem which authorities did not have the resources to address; it has been a slap on the back instead of the usual kick in the crutch for the DoE; and it has highlighted what can be done by targeting resources into certain areas" (RO 3).

Another analogous quotation is that: "EA took over an embryonic DoE policy and built it up. Cynics would say that this is just a 'tarting-up' exercise to encourage tenants to exercise their Tenants' Choice in landlords or HATs" (RO 2), which alludes to a possible 'danger' of too much success but a final comment is that: "EA does try to push forward with government policy, such as privatization and disposal but local politicians just want to get on with things with the minimum of interference. This will never change and consequently they will always be critical of this type of initiative. But most politicians have been pragmatic and have made the initiative a substantial success" (RO 2). There is little doubt among the ROs that EA has been very successful, but despite their conviction, it remains to be seen what the exact consequences of EA schemes have been in terms of effectiveness. This is attempted in the next chapter.

7.4 Central team, former staff and consultant interviews

This section outlines the views of various individuals who either played or play a key role in the formation and running of the EA Unit. The objective is to obtain feedback on issues which were raised through the local authority survey, so as to understand whether the people most able to effect change are aware of the existence of the problems brought out by the survey, and to analyze their responses and plans to cope with the circumstances. Other issues of importance are also addressed not least the effectiveness and the future of the scheme. The research is based on semi-structured interviews with EA Central team members; consultants; and former staff members involved in the key original decisions about the initiative. The responses are coded in the following manner (EA 1; EA 2; EA 3; EA 4; and EA 5/6) and the methodology is discussed fully in section chapter 3.

7.4.1 Economic issues

i) Redirecting and concentrating resources: In terms of targeting the Central team has been: "... at pains to dispel the idea of EA HIPs as 'topping-up' HIPs, although inevitably many authorities have come to depend greatly on the EA HIPs. But by targeting it on estates, we do feel that it is getting into the worst estates in contrast to the general HIPs system" (EA 2), adding that housing directors have confided to him in private that without EA HIPs, marginal investment would have gone into their worst estates. The Central team rejects the notion that the increase in number of authorities eligible for EA support (from 69 to all housing authorities), implies a 'watering down' of the concept of targeting resources. This had occurred because: "We found pockets of housing in need of change and investment such as in Bath; secondly, if EA was going to extend its other ideas, such as tenant consultation and participation, it would have to reach beyond the initial sixty nine authorities; and lastly, at the end of the day, the resources are still trained upon estates" (EA 2). Their opinion is that spatial targeting remains, but when the author suggested that based on survey results, it may not always be the worst estates which end-up being funded, the response was merely that: "Any scheme which authorities bid for should be their top priority" (EA 2). This ignores the fact that the very manner in which EA is set up may actually encourage authorities to submit bids *only* for certain estates which they feel have a chance of fulfilling EA stipulations, as suggested by the survey results (in chapter 5). Estates with severe structural defects may constitute the very 'worst' but would not be eligible for EA support.

Topslicing is a much-maligned issue brought-up by authorities convinced that the government is taking resources with one hand and offering it with strings attached on the other. This conviction has plagued EA since its inception (as discussed in chapter 6). Unlike the ROs which came out strongly in support of the view that topslicing occurred, the Central civil servants are somewhat reticent about this issue: "The question is hypothetical. If EA had not been around in 1986, would there have been £50m extra? Ministers would say no. It would not have been available because the HIPs figure had already been established." (EA 2) As for the correlation of declining HIPs and increasing EA HIPs: "The HIPs allocations were in decline and its original objectives to provide investment where it was needed had disappeared. The government is moving towards targeting increasingly more public money and refining the 'free element' available to councils" (EA 2), implying that the mechanism restricts choice, to the extent that investment is 'tied'.

But there does seem to be a degree of Central confusion about the importance of targeted resources to EA. On the one hand there is the belief that: "When the initiative was first announced, there was no mention made of cash. The idea was simply to bring together a team and various sources of funding [such as UP, MSC, private sector resources] and to find a way of co-ordinating it all ... It was only in late August, at the PESC round that ministers made a special plea for money to be set aside to help spread the scheme. As a result, a special fund of £45m borrowing approval and £5m from the Urban Programme monies was set aside" (EA 2). In other words, additional resources for EA were almost a side issue. On the other hand, another individual asserts that additional resources were being offered as the *key* to the whole initiative and that its availability was never in question - rather, it was a pre-requisite (EA 1). In the circumstances, probably the best conclusion that can be reached for the issue of topslicing is that: "It is impossible to say one way or the other. Would the ministers have made any extra resources available if EA was not around? It is a question of speculation" (EA 1). Nevertheless controversy remains and is likely to continue for the foreseeable future.

ii) Extra resources, privatization and 'additionality': The interviews suggest that the Central team has had to work hard to win its expanding share of resources (see Table 6.1), which is not surprising given the climate of political opinion that exists towards council housing: "It has been a hard battle each time" (EA 2). In support of its requests EA has been able to bring to bear upon the Treasury the fact that it has been very successful in attracting bids: "There are usually three to four times as many Form A bids as there are resources, which indicates that a large number of estates remain to be dealt with" (EA 2), and this is backed-up in the survey results (Pinto, 1992d, Table A6.2), where many bids were unsuccessful.

Additional reasons for the, no doubt, reluctant Treasury accession come from two former members of EA: "We 'muddled' the figures we sent them regarding private sector involvement. For example, that 'X' amount of units had been privatized but also that every scheme involved an element of privatization, in the sense that the various works were carried out by contractors. The fact that a lot of this was carried out by Direct Labour Organizations was ignored. Further arguments used include the fact that the existence of difficult to manage estates would affect adjacent properties and estates, which would not encourage others to continue to buy and lastly, that basically it was useful to continue to 'do-up' such estates" (EA 5/6). These arguments are very similar to those originally made to justify any EA resources at all (as discussed in chapter 4).

Clearly some base their explanation of EA's success in securing additional resources on the initiative's ability to pursue the privatization element. This appears to be because it is the most relevant factor for the Treasury officials yet paradoxically, this was one of the less successful aspects of EA - numerically at any rate (see chapter 6). They also note that: "The Treasury paid particular attention to the issue of 'additionality' for government initiatives in general ... the concern was to ensure that what was undertaken under EA could not be done from mainstream HIPs. [But] There is no doubt that many authorities were using EA HIPs to 'top-up' their housing programmes" (EA 5/6).

One of EA's leading members argues that they have obtained additional funds because: "We have been able to use those resources. There is nothing which annoys the Treasury more than to distribute resources only to find that they have not been fully utilized. There is also plenty of evidence to suggest that the money is producing good results on the ground" (EA 4). This 'evidence' is rather elusive to obtain, however, as no research has as yet been conducted to evaluate this. The next chapter will attempt to provide some idea of the degree to which EA is succeeding (see also Pinto, forthcoming).

iii) Capital allocations: When the author mentioned that according to the survey results 39% of authorities had underspent their EA resources, this was not questioned by EA Central. One of the responses was that: "The first year was always going to be difficult ... the situation [EA's inability to allocate all the HIPs] was explained to the Treasury and it was partly in order to compensate for the underspend that the Treasury allocated £75m in EA HIPs the following year. As a result of the informal arrangements we can now assure the Treasury that all the allocation will be used up. [But] The exact procedure has been kept from the Treasury so far." (EA 2). This contradicts William Waldegrave's letter to the AMA, assuring the chair of housing that the EA HIPs had been fully allocated in the early years (discussed in chapter 6).

When it was suggested that the survey results suggest that the EA HIPs system of targeting resources may be an inefficient method of allocation, the reaction confirms the suspicion that things did not proceed too well: "EA's budget in the first year was £50m. We allocated £45m. Since then we have fully allocated the resources. We underallocated because EA was still a new programme and it was a hard slog to get authorities to accept it ... Local authorities were all hopelessly optimistic about their abilities to spend and this was reflected in the amount of underspend ... As a result the two stage procedure was designed [Forms A and B]. Now we will not allocate resources until they [local authorities] come up with their prices. The result is that we do not underallocate" (EA 4). The Central team appears to be much more positive about the situation now.

They accept that programming difficulties may occur, partly because there are always risks involved for example, with contractors and the vagaries of the weather: "There are always uncertainties with major capital programmes and we cannot allow for the unknown" (EA 4). They confirm that EA now over-programmes to cater for slippage and monitors schemes closely for signs of emerging difficulties. They verify that: "Regional shifting of resources does occur ... mainly because of 'slippage'. Authorities are often over-optimistic about their abilities to spend on certain schemes and [as a result] these may even have to drop out altogether from that years' programme. This releases formerly committed resources and we have a choice of either writing them off or trying to allocate them to authorities that *can* make use of them and whose schemes match EA criteria [although there is a query over the 'and' part of the clause - see homeless discussion in chapter 6]. Some authorities even design schemes and hold them on 'the shelf'. We do not see anything wrong with that" (EA 4), not least because it can offer an escape route for EA. Not only is it an embarrassment when their resources are 'wasted', but full utilization of resource is also an important factor in DoE negotiations with the Treasury for additional or even continuing EA HIPs.

There is a feeling that things have improved greatly since 'regionalization' (the process of devolving EA power and control to the ROs) began. The interviews reveal that there has been an internal struggle between the ROs and the EA team about who should control the administration of the procedures. Both agents now agree that things would not have worked if it had all remained centralized: "There is a small team and they have to deal with over 300 EA schemes per annum, as well as all the bidding forms which they receive" (EA 1). In other words, EA would have been unable to cope had it not begun the process of devolution and there is confidence that even greater decentralization to the ROs will occur in future, although EA Central will remain 'pivotal' to the initiative's operation.

In future co-ordination of policy and objective is to be achieved through conferences and similar methods so as to encourage some degree of uniformity for what is, after all, a national initiative. EA Central will probably retain a budget for the larger, enterprise initiatives, while the regions will be allocated a slice of EA HIPs to do as they see fit under broad EA Central guide-lines. Both (EA 1) and (EA 2) believe that there will only be a couple of these 'enterprise' initiatives per region, which means that in the medium term, the ROs will have to cope with and process the more traditional type of EA scheme and continuation funding.

iv) Regional 'slices' and continuation funding: The slice of EA HIPs allocated to each DoE region normally reflects the previous years' allocations: "This is essentially because the continuation schemes are awarded first call on the year's resources. The provision for continuation funding was organized because it was clear that EA was not going to be able to turn around estates in a mere one or two years" (EA 2). In consequence: "EA began to encourage authorities to phase major works and to bid annually for those phases ... if EA folded then at least the phase completed could stand on its own. We had enough confidence to assume that it would be inconceivable for the Treasury to cut resources so drastically as to stop commitments to continuation funding. This is the only certainty!" (EA 2). If this is the case it is a pity that this confidence is not imparted to the local authorities, many of which are critical of the uncertainty.

As a 'rule of thumb', half of the total borrowing approval allocated by EA goes on continuation schemes and the remainder on new initiatives. The following quotation is particularly enlightening: "... the success of certain regions and authorities in bidding and securing substantial sums is related firstly, to the politics and secondly, to the performance of certain areas. Dealing with politics, the sheer antagonism to the idea of targeting and any sort of central interference was all-pervasive. Many [authorities] were reluctant EA partners and others were never going to be partners at all. Approximately half of the authorities originally invited to participate were very enthusiastic in the first year. More and more quickly warmed-up to it and the late-comers began to realize that they were looking very silly. They were crying that there was not enough cash around, yet other local authorities were seeing their estates brightened-up under EA. Pressure from tenants noticing changes across authority borders must also have been a factor in persuading certain authorities to get involved" (EA 2). This refutes again the EA claim that their decisions are based solely on the quality of the bids they receive (see Map 2 for those local authorities which were slow(er) in getting involved with the EA initiative).

It also appears that certain authorities acquire reputations: "The London authorities with one or two exceptions, were very slow in grasping EA and performed poorly. In allocating the money EA had to be certain that they would spend, otherwise EA itself would end up look silly to the Treasury. The performance of local authorities *is* a consideration in allocating EA funds, therefore, a number of the better-performing authorities have lots of schemes" (EA 2 - Emphasis Added). Even if authorities create thoughtful and well researched schemes which involve their tenants meaningfully, approval may still partly depend on their past performance, especially where large projects are concerned.

7.4.2 Administration and implementation

i) Administrative proceedings: Local authorities are greatly concerned about the EA procedures (Chapters 5 and 6). When this issue was raised during the interviews, the Central team's overall reaction was to attempt to rationalize them: "... someone has to ensure that authorities are spending on what they said they would [otherwise targeting would lose its value]. The second issue is that of public accountability ... There is a need for clear information and scrutiny via the various forms so as to verify the extent of underspend, overrun, variations in expenditure and so on" (EA 2). Another argument for retaining these procedures was advanced: "We have to have an understanding of the way the schemes are going and there is the issue of accountability since we are using public money" (EA 1).

EA Central staff go as far as agreeing that: "This is an extra burden on local authority managers but at least this way they maintain a degree of accountability as well as allowing EA advance warning of likely underspend", and continue that the purpose of: "Form A is to provide us with a macro view of what is there on the estate and an understanding of what and how much is needed. Form B transforms the bid into reality and EA ensures that there is no mismatch in the forms ... we get our quantity surveyors to scrutinise them for overpricing" (EA 2).

The next point raised by the interviewer regarding the application procedure was that it may actually force authorities to waste resources due to aborted schemes since, as EA Central themselves note, authorities heavily overbid EA resources. Their response is that: "Quite a lot of the information necessary for the bids should be available anyway" (EA 2). So while there is a degree of sympathy with local authorities' complaints over the time-consuming and costly nature of EA procedural forms, there is also a perception that they are not as onerous as authorities suggest.

The following quotation demonstrates an awareness of the potential difficulties as well as some attempt at amelioration: "We have tried not to make these [forms] too onerous but there *are* timing difficulties with the initiative ... to be really efficient, EA needs to know what its total resources are in September and to allocate it all by January so that by the first of April, authorities will have a full year to spend the allocation. This has been a clear problem. In the first year, we were not too sure of what was going to happen and we sometimes left local authorities with a handful of working days. The following year, the whole programme was delayed by six weeks as a result of the General Election. The way to resolve this has been to accept that one may get a small spend in the first year, the bulk of the spend in the second and a smaller, 'wrapping-up' spend in the third. Generally, the regions ought to know how local authorities are performing by September 30th. If the red light comes up we have a device whereby ... authorities are allowed to use [the] EA allocation to perform other works. Not many know about this device [namely the Central Reserve Fund]. It is kept quiet because of the

Treasury." (EA 2). Even so resources are not always fully utilized but the Central team supports the existing arrangements and argues that improvements are occurring all the time. The next section analyses these developments in detail.

1. Evolution of EA administration: Official recognition of the difficulties which exist *is* forthcoming from EA Central: "The procedures were 'cobbled together' with a fair amount of haste which is partly the reason why they have been evolving over time" (EA 1), and efforts *have* been made to streamline them, as illustrated via a brief description of the changes: "Procedures have changed from the first ... There was not so much bureaucracy in the first year. We just wrote to authorities inviting them to arrange visits. We took the intelligence gathered from the annual HIPs submissions, together with other information supplied by authorities and visited the estates in order to get a flavour of things" (EA 2). The EA Central procedure was then to: "Summarize verbally what we had seen, describe EA and its intentions and emphasize that the proposals had to be 'dressed in sexy clothes'. Every scheme proposed then went back to the centre together with supporting information. The minister would then examine each initiative and announce in the press releases how many and how much had been approved. Everything was centralized." (EA 2)

However, it seems that: "As the regions became more adept at understanding both the local authorities' and EA's objectives, pressure arose for them to have more say in the process. It also became increasingly clear that having to trawl everything to the centre would be impossible and it was decided to have an annual bidding round and allow the ROs to collect and prioritize the bids. The centre then took a macro view, looking across regional boundaries and ensuring that allocations were going to the estates that would benefit most and that they conformed to EA criteria. Things got more complex as procedures were added to ensure 'value for money' and architects and quantity surveyors were called-in to scrutinise bids." (EA 2) The ROs were then allocated tranches of the EA HIPs (see Map 6). The following section analyses how EA Central evaluates the Forms and is based upon interviews with a leading member of the EA Central team.

2. Form A: In defence of the procedures which authorities perceive to be slow and even unnecessary, the contention is that: "It would be somewhat artificial if we were to judge the schemes simply on the basis of whether they conform to EA criteria or not. There is no fixed format or procedure for selecting schemes for Form B stage" (EA 4). This officer is keen to stress that: "This is not a paper exercise. There should be a continuous process of general discussion about local authority proposals, months or years before they are submitted. As for the 'virgin' bids, the criteria for selection are not rigid, box-ticking exercises. We try to make things as flexible as possible but the paradox is that on one hand, authorities argue that government departments are mechanistic, yet at the same time, they believe that things ought to be well defined from the start ... Problems exist but these result from the employment of value judgements and flexibility" (EA 4), rather than EA procedures *per se*.

Nevertheless, there *are* certain important boxes/criteria in Form A such as: "The condition of the estate; the need for additional investment; the originality of the scheme etc. These are all factors but if for example, we came across a resource-rich authority, we might still take the decision to support it because of the possible consequences which this might have on their future management style or on the neighbouring authorities (EA 4). There is thus a series of considerations at Form A stage: "Up to this year, we have considered the recommendations made by the ROs and our aim has been to achieve consistency of approach since this is a national scheme. There are plans afoot to change the system so as to leave discretion entirely in the hands of the ROs at Form A so that they decide themselves which schemes should be funded" (EA 4). This points to welcome changes in EA, given the previous discussion in Chapters 5 and 6. It would certainly help speed-up the processing and approval of bids, resulting in a longer timescale for authorities to spend their total allocations. This can only be constructive.

3. Form B: The Central team argues that previously Form B: "... too was assessed by us although in more recent years this form has not, strictly speaking, been dealt with by the Central team. We only request that the ROs forward us a copy of the Form Bs and these are scanned to ensure cost consistency and that the schemes submitted are actually those that resources were originally applied for. Other issues we scrutinise include the degree to which tenants were consulted, the type of management arrangements provided and the value for money" (EA 4). A range of criteria must be met before final approval is obtained.

The author asked whether, in line with the survey results, EA really can be seen as being over-bureaucratic and leading to delays in the processing of forms. The reply is that: "Yes, ... these are likely if you have procedures. The real question is whether those delays are justified or unreasonable ... If you believe that EA is trying to do something desirable and that value for money assessments are of value, than this will inevitably build-in delay. I think it is a proper delay" (EA 4). And regarding the delays experienced by authorities in obtaining final approval: "I cannot say whether all the ROs are processing the forms as quickly and as efficiently as they ought to. If local authorities are unhappy they should inform us. What I do know is that authorities often fail to provide even basic information in their bids ... or do not know what the effects of the scheme are likely to be. This is unsatisfactory" (EA 4). In other words, there is a belief that blame for delays cannot be attached to any one agent and not necessarily to the current procedures either.

4. A and B into A/B: Chapter 6 discussed some advantages of amalgamating Forms A and B. There was agreement that: "Anything that reduces bureaucracy is good and the earlier this is done, the better" (EA 2). According to the LHU, the Central team has accepted that the two-stage procedure may not be the most satisfactory situation [LHU, mimeo], although nothing has been done so far. The reason for this appears to be because "... we came to the conclusion that it would not work. Form A requires relatively little information and time whereas if there was a single, more detailed procedure, authorities would once again complain about the costs involved for them if the bids were rejected" (EA 1). It seems that EA is unwilling to run the risk of altering the procedure and that things are unlikely to change in future.

ii) Timetabling arrangements: Problems do exist with the current timetable: "EA does have problems with the timespan, particularly with regard to tenant consultation." (EA 2). Nevertheless EA Central maintains that this has improved as the timetable has been advanced: "It is envisaged that in this year's round [1990/91], most authorities will be given the green light [final approval] on allocation by the first of April", and that some of the blame must rest with the authorities: "Some are very good, others are more pedantic ... [they] regard their procedures as inviolable and inevitably put themselves in a tight box which can't be escaped" (EA 2).

The argument runs deeper in that the Central team also realizes that: "Everything is tied in to a one year timescale in government" (EA 2). They do agree that in principle, there ought to be a longer timescale of operation but are resolute that: "Unfortunately, there is no way of changing it ... The timetable that we operate under is totally determined by the fact that Treasury itself operates under an annual budget. We have pushed back the timetable since the first year, when we realized that we were leaving authorities with far too little time to spend their allocations. Things have improved yet authorities still criticize the timetable" (EA 1). These comments clearly support the views obtained in the survey.

Also in defence, two former members of EA comment that: "No government department gets resources on more than an annual basis and we've always said that we will fund schemes for a maximum of three years [*sic.* originally two], which ought to provide ample time for authorities to gear themselves up. We have encouraged authorities to split their proposals into three phases for larger schemes and while it is true that we do not give guarantees of continuation funding, those schemes will have first call on resources. One must remember that there are no guarantees for HIPs funding either" (EA 5/6), which is certainly true, however, in that particular case, local authorities can decide for themselves exactly where, when and how much to set aside for priority schemes.

The head of EA, responding to whether authorities are justified in feeling that the timetable is both inadequate and makes programming problematic, argues that: "We invited authorities to bid in June for the next financial year. The dead-line was mid-September ... This was extended by a month to allow for late-comers ... We have tried to be flexible because tenants should not be penalized because of delays. Bids are selected for Form B stage but the decision cannot be made until the announcement of the results of the PESC negotiations. This normally happens in September, however, this year it was delayed until October/November. The Central role is to assess the hundreds of bids, prioritize and budget them. We responded to authorities in December/January, announcing whether they had been successful and inviting submission of Form Bs. It is then entirely up to the authorities to design the schemes in finer detail. This year, only a quarter of the new schemes have come in. We are nine months away from the date when Form B approvals were issued and they still have not come through! The fact that we have brought the timetable forward in response to their difficulties does not seem to make a jot of difference to their performance. Therefore, I do not accept that the timetable can make things that much more difficult" (EA 4). Equally both the ROs and EA Central cannot be emphatic that the procedures are improving and that the resources are being used as effectively as possible.

There is an appreciation of the potential difficulties experienced by authorities but there is equally a degree of cynicism towards this local authority criticism. On the bright side, (EA 2), (EA 1) and (EA 4) all insist that things will improve once again this year: "I suspect that this is the best timetabling arrangement possible [given the constraints]. Authorities should get a full year to spend their allocations unless they themselves 'bodge it up' for example, through their [slow] committee procedures. By January, most authorities will receive a friendly nod from the ROs. There is a good deal of informality. This is one of the good things about the ROs. Their local presence is invaluable. They know their [authorities'] performance, those that need help and those that need cajoling" (EA 2). The Central team recognizes the crucial importance of the ROs in enabling the effective implementation of the initiative.

On the negative side: "There was a lot of misunderstanding and misinformation put out by the ROs, especially the London RO. The EA scheme has been let-down by the London Office passing on incorrect information to authorities e.g., that they need to present bills of quantity whereas we just wanted estimates of total cost. There was also a good deal of 'in-fighting' over the regional share of EA HIPs ... The London RO has always moaned about the lack of resources for its authorities but it can't allocate them!" (EA 5/6). This confirms the survey indications that some ROs perform better than others. Moreover, just as certain authorities acquire reputations which make ROs unwilling to trust their abilities to spend EA HIPs, so EA nationally behaves in a similar manner towards ROs which do not perform adequately. Tenants in those authorities and regions are, therefore, lose out because of considerations other than levels of deprivation, need or indeed other categories which EA is fond of stating, such as the quality of the schemes and the degree to which they fulfill EA's current criteria.

iii) Constantly changing criteria?: All those interviewed at EA Central felt that this was not a valid criticism. In response to the accusation that local authorities feel that criteria and emphasis changes over time, there is the argument that: "We've said that we will fund all sorts of schemes as long as that is what the tenants want ... there are no 'hard and fast' rules." (EA 5/6). There is also the contention that some change has occurred but that this is justified: "Any good initiative requires time and government policy also changes. When EA became aware that the privatization element was not going to have an immediate impact, it reduced its profile and increased management's instead. TMCs also became important because of the tenant consultation issues. Some of these changes are bound to be influenced by central government but EA is always looking for innovation. If EA comes up with exactly the same things, it will not be supported [by the Treasury] hence for example, the idea of Tenant Management Boards" (EA 2), as well as enterprise initiatives.

The last view maintains that nothing has changed: "The criteria are not shifting. They have been set out in the Ministerial Guide-lines and the basic principle still applies namely, that those bids which go the furthest towards achieving EA objectives will be the ones most likely to receive EA funding. In the early days EA had to be satisfied with attempts to bring in greater tenant involvement and establish estate based management. It was a struggle to even do this and I suspect that some authorities did not consult as fully as they might have. EA was a new programme and I believe it was an achievement just to get authorities to introduce those measures" (EA 4). Over time, the balance of power has tipped in EA's favour: "Nowadays we do look to local authorities to 'go further down the line' ... As the programme has developed, despite the haziness, some authorities have been very acute in their perception of the way we operate. They have said to themselves, 'We've received funding for management, let's try concierges or co-operatives [instead]', and it wins them more resources. However, the criteria remain the same ... The authorities which win resources one year and are rejected the following year for submitting the same bids, will see it as shifting ground. Those who realize what the initiative is about, will understand why this occurs." (EA 4).

Taking up the issue of schemes being approved one year but not the following, the author asked whether it was feasible that this, together with the fact that various elements (such as the interior of dwellings) were sometimes funded, resulted in confusion and uncertainty over EA criteria. In reply: "The general rule is that we would fund works 'from the doorstep outward' because the rest is a matter for local authorities to take care of from their own capital and revenue accounts" (EA 2). At the same time, however, it is freely admitted that: "We have breached that 'line' from time to time. We have supported works such as roofs and windows so we are flexible. We ask authorities to work on the basis of three columns: things which they can and ought to meet from their own resources; things which we can and will fund; and things which we can have a debate on ... It is useful to retain flexibility and we have avoided listing things item by item" (EA 2). It is not surprising, therefore, that confusions arise from this situation but the onus seems to be upon local authorities to prove that what they propose 'fits' the EA ethos. Flexibility exists for authorities to exploit this aspect.

iv) Generating consultation

1. As relates to schemes and tenants: The aim of attempting to generate greater tenant consultation is one of the many laudable motives behind the EA initiative: "Greater tenant consultation and participation ... stems from an assumption that it is no good thrusting things upon local authorities and tenants. There is a need for consultation and an understanding that what we bureaucrats think as solutions are not always the best" (EA 2). At the same time, the survey findings that things have not worked exactly as anticipated (an issue analyzed in chapter 5) are supported fully and acknowledgement is obtained that this issue: "Is a very difficult 'chicken and egg' situation. Either consultation exercises raise tenants' expectations and do more damage than necessary or the architect goes out and destroys the estate. This is a great worry for the EA team. I don't think we can do anything about it." (EA 2). A further Central officer concurs with this view: "The issues which you draw-up are very proper [ie. about lack of consultation; the timetable; and little on-going consultation] and it is something which I have raised in meetings. However, my colleagues are of the opinion that these are supposed to be the authorities' worst estates and that there should be some consultation going on independently of the EA round" (EA 1). The assumption is that authorities are well aware of what tenants want, but this seems to run somewhat counter to the logic of trying to stimulate greater tenant consultation exercises in the first place.

The response, when the author mentioned that 68.9% of authorities surveyed indicated that EA had not resulted in greater consultation, was that: "... a lot of local authorities were [independently] moving towards greater tenant consultation and involvement" (EA 2); and when the author added that the evidence indicates that it may actually have resulted in less tenant consultation (see the discussion in chapter 5), this too was not disputed. The response was: "That is a worry for us. We are ploughing through and there is a concern that we are pushing authorities to do things which they can't logistically achieve. It is also a valid expectation for EA to underwrite the costs of tenant consultation if schemes are not accepted for funding" (EA 2). There is obviously much concern over this issue within EA itself.

This disquietude is by no means unanimous. One of those EA colleagues who plainly disagrees argues: "We have said that authorities ought to be consulting tenants. They argue that this tends to raise tenants' expectations. We say that this only happens if they do not explain fully to tenants the basis on which they are talking to the DoE ... What I suspect and know is happening, is that the department is being used as a weapon, with certain authorities informing their tenants that 'Unless you agree to the scheme, its impossible to meet the DoE's deadlines' ... A lot of authorities pay lip-service to the issue of tenant consultation ... We do not accept at all their argument about raising tenants' expectation" (EA 4).

When the author pointed out the evidence for less than effective consultation and that local authorities believe that it is EA's *modus operandi* that forces such a process to occur, the reply was: "They know that EA exists and that the initiative is likely to survive in the near future. We are talking about *their* priority estates so surely, they ought to have been talking to their tenants in advance about what are their needs and priorities. Are they really implying that if EA did not exist, they would not have been doing anything to find out about what is necessary on those estates? ... They need not wait until EA invites them to bid before they begin their consultation exercises" (EA 4 - Original Emphasis). This is a point which many authorities would counter by maintaining that they are not in a position to do so.

2. Other forms of consultation (with LAAs and HCC): This section confirms that when the EA initiative was formed, there was precious little consultation between EA and the other agents which it would have had to interact with, both in the very early days and subsequently. A personal view on the main forum for housing-related discussion between the DoE and the authorities, is that: "The HCC used to be a valid forum in the late 1960s and early 1970s but as councils became more politically active, the HCC became less of a valid forum and less used as a useful sounding board for new ideas. It has ceased to be a two-way forum and become a way for ministers to make announcements ... [As for the Local Authority Associations,] The AMA and London Boroughs Association were their own worst enemies - they staged confrontations, not consultations" (EA 2). This may be a reason for cautious dialogue but not for an utter *lack* of consultation with what would be their key partners. This clearly represents a major error on the part of those charged with the formation of the EA initiative.

In addition, the principle of consultation did not extend to EA itself consulting with the ROs and the local authorities over operational and other issues: "I suspect that there was no discussion. It was thrust upon them. This would explain their initial reaction to the initiative" (EA 2). Another Central team member was more pointed in commenting that: "There was no consultation with local authorities or their associations in instigating the initiative. Neither was there consultation with the Regional Offices" (EA 1), and accepts that the initiative and the procedures involved might have been more refined if the authorities, their associations and the ROs had been involved. The team did visit numerous authorities but this does not constitute a true form of consultation. It was more a process of informing authorities what EA's aims were rather than a discussion on how best to focus and operationalize it. Hope was expressed that this situation of minimal consultation on housing issues might change, but the priority of the last two Environment Ministers seems to have been the replacement of the Community Charge with a more acceptable form of local taxation.

7.4.3 EA and its remit

An opportunity was also provided for the Central team to evaluate the initiative's achievements as relate to its remit. This section should be read in conjunction with the discussion in chapter 6, which dealt with the extent to which EA is perceived to be meeting its objectives, form a local viewpoint.

i) Trusts and TMCs: As far as Trusts are concerned there is acknowledgement that: "These have been overshadowed and overtaken by HATs ... and there has been no interest shown in these by local authorities" (EA 2). HATs have all but been discontinued and it is unlikely that EA's scope and level of funding is commensurate with implementing Trusts. Turning to TMCs again: "There have been very, very few of these and we will have to rely heavily on the PEP and Estate Management Boards side of things to generate more interest and management by tenants" (EA 2). This is perhaps, a recognition that full tenant control is some way off and is confirmed by another member of EA: "Co-operatives proved quite hard to get going and partly as a result, Estate Management Boards are being promoted as an intermediary phase" (EA 3). Estate Management Boards seek to generate a formal procedure for generating tenant consultation and involvement in the running and operation of council estates (Zipfel, 1989). Few of these have thus far been organized, although they are an important development in terms of seeking to formalize tenant co-operation, involvement and decision-making over the management of their homes and environment.

ii) Private sector involvement: The general opinion is that while positive, this has not been as successful as was originally hoped for: "Where these have taken place, they have proved very successful but it has been found that there is a distinct difference between theory and what was found on the ground" (EA 1). It appears that: "Initially it seemed that there were lots of estates which could be taken over by the private sector and brought back for sale to first time buyers. However, actual examples of such schemes are few and only account for some 3,000 properties, which constitutes less than 0.05% of the total council stock." (EA 2) It seems that: "It was only when we got on the ground that the difficulties became fully apparent. There was already a good supply of housing in most regions; a lack of developer interest, even with Urban Development Grant support; the location of many estates made them unattractive; and few local authorities, Housing Associations and Building Societies linked together" (EA 2). There seems to have been little 'networking' in this respect and one must conclude that: "The potential has been undermined by actual practice ... lots of authorities still have not swallowed the 'bitter pill', but some authorities have become very pragmatic and there has been some change in attitude" (EA 2).

Similarly there are those who argue that: "There is no doubt that EA first emphasized private sector initiatives as the key [original] aspect of the initiative. The ministry then had to backtrack and to state that the other options listed under the initiative were equally valid for EA support. It was at this point that estate based management came more into its own ... even Sir George Young appeared to have been somewhat frustrated by the slow progress of the privatization element" (EA 5/6). The majority of the EA officials interviewed accept that privatization has *not* been an enormous success in numerical terms. This is in line with the opinions of the ROs and the local authorities.

iii) Homelessness: When the author suggested that according to the research, the homelessness initiative seemed to be incongruous and was introduced very late in the year, this was confirmed by the following statement: "We were facing an underspend of resources and it was decided to target them on the homeless" (EA 3). This represents further confirmation that there were allocation difficulties faced by EA and that homeless initiatives have been used as a method of 'mopping-up' any EA resources that might otherwise have been unused.

iv) Advise Ministers: The only comment made is that: "We are looking to do so but so far this has been insignificant" (EA 2), but see below.

v) New or relatively untried solutions: One view corresponded with that of the local authorities: "We have not come up with anything new. We are dependent upon authorities generating a bright spark. If someone was to come with something worth trying, we would support it" (EA 2). Another view about EA's contribution to any innovative issues is that: "It could be said that there were two spin-offs: Tenants' Choice and HATs. Both originated in the Tory's election manifesto, although the EA directorate has contributed to their formulation. In the case of Tenants' Choice, it probably originated from EA's desire to encourage the formation of co-operatives and Tenant Management Boards. Therefore, there was some involvement from the EA directorate ... HATs were primarily a central government initiative devolved to EA to deal with. There is no doubt whatsoever that the data provided in the various application forms have been used in the selection of suitable HATs candidates. The EA directorate is part of the DoE and information travels around, as is right and proper" (EA 5/6). Many authorities were greatly concerned about the possibility that the DoE would use the detailed information about their estates contained in Forms A to D, in order to select estates for designation as HATs. The above quotation suggests that this is likely to have been the case. The information was very pertinent to that purpose.

7.4.4 'Flagship' schemes and employment initiatives

Attitudes were also investigated with regard to the radical changes EA is currently undergoing: "If you can get into the social and economic issues and are able to generate some employment, than it can only be good for such estates. There is enough material in terms of human resources and the key must be to get the main governmental departments involved in order to 'pump-prime' the process" (EA 2). EA Central recognizes that co-ordination of the various authorities, voluntary organizations and central departments will be the most difficult aspect and feel that (EA 2): "There is a need for a [special] team in order to overcome departmental arguments ... It can happen ... [But] It will take an awful lot to get these schemes together and to get them going by lots of people and organizations. It would require a corporate approach which is not around. Ministers are keen to get this going next year but we will only see the beginnings of the new emphasis in the 1991/92 round. Lots of effort is being invested in this but the danger is that the initiative may be scrapped if it fails ... I think it is a brave idea".

A relevant comment on the reasons why EA has swung heavily in favour of generating these employment or enterprise initiatives is revealed in the context of the discussion on the reasons why the initiative has been able to secure additional resources: "It has been a hard battle each time. This year [the 1990/91 financial round], the Treasury was arguing that EA has now reached the worst estates and that they now want employment to be increased. This is why the new job opportunities angle has been added to EA so as to encapsulate the macro issues and not just management. Despite the existence of Urban Development Corporations and City Action Teams, there is still a public and media outcry about the many estates which have very high levels of unemployment and the idea is to try to bring in additional opportunities" (EA 2).

With respect to the future of the EA Unit, when it was posed that rumour had it that it would not survive much longer, the reaction was: "EA is still operating on a year to year basis. The directorate is reorganizing itself but this is because the 1988 Housing Act will dictate different workloads to civil servants ... [however;] As far as the financial changes and how they impact on EA, we have still to see the final papers, therefore, I can't say what will happen" (EA 2). EA does seem to be leaving the details to the last minute. To some extent this is inevitable, given that the legislation has not been finalized (at the time), but some believe that radical upheavals are unlikely in the near future: "I don't see any new developments in the next twelve months. The enterprise initiative will take a great deal of energy" (EA 2).

An interesting comment on the value of EA is put forward by (EA 1) who argues that many local authorities may be secretly glad of the initiative, quoting the case of a housing director using EA as the scapegoat for introducing changes in his authority - changes which would not otherwise have been possible but which were needed. Nevertheless it seems that the EA Central team believe that the initiative remains far from popular with authorities: "I recognize that EA, like many government initiatives, is not perfect but it is important to try to separate out the reasons for authorities grumbling about EA and criticizing it: A lot will depend on the kind of relationship which exists between the RO and the local authorities. It can come down to a matter of individuals and housing authorities just do not like EA *per se* - the fact that we control the funds which they believe they should have" (EA 4).

7.5 Conclusions

This chapter started by arguing that it is important to analyze EA Central and the DoE Regional Offices, both of which constitute important elements within the EA policy community. It then summarized the existing literature on the role of Regional Offices which suggests that they have an ambiguous role to play. Depending on the context, they can either be instruments of the centre or champions of local authority causes. Both roles are reflected in this chapter with respect to EA.

An advantage of semi-structured interviews over surveys is that they enable change and dynamism to enter the discussion. Despite the criticism of the operation of EA inherent in the survey results presented in chapter 5, the Regional Offices' administrative role (as regards EA) has evolved substantially. They have been given greater responsibility and flexibility. Examples include the creation of a Central Reserve Fund and the fact that they now have the option of over-programming the regional EA HIPs allocation, however, problems remain. Over time, the ROs' relationship with local authorities has also improved, a point recognised by local authorities. ROs have championed their authorities' EA bids and have become allies against bureaucracy and administrative delays. This is part of the reason why further responsibilities have been devolved from EA Central. The ROs maintain that they operate well with both the Central team and their colleagues in other ROs but that contact is minimal. This seems to be unfortunate because greater interaction might result in more efficient procedures and generally improved practice. The ROs consider their role to be critical to the implementation of EA schemes but that overall, EA Central also does a good job and has been quite flexible.

Turning next to the issue of implementation, the ROs acknowledge that the EA timetable has been problematic but that it has improved. They also affirm that the existing procedures may be slightly over-bureaucratic and that there may be a case for starting again and creating a new set of application forms. They also accept that tenant consultation has been one of the toughest problems of all to solve, but they deny the validity of the local authority claim that EA criteria keep changing.

Dealing with financial issues next, most ROs agree with local authorities that EA HIPs represents topsliced resource. An important finding is that regional under- and overallocation does occur and that one of the most affected of all is the London region. This can be seen from Map 6 where its share of EA HIPs and number of schemes is not commensurate with the high levels of housing deprivation that its authorities experience (Map 4). Another conclusion reached by those interviewed at the regional level is that financial targeting along EA HIPs lines works.

In terms of central-local issues, there are mixed views regarding what were central government's true intentions in creating special initiatives/allocations such as EA. Some accept that this results in centralization of control but other ROs stress that it is focused on proven need and thus that it is beneficial. They argue that EA has been successful in securing additional finance because of the high and continuing demand for schemes, because EA has lobbied effectively and because most authorities have responded positively and imaginatively to the initiative after a reluctant start. The ROs expect the operation of the initiative to improve with time, especially if further decentralization of functions to the ROs is forthcoming.

Some conclusions can also be drawn as regards the Central team. Starting with the financial side, EA Central refuses to accept that EA HIPs are topsliced or that the resources may not necessarily end up in the worst estates of all. Targeting is seen as an effective mechanism in directing resources to proven need and EA has worked hard to secure additional resources from the Treasury. Ironically, the issue of the degree of privatization achieved by EA has been the most important factor in persuading the Treasury to release further resources for the EA programme even though in fact, this is one of the initiative's least successful achievements. The Central team does not contradict either the local authority survey or the RO finding that underspending occurs. It merely agues that this only happened in its first year of existence and has not recurred subsequently. This is contradicted in the evidence put forward by the ROs.

Continuation funding constitutes half of the annual EA HIPs allocation and is normally based on the previous year's pattern of allocations. Interestingly just like authorities, ROs which do not perform adequately acquire reputations with EA Central of being unreliable. This has implications for the financial 'cut' (of EA HIPs) received by each region *and* the re-allocation of resources that are in danger of being underspent at the end of the financial year. The 'unreliable' regions are unlikely to be given the opportunity to make use of them.

EA Central stresses that administrative procedures have been decentralized to the ROs and that they have become more streamlined as a result. There is an awareness of the remaining problems for authorities but there is also a feeling that part of the difficulty (of slow administration and processing of bids) rests with local authorities themselves and that if they feel that the ROs are too slow, then those authorities should approach EA Central with their complaints. Great stress is laid on the fact that EA Central has to ensure public accountability, hence the reason for maintaining the existing procedural arrangements. Nevertheless, further decentralization or, in the DoE's terminology, 'regionalization' may occur, thus reducing some of the remaining delays.

Regarding the timetabling arrangements, EA emphasize that they have greatly adjusted it by 'bringing it forward' in the financial year in response to local authority criticism. They argue that if local authorities still have problems, it is their own fault: they should have been geared up to the fact that EA exists and it is the authorities' own procedures which create delays and other problems, not EA's timetable. Like the ROs, changing criteria was also not felt by EA Central to be a valid local authority criticism. EA Central argue that EA is about innovation, that there are no 'hard and fast' rules and that Ministerial Guide-lines have been issued. Another conclusion is that despite the speculation, EA Central is adamant that the two stage application procedure (forms A and B) will not be amalgamated in the future.

Turning to tenant consultation, this remains a key theme for EA Central but it is recognised that this continues to be a problem. Some team members argue that for this to work more effectively, local authorities should be subsidized, but others feel that it should be left to authorities to sort out their own housing priorities and to consult their tenants adequately. The latter view seems to run counter to the logic of creating an initiative (in part) to encourage authorities to develop their tenant consultation procedures. The chapter confirms that EA Central sought no consultation with other bodies such as the Housing Consultative Council and the Local Authority Associations and the Regional Offices prior to the creation of the EA mechanisms and that no great effort is being expended to remedy this error. The principle of consultation only operates in some directions as far as the EA initiative is concerned.

Lastly, EA's policy bias has changed towards employment/enterprise generation in public housing estates. Recent research demonstrates the necessity of such initiatives, especially as far as the long-term unemployed are concerned (see Pinto, 1991c; 1991d; 1992a and 1992b). There is unanimous agreement among all those interviewed that this is an useful and important departure since it is no longer adequate to see the problems in many of the estate supported by EA in purely housing terms. Unemployment is a key issue which must also be addressed, however, it has also been mooted that the move may have been influenced by the desire to maintain and/or increase Treasury support for the EA initiative. There are also those that suggest that the success of this emphasis may determine the future of the EA initiative.

8 The impact of Estate Action at the local level: Four case-studies

8.1 Introduction

This chapter develops from Chapters 4 to 7 in order to present an analysis of the operation and impact of the EA initiative at the micro or individual local authority level. In an attempt to present a thorough analysis of EA, the previous discussion has traced the initiative from its political and managerial origins, through to a national survey of its approach from a local authority perspective and finally to a discussion of the initiative at the regional (DoE Regional Offices) and central (EA Central) levels. It remains to conclude the empirical work by analyzing EA's impact in specific local situations.

As discussed in chapter 3, case-studies are considered to be vital in adding context, depth and dynamism to the analysis of EA - all important elements which do not come through with the survey methodology. In addition, public housing has traditionally not been very diligent in defining and maintaining management or output data so case-studies are useful in enabling both quantitative and qualitative information to be marshalled in support of the examination of the EA programme. Therefore four case-studies were selected comprising different management styles (estate based management, a concierge, an example of public/private sector partnership and a physical refurbishment scheme) in diverse contexts such as political control (Labour Conservative and SDP/Labour), level of housing deprivation, type of authority and DoE region (see Table 3.4).

The aim of the chapter is to unravel the notion of EA's impact or effectiveness at the case-study level. The term 'effectiveness' may be defined in terms of both EA's and local authorities' aims, but it cannot be defined purely in terms of statistical output measures. Even if this had been the intention of the book, the data and 'bench-marks' for statistical evaluation simply do not exist, therefore, one must make use of essentially qualitative data supplemented with quantitative data where possible. Furthermore, assessment of effectiveness must relate to various aspects which are central to the book, namely the way EA:

- impacts upon the estates and people's lives;
- is administered, organized and implemented;
- uses the resources available as well as possible; and
- impacts upon local authority housing management and housing policy.

In order to analyze the above dimensions of effectiveness, in-depth semi-structured interviews were conducted with key informed local authority personnel. The interviewees included the EA co-ordinating officer (two interviews), the assistant/director of housing departments, local councilors and the officers in charge of the financial programming of EA HIPs (see Appendix 3 in Pinto 1992d) for the semi-structured interview schedules used). For reasons of comparability, the structure of these interviews reflects and builds upon that of previous chapters.

The chapter provides an introductory description of the case-study authorities and what the four EA-funded schemes entail in financial and concrete terms. Section 8.3 begins to deal with the notion of effectiveness at the micro level. The first factors to be analyzed are the financial and procedural details of the four schemes in order to determine whether EA procedures were indeed slow and resulted in underspend as suggested by previous research. The discussion moves on to a brief discussion of the impact of EA schemes in terms of management statistics and supporting reference is also made to the results of the national survey. Thirdly, indications of whether EA has been a success in the actual estates is obtained from housing officers intimately involved with the changes occurring in the estates in question. Brief reference is also made to Pinto (1992d, Appendix 7) which contains the details of an attempt to canvass council tenants' opinions as to the developments occurring on their estates. Due to methodological weaknesses relating to the sample size, this information does not appear in the main body of the book. Finally the analysis continues with the aim of assessing EA's effectiveness in terms of the other criteria discussed above namely, procedural, financial and policy effectiveness.

8.2 The four case-studies

This section entails a summary of the background to the estates and the EA schemes selected for detailed analysis. The aim is to provide an understanding of the types of problems faced by the residents of such estates and the types of initiatives which have been encouraged by EA in order to counter the poor environment, physical condition of buildings and management style in such areas.

i) Goscote House (St. Peter's Estate): A concierge scheme

History: It seems that originally, "The area was the 'red-light' district for Leicester and had a close-knit community. The estate itself is very recent but because of the large number of high-rise units, it quickly came to acquire a bad reputation" (NS 1). The estate was built in four phases:

- 84 units built 1968-70 (2-3 bedrooms), all demolished in 1989
- 872 units in 4 tower blocks built 1971-73 (1, 2 and 3 bedrooms)
- 197 units in Goscote House, built in 1973 as a one-off scheme
- 49 low rise properties were the final development in 1980

However, over time: "The estate acquired such a bad reputation that even members of staff were reluctant to come to the estate, unless they had seen the work being done to renovate it" (NS 1). While the current estate manager (AB 1) maintains that the deterioration of the estate has little to do with the allocations policy, the previous manager has a different account for the reason why the estate came to become stigmatized: "The estate was originally quite stable because the whole community had been rehoused in the same estate. However, in the space of 18 months, the community became fragmented due to the influx of a mix of people from all over the authority. The previous social cohesion was lost" (NS 1).

It is suggested that the main driving force for change have been the Tenants' Association in conjunction with the council (AB 1) and that: "There was originally some concern about the newness of the block and, therefore, of its eligibility for EA funding. Nevertheless the place was undoubtedly 'difficult-to-let' with a very high turnover of tenants [20% p.a.], which meant that it fitted EA's bill. The block had been built exactly to DoE guide-lines with a resident caretaker. This was then increased to two and eventually to twenty four hours cover to little avail. The problem was that the council used the block to house people coming out of hostels and the like, so that Goscote began to acquire a certain type of tenant. The politicians were unwilling to change that policy and the [housing] department came to feel that the only alternative was radical change the security arrangement" (NS 1), which is why it began to consider concierge schemes.

The EA element: The Goscote House concierge scheme represents an initiative which EA has embraced and encouraged as being potentially very beneficial and cost-effective (Skilton, 1988). Concierges represent one of the lowest levels of decentralization possible, down to individual blocks. This particular block was one of the most problematic in the authority and is an added reason why it is worthwhile analyzing the degree to which the concierge has affected the situation.

St Peter's estate as a whole has benefited substantially from EA support for various schemes. Goscote House received an allocation of £210,000 in the 1986/88 financial round. 100% of the capital allocation came from EA and the particular works undertaken at Goscote House were the following: the creation of a bullet-proof glass door-entry system operated all day by a two-man shift. Two doors were installed (in case unauthorized persons managed to push past the first) which are opened by residents' magnetic keys whose code can be altered. Visitors must obtain permission from residents to enter the building.

Goscote House is subject to additional security measures. Three external cameras pan up and down the building; there is a camera in each lift; five cameras on the ground floor; and one in each of the 21 floors. All this is recorded and print-outs of anti-social and criminal behaviour can be obtained. Additional facilities provided by the council include a lounge with easy chairs which is mainly for parties and visitors' use; a TA room; a public telephone; and free a launderette service for residents' use.

ii) Canterbury Gardens (formerly Ladywell): A private sector scheme

History: The estate was built in 1950-51: "... but was going downhill due to the malaise which affected a lot of our property. A major part of our housing work until 1980-81 comprised of slum clearance but being geographically a small authority [until the reorganization in 1974], it meant that an awful lot of high-rise construction took place [*circa* 86 tower blocks]. People were at the time very willing to move into them, partly because they were of a much higher standard than the housing they'd left behind, but also because of a lack of choice. This major rehousing programme came to an end in the early 1980s with a dramatically reduced demand for housing. People now wanted houses instead of flats" (PW 2).

It appears that consequently: "Family flats [as in Ladywell] of which there was a surplus, became less and less in demand and people began to look to transfer out of the estate. Only those desperate to be housed moved in. The community began to break-up, not because of what the council was doing, but because peoples' aspirations began to change and a more transient type of tenant began to move in. We did attempt to improve things such as installing a new heating system and entry phones but these were soon smashed" (PW 2). It was at this point that the council began to think seriously about a more fundamental change to the estate.

The EA element: Disposals to the private sector and partnership schemes were a key principle behind EA's creation, this being very much in line with government housing policy. This choice of case-study was made all the more interesting because it is a labour-controlled council with a reputation for being 'pragmatic' and at the forefront of this type of scheme. The authority has obtained substantial resources via EA and it is, therefore, worthwhile analyzing the extent to which the EA-funded initiative has been successful. Canterbury Gardens received an allocation of £2.8m in the 1986-89 round with 100% of the capital allocation coming from EA.

The Ladywell Estate comprised 279 walk-up flats in seven three storey blocks. The estate was classified as 'difficult-to-let' with a run-down appearance, boarded up properties and a degree of vandalism. The council felt that 'the estate was no longer acceptable' (Form A, Part B, 25.2.1986), that the whole of the estate should be refurbished and proposed that approximately 50% of the estate be sold to a developer. The remainder of the stock would continue to be council property for rent and the developer would act as a contractor to the council. All the properties would be vacated and re-letting would commence once the estate had acquired a new image.

The council proposed comprehensive works on the estate firstly, to the flats and communal areas: renewing windows, doors, frames and skirtings; installing central heating and rewiring; new fittings for the kitchen and bathrooms including tumble driers; and an 'entry-phone' system leading to a carpeted lobby, stairs and landings. Secondly, the external shells/areas: demolishing unsafe balconies, cleaning and pointing all brickwork; new/rendered and painted stair shafts; replacement of bin shafts with free-standing bin stores; French windows to patios on all ground floor flats; subdivided gardens together with landscaping; and resurfacing the roadway, courtyards, and community centre playground (contained in Form A, 25.2.1986).

iii) Bengal House (Ocean Estate): A refurbishment scheme

History: The Ocean estate is one of the authority's largest with over 2,000 properties but: "Because of its size it eventually acquired a reputation as being unmanageable. There was a district housing office to try to better manage the properties, however, there was constant change in the officers assigned to manage the estate ... Within the estate itself, symptoms of this 'unmanageability' included a high turnover of voids, arrears, squatting and such like. At the same time, there was a centralized repairs service over which the Housing Department had little control ... Everything else was out of our hands" (MU 3).

The officer adds that: "The estate has quite a varied ethnic mix. [Although] There was a phase of racial harassment towards the Bengali community on the estate", and as regards the management side of things: "The decisive change came with the creation of a PEP management office in March 1987 together with a local repairs depot, over which the Housing Department has much greater control, allowing them to monitor the works or award them to private contractors" (MU 3).

The EA element: This scheme is interesting in that it represents an initiative outside of EA criteria as it involves little more than pure and simple refurbishment of the block. In other words, it is something which

EA insists should be undertaken from mainstream HIPs. It is worthwhile asking why this was approved. Additional points of interest include the fact that the scheme is on a PEP estate to ponder on whether the particular blend of the borough's politics (SDP/Liberal) may affect its perception of EA and its willingness to participate.

Ocean estate too benefited substantially from EA support. In the 1986-87 round it received £200,000 worth of allocation for the installation of central heating systems. In 1987-88 Channel House received an allocation of £1,335,000 for refurbishment works (including structural works, lift refurbishment, provision of central heating, roof recovering, new plumbing works, new kitchens and bathrooms and asbestos removal). Bengal House itself received an allocation of £2,771,000 in the 1987-88 round. All this capital allocation came from EA itself and the works undertaken included a new roof, new rendered façade, window replacement, enlarged refuse facilities and refurbishment of kitchens and bathrooms.

iv) Digmore Neighbourhood Office: An estate management scheme

History: When the authority took over the Digmore Estate from the New Town Corporation in 1985: "It found severe problems on the estate - so much so, that it was even considered seriously the demolition of a selection/whole of the estate ... Basically, no one went to Digmore unless they had no choice. Vandalism, voids and turnovers were very, very high and had been exacerbated by the Development Corporation's policies of the 'Sale of the Century' which had created lots of voids. Property was bought by individuals and private landlords who then left them void and derelict, and which the council has now had to buy back" (SO 4).

The situation forced the council to think seriously about: "... the idea of eventually forming a PEP. The council carried out various forms of consultation including a professional survey of the estate. The results highlighted very serious problems but many officers were surprised to find that a large percentage of tenants wanted to remain on the estate but wanted improvements. A project co-ordinator was employed by the council and having become aware of the existence of EA and the resources available through it, decided to bid for EA support." (SO 4).

The EA element: While awaiting PEP designation the authority decided to apply for EA resources and was successful. It has to be stressed that this is not the purest of examples of EA's influence, since the estate also has PEP status. Another difficulty which arose is that the bulk of the original work had been undertaken by the previous co-ordinator and the exact details of the EA procedures were, therefore, not entirely clear. This is an unavoidable problem which results from staff turnover. Nevertheless a key EA principle has been its determination to encourage decentralization via localized management and initiatives of this nature comprise approximately half of the EA-funded schemes. It is thus worthwhile analyzing the degree to which this has been an useful initiative. To this end, a scheme was chosen in an authority that previously had no plans to decentralize and where a localized management office is a novelty, in order to gauge the extent to which this has been a success. Digmore represents the most problematic council estate in the authority's stock which adds to its value as an indicative case-study for the effect of estate management.

Other important reasons for the selection of this area include the need to have a variety of regions and authorities for the case-studies. This area was also a Conservative-controlled district council which enabled a different slant on EA to be obtained. The Digmore estate has benefited from a substantial injection of EA support. In a period from 1987 to 1990 it has experienced three phases of continuous investment adding up to over £5m (including the creation of the local management office). It has also received PEP status (and the additional non-financial support that entails) and has been designated as an Estate Management Board site.

8.3 Effectiveness: Making use of the available data

This section analyses the scant statistical data available with which to address the issue of EA's effectiveness at the local level. It starts by collating all the available financial and procedural data and links the main findings to the discussions in previous chapters so as to use the case-studies to update the arguments. The subsequent section presents the data gathered as the result of an effort to obtain housing management statistics for the case-studies, however, information was available for only two authorities and even this had been compiled using incompatible definitions. This meant that the data had to be transformed into symbols indicating improvement or deterioration in the estates rather than exact quantification. This analysis is supplemented by reference to the results of the postal survey (Table 5.24). Lastly some indication was obtained as to the impact of EA schemes from the point of view of housing officers closely involved with the developments occurring in the estates in question.

8.3.1 Financial and programming details

By way of building the context and background to the schemes outlined above, Table 8.1 collates the basic information necessary for an understanding of the procedural, implementation and financial issues in dealing with EA. The first point to note is the degree to which information is missing. This seems to be primarily a reflection the fact that EA schemes are often hastily assembled by an *ad hoc* group of officers. The task is often delegated to individuals to organize and submit the information to EA and, therefore, the various EA forms are more likely to be misfiled. This says much about local authority organization and record-keeping but also reflects on the variable amount of information which is demanded of authorities by the various ROs - for example, one authority did not have to fill in Form B whereas the other, in the same region, did have to. EA's insistence that authorities submit the Quarterly Assessment forms (C) was not always heeded, regardless of the size of the allocation, although this may also have been a reflection of poor record-keeping and/or staff turn-over. The variability in information requested by the EA administration is the most striking aspect, backing the survey results (presented in chapter 5). It also reflects the fact that the EA initiative has evolved as it has gone along.

Table 8.1 also provides support for arguments presented earlier (Chapter five), relating to the processing of the various EA procedures. It is clear that by the time final approval was issued, there normally remained very little time for the authorities to actually spend their allocations, thus resulting in the underspending problems identified in other parts of the book. A third issue which is immediately noticeable is that at least two of the cases, the final costs of the schemes exceeded the original estimates. To some extent this is inevitable (due such factors as the weather, contractors, technical difficulties etc), but the point to note is that the authorities must meet all the additional costs from their own budgets. This also calls into attention EA's method of allocating funds. The information in Table 8.1 confirms many procedural and implementation issues discussed in preceding chapters. These will not be repeated here.

8.3.2 Housing statistics: A basic assessment of impact

This section deals with the officers' views regarding the end result of all the procedures and the effect of the EA schemes. It attempts to give an indication of the general achievements of the schemes employing the housing management indicators which are normally used to demonstrate improvements in housing conditions and should be analyzed in conjunction with the results of the survey (Table 5.24).

Although subjective in nature and prone to the problems of trying to separate out the 'EA effect' from 'other factors',Table 8.2 does illustrate that the situation appears to be improving on the estates as a result of the EA schemes. Every single management indicator (such as the reduction in rent arrears and the crime rate) records improvements occurring either one year later or in the time since. This is probably happening in conjunction with 'other' factors not taken into consideration. Nevertheless and despite the fact that only two case-studies returned the information, these results support the local authority survey findings presented earlier in Table 5.24.

Table 8.1: Case-studies: Procedural and financial issues

Basic Information on Schemes	Conc	Priv Sect	Refurb	Est Mmt
When built:	1973	1948	1961	1967-71
Design/Construction method	Wimpy	Trad.	Steel fr.	Radburn
Number of units on estate	1009	279	1975	1219
Number of units involved	197	141/160	95	981
Form A				
Date of EA invitation to submit	29.1.87	29.1.87	29.1.87	29.1. 87
Date of submission to RO/EA	N.A.	4.3.87	10.3.87	19.2. 87
Closing date	None	None	None	None
Form B				
Date when invited to go to Form B	None	None	26.8.87	30.6. 87
Date of submission to RO/EA	19.10.87	None	8.12.87	6.8. 87
Closing date	Flexible	Flexible	Flexible	Flexible
When final approval received	22.2.88	10.8.87	26.1.88	N.A.
Weeks to spend the allocation	5	15	8	N.A.
Weeks from A to final approval	N.A.	21	52	N.A.
Form C				
Number of forms sent to EA	5	3	5	2
Spending going to plan?	No	Yes	No	Yes
Amount bid for (000's):	186	2,863	2,711	5,566
Amount approved (000's):	210	2,863	2,584	5,566
Final cost (000's):	258	2,763	2,631	5,566
EA's contribution	100%	100%	100%	100%

Source: Interviews and Estate Action Forms A and B

Table 8.2: Management indicators: Before/after the EA scheme

Concierge:	Arrear	Re-lets	Voids	Transf	RTBs:	Vandal	Crime
Beforehand	--	--	--	0	--	--	--
1 year later	+	++	+	+	0	++	++
Since then	+	+	+	+	0	+	+

Estate Mmt:	Arrear	Re-lets	Voids	Transf	RTBs:	Vandal	Crime
Beforehand	--	--	--	--	+	--	--
1 year later	0	0	+	+	0	0	+
Since then	++	++	++	+	+	+	++

Before scheme: Very high/Much worse (--); High/worse (-); Medium/No change (0); Low/Improved (+); Very Low/Much improved (++)
Note: No data returned for refurbishment and private sector schemes

8.3.3 Impact on estates: Quotations from informed housing officers

A worthwhile exercise is also to ask the housing officers who are intimately aware of and involved with, the developments taking place in the estates for their opinions regarding the extent to which they perceive improvement taking place in the EA estates. Their impressions about the achievements in the various case-studies are recorded below:

• *Concierge:* "A tenant satisfaction survey was carried out in February 1989 but only 27 tenants responded. All were favourably impressed with the scheme, although some still complained about the allocation policy. Even the existing staff members have built a lot of bridges with the tenants ... There have been no burglaries and no more missiles thrown out of the windows" (NS 1).

• *Private Sector:* "There have been no studies but is self-evident that it has been a success. Void levels have fallen dramatically and it is now 100% occupied. It has also enabled us to free under-occupied properties and meet housing need as a result. There are only two transfer requests at the moment" (PW 2).

• *Refurbishment:* "Yes, certainly the estate has improved. There was no central heating and the windows were draughty before. Now external cladding has also been added and this has made a difference. It has not solved the management problems for example, the homeless and there are still families housed on the seventh floor of the building, but there have been improvements. Before all the four blocks were regarded as difficult-to-let. This is no longer the case. There is now a high demand for these dwellings which is reflected in the fact that there are now 12 'right to buy' applications where there were none before." (MU/SR 3)

• *Estate Management:* "We believe that it has been a success. The next bid is going to be on very similar intensive management lines" (SO 4).

These comments imply substantial improvements in the estates. However, an important opinion must be that of the residents themselves - the people who live in the estate and experience the changes. Consequently part of the case-study research involved an attempt to obtain an indication of the tenant opinion as this was felt to be of relevance. An attempt has been made to encompass this issue (see Pinto 1992d, Appendix 7 for a discussion of each element of the tenant survey analysis; and Appendix 4 for a copy of the survey), however, it was not considered to be sufficiently robust to be discussed in great detail. Nevertheless, the tenant findings represent useful, albeit rudimentary, indicators of tenant satisfaction with their living environment. The tenants' responses both support and enhance the housing management statistics provided by the housing officers for the four case-studies (Table 8.2); the positive EA Central, RO, and local authority comments; and the survey results (Table 5.24).

Taken together this constitutes an incomplete but substantive body of evidence that suggests that, not only is the situation improving in all the four case-studies (and beyond according to the survey results) but more importantly, that these schemes are actually meeting tenants' individual wants and needs. It is extremely difficult (if not impossible) to try to extricate the pure 'EA' impact from other factors occurring independently of the initiative. For example, to what extent does the improvement simply reflect the fact that these estates were in need of additional investment? Most of them were severely run-down and any focused and substantial investment in environmental, dwelling or managerial terms would probably have resulted in substantial improvements. Effectiveness cannot stop at this stage.

Having concluded in the previous section that EA schemes seem to have beneficial effects for the estates and the residents, nevertheless, any discussion on the effectiveness of EA must look at other dimensions. Three other critical determinants of the effectiveness of EA, based on both their aims and those of local authorities, must relate to the following issues: firstly, the procedures, administration and implementation - in other words, whether these are as well designed as possible; secondly, financial effectiveness - in other words, whether the targeted resources available to EA are used thoroughly; and thirdly, policy effectiveness - or what impacts there have been upon local authority housing management and wider housing policy. These are now discussion in turn.

8.4 Procedural effectiveness

Procedural effectiveness refers to the extent to which authorities believe that EA Central has organized the administrative procedures, the timetabling arrangements, tenant consultation and other implementation or procedural issues as well as possible. This section also seeks to link up with and refine earlier arguments (based on the national survey and the analysis of Regional Offices and EA Central) by adding the dimension of specific authorities, estates and schemes, thereby verifying the preceding research or obtaining perspectives not previously discussed. Therefore the following discussions of effectiveness not only report on the findings at the local level but also seek to integrate them with those of previous chapters where relevant.

As described in chapter 3, this part of the case-studies involved detailed semi-structured interviews with key decision-makers in the local authority administrations (see chapter 3). The interviewees which are quoted have their own letter and number code. The letters refer to the individuals interviewed and the numbers 1 to 4 identify the different case-studies (see Table 3.4). This section will analyze the local procedures involved in selecting estates which are eligible for EA support; the operation of the timetable; the quality of tenant consultation; EA's growing influence in housing circles; and the other relevant procedural factors.

8.4.1 Selecting EA candidates

In all four cases it was the Housing Department that assumed the lead role in co-ordinating bids, selecting the candidates and collecting the necessary statistical information. This requires the full co-operation of other local authority departments (eg. the architect's regarding costings). The general agreement is that: "If authorities are to operate within EA deadlines, a good deal of co-operation and willingness to succeed must be available from other departments" (MU/SR 3). This was soon appreciated and the departments have, in the main, acted in unison and authorities are now finding that: "It is getting easier to liaise with the others. This is both because of the experience gained of dealing with EA and there has been limited staff turnover" (NS 1), which facilitates matters. Similarly it was felt in another authority that: "It has not been too much of a problem ... They [other departments] have been very reasonable and realize that this is the only way to succeed" (SO 4).

Authorities stress that they were aware of *which* estates needed attention and *what* was needed before EA was inaugurated and it thus was inevitable that some candidates for EA bids would be chosen almost irrespective of the EA criteria. In one case a bid was made in the full knowledge that it did *not* conform to EA criteria: "... the estate had already been prioritized by a comprehensive GLC report and the authority undertook to push this forward under the EA programme ... the scheme was, therefore, a top priority for the neighbourhood and for the authority as a whole" (MU/SR 3), but not for EA, although it was still supported.

Normally it was only once authorities became aware of the EA initiative that an attempt was made to ensure that schemes submitted would be eligible under its criteria: "By 1985 ... a number of estates 'at risk' had been identified by the housing strategy ... It was at this point the EA/UHRU came along and we realized that the estate would fit" (PW 2). In another case: "The original impetus for a high security system came from the tenants themselves following a sit-in and a petition" (NS 1). In all four cases, the officers maintain that EA contributed little other than providing allocations which enabled the schemes to occur. This is in line with the survey results presented in the latter part of chapter 5, regarding the primary reasons for the improvements in the estates.

8.4.2 Timetabling

Regarding the adequacy of the timetable, views are mixed at the local level. An officer states that: "It is actually getting worse. It is now ludicrous because EA expects us to drop everything else and to devote our time exclusively to developing EA bids" (NS 1), but authorities largely agree with the ROs and EA Central that things are changing (see also chapter 7): "It has improved. If EA allocates things as last year, when we received Form A in December 1988, then we have a reasonable amount of time to plan things - to be fair to them we do not have to wait for them to invite us to prepare bids" (PW 2), a point stressed by the EA Central team.

Nevertheless there remains a feeling that: "There is still room for improvement ... and the proposed decentralization to ROs should help. I appreciate EA's argument that authorities ought to have 'cottoned on' to EA and to have the schemes ready for submission, rather than waiting for an invitation ... Unfortunately, the situation is not as simple as that" (SR 3). This view is supported by the following: "We submitted Form A some while ago. Its already December and we have not been informed whether to develop the scheme or not. By the time this is done it will be into the financial year once again ... in the majority of cases, schemes are only fully approved in September or thereabout. So although the timetable seems to have improved, it is not that much better" (SO 4). Clearly this still causes difficulties and the Central team is adamant that the timetable cannot be brought forward any more than it already has. This issue remains to be handled effectively (but see the concluding chapter).

8.4.3 Administrative burdens and criteria

The case-studies also confirm the survey results *apropos* the administrative load. All agree that: "This is still large and onerous. The whole two stage process is cumbersome because even at Form B, it [the bid] is speculative. The authority must make a decision whether or not to work on the scheme prior to receiving official approval. The vetting of application forms does not need to be so detailed ... that is what the tenders are supposed to be for - to ensure that the prices and costings are competitive" (TH 3). This call for more relaxed vetting arrangements could help matters: "I suspect that they just look in detail at those bits that really matter to them but an awful lot of information looks suspect in terms of relevance to the bid" (SO 4). There also remains a need to streamline the application forms. There is common agreement between the ROs and the local authorities about this point.

An authority even insists that contrary to RO/EA claims, these administrative aspects have become progressively worse: "This too is becoming a heavier burden. They get longer every year. The last form I received was 20 pages long!" (NS 4). At least there is a realization that: "... all their administrative procedures are necessary, however, they still get on our nerves, for example, when they change Form A and we have to complete it again. There is also the 'pedantics of the statistics' where they often request very exact measurements which are time-consuming" (DP/MW 1). Then again others believe that: "This is no more difficult for us than forming HIPs submissions. We do not see this as being an EA problem - its very much at the local authorities' door" (PW 2), since authorities should collate management statistics to analyze performance.

A whole spectrum of opinion is obtained on the nature of EA criteria: "The criteria are still a bit blurred. They [EA/ROs] are trying to be more hard-line, but even during our meetings they are only prepared to say that anything would be considered. They do not tell us what we should not bid for and the schemes are rejected. I guess this is because they never know if they will get sufficient schemes and need the uncertainty to mop-up the rest of their allocation" (SR 3). This vagueness naturally raises difficulties: "This causes a problem, especially if they spring it upon you without warning ... The biggest change has been the reduction of EA funding from 100%; to 75%; to the current 50% threshold ... perhaps some warning [of changes] would have been valid" (PW 2).

On the positive side and in support of the ROs views regarding changes to EA criteria (see also chapter 7): "... this element has improved. Their publicity has got better" (NS 1). There is also the view that: "This has not been too problematic. I submitted a Form A this year but by then the Ministerial Guide-lines had already been published so I can't quibble. We knew about the emphasis on employment and we are in partnership with PEP who emphasize local management. The fact that PEP advises us ... has been additionally helpful in focusing our bids" (PW 4). More could still be done to reduce this uncertainty, perhaps along the lines proposed in chapter 6, namely a DoE letter specifying exactly what will be approved, although this too has its disadvantages in terms of affecting flexibility.

8.4.4 Tenant consultation

In contradiction to the survey results, all four maintain that rigorous tenant consultation exercises had been carried out before submission of Form A bids, however, upon close examination, the evidence is that these have all been carried out *independently* and *irrespective* of EA. It was clearly not because EA was forcing authorities to be more rigorous in their attitude to consultation that this took place. Moreover, there is as previously discussed, some argument as to whether EA's present structure actually *hinders* efficiency in consultation (as discussed in chapters 5, 6 and 7). Some relevant quotations illustrate these points: "The consultation process involved a survey which identified the key priorities for the residents, then a series of public meetings which the Director and other departments attended and finally, the project co-ordinator undertook consultative exercises block by block. However, all this occurred *before* EA came along and the authority decided to bid for their resources" (SJ 4, Emphasis Added). A second comment likewise highlights the difficulties arising from the current EA structure: "We are aware that EA tries to promote this, however, there was no tenant consultation involved in submitting the bid at Form A stage. This was partly because the GLC had itself conducted a large campaign of tenant consultation ... the bid was also fairly speculative so there was no point in doing it; and lastly, EA left us little time in which to perform this. We received the invitation to submit bids in February and it had to be in by March" (MU/SR 3). This confirms the survey findings that few (31%) indicated that EA involvement had resulted in greater tenant consultation.

Very little change was made to the schemes at Form B, except where a 'design day' was held for the various proposals' (LA 1); and where the costs were revised but not the scheme itself (LA 4). The reason why so little change actually occurred at this stage can be understood from another quotation which also sheds light on the limited on-going consultation: "Once we are informed that we have got through to the next stage [Form B], we must then 'go to tender'. This is a problem because the timescale involved is very short. Tenants could not make any changes to the scheme ... otherwise tenant consultation exercises would have been mounted" (MU/SR 3).

These point to a contradiction within the research. On the one hand, the survey results indicate that most of the consultation actually occurs at Form B stage (as per chapters 5 and 6), yet the case-study results indicate that little consultation actually occurs at this stage. This probably reflects the choice of case-study authorities and schemes - all of which date back to EA's first year. All the case-studies formed part of the original batch of EA bids and were all top priorities for the councils involved. As such, they were likely to have been well research, planned and their tenants well consulted, but this would have occurred *prior* to the formation of EA. Such schemes would be exhausted in later years and consultation would have to occur within the EA-defined timespan, thus leading to the situation revealed in the survey results - the problems / solutions may have been less well researched subsequently.

Despite *some* RO and Central opinions to the contrary, the local authorities perceive that this issue has *not* improved significantly: "This is a major problem. We have tried to avoid raising expectations too highly, while at the same time keeping the tenants informed about the state of the bid" (SO 4). The result is that: "We still manage to consult at an early stage but it is becoming more difficult ... so we agree on the broad details but on smaller issues, we simply have to go ahead without necessarily consulting the tenants. This is happening increasingly ... Things would improve if the authority had the ability to work-up the schemes in advance of EA invitation and hold them on the 'shelf'. This is not possible for us" (NS 1), primarily because of the pressure of the work-load and the lack of spare capacity.

Even if tenant consultation occurs at Form B, this will not necessarily be adequate: "... Tenant consultation is extremely tentative and needs to be qualified to the tenants. There is undoubtedly an element of raising the tenants' expectations - perhaps falsely. This also happens on our own capital programmes but the difference is that EA gives a very high profile to tenant consultation ... [which] is neither better nor more effective under

EA" (SR 3). Another view corroborating the survey results was aired: "We have definitely had greater tenant consultation in these schemes although this is partly because all of them have been so major ... I would not say that it is because of Estate Action" (PW 2).

8.4.5 EA's influence in 'shaping' schemes

There was variable EA/RO involvement in the case-studies. In one case the RO was fairly instrumental: "... there was a great deal of discussion with the DoE and the former estate co-ordinator built a close relation with the Manchester RO as well as the national office. There were about 20 visits by various DoE officials which must have influenced the final form of the scheme" (SO 3). This was important but more limited in another case-study: "We have a very good working relationship with the RO ... [But] It is important to point out that the council was quite advanced in its plans *before* EA/UHRU came along and our schemes fell into its remit. This is why we've done very well out of the initiative. In actual fact it was EA that approached us and the Regional Office played its part in steering them towards us, and us towards EA. However, our ideas were *not* stimulated by EA" (PW 4, Original Emphasis).

By contrast, DoE influence was less significant in the other authorities, merely involving visits at a late stage. The nature of the relationship has evolved and many authorities now maintain a more or less continuous dialogue with the ROs in order to 'sift out' many of the unworkable schemes unofficially before too much work and effort is expended. This is a welcome development which will grow in importance with further moves towards decentralization and larger EA schemes.

The authorities generally discern that the ROs have been forceful in securing successful bids for them at Form B stage: "The RO was quite influential in enabling us to obtain the funding. They gave us helpful suggestions about how to complete the bid and make it look good to Estate Action" (TS 1). A similar view is held in the Conservative-controlled authority as discussed above. However, a different sort of argument also comes through: "The RO is in a strong position at this stage and we went to various meetings ... the DoE [then] sent us a 'special' form asking all sorts of questions. Therefore, we felt that we were constantly having to go through a series of hoops - the case for investment stood for itself without the need for further elaboration." (MU/SR 3) Inevitably there is no simple relationship - it varies between regions, authorities, schemes and officers.

8.4.6 Other procedural factors

i) The Committee Stage and tender documentation: Proposals involving major capital works must first be approved by the appropriate councilors but according to the interviews, nothing unusual occurs at the Committee approval stage: "The tender process is no different from other schemes" (SO 4), and it seems that: "It simply goes through the normal committee cycle" (NS 1). Special problems still can present themselves: "In large, multimillion pound schemes, a bill of quantity is necessary; as are tender documents and negotiations with contractors. Within the space of about a month we have to make a judgement about the likely costs. There could be problems involved if the DoE pushes us to get the work done in a short period of time. This may for example, contribute to an increase in costs" (MU/SR 3). More typically: "The process is very much council-led ... We invited ten developers to listen to our proposals for the concept of the joint venture and to submit tenders ... [regarding] how much it would cost to refurbish our half and what they would offer us for selling them the other half. When the tenders came back ... the design was finalized, [and] the rehousing of tenants began." (PW 2). Two officers note that there was a 'strong correlation' between the location of EA schemes and the ward of their Chair of Housing. No comment can be made on this point here.

ii) Staff/Employment issues: Complications arising from new employment and/or changed job descriptions were minor. No one was made redundant because the EA schemes either involved transfers of staff or new appointments which the unions were satisfied with. The main changes occurred in the estate based management scheme where: "I don't recall there being any difficulties in negotiating with the unions as most of the posts were created anew. Some clerical staff were 'volunteered' for the local office. The whole staff issue was eased by an understanding that people could go back [to the central office] after 12 months if they did not like it." (SO 4) In general terms there was the feeling that: "The most difficult aspect is the CRS because it has to link with Employment Training. It is very hard to work with and involves a number of different agents: the ROs, EA and the Training Commission [now the Training and Enterprise Councils] and they do not always talk to each other" (SL 4). This quotation refers to a difficulty in co-ordinating various agencies and bodes ill for EA's new emphasis on 'flagship' initiatives. Success depends on strong links developing between all these agencies.

iii) Problems specific to management structures: Only the decentralized authority noted potential implementation difficulties arising from its present management arrangements: "Perhaps additional difficulties are created by the fact that we have a neighbourhood structure. We do not have a corporate housing strategy and each Neighbourhood Office is free to decide its programme. Only the Housing Committee has control over the types of bids made to EA and it is unlikely to reject the proposals submitted by the Neighbourhood Offices. The disadvantages of this situation outweigh the advantages. They can't afford to underspend; ... their capital allocations are relatively small, [and] it could discourage the Neighbourhoods from undertaking large-scale schemes; and there is also the temptation to over-programme capital commitments. This means that many Form As are sent out which we know will not get EA approval. However, in fairness, we have managed to get a lot of schemes approved which do not fit EA criteria" (SR 3). On the other hand, decentralizing authorities may benefit by bidding for estate based schemes, thus using EA to 'subsidize' their housing strategies.

iv) The EA co-ordinators' influence and capitalising upon EA: An attempt was made to elucidate the degree of influence wielded by housing officers closely involved with the EA initiative regarding for example, the selection of estates, types of initiatives and sway over councilors. In actual fact the officers felt that their influence by virtue of their familiarity with the initiative, was marginal. The types of scheme and estate are pre-defined: "In selecting estates, we looked at the Ministerial Guide-lines and at ways of putting schemes into EA's rubric and objectives" (SO 4), besides which, their authorities' priorities are normally self-evident: "The schemes we submit are those that demonstrate the greatest need. Neither have we had to look for schemes to 'fit' the EA bill because there isn't a shortage of these. I have only been influential in deciding the best way to present bids to EA and eliminating those elements I know will not be funded" (PW 2).

The survey results suggest that authorities have used EA to establish predominantly such schemes as were *acceptable* to themselves and which *conformed* to their policies. Such a view is fully supported in the case-studies: "The authority has only done what was palatable to itself. This has been easy because we were decentralizing and largely pursuing the same changes as EA was trying to promote. It was also the fact that the DoE was offering us some cash to do the things that a shrinking HIPs wouldn't allow us to" (NS 1). Another typical quotation is that: "Some of our schemes have been little more than straight-forward refurbishment [namely,] just putting things together to fit the bill. We just wanted the cash, so we do use EA to some extent by twisting things slightly ... We have simply told them what they wanted to hear" (PW 2). Other authorities were defensive: "We have not 'manipulated' EA! We have merely submitted our bids - they always had the option of rejecting them" (SR 3). Another preferred to put it slightly differently, "Yes, there is an element of what I would call 'capitalising' upon what EA is trying to do" (SO 4). All this forms part of the housing 'game'.

The benefits can cut both ways. An officer implied that his authority had become more receptive to certain types of initiative as a result of its involvement with EA: "We have pursued some ideas with EA's criteria in mind. For example, we were prepared to go ahead with a housing co-operative because we knew that it was likely that we'd receive an allocation. Perhaps we would not have been so open-minded if EA was not around" (PW 2). These quotations suggest that although in the majority of cases, authorities are using EA resources to fund projects which they suggest they would have themselves carried out, there have been instances where EA has been influential in changing the agenda or increasing the options available to councils. This issue is analyzed in detail in below.

8.5 Financial effectiveness at the micro/authority level

As discussed earlier, the notion of financial effectiveness is used here simply to examine the extent to which EA is perceived to be using the EA HIPs targeted resources competently. EA HIPs represent specific allocations of resources which are directed by central government at perceived problems in this case, the most problem prone public housing estates. This involves the creation and operation of a different financial mechanism from the 'traditional' HIPs. Previous work has demonstrated that EA resources are achieving positive outcomes, however, that is not the same as suggesting that those resources are being utilized effectively.

Chapter 5 illustrated the argument that problems seem to exist with the 'targeted' mechanism of allocating resources. The Regional Offices confirm this but the EA Central team argues that the problems have been overcome. This section analyses the extent to which this is truly the case by discussing whether targeting works against local discretion; the effects of continuation funding upon local capital programming; the difficulties that may arise as a result of delayed notification by EA of scheme approval; whether authorities should have to contribute to the schemes; and concludes with some speculations on the likely effects of the latest Housing Act on the financial operation of the initiative.

8.5.1 Targeting: Central control and local discretion

All four authorities insisted that: "The resources are definitely topsliced and it definitely increases central control" (TP 1). This was rather taken for granted and the individuals interviewed were more concerned to discuss what they considered to be the real issue: "It does not matter whether EA HIPs [funds] are topsliced. What is certain is that EA does not compensate for the cash that has been whittled away in the last decade or so. Where they have got the resources from is an irrelevance" (PW 2).

There is in fact, a degree of self-interest in maintaining the *status quo* for the fortunate few: "We've managed to get £10m from EA HIPs ... we don't want to be too critical. We would never have got nearly as much from the HIPs mechanism." (SR 3). For another authority that normally receives very little under HIPs, EA has been a godsend: "... the authorities' particular needs are their worst estates, nevertheless, they are miffed about the fact that the resources get topsliced. For us it is the *only* way to put together a housing package and programm e" (SJ 4, Emphasis Added). Clearly there are advantages to this instrument of spatial targeting over and above those discussed earlier in the chapter, where positive developments are occurring.

Despite the fact that the clock cannot be turned back, some authorities prefer the HIPs system of capital allocation to targeted EA HIPs because: "There is no doubt that it is much easier to plan the housing programme via the HIPs mechanism" (PW 2). A further observation illustrates why authorities are so concerned about targeted mechanisms of capital allocation: "HIPs carry permission to spend and leaves authorities free to decide how to use these. EA HIPs is completely different. There is much less flexibility and the DoE gains control over part of the capital programme. There is also the administration necessary and the inconvenience of the annual process. HIPs comes in December. EA HIPs may come at any time and because of its timetable, is an inflexible and unpredictable system" (SR 3).

It is not just a matter of inconvenience and cost. It is also an issue about control and decision-making in council housing programmes. A contrast to the opinions discussed above is offered by admittedly, a small authority with only one scheme to plan and programme: "It is not too much of a problem because you can predict when you will receive the final approval from EA and simply fit it into the programming cycle. This is aided by the fact that the ROs are becoming more free at telling you the allocation you are likely to obtain in advance ... but the official letters are woefully slow in arriving" (SJ 4), so it too experiences certain difficulties.

8.5.2 The effect of EA HIPs on rolling capital programmes

EA operates on an annual basis. According to the case-studies difficulties arise because it: "... allocates on a very different basis [to HIPs] - allocations are for specific projects. Each neighbourhood must decide how it wants to use its HIPs resources. In the case of EA bids, however, they must programme on the *assumption* that they will receive additional borrowing approvals. We recommend that they work on schemes which will go though in the main programme anyway, if EA backing falls through" (SR 3), thus recouping what would otherwise be lost investment. Another officer states that there is little doubt that: "The fact that EA operates annually can be disruptive of that [housing] plan. It is a very, very unsatisfactory way of programming a capital strategy. It's bad enough trying to figure out what the reduction in HIPs allocation is going to be" (SR 3). Despite the difficulties that can arise, not all authorities feel it to be a huge disadvantage: "It is only a minor problem - the programming in particular is short term ... but in general the [two] systems are not so different in terms of the programming" (SJ 4).

There are indications that authorities concur with suggestions by both EA Central and the ROs (in chapter 7) that things are improving: "In terms of the procedures, there have been improvements with Form A dates being moved forward to approximately the same time as the other allocations. However, it is still taking EA much too long to process the bids, especially the continuation funding bids" (PW 2). Another officer agrees, illustrating the remaining problems: "While this will help planning and programming, it would be better if there was some degree of certainty. The potential for much abortive work would be controlled if uncertainty was removed. We have experienced severe delays in the past because it has taken them [EA] so long to process Forms B. It means that the tender documents have expired and we've either had to re-tender or renegotiate, usually at higher prices ... it would be better if we had a three year rolling capital programme ... We operate on 'guesstimates' but even then, a pattern does not exist for EA HIPs as it does for HIPs" (SR 3). Problems remain which must be overcome in order to improve the operation of the initiative.

8.5.3 Continuation funding

The lack of guarantees of EA funding for schemes in subsequent years and phases is also regarded as being as much of a problem as suggested by the survey results: "We simply do not have the resources to carry schemes forward on our own. This means that we have to trust EA to approve the continuation funding ... We do not hold back uncommitted resources until we have received final approval ... This would be impractical and might result in underspending" (PW 2). A suggestion is made about how to improve this: "... ROs have on occasion given us a letter which indicates the level of continuation funding to be expected. This should be a more common practice - EA could qualify it by saying: 'subject to further allocations from the Treasury' or whatever else it likes but at least there would be a little more certainty for authorities" (SR 3). If such a letter, (with the appropriate caveats) could help, then perhaps this should be instituted.

Authorities are prepared to make serious representations if the DoE were to simply refuse them continuation funding: "I am sure that the council would not pick-up the 'tab' if continuation approval did not come through. There could be severe repercussions but the DoE simply tells us not to worry" (SJ 4). The likely course of action would probably be that: "We would start by making some sort of representation to the DoE ... As to whether there would be any problems, that would depend on how the capital programme stood. Schemes might have to be shelved or delayed" (SR 3). But in fairness: "... they have always come forward with the allocations and even provided written statements more or less to the effect" (TP 1); and there is a determination that in future, "... we have to tie down EA into giving an indication of the likely level of continuation fun ding" (SR 3). This appears to be a wise course of action since 24.5% authorities surveyed suggest that on certain occasions, continuation funding was *not* obtained from EA (see chapter 5 for further details).

8.5.4 Difficulties arising from late approval

The experience of local authorities varies but all four acknowledged a degree of EA HIPs underspend. As discussed previously, in some ways this is inevitable - the important issue is to what extent this occurs because of the manner in which EA operates. Experience varies from: "We do not underspend significantly - last year 97% of the allocation was spent ... it is not unusual for the balance to be slightly out" (SO 4), to: "We've had lots of problems but we've always managed to get around them by carrying the allocation forward ... The real problem is in the form of a loss of credibility with the tenants. It is a stupid way of doing things and as schemes become larger in size and scope [as is expected], so will bigger problems be presented to authorities and EA" (NS 1).

Underspend as a result of late notification of approval by the DoE is reconfirmed as a serious problem at the locality. The following quotation captures the dilemma: "The level of allocation must be tied very closely to what we can spend [this estimate can be seriously flawed because of delays], otherwise we run out of time. The contractors also have to gear themselves up. When we submit Form Bs, we must have a quick response partly because tenders are only valid for a period of about 13 weeks. If anything goes wrong, we may have to go through the whole process again or to renegotiate the costs. In principle the EA allocation is not tied specifically to a scheme and as a result of delays, we may use the allocation to supplement mainstream HIPs. Although we may benefit from undertaking other schemes we must finish the original EA scheme from our own resources the following year. No additional allocation is made by EA" (SR 3). Ear-marked resources must then be diverted to meet the EA obligations, which means that programmed schemes may have to be delayed or scrapped.

One authority was very pragmatic in its attitude to the above: "... in order to avoid underspend, we may not accept all the allocation offered by EA. Another way to cope is to pay the staff overtime to put the programme together and get the work done in the time available. A last method is to simply have schemes on the 'shelf' which can be pulled out and slotted in ... [but] the best thing to do is only to accept the level of allocation which we can spend in the time remaining ... If we were to underspend, then such schemes have first call on the next year's programme but ... Normally we are able to accept additional resources when EA underallocates because we can pull out pre-prepared schemes" (SJ 4). This authority is in a fortunate position relative to the others who argue that this is simply not an option available to them because of the lack of spare resources.

Although evidence has been obtained about the problems faced by authorities in using the resources they manage to obtain through EA, the four case-studies echo the survey findings in indicating that they have coped reasonably well: "We have never underspent EA HIPs resources.

We've been on the margins but fortunately we have been able to transfer these bits" (PW 2). The fact that they have to take 'flyers' (by starting schemes prior to receiving EA approval and hope for the best) also helps. Similarly: "On one or two occasions we have had problems with tenders and various procedures but by and large, we have either managed to spend all our EA HIPs or it has been carried forward ... If the amounts involved were substantial and if there was regular underspend, then there would be a problem ... the difficulties would surface the following year" (SR 3). It is obvious that authorities regularly experience difficulties: "To my knowledge, the authority has not underspent although we certainly have adjusted the figures to make it look as if we are on schedule" (SJ 4).

It helps if the financial situation is monitored closely and some forward planning is attempted: "As the end of the financial year approaches, we have two meetings per week to review the performance of contracts ... We do have other proposals ready around January or February which we can use just in case. There is then less adherence to what complies with the council's policy. More important is what 'fits' the spend profile because it is a matter of short-term gain. Councilors sometimes complain about this but this is the practicality of the financial system" (SJ 4). The general attitude is that little can be done to forestall these difficulties but that dialogue helps: "These days there is more contact between authorities and ROs. This is the only way to keep things going, especially towards the end of the financial year. There has been a learning curve for both organizations" (SR 3).

To conclude while the case-study authorities have not underspent wildly, problems still recur and a variety of methods have been devised to 'mop-up' the potential underspend. The danger must be that if schemes become larger in scope as is planned, the authorities' flexibility at the margin will be reduced and that much more resource will be wasted.

8.5.5 The authorities' contribution and revenue costs

An important change in EA policy has been its insistence that authorities must also subsidize schemes from their own resources. Much dismay was recorded about this particular rule: "The contribution expected is onerous [50%] ... A high input is necessary to achieve any sort of result in the estates but if the rule is applied more strictly, schemes will be compromised. Either we'll extend the completion dates by bringing down the size of the phases or by reducing the level of input to something which is affordable to the council. The new emphasis on 'flagship' schemes does not seem to square with this rule, especially as councils continue to be restrained in terms of their capital investment" (TP 1), via the shrinking capital receipts and HIPs allocations. In other words, councils will simply be unable to meet half of the costs of these larger initiatives. This does not appear to have been fully considered by EA Central.

But even for the 'ordinary' schemes, strong views were recorded along the same lines: "Our feeling can be likened to a culture shock ... we were greatly disappointed that this was changed and we had to re-adjust our bids accordingly. This is doubly annoying because the dwindling size of mainstream [HIPs] allocations means that it is very difficult to support our contribution. That is part of the reason why we have had to sell half of the estates in some of our bigger schemes. This rule certainly acts against the generation of bigger schemes" (PW 2). But at least: "The DoE has said that a 50% contribution is the bench-mark figure ... the 50% rule is not a rigid one and its up to the authority to decide whether it can afford it" (SR 3).

Finally the opinions regarding the revenue costs associated with many EA schemes are well summarized in the following quotation: "EA has never covered these costs. It wants greater management presence and localization but it does not want to take account of local authorities' abilities to afford those increased costs. We have been able to open two new area offices through EA, but only by splitting two existing area offices and transferring staff. We have also had to employ extra staff but we have somehow been able to afford the extra costs" (PW 2). For others, the fact that EA refuses to meet any resultant revenue costs: "... is not really a constraint because the council had a policy of decentralizing anyway so it must have felt able to cope with the increased revenue costs" (TP 1). However, EA help with such costs would probably encourage more authorities to experiment and innovate with alternative housing management initiatives such as decentralization.

8.5.6 Speculations on recent financial effects

i) On EA finance: During the final period of research (until January 1990), a great deal of uncertainty surrounded the extent to which the latest legislation would affect EA and how this would be translated into interaction with local authorities: "Nobody really knows but it seems that the DoE will give us an authority-wide annual capital guide-line rather than being merely for housing investment. It will be made up of Basic Credit Approvals [BCAs], capital receipts accumulated and any additional resources will come through Special Credit Approvals [SCAs - as discussed in the financial part of chapter 2]. We should be able to start the year knowing what is the total amount that they will allow us to borrow" (PW 2). Another high level housing officer admits: "I have no idea of the likely impacts of the latest Housing Bill on EA. There were rumours that EA would be abolished because the Treasury was arguing that EA had been designed to get authorities to think about new and alternative management initiatives and that it had gone as far as it could go. However, EA has moved the 'goal-posts' yet again with the introduction of the employment initiatives. The problem is that there will be even more agencies involved and the procedures will become even more complex and cumbersome" (SR 3). This must be an issue which EA Central itself is pondering on.

One officer did have definite views about the likely effects: "Because EA resources will come under the BCA in future, it will become more difficult to programme with confidence. In the past we were able to programme independently of other resources or commitments ... we have been able to develop a model and get a pattern going on its own momentum. With the new system and the likelihood that we will receive substantially less capital allocations, the whole thing is back in the melting pot. Even if we receive EA allocations, the whole process will be much more subject to political involvement and decisions" (TP 1). The main point to come out of the interviews was the *vagueness* and *uncertainty* despite the fact that SCAs and BCAs were about to be introduced.

ii) On EA's timetable: Uncertainty about the changes has also resulted in confusion about the likely impacts on the timetable - a key element behind the current implementation difficulties. One interviewee felt that: "SCAs will force future EA schemes to comply with within-year spend. The emphasis will be on bidding for schemes small enough to be completed within the year. Any schemes which involve longer timescales will fall into the BCAs ... So large scale 'enterprise' schemes will have to be broken into small phases" (TP 1). This would also work to make EA s emphasis on enterprise schemes dubious but more positive consequences were also envisaged: "It should result in a less tight timetable as well as greater scope to plan the initiatives although problems will remain." (PW 2). A further advantage foreseen in contradiction to the above (and which underlines the obvious uncertainty), is that: "Under the new system, the SCAs don't have to be done on an annual basis. If EA was to come under the SCA system, an allocation could be made over two or three years. Such a system would be a lot better" (SR 3).

Other views about the likely future impact include the belief that: "Next year will be EA's test. It may well fold if the enterprise initiative does not work" (SR 3); and another authority felt that: "The government will try anything to undermine local authority control and it is likely that these [topsliced] financial systems will continue to exist. EA may not last much longer but targeting will continue under another banner" (TP 1). What is beyond doubt, is that authorities are very unsure about how the changes will affect their relationship with EA. This is particularly disturbing because the new financial régime was then due to come into effect three months hence. The changes are likely to result in turbulence and yet more underallocation and underspending under the EA programme.

iii) EA in context of recent housing legislation: Suspicions about the government's 'true' motives via EA and its implications for centre-local relations resurface time and again: "EA is a mechanism whereby Government can reduce total expenditure. It can argue that it is not cutting resources - it is 'targeting' them, but this also removes control from local authorities. While targeting does put in more resources these are channelled to the areas which the government sees as requiring them" (PW 2).

EA is additionally regarded as being part of a chaotic but purposeful housing strategy: "EA is about greater control. It is not part of a central government strategy designed in steps and stages. Government housing policy has come together almost by chance. In this sense, EA accidently fits very well with the Housing Act, 1988 which is the clearest expression of government's housing ideology" (LJ/SR 3). This quotation refers to the recent housing legislation discussed in chapter 2 which argues that the government may now have 'de-municipalization' in mind. A more directly critical view is that: "I can't imagine that council housing is being helped in any way by EA. It ... is improving those estates that don't have a 'cat in hell's' chance of being renovated, but EA can also be seen as a central government con. There may be a hidden agenda such as to try to bump-up the 'right to buy'. We always expected the information we provide via EA to be used by the DoE for other purposes, such as to help in the designation of HATs" (DP/MW 1). Deep suspicions continue after five years and stem from a complete absence of consultation at the preliminary stages of the initiative (as identified in the latter part of chapter 4).

iv) Change in emphasis: employment and 'enterprise' initiatives: There were unanimously favourable opinions about the concept of stimulating employment and training opportunities in housing estates: "It represents a recognition that ... the factors which contribute to well-being are broader than the dwellings themselves and include socio-economic factors ... I do not think anyone can quibble with the principle" (PW 2). Likewise: "The basic concept cannot be criticized - simply upgrading the dwellings and environment is not enough. That is merely the tip of the iceberg and we must consider the wider socio-economic issues." (SR 3).

Such views augur well for they fit snugly with those expressed by both EA Central and the ROs (chapter 7), but they also point to what some suspect the government may have been hoping for: "The problem arises if gaps are left between the good estates and the 'flagship' estates. There is a potential for even greater physical deprivation to occur. Herein lies the link with the Housing Act, 1988. If councils do not sort these out, the tenants in the intermediary estates will simply buy their own properties or get themselves a different landlord. The government *did* have a clear strategy in mind for council housing. In the beginning there were calls for a need to restrain public expenditure; then cuts in HIPs; then the 'right to buy'. Shelter is a basic need and the government could not overtly and speedily attack it as it would not have been politically acceptable. Nowadays they just build upon the councils' poor image and let them take the blame." (PW 2). Such deep-felt mistrust of government policy and where EA fits into that, is widespread among the housing officers interviewed at all levels of the hierarchy.

The second issue relates to whether authorities feel that such an emphasis on enterprise schemes is viable. The qualified optimists suggest that: "It is workable. I do not see any reason why we cannot work with the various other local and central departments if there is support for it at the highest levels of the authority" (SL 4) and secondly, that: "I suspect it will not be too difficult to get these up and running but the failure rates will be high" (DP/MW 1). The others did anticipate problems in implementing 'flagship' schemes: "The mechanics of the idea have not been thought through properly, such as how to combine the employment and training elements with the capital works issues ... Its good if you can set up some shops on these estates thus providing the opportunity for some training but what happens when the scheme is completed? What about their wages and conditions? There are a number of other problems such as the number of agents involved, the various council departments as well as the civil service. There will be an additional layer of bureaucracy' (LJ/SR 3).

It is clear from this research that effective interaction between EA, the ROs, the local authorities and the tenants is difficult enough to generate. To introduce additional institutions (such as the Training and Enterprise Councils) and central departments (such as the Department of Employment and the Department of Education and Science), will be an extremely difficult undertaking which will require exceptional goodwill and co-operation on all sides and at all levels. Unfortunately these organization tend to be known less for their collaboration and more for their intense desire to protect their policy 'turf'.

A host of other factors bearing upon the success or otherwise, of the new emphasis can be identified: "EA is going to be hoist by its own petard. Its timetable and spending arrangements are far from perfect but authorities move their sums around and make the thing work. However, if we are talking about large sums such as £3m or more, if one does not get the whole scheme right, it can result in very serious problems indeed ... The crucial point is whether authorities will be prepared to risk so much if there are no guarantees of funding or of continuation funding. Larger, complicated bids will only be submitted if the authority is certain of the value of the initiative and that it will fund the initiative from mainstream HIPs if EA was to reject them" (LJ/SR 3). Nevertheless recognizing a need to become involved in issues other than housing is an important first step, but one which brings an awareness that there are even wider considerations which should be addressed more fully than has been the case thus far.

v) EA's prospective medium-term: Some interviewees were optimistic, if somewhat cynical about the future of the initiative: "EA is going to be around for a while because of the element of central control it gives the government and because it has had some success. It represents a very obvious return on the government's investment. When the DoE takes the ministers around the estates and shows them the effects, it is easy for ministers to be impressed and thus to want to keep supporting EA" (SL 4). In an analogous vein: "Let's face it, ministers are only interested in those things which they can be associated with and can present to the press and public. That is exactly what these 'flagship' schemes are about. That is the way its [EA] going in the future and thus will survive a bit longer" (PW 2).

In terms of government policy, EA can be seen in a interesting way: "Coercion on the part of the government is one of the important reasons why HATs have been unsuccessful. EA's emphasis of flagship initiatives will have exactly the same effect - it will concentrate resources and deal with the wider socio-economic issues as HATs were envisaged to. The difference is that it will not be as intrusive and coercive" (PW 2). Inevitably there is another view which springs from a conviction that EA has not fully met government objectives (as suggested in chapter 6): "At some point the Treasury is going to ask if EA is good value for money and it will 'get the chop' because housing as an issue has gone 'off the boil' in governmental terms, as witnessed in the last election. Unfortunately, housing was not much discussed in either the Labour or Conservative manifestos" (DP/MW 1). This echoes the civil servants' views (in chapter 7) in fearing that central government's concern is rapidly drifting away from housing. The latest information is that when Michael Heseltine came back to the DoE, the EA initiative has been given a further boost.

8.6 Policy effectiveness: The results of partnership

It was argued earlier in the chapter that it is not sufficient to analyze EA in terms of the official's (and to a lesser extent, tenants') views on the effectiveness of EA schemes in their authorities. One must also analyze the effectiveness of EA's procedures and financial mechanisms. This chapter has now done so, however, it remains to draw out the degree to which EA had been influential to local housing authorities in wider, policy respects. Accordingly a variety of issues are discussed to ascertain the ways in which involvement with EA may have had 'knock-on' effects in terms of the authorities' attitudes to housing management, difficult-to-let estates and general housing policy.

The discussion begins by assessing just how important EA HIPs resources have become to local authorities; goes on to discuss the extent to which EA has helped achieve stated government policy for housing authorities; how much council attitudes to difficult-to-let estates have changed; why the government has been so keen on creating other specific schemes similar to EA; and whether, thorough the EA programme housing aid is really targeted at the areas most in need of them.

8.6.1 Impact of EA resources: Collaboration and significance

All authorities made it abundantly clear that resources figured prominently in their relationship with EA: "Our HIPs allocation was very low and the authority was not earning very much out of capital receipts so the idea was to obtain additional resources in order to fulfil our own policies. EA was always seen as an additional source of funding" (LJ/SR 3). Housing executives in two other authorities aired similar views but the next quotation illustrates EA's importance in a wider context: "In our case it was both the fact that additional resources were available and the fact that we were trying to develop a 'package' for our estates. EA provided us with a vehicle to push forward with our plans. Our own housing investment was decreasing so we were seeking to obtain additional finance to keep our management impetus going." (DP/MW 1)

When asked whether it was the resources that had convinced firstly, the Housing Department and secondly, the local politicians to become involved in EA, one authority contained itself to stating: "Yes on both counts" (SL 4). Others preferred to expand on their initial attitudes to EA: "In the early days of UHRU, there was a view among local authorities that its primary purpose was to privatize estates. In some ways, our proposal was to test the DoE and to see if they were serious about renovating estates, as opposed to selling them off ... We are a small, pragmatic Labour council. If someone offers cash which will benefit the tenants we will go for it" (PW 2). A parallel view was that: "Councilors didn't need much convincing. They saw it as another pot they could dip into ... there was no disagreement between Labour and the Liberals over the desirability of estate based management ... we were lucky that we had already begun to decentralize ... Our members never saw it as anything more than an additional source of cash. We've had an element of decentralization to our [EA] schemes but this has been coincidental - this is what the authority was trying to do anyway" (LJ/SR 3).

EA's significance to authorities cannot be overstated - the value of EA HIPs as a proportion of mainstream HIPs (excluding capital receipts), ranged from 20% to about 160%. The following quotation suffices in demonstrating the increasing importance of EA HIPs: "Absolutely crucial! In the first year the value of EA HIPs was £4.5m which is equivalent to 25% of the HIPs. This year we expect to receive 50% of our investment from this source [1989-90: £4.5m EA HIPs / £8.17m HIPs]. This excludes a further £9m in capital receipts, which would mean that EA HIPs constitutes approximately a quarter of all the potential capital investment" (PW 2). The other issue of course, is that it also *concentrates* resources: "We would not have had the cash to put into these estates and certainly not at the same level. If we had gone ahead on our own, the estates would not have looked very different or special because of the usual conflict over resources. The advantage of the EA system is that its resources are sacrosanct to that particular project" (TP 1). Further advantages are clearly that such funding is scheme-specific *and* free of the usual political conflicts.

An issue worth further investigation is the extent to which EA involvement has skewed investment in favour of certain areas or estates. One officer insists that: "The proportion of capital resource spent on such estates has not swung towards difficult-to-let estates. The bulk of the investment is going to post-WW1 properties which are highly desirable and much sought-after" (DP/MW 1) but the majority did feel that: "The proportion has to have increased ..., however, this is due to the way problems have arisen rather than because of EA itself. If we had the same real levels of funding as in 1979, then the proportion going into such areas would have been the same" (PW 2). The fourth case-study with its particular background, does indicate that now: "A much greater proportion of resources go to these estates" (SL 4). When all the 'ifs' and 'buts' are removed, it must be the case that more investment (as a proportion) is now finding its way into these sections of council housing. That is without doubt part of what EA was supposed to achieve.

8.6.2 EA's impact in achieving government policy

i) The clarity of EA's policy statement: This section tries to gauge the degree to which EA's objectives were clear to local authorities when it was launched. Two interviewees indicated that they were very uncertain: "Not many people claim to know what EA was exactly about. There was a belief that it was about selling estates. It has not turned out that way. In the first year, it was fishing about for schemes to spend on" (PW 2), and also: "There was quite a lot of ambiguity surrounding EA. We didn't quite appreciate how it fitted into their [Conservatives'] policy to de-municipalization. While it was seen as another form of central control, it was not recognised in its wider context. It has become another instrument of fulfilling Tory ideology. The Treasury has now forced them [EA] to move forward with sales and disposals and to begin to achieve what it is supposed to be about" (LJ/SR 3). A third authority did not experience difficulties over the clarity of the policy but acknowledges its debt to other organizations: "The philosophy has been quite clear - their approach has varied according to the differing circumstances, as they had stated. Things have been facilitated by the back-up we have had in particular from PEP and our Regional Office which have been very supportive" (SL 4). Clearly, not all housing authorities flounder in confusion but a little 'steering' does seem to help, particularly where the concepts are untried.

ii) Influencing attitudes to the value of management: Three authorities were concerned to make the point that in their case, an emphasis on management had already begun to occur independently of EA. Where EA has been positive is in extending the process: "EA has enabled us to decentralize even further ... What is important is that it has given us the financial opportunity to pursue our plans and policies" (PW 2). The fourth authority also acknowledges EA's positive influence in this respect: "EA has been a strong incentive for us ... The principle of decentralization had been debated but it is the availability of resources that actually makes you get on with it. Because the scheme has been successful and promoted tenant consultation, the point has been made to both officers and councilors that tenant involvement can be made to work successfully." (PL 4). The EA Unit has been useful in this respect and not purely in facilitating matters financially.

iii) Influencing the predisposition to private sector involvement: It is significant to note that no single officer now expresses vehement opposition to the principle of private sector involvement and disposal of council housing or land. An attitude of pragmatism seems to have developed as exemplified by one of the Labour-controlled authorities: "We do not plan to dispose of our stock. That is basically against the members' view but we have been pragmatic. The units which we have sold have been genuinely surplus to our needs. Except for 43 units, all have been family flats, the least popular and least in demand by our tenants. We do this as a last resort" (SL 2), and manage to obtain significant EA backing as a bonus. The SDP/Liberal controlled council made a point of stressing that it had been pursuing this option *independently* of EA: "... private sector involvement has been going on for some time, prior even to the change in balance of local political control towards the Liberals ... As councils are pressed [financially], this is an option which we had to explore. We are currently negotiating the transfer of a set of empty dwellings to Housing Associations." (LJ/SR 3)

But an awareness that such deals are much harder to organize than expected is reinforced by the authority that on the face of it, would be the most likely to pursue this option to the fullest: "Our experience has demonstrated how difficult it is to try to involve the private sector. Even the DoE has accepted that this has failed. The market is flat and its very difficult to get it going. Nothing works" (SL 4). He is not the only person have arrived at this conclusion (see preceding chapter regarding Sir George Young's disappointment with the lack of progress with privatization).

iv) Undermining council housing policy? The themes of 'pragmatism and realism' recur in authorities' responses regarding whether EA involvement erodes or enhances wider housing policy. On one hand there is the belief that: "EA does not undermine our housing programme at all, in the sense that we have not been forced to do anything which we did not want to ... We have not had to compromise except to an insignificant extent." (LJ/SR 3). Others were less enthusiastic: "It may mean that we invest in areas which are not our own highest priorities. We face the choice of either doing something or nothing at all. EA may not be achieving its aim of targeting resources onto the worst estates but this is be academic since estates suffer from different things anyway" (DP/MW 1). This underpins the observations obtained in the survey about resources not necessarily being used where authorities, given the choice, would have invested them (chapter 5).

The 'love/hate' relationship between authorities of all types and EA is neatly encapsulated by the following quotation: "If we had not had EA moneys we would have had to continue with properties which were unpopular, standing empty or not meeting housing need ... Refurbishing those units means that we have retained income for the city as a whole, through rents and rates. There have also been spill-over effects. These developments have helped bring-up the whole area by pulling in additional housing investment together with other things such as office development. However, it must be stated that if we had equivalent resources in basic HIPs, we would have done exactly the same thing ... These were all developments which the council was prepared to undertake prior to the creation of UHRU" (PW 2). The above two paragraphs illustrate EA's difficult position. Authorities do not give it credit for positive developments because most believe that these developments would have occurred anyway; would have been done elsewhere; or would have been undertaken more effectively without EA involvement.

In all the case-studies there was the impression that authorities *tolerate* EA: "There is no doubt that EA has helped to deliver what the tenants want in particular estates. If we had sufficient resource we would have done the whole of the areas. As it is, we now have to sell about 50% of the estates to meet our contributions. On the other hand, without EA we may well have had to sell them entirely!" (PW 2) But to conclude, there seems to be a threshold beyond which the advantages of partnership may evaporate: "Overall, EA has been positive in our estates in terms of the environmental issues and the facilities ... because it has created more housing finance and helped get additional works done. However, now that authorities have to contribute a proportion of the allocation from their own HIPs, our relationship with EA must be reappraised. If our top priorities are compromised or delayed while we must also contribute financially, then this is a penalty and a judgement must be made about whether it is worthwhile continuing to participate in EA" (DP/MW 1). There also remains the feeling that: "There is an element of tokenism about it. It can attract attention away from the housing under-investment which is apparent in all sectors of the [housing] stock." (SL 4)

v) Overall effect on authorities: In terms of an authority-wide perspective on EA, there is common agreement that it has been positive overall: "Many of our tenants are now living in improved dwellings and environments. It has halted the slide into the trough and even helped reverse the decline of certain areas ... Both the security and the image of the places have also improved" (NS 1). Moreover: "We have been able to refurbish estates which we would not otherwise have been able to and it has allowed us to do the things which we'd never had the money for before, such as establishing two additional area offices" (PW 2). Lastly there is the view that: "The experience ... has been obviously constructive because the authority has been able to capitalise on EA funding ... Obviously, it has also allowed improvements to the houses, the environment and established local management facilities" (SO 4).

But there are also perspectives about the negative side of involvement with EA. At one extreme there is the following opinion: "There has been little that I consider negative other than that there is not enough of it [EA HIPs]. There are all sorts of other works which are necessary and EA involvement does not necessarily result in the comprehensive improvement of the area or estate" (SO 4). The intermediate level of criticism is: "We need to get away from the annual financial cycle, EA is becoming more tight-fisted over time and environmental issues are now being neglected" (NS 1), and at the most extreme level, there is a sustained critique about the price of EA involvement: "It is yet another way for central government to control local authorities. It is not actually providing more resources on a national scale. It merely redistributes them. It has been very advantageous to us, but not overall. EA is administratively cumbersome and bureaucratic, it does not reflect the need for housing investment, it is a way for the government to promote its own views and ideology and it is also concentrating resources in order to dangle the carrot of the 'right to buy' and 'Pick a Landlord'. Its another instrument aimed at breaking-up 'monolithic' council estates and its main advantage to central government is the element of control which it presents" (SR 3). No doubt many councils can identify experiences which relate to the last quotation but the (somewhat reluctant) general opinion, is that EA has been beneficial to the authorities, estates and the residents. The results of the research certainly uphold such a conclusion.

vi) Impact of schemes and replicability: Despite the confident assertion that the schemes are having propitious impacts on the ground, only one authority actually had instituted any sort of systematic evaluative process to assess the impact of the schemes: "*Capita* are involved in evaluating the schemes ... [and] *Harris* have been commissioned to conduct a 'snapshot' study of the estate. We are also independently monitoring the estate and collecting 'soft' data" (SL 4). Two other authorities were concerned to emphasize that: "We are very pleased with the results ... The residents are also happy but at the end of the day, they are *our* own schemes" (PW 2, Original Emphasis); and similarly: "EA-funded schemes are no different to the others in our authority. They are just an extension of our capital programme" (PL 4). Another point is that: "The other big problem for the authority is now going to be how to keep the momentum going or even how to maintain the improvements because otherwise, with the capital constraints the estates will regress once again" (DP/MW 1). There are no grounds for complacency regarding EA's achievements. It is not certain that resources will be available to maintain the gains.

One authority down-plays the discussion of whether it had plans to build upon the experience of the EA-funded model for the rest of the stock: "The authority is building upon its own experience of decentralization, not upon anything which EA has taught us" (LJ/SR 3). Another did have plans to replicate certain aspects: "The only things we have undertaken which were different or novel, as opposed to things which we were trying anyway, were environmental improvements ... whether these will be built-upon and used elsewhere, ... is difficult to say because there will always be different situations and estates with different lay outs" (DP/MW 1). However, another authority did see much merit in copying the estate based management model: "Yes, we are using essentially the same model. We are also trying to tease out the lessons with which to develop the most appropriate style of management" (SL 4). So EA has also had a degree of influence in this respect. Some authorities are now confident and willing enough to attempt some of the schemes on their own.

8.6.3 Changing attitudes to 'difficult' estates

It has been argued that part of the rationale for conceiving the EA project was the fact that the DoE did not feel that sufficient investment was flowing into certain estates and hence, that there was a need for a 'targeting' mechanism (chapter 4.3iii). One authority agreed partially with such a DoE assessment: "Yes they have [been neglected], but only because there was a lack of resources. The [councilors'] priorities were such that virtually all the allocation went on private sector housing" (SL 4). This points to what all the others also perceive to be at the base of the problem, namely lack of capital.

The other three authorities rejected vigorously the notion that 'problem' estates were previously neglected and chose to attack central government policy instead: "The council spent an incredible amount on maintaining the property. The problem is that it could not keep pace with the investment that was required. This is because of the capital constraints which central government has imposed upon councils. EA has not affected our attitudes - it has just released resources. The government has develop all sorts of other schemes on similar principles which we cannot afford to ignore" (DP/MW 1). One must expect these DoE schemes, such as the Private Sector Renewal and Homeless Initiatives, to also demonstrate some of the problems (and advantages) discussed with respect to EA. Another interviewee stresses that it is quite wrong for the Government to blame Housing Departments: "The problems associated with these estates are not necessarily related to housing. They have wider socio-economic connotations and the DoE cannot argue that we did not put cash into these estates. The problems were then not identifiable to such an extent. We were targeting cash to these areas but it wasn't enough to do what was necessary. We were also squeezed by the cuts in revenue and the change in demand for houses [not flats]" (PW 2).

Naturally different opinions exist regarding whether the initiative (and its objectives and principles) has influenced their stance and behaviour towards 'difficult' estates. Two authorities are in agreement that: "EA has not greatly modified our attitudes to our estates primarily because they were fairly similar anyway, such as an emphasis on the environment " (DP/MW 1). One officer is clear about the value of EA in influencing his authority: "The councilors have seen the benefit of a comprehensive package instead of just capital works, such as security and environmental works" (SL 4), but the larger authorities were convinced that: "We've already done all that EA proposes and we would have done it more comprehensively if more cash had been provided for authorities" (DP/MW 1). Such views are largely supported in another case-study authority: "The council had various aims regarding housing management. It simply lacked the cash to do those things" (PW 2). But the smallest authority viewed this issue as one of the advantages of the initiative: "EA has very definitely forced 'problem' estates, management and new housing management initiatives into the authority's agenda" (SL 4), which must be regarded positively.

8.6.4 Focussing resources to where they are most needed?

i) The popularity of targeting: Central control? Suspicions abound as regards the DoE's keenness to target a greater proportion of capital allocations: "Apart from the underlying political motives, it is an attempt to undermine the public rented stock. Nobody would consider buying our estates until we have carried out the EA-funded types of work" (TP 1). Another view much in currency is that: "This is all to do with control and centralization. Many powerful central mechanisms have now been removed [eg. various housing subsidies]. EA is one means of attempting to bring that back and to reassert central control" (PW 2).

There is also the opinion that targeting is all about tokenism along with control: "The government must maintain political credibility and if these [schemes] work, it can say that it is doing something [about those Inner Cities]. On the other hand, if authorities do not respond, central government can always argue that it is the authorities' fault. In principle EA is a laudable idea ... [but] The government is trying to give the impression that it is doing something, whereas it is actually offering 'small beer' ... EA is part of an approach to target resources into specific areas. However, the question is whether it is intended just to 'do up' estates or whether it is to 'set them up' by making them more financially attractive for third parties and for tenants to exercise their latest powers ... via EA, the government is dictating to us what we can spend our capital resources on" (SR 3). A whole gamut of fears are expressed in the quotation above and one officer also retorted, regarding EA's primary focus: "I firmly believe that EA exists because it allows the government to decide which authorities and which schemes get resources, as well as how much and how it should be spent. If you do not 'play ball', you lose resources. Its all about central government wanting to control what councils do *and* how they do it!" (DP/MW 1, Original Emphasis). There is little need to elaborate on these points.

Positive views also exists as to the government's concern with targeted resources: "Everyone suffers from reduced resources but it provides the incentive for most councils to actually do something. If it wasn't for this method, they would simply carry on as they have done for years and years" (SJ 4). A very high degree of consensus does exits, regardless of political background, about the main reason why EA's resources have been increasing in the recent past and what the government is hoping to achieve through EA. The key question is whether EA is motivated mainly by political or managerial considerations. There are as many views as there are case-studies. None is particularly complimentary to EA:

• the *'conspiracy'* view: "EA resources are simply increasing because the scheme allows them [central government] to target capital funds to where they want them to go. It takes discretion away from authorities and enables central government to manipulate things and pick and choose the authorities, towns, estates and schemes they like." (DP/MW 1);

• the *'Cynical'* view regarding EA as a whole: "EA is part of the move towards targeting resources to specific areas and no doubt the government hopes that either tenants or other landlords will want to take-over the properties once the estates have been improved to a satisfactory condition ... its underpinned by a belief that local government should not be left to make-up its mind about local issues" (LJ/SR 3);

• the *'symbolic'* view: "The basic HIPs allocations are being cut. The government has realized that it cannot go much further without a major political outcry. By 'topslicing' and 'targeting', it can spend resources in ways which meet the government's own criteria. and it is a means of increasing central controls over local expenditure in a subtle way. It basically results in a step backwards to the pre-HIPs system of project control, where the government decides which individual schemes are approved" (PW 2); and finally

• the *'Yes, but'* view regarding the schemes: "It is fair to say that it gives the government more control over what is going on. However, the schemes have been quite successful, therefore, EA is having an impact and is value for money" (SL 4). All agree that centralization does occur, although they stress different elements.

ii) Outcome of use of targeting: It has already been argued that it is not always the estates in greatest need or the councils' highest priorities which are subject to EA bids and funding (in the penultimate section of chapter 5). Such a position is supported by the experience in the case-studies: "As an estimate none of our EA schemes could be considered to be in our worst 20% of the housing stock, except for two. Our very worst stock has been left aside because it would need very substantial investment on its structure and we know that we wouldn't get approval for those buildings" (LJ/SR 3). In a perfect world: "It would be even better if we had more control over the way that resources are targeted. However, given the under-investment in public sector housing, targeting resources to the worst areas is better than not targeting them." (SL 4). This highlights a weakness (and a strength) in the targeting system: "We have to juggle between letting some estates sink completely or do a bit for all the estates. In one case, without substantial EA funding, we probably would have sold the lot or demolished and sold the vacant plot ... Therefore, EA has produced effective targeting on EA's criteria but it may be concentrating resources too narrowly since there are too few overall resources" (PW 2). A last authority with only two problem estates stated: "Its always our worst estates that get EA HIPs" (SL 4), implying that targeting works as optimally intended.

A slightly different but revealing line of criticism, is offered by the second case-study: "Authorities do not need to be told about how to target resources. Ministers have recognised that there are special problems but there is then a question of what is perceived as being the priority. We started a programme to deal with central heating. That was identified as being a priority but the DoE ignores the fact that we were targeting resources to where our tenants saw a problem. We targeted the estates that are now EA-supported before EA even existed ... Their view of 'effective' is only if the scheme fits their criteria. Why shouldn't local authorities do what their tenants want, as opposed to conforming to national objectives?" (PW 2) A word of warning is timely for those who disapprove of the concept: "The latest housing finance Act has important consequences ... which mean that the authority will come to rely even more on targeted allocations" (SJ 4). All sorts of targeted initiatives now exist and the amount of this type of resource is, therefore, also increasing.

iii) Are resources really focussed to where they are most needed? When phrased in such a way, a more positive response is forthcoming from those interviewed: "The estates which have received EA funding are the ones which would have been high in our priorities but I cannot in all honesty say that they are necessarily those which we, as a housing authority, would have chosen if we had a choice ... In the first year the bids made were for schemes ... [which] definitely aligned themselves closely to EA criteria, such as those which had local management" (SR 3), but this was not necessarily the case with subsequent bids.

Other positive opinions were also obtained: "By and large, these are the estates which were in greatest need ... In future the bids will begin to reflect a need for balance or fairness across the city. This may not necessarily be the same as the neediest estates." (TP 1). Also: "The more targeted it is the more it focuses views. EA has been a phenomenal success in this authority in terms of tenant involvement, the appearance and management of the estate" (SJ 4). A further comment from the same authority illustrates how useful the notion of targeting mechanisms can be: "The point is that this housing problem had been known for quite a while ... people were aware of the structural and social problems. The only thing that was missing was the political will to meet the requirements which dealing with such estates would pose ... Since most of the councilors were Conservative [whereas the bulk of the resources would be directed at the Labour-controlled estate], they wanted to show the electorate that the cash was being spent evenly, not just on the worst estates" (SJ 4). Herein lies a further advantage of targeting - in this particular case, as a way around the political impasse. At their best, instruments for spatial targeting can be very useful tools.

8.7 Conclusions

Chapter 8 completes the empirical part of the book. This chapter has concentrated on analyzing the effectiveness of the EA initiative at the micro level by using case-studies and semi-structured interviews with key local authority officials. Effectiveness was defined in terms of both quantitative information (such as procedural, financial and housing management statistics) and qualitative evidence (effectiveness of the procedures, the financial mechanism and EA's impact in influencing housing policy). The chapter began by describing the four case-studies (estate based management, concierge, refurbishment and public/private sector schemes) in terms of the history of the estates and the EA elements, so as to provide important background for the subsequent discussion. All were estates in need of substantial investment from the environmental, physical fabric and housing management viewpoints.

Section 8.3 started to grapple with the notion of effectiveness by dealing with the quantifiable side of the question. There is a dearth of statistical information on EA schemes but an attempt to compile financial and procedural details on the four schemes revealed that there is very poor record keeping on the part of both the local authorities (many of the EA application forms were missing) and the Regional Offices (some standard application forms were sometimes not requested). The data that are available back the findings of the local authority survey that delays were endemic and that this affected the procedural and financial operation of the initiative, certainly in the first years of EA's operation. This has subsequently improved.

Only two authorities had actually collated housing management statistics for the schemes but the results (albeit subject to caveats) demonstrate that EA resources and schemes are having a considerable impact. This result is in line with earlier survey findings (Table 5.24). All the housing officers who were approached for their opinions about the developments which have occurred in the four estates find that the improvements are noteworthy. Some reference was also made to a rudimentary attempt to canvass the opinion of the residents themselves (Pinto, 1992d, Appendix 7). All the schemes received very positive ratings by the residents in terms of the effects on the environment, the changes to the inside and outside of their dwellings and the contribution of the new management arrangements. The overall conclusion at this stage was that pronounced improvements were occurring in the four estates but that the discussion of EA effectiveness had to be extended further. Three other dimensions of 'effectiveness' were then analyzed.

Section 8.4 moved to a discussion of the 'procedural' effectiveness or the degree to which EA's procedures can be considered to work as well as possible. The conclusions were mixed. It was always the Housing Departments that assumed the 'lead' role in interacting with EA but the other departments have generally been very supportive and responsive. Regarding the timetabling arrangements, most authorities agreed with the EA Central and Regional Office claims that it was getting better but maintained that there is still room for improvement (see the concluding chapter for some recommendations). Local authorities still argued that the EA administrative burden was onerous, that the application forms could be streamlined and amalgamated and that EA's criteria for selecting bids submitted was still vague.

All the local authorities argued that their tenant consultation exercises for the case-studies were conducted rigorously but that this occurred irrespective of EA. Even if this is true, it is likely to characterize only the first year of EA's existence because the bids submitted were essentially the authorities' most long-standing housing problems which also tended to be focused on the better-researched housing estates. Tenant consultation is unlikely to have been as effective with the subsequent bids because of the limited time available to prepare bids. This has ensured that effective tenant consultation remains a problem. EA's influence in shaping housing schemes ranged from nil to estate visits - it was the Regional Offices which were much more influential in determining the nature of EA bids. Lastly the Committee Stage, the preparation of tender documentation for EA schemes and the staffing, union and employment issues relating to EA were minor for the case-studies and most authorities have sought to 'capitalise' upon the EA programme, but only where the schemes proposed conformed to their housing policies. There is some doubt as to whether this would necessarily be the case in the future.

Section 9.5 analyzed the issue of 'financial' effectiveness or the extent to which the EA HIPs targeting mechanism operated well. In contradiction to the Treasury's argument that they represent additional funds, all those interviewed argued that EA HIPs was topsliced or recycled. Nevertheless, the conflict hinges on how far one considers that the 'old' money would have been available to local authorities without EA. It is unlikely that the authorities participating in the EA initiative would have received the same levels of housing allocation without the existence of the programme. Turning next to the notion of 'continuation funding', while this procedure may enable EA to circumvent its one year financial timescale (thus enabling it to fund longer scale projects), it was still regarded locally as being cumbersome and restrictive. Despite the decentralization of responsibilities from EA Central to the Regional Offices, delays in processing forms remained common and as a result, some authorities continue to underspend and/or have to renegotiate tender agreements with contractors. Even though this has improved substantially since EA's first year when £5m in EA HIPs allocations were lost, this is remains a worrying inefficiency.

In addition local authorities complained that the 50% contribution to EA schemes which is expected of them is too onerous, that it will work against EA's new emphasis on large enterprise schemes (since authorities will have difficulties in meeting their half) and that it would be a great advance if EA could find a way of subsidizing the increased revenue costs which are implicit in the new management practices encouraged by EA Central. A great deal of uncertainty surrounds the introduction of the latest Local Government and Housing Act and its financial implications for the operation of the initiative. No one knew whether it would improve EA's financial effectiveness, but then neither did EA Central nor the Regional Offices. Local authorities are still suspicious of the government's 'true' reasons for creating targeted housing programmes, however, the new emphasis on employment is welcomed in all the case-studies and most of the local officials are optimistic that EA will be around for a few years more, which is much longer than such initiatives normally last for.

The chapter then analyzed EA's 'policy' effectiveness or the extent to which the existence of the EA programme has had other, less direct but nevertheless, important policy impacts upon local authorities, such as influencing their attitudes to the importance of localized management, difficult-to-let estates and so on. One of the conclusions is that the authorities' main reason for being involved with EA continues to be the possibility of acquiring additional housing resources at a time of severe fiscal retrenchment. Also as EA HIPs have increased over time, so have these targeted resources come to become critical to local authorities' ability to maintain their housing programmes. EA HIPs now constitute between 20-160% of authorities' HIPs allocations. The advantages identified are that targeting results in the concentration of resources, funds are 'ear-marked' for specific projects and are thus freed from the usual local political conflicts and finally, much more resource is now directed at problem housing estates.

Most authorities contend that decentralization of management practices was occurring independently of EA but that the programme has enabled them to go even further by releasing resources. One case-study did find that the benefits of estate based management had been debated but that it would not have happened for financial and the political reasons. Significantly, none of the case-studies reject the option of privatization out of hand. All are now quite pragmatic about this issue and accept that this is a strategy that may have to be employed in times of retrenchment, although the ones that have dabbled with the principle conclude that privatization is very hard to achieve in the type of housing estate which attracts EA support. As to the issue of whether involvement with EA results in compromised local housing policies, there are mixed views. The 'love/hate' relationship continues but local authorities accept that overall, EA has been positive to their authorities. Some of their housing estates have been refurbished, they are better managed and the quality of the tenants' lives has improved, however, three out of four still reject the argument that such estates were neglected in the past. Nevertheless since the creation of the EA programme, problem estates do seem to have been accorded higher priority in the participating authorities and more resources have undoubtedly been funneled their direction.

All the authorities still mistrust the underlying political motives behind the creation of targeted initiatives such as EA. There is a belief that this is often 'tokenistic' (although with its current level of resources, this criticism can no longer be applied to EA) and that it inevitably results in further increases in government control over the housing sphere. Turning lastly to the issue of targeting, it is not the case that EA has directed resources at the very worst council housing estates, for that would involve a change in EA policy which would enable authorities to direct resources at the structural problems inherent in many types of housing design. It may also be true that housing resources have been focused too narrowly and that the setting of priorities has been removed from the local level to the national one. Nevertheless all the case-study estates have been high priorities for the local authorities in question, concentrated levels of resources have been directed at the refurbishing and management of problem estates and this funding effectively by-passes the usual political conflicts and processes.

Part 3
CONCLUSIONS AND IMPLICATIONS

9 Synthesis, conclusions and future research

9.1 Introduction

A wealth of material has been presented in the previous empirical chapters. This was necessary because this book has investigated a recently established housing programme about which very little has been written in the academic literature. The main emphasis of the empirical chapters has been on the presentation of the survey and interview material. The thrust of this final chapter is to synthesize the main findings (from the local authority survey, the semi-structured interviews with both the DoE Regional Officials and the EA Central team based in Marsham Street and the case-study authorities) and to use them to address the five issues introduced at the start of the book, namely: EA and the issue of central-local relations, the managerial implications, the implementation of EA schemes, the operation of the financial mechanism of targeted EA HIPs and EA's impact in influencing housing policy at the local level.

Effort is also put into discussing the implications of the findings of the research for the theoretical frameworks introduced earlier in the book. Chapter 3 analyzed various concepts which are of relevance to an understanding of the way the EA initiative operates: the Agency/Partner debate, the Dual State Thesis, the conception of Local Social Development and the analysis of Sub-Central Government are all plausible arguments in explaining the purpose, mechanisms and implementation of EA. The findings of this book have implications for our understanding of those theories and the section part of the chapter discusses the significance of the research in broadening our comprehension of the applicability of such concepts. Inevitably this book has not been able to cover every important aspect of the EA programme, not least because EA has evolved since the research began, however, the conclusions point to other issues which must be analyzed in order to develop our understanding of this important central housing initiative.

9.2 Overall conclusions: Synthesizing the evidence

The book has employed a mixture of methodologies in order to investigate a housing programme of which little has been known. This has meant that as a first stage, the origins of the initiative had to be investigated. As there was no published information on this issue, semi-structured interviews had to be employed and the results are presented in chapter 4.

Discussion of EA's policy community revealed that there are three key elements to the EA programme: the local authorities, EA Central and the DoE Regional Offices (chapter 3). Therefore the purpose of the second stage of the research was to obtain a through understanding of the operation of the initiative at the aggregate level. This meant that a postal survey methodology had to be employed which could deal with a range of issues while also reaching all the authorities which were participating in the initiative (chapter 5). This resulted in the identification of the key areas of concern to local authorities and the implementation, financial, central-local issues to be pursued in the subsequent investigation (ch 6).

The method that was considered to be most apposite at the next stage was the use of semi-structure interviews (chapter 7). This was for two reasons. Firstly, there were just 10 Regional Offices and only a limited number of key EA Central personnel which had to be investigated and secondly, the survey had identified the key issues (such as the quality of tenant consultation and the underspending of resources) which had to be pursued on an interactive basis with those responsible for determining EA policy. Semi-structured interviewing was a demanding and time-consuming technique, but one which added depth and dynamism to the analysis.

The element which remained to be dealt with, was that of specific localities and the extent to which the EA programme was having positive impacts. This was achieved through the use of case-study research concentrating on an estate management scheme, a concierge, a public/private sector initiative and a refurbishment scheme (chapter 8). The use of case-studies was deemed to be the most relevant method because it could also add the dimensions of background, politics, history of the estates and the impact of the EA initiative on the basis of statistical, procedural, financial and policy effectiveness criteria.

The biggest disadvantage of such a methodology, despite the detailed conclusions provided for each empirical chapter, is that its very nature requires a synthesis of the main issues arising from the four sources of evidence. This is the task set for the concluding chapter and is undertaken by reference to Table 9.1 which is integral to the analysis to follow. Table 9.1 refers to the five main issues posed at the start of the book and presents the main conclusions by pulling out the results of the four sources of evidence. Symbols are used for clarity and simplicity.

Table 9.1 Overall synthesis: Conclusions and source of evidence

Thesis themes and main issues:	Postal Survey	DoE Region	EA Central	Case Studies
A) Administrative/implementation issues				
1. Quality of the timetabling	--	-	+	-
2. Whether EA keeps changing its criteria	--	+	+	-
3. Quality of administration	--	-	++	-
B) Management issues				
1. EA's impact on number of schemes	+	+	+	+
2. EA's impact in aiding innovation	-	+	+	+
3. EA's impact in aiding decentralisation	+	++	++	++
4. EA's impact in aiding tenant consultation	--	-	+	-/++
5. EA's overall impact on management	++	++	++	++
C) Financial issues				
1. Whether EA HIPs is additional or topsliced	--	--	++	--
2. Whether EA results in underallocation	--	-	-/+	-
3. Whether EA results in underspending		--	-	- -
4. Problems due to continuation funding		--	++	++ -
5. Quality of EA's targeting		+	++	+++
D) Housing policy issues				
1. Whether EA results in more investment	-/+	++	++	++
2. Whether influences management styles	0	+	++	+
3. Degree of replication of EA schemes	-	++	++	+
4. Impact on run-down estates	++	++	++	++
5. EA's overall impact on policy	+/++	++	++	++
E) Centre-local relations				
1. Degree of conflict	--	+	+	-/+
2. Degree of co-operation	-	++	+	+
3. Degree of privatisation	--	+	+	+
4. Number of alternative organisations	--	+	+	+
5. EA's impact on local policies/autonomy	-	0	0	-/--

Code: Very Poor (--); Poor (-); Neutral (0); Good (+); Very Good (++)

9.2.1 Implementation issues

1. Fairly clear-cut conclusions can be reached on the implementation issues. The evidence on the timetable, administrative issues and the changing nature of the criteria does suggest that EA is administratively cumbersome and that the implementation process could be improved (see Table 9.1). Confirmation of this is obtained from the survey, the ROs and the case-studies. At the same time, the evidence of chapters 7 and 8 also indicates that EA has been aware of the difficulties which operate on local authorities and that there has been some attempt to adjust the EA *timetable* so that it coincides more closely with that of the HIPs timetable. Authorities argue that this has greatly improved the situation, although many remain unhappy with it. EA Central itself maintains that the timetable is dictated by the way the Treasury/government operates; that this is now the best possible timetable that can be achieved; and lastly, that authorities are partly to blame for their difficulties.

2. The effect of *changing EA criteria* is heavily criticized by authorities in the survey. However the changes are defended by both the ROs and EA Central who contend that they are justified because EA in supposed to encourage 'innovation' and as such, has be free to generate different elements. There should be no 'hard and fast' rules. What is supported by EA is dictated by what tenants want and what is needed in the particular estate. This suggests that the burden is on local authorities to prove that what they wish to undertake is genuinely needed and supported by their tenants. In addition EA has taken two important steps to clarify the situation. Firstly, it has issued Guide-lines for EA bids which at least one of the case-study authorities finds adequate in clarifying its queries over EA criteria. As long as authorities are aware of these issues, the problem should diminish. Secondly, EA has begun publish guide-lines which focus on implementation (see DoE, 1989b; 1990b and 1990c) which have proved to be very useful to authorities. This difficulty should, therefore, become less important in the future.

3. The survey results indicate that authorities are very concerned about *EA administration*, although the case-study evidence is that this has slowly improved over time. EA has tried to 'decentralize' the administrative burden. The small EA Central team has (somewhat reluctantly) agreed that it cannot cope with so many bids and continuation schemes. The result is that the implementation structure presented in Figure 3.1 has changed to the one depicted in Figure 9.1, which is much more streamlined. The Regional Offices are now in charge of virtually all the administrative elements: they prioritize the local authority bids, consult with the authorities, determine which schemes to fund (subject to EA Central veto), monitor progress and finance of schemes, and are also in charge of the continuation schemes. Two important developments to come

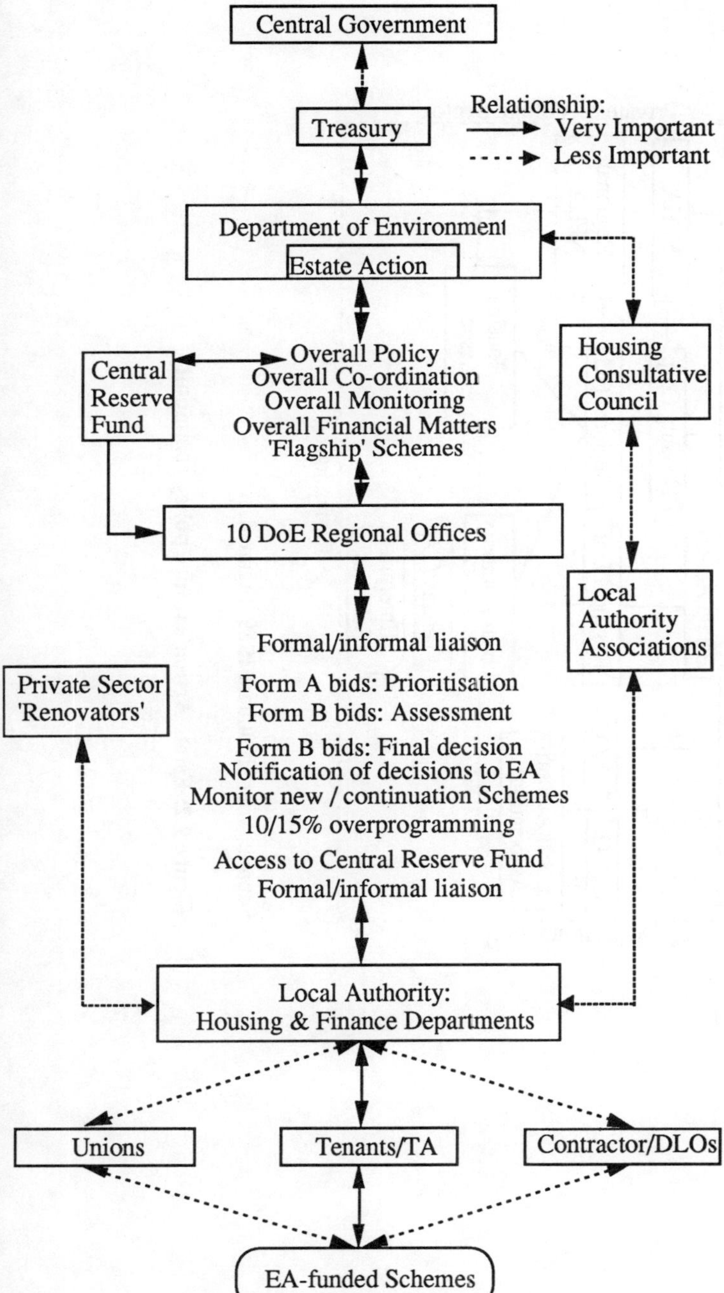

Figure 9.1: Evolution of relationships in the EA policy context

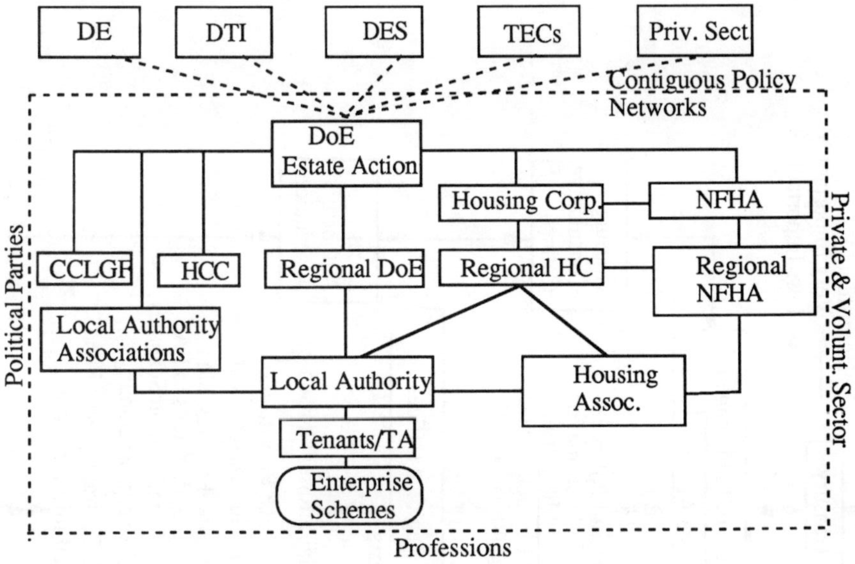

Source: After Houlihan, 1989, Figure 4.1

Figure 9.2: Estate Action's future policy community

out of the EA Central and Regional Office interviews, are the fact that in order to reduce underspending, the Regional Offices can overallocate their EA HIPs slice by 15% (more in the case of London); and a Central Reserve Fund has been created which 'pools' all the EA HIPs resources which are very likely to be underspent. This is then offered to those regions which can spend the allocation late in the financial year before the EA HIPs is 'lost'.

This new structure has arisen because the ROs now understand the EA initiative's 'ethos', have developed a good working relationship with local authorities and are, therefore, seen to be capable of taking on a much more comprehensive role as regards the day to day operation of EA. This is much more satisfactory to all concerned although local authorities stress that delays still occur and that further improvements could be made for example, to the application Forms, the need to prepare tender documentation and the processing of bids.

The evolution and contrasts between Figures 3.1/9.1 and 3.2/9.2 merit further comment. Figure 3.2 represents what the literature (such as Houlihan, 1988) suggests is the overall public or social housing policy community, both in terms of the main relationships and the key organizations. Following EA's recent change in emphasis towards larger scale, enterprise initiatives, it would be more appropriate to suggest that the overall policy community (certainly as far as the EA initiative in concerned), has become more complicated. While still concentrating on housing issues, EA has accepted the logic that housing problems cannot be considered in isolation and that an attempt must also be made (albeit through housing initiatives) to improve the situation in problem estates by also dealing with training and employment issues. This means that EA must increasingly operate in an inter-departmental manner which goes beyond the previous model of policy community.

The argument is that as soon as the DoE goes beyond the accepted 'housing' threshold into areas such as employment and training, it has to interact with other departments such as the Department of Employment (and to a lesser extent, the Department of Trade and Industry and the Department of Education and Science). With the creation of the business-led Training and Enterprise Councils (TECs) now in charge of the Youth Training and Employment Training budgets, EA and local authorities must communicate with TECs in order to support the employment and training initiatives, such as Community Refurbishment Schemes (CRSs). CRSs involve the refurbishment of housing estates using an element of local labour which is trained as a result. This means that the EA Central team will have to liaise with the private sector. If the CRS schemes are to be the main model of EA involvement in these issues, then EA Central will also have to become involved with private sector developers such as Regalian, Laing's and Wimpey's (see Pinto, 1991c and for the Scottish equivalent see Pinto, 1991d). The other point to note in this respect is that in principle, there is a great deal of scope for CRS type involvement. A

£19bn backlog of council housing disrepair exists alongside the highest concentrations of unemployment in the country. However, turning back to the issue of the policy community, while it is widely accepted that employment and training elements should be build into EA schemes, this development also throws up potential difficulties in implementation as it results in a widening of the EA policy community.

The overall social housing policy community was translated into the EA policy community in Figure 3.1. Based on the implementation conclusions of the research, however, several aspects of Figure 3.1 can be refined and transformed into Figure 9.1. Firstly, The relationship with the Housing Consultative Council and the Local Authority Associations is very weak and ineffectual. These organizations have failed to influence the operation of the EA programme, rather the DoE Regional Offices have been more important in this respect (this issue is developed below). The relationship with the private sector renovators is not particularly strong either. Privatization of housing blocks or estates has not occurred to any notable extend. The other aspect of private sector involvement has been the CRSs. However, while there is renewed interest in this type of scheme and a lot of potential exists, after a good start, the number of CRSs supported through EA became insignificant, mainly due to the change-over from the Community Programme to Employment Training (see Pinto, 1991c). This has meant that the link with the Private Sector Renovators has been similarly weak.

Other aspects of EA's relationships have been found to be non-existent. Both the case-studies and the local authority survey demonstrate that very few housing jobs have been formed or restructured as a result of new management styles such as estate based management. This has meant that Union issues have been minimal, as has the role of contractors/Direct Labour Organizations (see Figure 9.1), however, this finding conflicts with Anne Powers' work on estate based management (Personal Communication). Lastly, the only local government department that matters is the Housing department with some involvement from Finance due to the complexity of EA HIPs capital programming.

By the same token, other relationships have been intensified. The key evolution is the demise of the role of EA Central as that of the Regional Offices has expanded out of recognition with the decentralization of EA Central functions, the creation of the Central Reserve Fund and the opportunity to overcommit EA HIPs. The Regional Offices are now in charge of all aspects of administration, liaison with local authorities, implementation and monitoring of schemes. EA Central retains strategic control of the EA programme. Decentralization is a very positive development. Apart from making for more efficient procedures, it enables the relatively small EA Central team to concentrate on what it can do best namely, devote its time to issues such as policy development, lobbying the Treasury for further resources, research and co-ordination. The other area of 'intensification' is the importance attached to tenant consultation. While there may be questions as to the quality of tenant consultation, the importance attached to this issue by EA and its reaffirmation via the pioneering of Estate Management Boards controlled by tenants, means that this issue remains central to the EA programme and, therefore, crucial to authorities wishing to participate in the programme.

The evidence presented in the empirical chapters (4 to 8) leads to a number of possible recommendations: first, it is obvious that a key improvement would be the creation of a mechanism which would generate more effective *consultation* between the main agents, namely the local authorities, LAAs, ROs and EA Central team. Only then would each of the key players be aware of the problems, the changes taking place and be able to share best practice. This would help reduce the mistrust and antipathy which has always plagued the initiative, something which becomes absolutely essential with the recent change of emphasis towards 'enterprise' initiatives. This necessitates effective co-ordination and co-operation between these agencies and others besides, such as Tenants' Associations and Training and Enterprise Councils.

Second, EA's 'rule' that local authorities should contribute 50% of the capital costs for each scheme could be modified. While it is true that EA uses discretion in deciding each authority's capital contribution, this may still be problematic in, for example, discouraging authorities from bidding for large schemes and thus is likely to work against EA's emphasis on comprehensive 'enterprise' initiatives. It would be better if some account were taken of authorities' differing abilities to afford the contribution. A more effective strategy would be to replace it with a *sliding scale of support* with those authorities with relatively greater need and fewer resources able to secure greater EA support. This would build upon and extend the notion of 'targeting' resources.

Third, EA proposes nationally conceived solutions to nationally perceived problems. This works if the needs experienced by housing authorities happens to fall into those slots - it is not so good otherwise. *Two improvements* might be to: a) take greater account of local needs so that authorities can be a little more flexible about the projects and works which are conceived and also, EA could be more flexible about what it supports; and b) a willingness to move away from an insistence on 'innovation'. Depending on the context, tried and tested schemes may be even more relevant and effective.

Fourth, EA's timetable has been discussed in detail and the problems identified. Suffice to say that with the constraints faced by EA and the fact that government budgets operate annually, the best practical advice is for authorities to begin *planning and designing the EA bids/schemes long before EA invites them to do so.* In terms of using resources as effectively as possible, authorities should consider formulating only those schemes which they are prepared to fund from mainstream capital allocations if EA approval is not obtained. The advantages are that with the certainty of being funded, there would be much more forward planning and greater tenant consultation. It would reduce the risk of disappointing tenants and also help eliminate underallocation and underspending as far as possible.

Fifth, the above approach would facilitate other useful changes. Currently until final approval arrives, there is a lack of certainty at the point when authorities are ready to spend the allocation. Perhaps what is needed is a more *comprehensive Form A* (this would not be a problem to authorities committed to supporting the schemes), which would mean that when authorities get Form A approval, they can be certain of receiving EA funding. This places a greater onus upon authorities to generate more forward planning and costing, but the DoE could then 'ear-mark' a certain amount of resources for the scheme, based on those detailed Form A figures. It would be worth the extra month or so which would be necessary for the ROs to process the forms and also result in greater certainty for all concerned. If, as EA Central recommends, local authorities maintain a continuous dialogue with the Regional Offices, local authorities are less likely to lose investment on bids which do not succeed.

Sixth, the EA bid process is separate from the HIPs round and involves a different timescale. It has been demonstrated that the one year timetable results in a plethora of difficulties, not least a scramble to spend all the EA HIPs allocation at the end of the financial year. At the time of writing, it still remains unclear how the new financial régime will affect EA (but see chapters 7 and 8). It is to be hoped that in future there will be a *project timescale* to work to, for the large and complex schemes which the government has in mind. This is important so that authorities do not rush, underspend and have, as currently happens, to repair peoples' roofs and windows during winter. A sensible and compatible timetable will become even more crucial.

Seventh, an obvious difficulty is that the DoE insists on 'hard' tender figures and documentation before allocations are approved. While the motives are understandable, this constitutes a problem. An improvement might be to allocate approvals based on Quantity Surveyor *estimates* and on housing authorities undertakings that the project costs will not exceed those estimates. There would thus be an incentive for authorities to assess those estimates as minutely and accurately as possible since they would be responsible for meeting any extra costs arising. While this would also accelerate the whole process, the real advantages would lie in the fact that it would allow for both greater certainty and better forward planning.

9.2.2 Management issues

In chapter 4 the argument was introduced that political motives were involved in the formation of the EA initiative but that the managerial issues were uppermost in the minds of the civil servants. A key general concern at the time, was that of improving the management organization in 'run-down' estates. For its part central government does not believe in the traditional, centralized and hierarchical model of council housing management and in line with government's objectives of creating a new sector of 'social' housing (see chapter 2), EA attempts to provide incentives for authorities to experiment and innovate with alternative forms of housing management and ownership, as set out in EA's remit.

1. The general opinion obtained from the survey (see also chapter 6) is that authorities are primarily implementing those schemes and initiatives which conform to their housing policies although some indicate that, were it not for EA considerations, they might have implemented them elsewhere. A related point is that if there is a further tightening of the financial situation confronting authorities, this degree of freedom may well be impaired in future. All the sources of evidence also suggest that EA has enabled *more schemes* to occur than would otherwise be the case. This is an important finding in EA's favour (see Table 9.1).

2. As regards helping authorities to *innovate*, the results of the survey would suggest that the EA initiative has had little impact and that the great majority of schemes were either 'under discussion for future implementation' or 'in the process of being implemented from mainstream HIPs'. This would imply that a large proportion of EA HIPs is simply 'dead-weight' investment, however, both the ROs and EA Central disagree with this conclusion.

3. The survey suggests instead that the options placed in front of authorities together with the resources, have forced authorities to both consider and implement different types of management and ownership schemes. Whether EA really aids innovation depends on the authorities' attitudes to it. The results of the case-studies suggest that there is truth in this argument and that some authorities have been able to put into effect schemes (such as Co-operatives and 50% sales to the private sector) because of EA's very existence. Therefore EA has helped both the process of innovation and *decentralization* in run-down estates (see Table 9.1).

4. In dealing with the topic of management efficiency, a key issue of concern is that of *tenant consultation*. The local authorities examined in the survey suggest that although improving the level and quality of tenant consultation is a key EA objective, most believe that this has not occurred in their authorities mainly because the 'Authority/officers were satisfied with the existing levels of consultation' and secondly, that effective tenant consultation may have been impaired by the way EA operates. Further research suggests that EA has had a positive impact in pushing authorities to confront this issue more fully.

Both the ROs and EA Central argue that local authorities may be underplaying EA's impact in this respect and the evidence of the case-studies indicates that certainly in EA's first year of operation, the level of tenant consultation was very great indeed. Undoubtedly this is in part because the schemes implemented in EA's first couple of years of operation would have been the authorities' top priorities. As such, they are likely to have been researched and the tenants reasonably well consulted, although this may not necessarily be the case with subsequent bids (see discussion in chapter 8). Nevertheless the fact that EA has given this issue so much emphasis, made it a pre-requisite for EA funding, required local authorities to monitor impacts and encouraged local authorities to create Estate Management Boards among other factors, simply has to have impacted upon the tenant consultation practices of many authorities. Nevertheless this remains a difficult issue and the evidence from all the other sources suggests that the quality of tenant consultation could be improved and that more attention needs to be given to this issue, an opinion with which both the ROs and some EA Central officials concur.

5. In any event, EA is having a very positive overall *impact* on management. Despite the fears about the true aims of the initiative, those authorities which are experimenting, for example, with security and environmental works, concierges and estate based management, report very encouraging results. This is true of the national survey (chapter 5), local authority staff views (5 and 8), RO and EA Central assessments (7), tenant opinions and case-study schemes (8). In view of this consistent evidence and despite all the other difficulties identified in the empirical chapters, there can be no denying that targeting resources in specific ways and localities does work. It would work more effectively if the recommendations presented in the section above were implemented. The value of this achievement should not be underrated. The 1980s was the decade when the key council housing concerns were related to the issue of management and the Estate Action has made a contribution to an understanding of how to improve management organization and style in the most problematic portions of council housing.

9.2.3 Financial issues

Chapter 4 has introduced the argument that there is a feeling amongst politicians and civil servants that the HIPs system of block allocations was failing to provide sufficient resources for what the government saw as a housing priority, namely run-down council estates. In terms of the government's objective of achieving economic or financial effectiveness in public resource use, a key idea is that of 'targeting' resources. Much is being said about targeting but there has been virtually no research on it. The government's key targeting mechanism in the housing field is that of EA HIPs, whose experience is useful in that it also sheds light on similar systems, such as the Homeless Initiative (see Figure 3.2).

1. The research has demonstrated that all local authorities agree that EA HIPs resources are *topsliced* from mainstream HIPs, centralized and redistributed according to government or DoE determined priorities (see Table 9.1). This is a criticism that has dogged the EA initiative since its inception and the mechanism is resented by authorities who regard this as clear-cut evidence of further centralization of control and autonomy. The authorities in both the survey and the balance of the Regional Officers' opinions suggest that virtually everyone now accepts the notion of 'topsliced' finance and secondly, the increased central control that it implies. Only the Treasury and EA Central maintain that EA resources are 'additional', rather than re-circulated. This perception has never been shaken off and has made EA's role more difficult to implement. Nevertheless the dire local government financial climate has made certain authorities that had originally refused to participate with the initiative swallow their pride and also bid for EA HIPs (see Table 4.1).

There are additional problems which can arise from the EA HIPs mechanism. The analysis in chapters 5 to 8 makes it abundantly clear that a side-effect of targeting resources is that in the case of EA, there are two timetables in operation - one linked to the general capital allocation system and another relating to the targeted resources - which are not necessarily compatible and may be very difficult to co-ordinate and synchronize. This has already been discussed in detail above. Two important problems may spring from this difficulty and these are discussed next.

2. Firstly, the Regional Offices may *underallocate* the targeted resources. The survey results suggest that this does happen. EA Central itself confirms that it occurs, although it argues that it only happened in the first year when about £5m was underallocated. EA Central argues that this has not occurred in subsequent years because ROs can now over-programme their allocations (by 15%) and there is now a Central Reserve Fund which pools all the potential underspend and allows EA to re-allocate it before the end of the financial year (see Figure 9.1). The ROs also reveal that underallocation occurs and the contention is that this is almost inevitable, although the London RO is particularly prone to underallocate. The research indicates that certain authorities obtain 'reputations' based on whether they can achieve spend. In turn, this affects their success rate in the EA bid process since a 'credibility' factor comes into play. A similar sort of reputation can develop among the ROs themselves. For example, the London RO complains that EA Central does not allow it to invite its authorities to submit bids for resources which become available at the last minute (via the Central Reserve Fund mechanism). This has implications for those authorities excluded and thus for their residents.

3. Secondly, the local authorities may *underspend* EA HIPs. One must not lose sight of the fact that under/overspending also occurred under the HIPs system (see Gay, 1985; Malpass and Murie, 1987), although authorities

suggest that the problem is much greater with the EA schemes, mainly because of the uncertainty of it all. All the evidence from the survey and the EA Central and RO interviews bear out the fact that underspending occurs. As to the reason, the local authorities blame delays and inefficient procedures on the part of EA while naturally, EA Central and the ROs point in the opposite direction. In one of the case-study authorities, it was argued that authorities had only themselves to blame, although this authority only had one EA scheme to programme. The recommendations presented earlier would help the situation.

4. In addition an important issue is that of *continuation funding*. The survey indicates that authorities were very critical of the EA constraint of two years of funding per scheme (see Table 9.1). The EA team has sensibly accepted that schemes may take longer and now encourages authorities to think in terms of bidding for different phases each year. This enables substantial schemes to be take place over several years. The other important development is that all the control, supervision and monitoring of continuation funding schemes has now been devolved to the ROs. This is a measure which has come about through the ROs' insistence that they were better placed to deal with this aspect. Both the ROs and EA Central argue that this is no longer an issue but the authorities are not so easily convinced. They maintain that there are still no guarantees of 'promised' continuation funding being received and that this hampers their financial programming and threatens the success of the new type of 'enterprise' or 'flagship' initiative which EA hopes to generate in future. EA Central counters that it is almost inconceivable that the Treasury would disband the EA initiative without meeting its continuation funding obligations. If this is the case, perhaps it could be better advertised to authorities.

5. It is becoming increasingly common for central government initiatives to be *targeted* at specific areas, groups of people, types of housing etc. The DoE has several such instruments employing the technique of 'topslicing and targeting'. The conclusions of this book point to the fact that these may well work in terms of their objectives but that unless careful attention is given to the issues of local authority timetables, council procedures, political processes and consultation, the government's objective of financial efficiency may be compromised because of problems such as underallocation and underspending, not to mention mistrust and reluctant co-operation. The importance of consulting with local authorities, their associations, the tenants and the Regional Offices cannot be over stressed.

That said, the government's concern that more resources should be directed to run-down estates and that the EA initiative would be a good vehicle for this, must have been fulfilled. By originally targeting 69 authorities, (and later on) by requiring that bids for EA support must only be made for estates with certain indices of deprivation (see Table 6.3), and lastly, by securing an increasing supply of EA HIPs allocations from the Treasury, the EA initiative has ensured that this aim was met.

The survey results imply that the notion of targeting was not being fully effective, since a number of authorities argued that they would have used the EA HIPs resources in different areas/estates or in different schemes/ways. However both the ROs and EA Central insist that the policy of targeting has been very successful. In addition the case-studies reveal that the EA scheme estates were the four authorities' greatest priorities and that even where they weren't, the estates were in severe need of additional investment. The local authorities maintain that they would have directed more resources into these estates if their financial situation had enabled them and one of the biggest critiques of EA, in terms of financial targeting, must be that it shirks the responsibility for investing in structural disrepair. EA argues that it only concerned with management and innovation and that the costs of structural repair must come from the local authorities' own mainstream HIPs, yet numerous reports have highlighted not only the severe problems which exist, but also the huge level of expenditure which is necessary. The government has yet to come to terms with this major issue.

9.2.4 Housing policy issues

1. We start with the level of *investment* as this links with the previous conclusion that as far as targeting was concerned, EA was meeting much success in directing resources towards the areas it felt was in need of them. A major finding is that there can be little doubt that more investment is now finding its way into run-down estates (see Table 9.1). Local authorities see this as being one of the essential virtues of the initiative. While they argue vigorously that these estates would have been given much greater priority if centrally determined financial resources had been more directly and freely available, the case-studies in particular, leave little doubt that a large proportion of local authority resources is being directed in the way the government hoped.

This is not simply because EA HIPs are targeted at particular authorities and tied to public housing estates exhibiting above average problems of various sorts. The way EA has changed over time has accentuated the direction of the authorities' own investment. The survey material has revealed that to start with, virtually all the capital allocation was provided through EA HIPs but that in subsequent years, EA began to 'encourage' authorities to meet approximately 50% of the investment from their own mainstream HIPs. This has meant that an even greater level of commitment, both financial and political, was required to maintain the authorities' involvement with the EA initiative. While authorities bitterly criticize this development (indeed, this has encouraged a few to part company with the initiative), all the same, the great majority have gone along with it and committed their resources accordingly. The tenants in the most run-down estates have benefited.

2. The survey information reveals that authorities were engaged with EA primarily to obtain additional resources, although the second most important factor was because of the fact that it espoused decentralized or innovative *management* structures. However, the implication is that EA was not affecting authorities in terms of the management issues because they planned to implement these anyway. EA merely released the resources to make this possible. Of course, a different perspective was obtained from the ROs and EA Central. The case-studies suggest that EA involvement (not least the availability of resources), certainly affected the predisposition of some authorities to undertake initiatives such as private sector involvement and co-operatives; and one case-study had been convinced of the value of setting up localized management structures and involving the tenants more closely. EA has certainly begun to affect some authorities' perception of management issues very positively, as evident from Table 9.1.

3. As regards the issue of whether authorities have been encouraged to *replicate* EA management models, most authorities maintain in the survey and in the case-studies that the schemes they were implementing were their own schemes and not EA's. Nevertheless, one authority was definitely planning to bid for a similar scheme (because of its success) and the others were also considering replicating the schemes analyzed in the case-studies.

4. Bearing in mind the methodological caveats discussed in chapter 3, the management indices discussed in the survey; the ROs' and EA Central's opinion (based primarily on the information provided through the Annual Assessment Forms); the local authority housing officials; and the tenants' opinions, another key finding of the book is that the EA impact on the *run-down estates* and overall, has been very positive (see Table 9.1). With hindsight, the research might have benefited if there had been a more rigorous discussion of issues such as: the counterfactuals (what would have happened without EA); the opportunity costs (what alternative uses the same amount of money, including the bureaucratic elements, might have produced); and some comparison with what has happened on other estates without EA funding, both within the authorities and elsewhere. Nevertheless there is strong, consistent evidence across the four methods used to suggest that involvement with the EA initiative has resulted in very positive effects in terms of the impact on run-down estates.

5. We come now to the *overall effects* of EA identified in the Table 9.1. Traditionally authorities' attempts at ameliorating the situation in 'problem' estates have been flawed. They have been half-hearted and have often excluded the tenants altogether from the proposed alternatives, thus

it was almost inevitable that their impact would be limited. For all its administrative and implementation difficulties, the EA initiative has presented various 'tried and tested' management models to local authorities; provided capital allocations to carry them out; forced authorities to consider alternatives and make novel choices; courted tenant consultation; and insisted upon authorities providing firm tenders and monitoring the financial and management developments closely. It is, therefore, not surprising that Table 9.1 demonstrates that EA's overall impact on management is viewed as having been very positive.

As the discussion in this section has pointed out, the EA initiative has been very successful from the point of view of the government's pro-council housing aims. This is part of the reason why EA has survived so long for this type of initiative, that the Treasury has been forced to relax its rigid policy towards investment in public housing and to provide additional resources for it (amounting to £450m over five years). As far as the more radical housing objectives are concerned (such as transfers of portions of the housing stock to Trust and Housing Associations), the success has been very limited and the initiative may not survive close inspection by politicians keen on rapid and substantial change to council housing.

9.2.5 Central-local relations

1. It is clear that the initial reaction by local authorities to EA was one of dismay and *conflict* (see chapter four). Some authorities were so set against the initiative and in particular, its principles of topslicing resources and partnership with the private sector, that they refused to participate at all. What has happened, however, is that in the subsequent time, most authorities have had the opportunity to reflect on the various housing options that are possible to undertake under EA (see Table 9.1). Most came to appreciated the scope offered by the initiative to further their housing policies and have sought to capitalise on it as far as possible.

The realization that it could be profitable to 'do business' with EA has meant that there has been a steady diminution in the level of overt conflict and criticism of the EA initiative and the onus has shifted perceptibly from ridiculing the initiative, to more constructive suggestions of how to improve its operation. Because there was a ready-made channel for authorities' views to be aired and passed on to EA Central, through the Regional Offices, not much use was made of the Local Authority Associations, although they were involved. The ROs in particular, note that there has been a complete change in the local authority attitude to EA and that the words 'pragmatism' and 'realism' frequently cross their lips.

2. This *co-operation* has arisen, of course, because most authorities were predominantly motivated by the fact that EA provided an additional source of finance, rather than the other aspects that the initiative espoused

(chapters 5 and 6). Throughout the empirical chapters, it is apparent that authorities are being forced by the capital restrictions and reductions to engage in the initiative and that they have managed to do so mainly on their own terms, but with time, EA has begun to gain the upper hand in the relationship. Authorities make more EA bids and even formerly dissenting authorities now actively bid to EA. EA HIPs allocations have steadily increased while HIPs have dried-up and capital restrictions constrain financial flexibility. With so few alternative sources of finance, authorities have had to consider and often implement, many of the options offered under EA, particularly in view of the fact that EA expects authorities contribute and to innovate.

All the local authorities (those surveyed and the case-studies) agree that EA's 'power' is bound to increase, resulting in further centralization of control (chapters 5, 6 and 8), rather than rolling back of the frontiers of the state. Local authorities must dance to a central government tune, nevertheless, most have benefited from it and have been able to fulfil their aims (and EA's) without compromising their housing policies. Such a trick becomes harder with time and as EA's expectations of such authorities rise. The topslicing and targeting mechanism in conjunction with capital restrictions undoubtedly provide great scope for central direction and control.

3. As regards the issue of *privatization*, because of the hitherto lack of research on EA, the popular or conventional view as to what the EA initiative is about, has generally been as follows:

> To ensure that local authorities would not be slow in disposing of their estates, the Department of the Environment set up the Urban Housing Renewal Unit (UHRU) in 1985 both to promote emptying and selling local authority housing (so that it could be refurbished and resold) and to oversee the handing over of estates to trusts. Within a year, 42 local authorities (half of which were Labour controlled) had embarked on 80 estate sale schemes under UHRU, although with only £50 million at its disposal in 1985/86 UHRU could not be expected to have much impact on a £20bn repair problem. (Balchin, 1989, p.224)

Such a view wildly over-estimates the extent to which EA has resulted in disposals to the private sector *and* completely ignores the fact that the main emphasis has shifted perceptibly to the encouragement of estate management. More importantly, it also misses the point regarding the extent to which EA has contributed to the acceptance of the notion of privatization of council estates. With limited (but increasing) resources, EA has played a crucial role in conditioning authorities to the concept and value of selling either parts of their housing stock or land parcels.

Whereas such a notion was absolutely taboo when EA was formed (and indeed was part of the reason why a number of authorities refused to participate with it), the case-studies demonstrate that this has gained credibility and even acceptance among many authorities as a perfectly sound option to consider, especially at times of fiscal stress. This is reflected in the 'pragmatism' demonstrated by authorities of all political backgrounds throughout the research and also implies that authorities are increasingly willing to form partnerships with the private sector, despite the findings of the survey, where this was the housing authorities' least popular option to undertake under the EA initiative. In terms of the wider housing policy, experience and involvement with EA may also mean that authorities look more pragmatically upon such policies as Tenants' Choice, Voluntary Transfers and Housing Action Trusts.

4. As regards EA's aims of encouraging innovation and help stimulate *alternative management organizations*, in line with government's social housing policy, the overall conclusion is that EA has also had a degree of success in this respect (see Table 9.1). The survey results indicate that authorities have only been pursuing the initiatives which were in line with their housing policies, some of which involved the formation of co-operatives and concierges. They do agree that EA has enable more schemes to take place, which implies a degree of success for EA. Both EA Central and the ROs have no doubts that they have been influential in this respect and the evidence from the case-studies confirm some authorities' greater willingness to experiment with alternative organizations. In most cases this is done willingly but in others, it is because of a lack of alternative, since the authorities do not have the resources to undertake the schemes on their own. None have considered radical options such as the transfer of stock/estates to Trusts.

5. One of the biggest criticisms of the EA initiative to start with, was the fact that it was believed that the financial mechanism of topslicing and redistribution via DoE determined criteria of what was relevant, resulted in centralization, a reduction in *local autonomy* and interference with local policies and priorities. Such a view comes through very clearly in the survey (see chapters 5 and 6) and in the case-studies (chapter 8). As mentioned above, there is also the expectation that the level of EA control will accentuate because increasingly more authorities bid for EA support and because alternative sources of funding are harder to find or yield less resource.

These arguments have by no means disappeared and remain a thorn in the operation of EA. The Central team exhausts itself in arguing that EA HIPs is separate from and additional to, mainstream HIPs with little success. There is some recognition on the part of the case-study authorities that they are not forced to comply with EA. They are aware that they have complete freedom over the decision on whether to get involved and what to bid for, nevertheless, in both the survey and the case-studies, authorities maintain that there has been a degree of compromise in local priorities and a reduction in local autonomy.

Authorities argue that both these trends will increase in future (see survey and case-studies), however, the reason why most authorities are not more critical of these issues is because of the 'umbrella-like' nature of EA where virtually anything can be funded, provided it is presented in the right way and with the right phrases. In this respect, the ambiguity over EA criteria works in the authorities' favour. In addition, the ROs have become very adept at advising authorities on the presentation of their bids and now, with further decentralization, the ROs' knowledge and understanding of local needs and priorities will further aid matters. A great deal of scope exists within EA for local authorities to benefit from EA support without necessarily feeling as if it compromises local policies unduly. That is precisely why (together with the additional resources) many authorities which originally refused to participate are now heavily committed to the EA initiative.

To conclude this section, the few housing commentators who have paid attention to the EA initiative have pointed to the fact that its resources are topsliced, that they are inadequate in view of the scale of housing disrepair and that it is anti-council housing. This book has shown (apart from the fact that there is a series of other elements which are just as important) that while the first two issues may be correct, despite its remit, the third is far from clear-cut (see also Table 9.1). The essential point to note is that it is simplistic to try to conclude on whether the EA initiative is 'pro-' or 'anti-' council housing. The evidence presented in this book clearly demonstrates that although the programme is highly politicized, both views of EA are partly true. EA can and sometimes does, work against local determination of housing policy. However, housing authorities can also and have, made the initiative work for themselves and their tenants.

9.3 Implications for the theoretical context

This work has not sought a direct appraisal of theory. Although there has been a discussion of theories of the local state and central-local relations, this is meant to provide a conceptual backdrop, rather than a rigid theoretical perspective. However, this section presents an attempt to link the overview of the main findings of the book to the theoretical perspectives introduced earlier in the book (chapter 3). This link is attempted via reference to each of the theoretical concepts so as to draw out the implications of the research for the theories.

1. As far as the *'Agent/Partner'* debate is concerned, using Estate Action as an example of a central housing policy, the main finding is that local government is neither agent nor partner, but both in different contexts and

at different times. This dichotomy is also unhelpful because it ignores the crucial function performed by another level in the governmental framework, namely the role of the DoE Regional Offices in the EA initiative, its degree of flexibility, decision-making and impact. The research has also demonstrated that authorities have the option of either ignoring central government initiatives/policy, or of only implementing those aspects which are acceptable to its local electorate/local policy thus resisting central control and maintaining their own agenda. Beyond a certain time, the pressures may become too great, especially if there are few or no alternative financial sources to tap into.

2. The *'Dual State Thesis'* acknowledges that state activities have greatly increased, that the 'state' is organizationally complex and fragmented into elected branches (such as local government) and non-elected branches (such as EA Central and the Regional Offices) which is more in line with the EA policy context. It argues that state intervention at central level occurs through a process of corporatist mediation and is primarily concerned with social investment. This may well be the case since EA can be seen as being about investing in social housing and the evidence of chapter 4 has pointed out the government's obvious concern about the inner city riots of the 1980s and the need to direct further resources in the direction of public housing estates. The Dual State Thesis argues that at the local level, however, state activity is geared towards social consumption by individuals or sections of the population and that such policies are developed through a process of neo-pluralist activity at the local level and is addressed at issues of social rights and needs (Saunders, 1984; 1986).

The research suggests that this process may not be very applicable with respect to certain central government policies. The EA initiative, its policies, funds, aims and organization were all centrally determined. In part it was designed to address the centrally defined issue of directing a greater amount of resources to the 69 authorities in greatest need of them. Local authorities were perceived as not wanting to invest more of their resources in run-down estates. Through policies such as the EA initiative, Saunders' locally based 'consumption classes' (such as council tenants) are by-passed by centrally prescribed policies, even though such policies may be aimed at this particular consumption class.

This is certainly the case for the great majority of council tenants because only those tenants who live in estates which conform to EA's eligibility criteria are 'enfranchised' by such initiatives (and then only indirectly), and able to influence the policy process. Any additional investment allocations which authorities obtain from EA are determined by central priorities and since local authorities are expected to contribute to EA schemes, their 'free' (HIPs) resources are also directed in the manner that central government desires. In this case, central government wishes only local authority tenants who live in EA designated authorities and estates to be consulted in the policy process, but the general council tenant and the rest of the local government electorate is not involved. Even within this sub-set of council tenants, the options and opportunities are also largely centrally determined. EA may wish those tenants to be consulted but it will not necessarily support whatever the tenant associations or the majority of tenants wish. Neo-pluralist perspectives can thus be applied only in a very limited manner.

It would be true to argue that local politicians are involved in deciding whether to be involved with the EA initiative or not. It has even been suggested in the research that it tends to be the ward represented by the local Chair of Housing which benefits most from EA support, implying that local politicians have some control over where the greatest emphasis is to lie in terms of EA bids. Nevertheless, this is not to imply that EA related policies arise primarily through competitive political activity or that activity in run-down estates is necessarily influenced by the locally-based council housing consumption classes, therefore, the concept does not appear to be applicable with respect to the operation of EA. Policy and priorities, as regards EA investment and schemes, is centrally determined. The key local concern in co-operating with EA, has always been that through the initiative, authorities might be able to obtain additional housing investment. However this decision also brings with it major implications for the direction of housing policy and housing investment which in part, wrests control away from local politicians, local consumption classes or whatever the local policy basis (even if it conformed to local policies).

3. A similar conclusion may be reached as regards those theories which point to the importance of *'Uneven Social Development'* or the importance of 'local variation' in determining outcome. Dickens *et al.* (1985) argue that it is crucially important to analyze local social relations and the nature of local social institutions, as these influence the form and course of housing action. EA by-passes local variation and social processes. Local consumers such as housing tenants may have genuine local grievances, address their actions at local state institutions such as local housing departments and it may also be the case that (p.233):

> Each episode also needs to be understood as something with a complex pre-history and equally complex wider implications both for housing consumers themselves and for the shape of housing consumption.

However, no matter what the general history of local politics or the specific previous actions of council tenants as regards rents, squatting and other protests, the history of these will not determine local actions with regard to certain policies such as the EA initiative. The initial targeting of 69 authorities was done on the basis of the local situation (annual HIPs returns), but this dealt with indicators such as the level of voids, arrears and difficult-to-let properties which were compared nationally and not on the basis of other relevant factors such as history of tenant activity or balance of local politics. EA criteria were all centrally defined and there was no consultation with either ROs or local authorities (see chapter 4). Local politicians had little say in the process except in whether to accept or reject EA involvement, and even here, we have seen that authorities have increasingly had little financial choice but to accept involvement in EA. Once agreed, the housing officers are allowed to determine which estates and schemes to bid for, however, these are made within the boundaries specified by EA criteria. Local processes of variation and history are thus by-passed, except where they run tangentially to EA's priorities.

This is not to deny completely the persuasive arguments that the housing question itself will vary according to time and space and that it is unrealistic to suppose that local variations have no local effects. There is still local variation. For example, because of its decentralized neighbourhood structure, the London Borough of Tower Hamlets makes a much larger number of bids than other authorities and partly as a result, it has also been disproportionately successful in gaining EA support (see Pinto, 1992d, Appendix 8). Nevertheless, initiatives such as EA work against the importance of local variation and the relevance of historical factors, because the agenda for action and the policy alternatives are reduced to those determined and laid out nationally by EA.

Local authorities which follow the desires of their politicians in responding to activities on the part of their tenants' and their requests, for example for intensive management structures, may be successful in biding for EA resources once or twice (and then only because that particular local priority coincides with EA's own aims). Nevertheless, although that authority may be responding to local circumstances, it will find that EA will not support many more such bids unless the authority is prepared to introduce other aspects which EA espouses, such as private sector involvement or the creation of management co-operatives. This may run completely counter to local policies and residents' wishes, however, there may well be little choice in the matter if the authority hopes to attract further EA support in order to maintain and improve its run-down estates.

4. Section 3.3 also discussed the relevance of the 'Sub-Central Government' literature generally and then 'fitted' the housing context within this literature by arguing that the notion of policy communities is particularly relevant and highlighting Houlihan's (1988) conception of the Housing Policy Community. Some conclusions may also be drawn as regards the operation of the EA policy community (see Figures 3.1, 3.3 and 9.1):

Firstly, some elements of the EA policy community are more relevant than others. The private sector was hardly of any importance and generally only became involved at the request of local authorities (at tender stage) and the relationship was contractual in nature. The trade unions were similarly unimportant as very few jobs were created anew for EA schemes. In the great majority of cases, posts were simply decentralized and in one of the case-studies, the officers had the option of moving back to their old posts if so desired (see previous discussion in chapter 8).

Turning to the Local Authority Associations (LAAs) and the Housing Consultative Council (HCC), these have not been very effective since the late 1970s and their role was similarly marginal with respect to EA. This is by no means surprising given the political climate as regards the notions of consultation and corporatism (see Rhodes, 1988). The HCC did try to bring attention to EA's less than perfect operation (see HCC, mimeo), however, this did not get far and it was completely ineffectual in influencing the way EA operates. Firstly, the DoE and EA Central largely ignored it and secondly, the authorities found other, more powerful allies in attempting to influence central government policy. This role has largely been taken over by the Regional Offices for two reasons. Section 7.2 has discussed the ambiguity of the Regional Offices' role. This has meant that they have served as a direct and vocal route (for local authorities) into EA Central. Also the Regional Offices have long felt that they could perform certain roles more effectively without EA Central supervision or control (chapter 7). Taken together, these two issues have meant that local authorities found a much more effective ally in the Regional Offices, rather than through the traditional route of the LAAs and the largely defunct HCC.

There was virtually no professional conflict between the various local government departments in an attempt to protect their policy 'turf'. The 'lead' role in dealing with, co-ordinating and erecting EA schemes was always taken by the housing department with a great deal of co-operation from the other departments (particularly finance and planning), once they became aware of the quirks of the EA initiative, not least its timetable.

The EA policy community is not static and has evolved. There are several components to this issue: firstly, local authorities have come to accept that EA is not going to disappear, that it can provide crucial resources, that they need to work with it and they have also began to get used to EA's operational mechanism and to adjust accordingly. Nevertheless because EA's operation was so different from what they were hitherto accustomed, there has been a 'learning curve' involved in dealing with initiatives such as EA and over time, authorities have been able to modify their operation and procedures in order to create greater flexibility and thus make better use of the EA initiative. This has also made the process of implementation smoother.

Another important finding is that while the literature has been at pains to stress the fact at the Regional Offices have more than a passive, implementing and mediating role (see chapter 7; Young, 1982; Houlihan, 1983; 1984; and Rhodes, 1988). An interesting development which has not been picked up, is that the DoE ROs have almost 'usurped' EA Central with regard to the EA initiative. The important point is that rather than merely administering the more mundane aspects of EA, the ROs have been able to amass a greater degree of autonomy at the expense of EA Central. Over time, EA Central has been persuaded of the fact that the work load was becoming unrealistic for a small central team and that the ROs would be better placed to control various operations of the EA scheme.

More and more powers and functions have been devolved and in due course, EA Central will only retain control of overall policy to ensure consistency and direction in what is after all, a national housing policy. The ROs now have a fair degree of power and have moved far beyond being largely concerned with informing authorities of the existence and role of the EA initiative. They now administer most of the operational matters, monitor the progress of schemes, have complete control over continuation funding schemes and have recently acquired final decision-making over new schemes. EA Central has been forced into a position where it had to accept this progression, in part because the Regional Offices became so adept at this new role; partly because they were soon overwhelmed by the amount of bids and paperwork involved in the various application forms; and partly because local authorities were keen on and encouraged such a process (see the contrast of Figure 3.1 and Figure 9.1). Essentially, EA is only left with a policy-making or strategic role, however, as discussed above, this can be seen as a positive development.

Lastly, with its new emphasis on large 'enterprise' initiatives involving the generation of employment and training elements within the housing schemes, the EA policy community is set to change radically. In future the EA initiative will undoubtedly come into greater contact with institutions with which it has had limited contact thus far, such as the House Builders' Federation, the Housing Corporation and the National Federation of Housing Associations. This will require EA Central and the Regional Offices to be able to operate interactively with these organizations whilst not jeopardizing their contacts with local authorities and being able to meet tenants' needs and aspirations (see Figure 9.2). The EA initiative will need to become involved with private, voluntary and central organizations (such as Training and Enterprise Councils, The Department of Trade and Industry; the Department of Employment and the Home Office), all of which have a legitimate interest in public housing estates. How EA handles this transition will determine its future viability.

9.4 Future research

This research has made a detailed examination of the Estate Action initiative. From its findings a number of fertile avenues for future research can be explored:

• *Privatization:* various chapters have discussed the fact that authorities have become more willing to pursue EA's controversial elements over time, therefore, an important question is whether public/private partnerships in general and privatization in particular, will accelerate under greater fiscal restriction.

• *The effects on (other) estates:* Estate Action is targeted at the most problematic council estates but little is known of the effects of such a policy on the 'intermediate' estates, in terms of resource allocation, management and maintenance. A key question is whether finite resources are merely displaced and the same malign process of neglect starts elsewhere both within and between the authorities. Greater attention must also be given to the opportunity costs associated with EA HIPs.

• *Enterprise/employment generation:* Economic development has largely by-passed council estates where the skill and employment levels remain low. Employment generation is now EA's overriding commitment and although laudable in principle, one must examine why this has occurred, its scope, ease of implementation and effectiveness. Attention must also be focused on issues such as educational attainment and skill levels so as to determine ways of improving both.

• *Partnership and co-ordination:* Enterprise initiatives inevitably depend upon effective co-ordination between various agencies such as government departments, local authorities, voluntary and community organizations and Training and Enterprise Councils (see Figure 9.2). Workable and effective partnerships will be of crucial importance in the future and an analysis must be made of similar policies (such as inner city policy involving a multi-organizational context) to learn the key lessons and to incorporate them for the benefit of the EA initiative.

Bibliography

Allen, J. and Hamnett, C. (eds.) (1991) *Housing and Labour Markets: Building the connections*, London, Unwin Hyman.

Anderson, J., Duncan, S.S. and Hudson, R. (eds.) (1983) *Redundant Spaces in Cities and Regions*, London, Academic Press.

Andrews, C.L. (1979) *Tenant and Town Hall*, London, HMSO.

Archbishop of Canterbury's Commission on Urban Priority Areas (1985) *Faith in the City: A call for action by church and nation*, London, Central Board of Finance of the Church of England.

Architects' Journal (1986) "Privatising the Public Sector", 20 & 27 August, Vol. 184, Nos. 34 & 35.

AMA (Association of Metropolitan Authorities) (1983) *Defects in Housing 1: Non-traditional Dwellings of the 1940s and 1950s*, London, AMA.

AMA (1984) *Defects in Housing 2: Industrialised and System-built Dwellings in the 1960s and 1970s*, London, AMA.

AMA (1985) *Defects in Housing 3: Repair and Modernisation of Traditionally Built Dwellings*, London, AMA.

AMA (mimeo a) *Letter by AMA Chairman (Mr Maurice Barnes) to the Minister for Housing and Planning*, (Mr William Waldegrave MP), dated 9.Dec.1987.

AMA (mimeo b) *Housing Investment Programme: 1988/89*, Housing Circular 79/1987, AMA.

Audit Commission for Local Authorities in England and Wales (1984) *Bringing Council Tenants' Arrears Under Control*, London, HMSO.

Audit Commission (1986a) *Managing the Crisis in Council Housing*, London, HMSO.

Audit Commission (1986b) *The Management of London's Authorities: Preventing the Breakdown of Services*, London, HMSO.

Audit Commission (1986c) *Improving Council Housing Maintenance*, London, HMSO.

Aughton, H. [2nd ed.] (1986) *Housing Finance: A Basic Guide,* London, Shelter.

Balchin, P. N. [2nd ed.] (1989) *Housing Policy: An introduction*, London, Routledge.

Ball, M. (1983) *Housing Policy and Economic Power: The political economy of owner occupation*, London, Methuen.

Ball, M., Harloe, M. and Martens, M. (1988) *Housing and social change in Europe and the USA,* London, Routledge.

Bassett, K. and Short, J. (1980) *Housing and Residential Structure*, London, Routledge & Keegan Paul.

Bennett R.J. (ed.) (1990) *Decentralisation, Local Government and Markets: Towards a post-welfare agenda?,* Oxford, University Press.

Benson, J. (1982) "A framework for policy analysis" in Rogers, D., Whitton, D. *et al.* , *Interorganisational Coordination*, Ames, Iowa, Iowa State University Press, pp137-76.

Birchall, J. (1988) *Building Communities the Co-operative Way*, London, Routledge & Kegan Paul.

Boddy, M. (1980) *The Building Societies*, London, Macmillan.

Boddy, M. and Fudge, C. (eds.) (1984) *Local Socialism?,* London, Macmillan.

Bonnerjea, L. (1987) *The Future of Social Housing*, London School of Economics, Department of Social Science and Administration, Discussion Paper No. 1, April 1987.

Bramley, G., Leather, P. and Hill, M. (1981) *Developments in Housing Finance,* Working Paper No. 24, Bristol, Bristol University, School of Advanced Urban Studies.

Brindley, T. and Stoker, G. (1988) "Housing Renewal Policy in the 1980s: The scope and limitations of privatisation", *Local Government Studies*, 14(5), pp45-67.

Bulos, M. and Walker, S. (eds.) (1987) *The Legacy and Opportunity for High Rise Housing in Europe: The management of innovation*, London, Housing Studies Group, Polytechnic of the South Bank.

Burbidge, M., Curtis, A., Kirby, K., and Wilson, S. (1981) *An Investigation of Difficult to Let Housing: Vol. 1 General Findings; Vol. 2: Case Studies of Post-War Estates; Vol. 3: Case Studies of Pre-War Estates*, London, HMSO.

Cameron, S.J. (1987) *Recent Approaches to Problem Council Housing in Tyneside*, Newcastle University, Department of Town and Country Planning, Working Paper Series No. 3.

Cantle, T. (1986) "The Deterioration of Public Housing" in Malpass, P. (ed.) *The Housing Crisis*, London, Croom Helm, pp67-85.

CES (Centre for Environmental Studies) (1984) *Outer Estates in Britain: interim report - comparison of 4 outer estates*, Paper 23, London, CES.

CHAC (Housing Management Sub-Committee of the Central Housing Advisory Committee of the Ministry of Housing and Local Government) (1945) *Management of Municipal Housing Estates: Second report*, London, HMSO.
CHAC (1953) *Living in Flats,* London, HMSO.
CHAC (1955) *Unsatisfactory Tenants: Sixth report*, London, HMSO.
CHAC (1953) *Councils and their Houses: Eighth report*, London, HMSO.
Chandler, L.A. (1988) *Public Policy-Making for Local Government*, London, Croom Helm.
Clapham, D. and Maclennan, D. (1983) "Residualisation of public housing: A non-issue", *Housing Review*, 32, pp9-10.
Clapham, D. and Kintrea, K. (1986) "Rationing, Choice and Constraint: The allocation of public housing in Glasgow", *Journal of Social Policy*, 15, pp51-67.
Clapham, D., Kemp, P. and Kintrea, K. (1987) "Co-operative Ownership of Former Council Housing", *Policy and Politics*, Vol. 15(4), pp207- 220.
Clapham, D. and English, J. (eds.) (1987) *Public Housing: Current Trends and Future Developments*, London, Croom Helm.
Clapham, D. (1987a) "Trends in Housing Management" in Clapham, D. and English, J. (1987).
Clapham, D. (1987b) "The New Face of Public Housing" in Clapham, D. and English, J. (1987).
Clapham, D. (1989) *Goodbye Council Housing?*, The Fabian Series, London, Hutchinson.
Cochrane, A. (1985) "The Attack on Local Government: What it is and what it isn't", *Critical Social Policy*, Issue 12, Vol. 4 (3).
Cockburn, C. (1977) *The Local State,* London, Pluto Press.
Coleman, A. (1985) *Utopia on trial: Vision and Reality in Planned Housing*, London, Hilary Shipman.
Coleman, D. A. (1988) *Housing Policy: Unfinished business*, London, Bow Publications.
Coleman, D. A.(1989) "The New Housing Policy - a critique", *Housing Studies*, Vol. 4(1), pp44-57.
Cooper, S. (1985) *Public Housing and Private Property*, London, Gower.
Cullingworth, J.B. (1966) *Housing and Local Government*, London, Allen & Unwin.
DoE (Department of the Environment) (1977) *Housing Policy: A Consultative Document*, London, HMSO.
DoE (1978) *Organising a Comprehensive Housing Service*, London, HMSO.
DoE (1982) *English House Condition Survey 1981 Part 1,* Report of the Physical Conditions Survey, London, HMSO.
DoE (1985a) *The Urban Housing Renewal Unit,* London, HMSO.
DoE (1985b) *New Homes from Old: Urban Housing Renewal Unit,* London, HMSO.

DoE (1986) *Urban Housing Renewal Unit Annual report 1985-86*, London, HMSO.
DoE (1987a) *Estate Action 2nd Annual Report 1986-87*, London, HMSO
DoE (1987b) *An Inquiry into the Condition of the Local Authority Housing Stock in England 1985*, London, HMSO;
DoE (1987c) *The PEP Guide to Local Housing Management Vols. 1 to 3*, London, HMSO.
DoE (1988a) *Estate Action 3rd Annual Report 1987-88*, London, HMSO.
DoE (1988b) *New Financial Regime for Local Housing Authorities: A consultation paper*, London, HMSO.
DoE (1989a) *Estate Action 4th Annual Report 1988-89*, London, HMSO.
DoE (1989b) *Handbook of Estate Improvement: Appraising Options*, London, HMSO.
DoE (1990a) *Estate Action 5th Annual Report 1989-90*, London, HMSO.
DoE (1990b) *Handbook of Estate Improvement: External Areas*, London, HMSO.
DoE (1990c) *Handbook of Estate Improvement: Dwellings*, HMSO.
DoE (undated) *A Guide to Community Refurbishment Schemes*, London, HMSO.
Dickens, P., Duncan, S.S., Goodwin, M. and Gray, F. (1985) *Housing, States and Localities*, London, Methuen.
Doling, J. and Davies, M. (1984) *Public Control of Privately Rented Housing*, Aldershot, Gower.
Doling, J., Ford, J. and Stafford, B. (1988) *The Property Owning Democracy*, Aldershot, Avebury.
Donnison, D. and Ugerson, C. (1982) *Housing Policy*, London, Penguin.
Duncan, S. and Kirby, K. (1983) *Preventing Rent Arrears*, London, HMSO.
Duncan, S.S. and Goodwin, M. (1982) "The local state and restructuring social relations: theory and practice", *International Journal of Urban Regional Research*, Vol. 6, pp157-85.
Duncan, S.S. and Goodwin, M. (1988) *The Local State and Uneven Development: Behind the local government crisis*, Cambridge, Polity Press
Dunleavy, P. (1980) *Urban Political Analysis*, London, Macmillan.
Dunleavy, P. (1981) *The Politics of Mass Housing in Britain, 1945-75*, Oxford, Clarendon Press.
Dunleavy, P. (1984) "The Limits to Local Government" in Boddy, M. and Fudge, C. (1984) pp49-81.
Dunleavy, P. and O'Leary, B. (1987) *Theories of the State: The politics of liberal democracy*, Basingstoke, Macmillan Education.
English, J. (ed.) (1982) *The Future of Council Housing*, London, Croom Helm.
Flynn, R. (1986) "Urban Politics the Local State and Consumption: The problem in recent social and political theory" in Goldsmith, M. and Villadsen, S. (1986).

Forrest, R. and Murie, A. (1983) "Residualisation and Council Housing: Aspects of Changing Social Relations of Housing and Tenure", *Journal of Social Policy,* 12, pp453-68.

Forrest, R. and Murie, A. (1984) *Right to buy? Issues of Need, Equity and Polarisation in the Sale of Council Houses,* University of Bristol, SAUS.

Forrest, R. (1987) "Privatisation, Marginality and Council Housing" in Clapham, D. and English, J. (1987) pp67-85.

Forrest, R. and Murie, A. (1988) *Selling the Welfare State: The privatisation of public housing,* London, Routledge.

Forrest, R. and Murie, A. (1990) *Residualisation and Council Housing: A statistical Update*, School of Advanced Urban Studies, Working Paper No. 91.

Gay, O. (1985) *Housing Investment Programmes and Capital Receipts*, Background Paper No. 162, London, House of Commons Library Research Division.

Gay, O. (1988) *Council Housing: does it have a future?,* Background Paper No. 213, London, House of Commons Library Research Division.

Gay, O. (1989) *Housing Associations,* Background Paper No. 227, London, House of Commons Library Research Division.

Gibson, M. (1986) "Housing Renewal: Privatisation and Beyond", in Malpass, P. (1986), pp86-124.

Gifford, Lord (1986) *The Broadwater Farm Inquiry Report,* London, Borough of Haringey.

Gifford, Lord (1989) *Broadwater Farm Revisited,* London, Karia Press.

Ginsburgh, N. (1989) "The Housing Act,1988 and its Policy Context: A critical commentary", *Critical Social Policy,* Issue 25, Vol. 9(1), pp56-81.

Glennerster, H. (1990) "A Decentralised Housing Service: What Does it Mean?" in R.J. Bennett (1990), pp207-220.

Glennerster, H., Power, A. and Travers, T. (1989) *A New Era for Social Policy: A new enlightenment or a new Leviathan?,* Welfare State Programme Discussion Paper No. 39, STICERD, London, LSE.

Goldsmith, M. and Villadsen, S. [(eds.) (1986) *Urban Political Theory and the Management of Fiscal Stress,* Aldershot, Gower.

Grant, C. (1988) "Old HAT?", *Roof,* 13(4), pp22-24.

Griffiths, D. and Holmes, C. (1985) *A New Labour Housing Policy*, Fabian Tract 505, London, Fabian Society.

Gross, S. and Lansley, S. (1981) *What Price Housing?*, London, SHAC.

Ham, C. and Hill, M. (1984) *The Policy Process in the Modern Capitalist State,* Whitstable, Harvester Press.

Hambleton, R. (1983) "Planning Systems and Policy Implementation", *Journal of Public Policy,* Vol. 3, pp397-418.

Hambleton, R. and Hoggett, P. (eds.) (1984) *Decentralisation and Democracy: Localising Public Services,* Occasional Paper 28, Bristol University, SAUS.

Hambleton, R. and Hoggett, P. (1987) *The Politics of Decentralisation: Theory and Practice of a Radical Local Government Initiative,* Working Paper 46, Bristol University, SAUS.

Hamnett, C. and Randolph, B. (1987) "The Residualisation of Council Housing in Inner London 1971-81", in Clapham, D. and English, J. (1987), pp32-50.

Hardcastle, P. (1986) "Going Private", *Building Refurb.,* Vol. 6, pp40-41.

Harloe, M. (1988) "The Changing Role of Social Rented Housing", in Ball, M., Harloe, M. and Martens, M. (1988).

Healy, P., McDougall, G. and Thomas, M.J. (eds.) (1982) *Planning Theory: prospects for the 1990s,* Oxford, Pergamon Press.

Henney, A. (1985) *Trusts the Tenant: Devolving municipal housing,* No. 68, London, Centre for Policy Studies.

Hills, J. (1987) *Subsidies to social housing in England: their behavioural implications,* Welfare State Programme Paper no.24, STICERD, London, LSE.

Hills, J. (1988) *Twenty-first century housing subsidies: durable rent-fixing and subsidy arrangements for social housing,* Welfare State Programme Paper No. 33, STICERD, London, LSE.

H.M. Treasury (1986) *The Government's Expenditure Plans 1986-87 to 1988-89*, London, HMSO.

H.M. Treasury (1990) *The Government's Expenditure Plans 1990-91 to 1992-93*, London, HMSO.

Hogwood, B.W., and Keating, M. (eds.) (1982) *Regional Government in England,* Oxford, Clarendon Press.

Holmans, A. (1987) *Housing Policy in Britain,* London, Croom Helm.

Hough, M. and Mayhew, P. (1983) *The British Crime Survey,* Home Office Research Study: 76, London, HMSO.

Houlihan, B. (1983) "The Professionalisation of Housing Policy Making: The impact of housing investment programmes and professionals", *Public Administration Bulletin,* No. 41, April.

Houlihan, B. (1984) "The Regional Offices of the DoE - Policemen or Mediators? Study of Local Housing Policy", *Public Administration,* Vol. 62, pp401-421.

Houlihan, B. (1988) *Housing Policy and Central-Local Government Relations,* Aldershot, Gower.

HCC (Housing Consultative Council) (mimeo) *The operation of Estate Action/ Urban Housing Renewal Unit,* paper by ALA, AMA & LBA, (HCC (HIP) (87) (17)).

HRG (Housing Research Group) (1981) *Could Local Authorities be Better Landlords?,* London, City University.

HSAG (Housing Services Advisory Group) (1978) *Organising a Comprehensive Housing Service,* London, HMSO.

Hughes, D.J. (2nd ed.) (1987) *Public Sector Housing Law,* London, Butterworths.

Institute of Housing (1987) *Preparing for Change,* London, Institute of Housing.

Johnston, R.J. (1971) *Urban Residential Patterns,* London, Bell.

Jones, G. W. and Stewart, J. (2nd ed.) (1985) *The Case for Local Government,* London, Allen & Unwin.

Karn, V. (1985) "Housing", in Ranson, S., Jones, G. and Walsh, K. (1985), pp163-184.

Karn, V. (1988) "The Baby in the Bathwater? Housing reform 1988", *Housing Review,* Vol. 37(3), pp85-89.

Kirby, K., Finch, H. and Wood, D. (1988) *The Organisation of Housing Management in English Local Authorities,* London, HMSO.

Kleinman, M. (1988) *The changing role of council housing in England: a study of supply, access and allocation, 1976-1985,* Unpublished Ph.D., London School of Economics, London.

Laffin, M. (1985) *Professionalism and Policy in Central-Local Government Relations,* Farnborough, Gower Press.

Lavery, C. (1987) "The Legacy of High Rise", *Housing and Planning Review Special,* Vol. 42(1), pp4-8.

Lawless, P. (1988) "British Inner Urban Policy Post 1979: A critique", *Policy and Politics,* Vol. 16(4), pp261-275.

Lenaghan, J.P. (1986) *The Priority Estates Project: analysis of its origins, development and implementation,* MSc. Policy Studies, Bristol University, SAUS.

LHU (London Housing Unit) (1987a) *Tenants' Choice: New initiatives in London's public housing,* London, LHU.

LHU (1987b) *Coops in Local Authority Housing,* London, LHU.

LHU (mimeo) *Notes on the Estate Action seminar held by the Department of Environment for the London Associations,* LHU, 19th Feb. 1988

Loughlin, M. (1986) *Local Government in Modern States,* London, Sweet & Maxwell.

McArthur, A. and McGregor, A. (1989) "Regenerating Public Sector Estates: The role of community enterprise", *Local Economy,* Vol. 14(1), pp29-43.

Maclennan, D. *et al.* (1989) *The Nature and Effectiveness of Housing Management in England: A report to the Department of the Environment,* London, HMSO.

McCoshan, A. and Pinto, R.R. (eds.) (1991) *Past Experiences and Possible Scenarios for Local Services*, LSE Geography Department Working Paper, No. 24.

McFarlane, R. (1986) *Councils Support Coops,* CLES Report 2, Manchester, CLES.

Macey, J. (1982) *Housing Management,* London, The Estates Gazette.

Malpass, P. (ed.) (1986) *The Housing Crisis,* London, Croom Helm.

Malpass, P. and Murie, A. (2nd ed.) (1987) *Housing Policy and Practice,* Macmillan Education.

Malpass, P. (1990) *Reshaping Housing Policy: Subsidies, rents and residualisation,* London, Routledge.

Mason, D. (1989) "Keeping on the Right", *Housing Review,* Vol. 38(4), pp97-99.

Meehan, C. (1988) *Trying it on: Housing Action Trusts (HATS): the struggle begins,* London, London Housing Unit/Shelter.

Merrett, S. (1979) *State Housing in Britain,* London, Routledge & Kegan Paul.

Minford, P., Peel, M. and Ashton, P. (1987) *The Housing Morass: regulation, immobility and unemployment,* Hobart Paperback 25, London, Institute of Economic Affairs.

National Consumer Council (1979) *Soonest Mended: A review of repair, maintenance and improvement of council housing,* London, NCC.

National Federation of Housing Associations (1985) *Inquiry into British Housing* , Chaired by HRH Duke of Edinburgh - (1): *The Evidence,* London, NFHA.

National Federation of Housing Associations (1986) *Inquiry into British Housing*, Chaired by HRH The Duke of Edinburgh (2): *Supplement,* London, NFHA.

Pinto, R.R. (1990) "An Evaluation of the Estate Action Initiative: Aims versus achievements", *Housing Review,* Vol. 39(2), pp45-48.

Pinto, R.R. (1991a) "Centre/Local Interaction in Renovating Run-down Estates: The view of local housing authorities on the Estate Action initiative", *Local Government Studies,* Jan/Feb, Vol. 17(1), pp45-62.

Pinto, R.R. (1991b) "The Revolution in Social Housing?" in McCoshan, A. and Pinto, R.R. (eds.) *Past Experiences and Possible Scenarios for Local Services*, LSE Geography Department Working Paper, No. 24.

Pinto, R.R. (1991c) *Accessing the Long Term Urban Unemployed: Unlocking the potential in English social housing estates*, Centre for Economic Performance, Working Paper No. 145, London, LSE.

Pinto, R.R. (1991d) *Tackling Long Term Urban Unemployment: The Scottish Experience*, Centre for Economic Performance, Working Paper No. 146, London, LSE.

Pinto R.R. (1992a) *Duration of Unemployment and Housing Tenure: An Analysis of the Labour Force Survey*, Centre for Economic Performance, Working Paper No. 263, London, LSE.

Pinto R.R. (1992b) *Linking Problem Housing Estates to Labour Markets: A model of Employment and Training Initiatives*, Centre for Economic Performance, Working Paper No. 264, London, LSE.

Pinto, R.R. (1992c) *The Provision, Ownership and Management of Social Housing: Towards the renaissance of council housing in Britain?*, LSE Geography Department Working Paper, No. 25.

Pinto, R.R. (1992d) *The Impact of Estate Action on Developments in Council Housing, Management and Effectiveness*, Ph.D. Thesis, London School of Economics.

Pinto, R.R. (forthcoming) "An Analysis of the Impact of Estate Action Schemes", *Local Government Studies*

Power, A. (1984) *Local Housing Management: A Priority Estates Project Survey,* London, HMSO.

Power, A. (1987a) *The Crisis in Public Housing Management: Is Public Housing Manageable?,* Welfare State Discussion Paper No. 21, STICERD, London, LSE.

Power, A. (1987b) *Property Before People: the Management of Twentieth Century Council Housing,* London, Allen & Unwin.

Power, A. (1988) *Council Housing: Conflict, change and decision making,* Welfare State Discussion Paper No. 27, STICERD, London, LSE.

Power, A. with PEP Associates (1991) *Housing Management: A Guide to Quality and Creativity*, Hong Kong, Longman.

Ranson, S., Jones, G. and Walsh, K. (eds.) (1985) *Between Centre and Locality: The politics of public policy,* London, for the Institute of Local Government Studies, University of Birmingham [by] Allen & Unwin.

Rao, N. (1990) *The Changing Role of Local Housing Authorities: An interim assessment*, Policy Studies Institute for Joseph Rowntree Memorial Trust.

Reynolds, F. (1986) *The Problem Housing Estate: An account of Omega and its people,* London, Gower.

Rhodes, R.A.W. (1981) *Control and Power in Central-Local Government Relations,* Aldershot, Gower.

Rhodes, R.A.W. (1988) *Beyond Westminster and Whitehall: The sub-central governments of Britain,* London, Allen & Unwin.

Richardson, A. (1977) *Tenant Participation in Council Housing Management,* London, HMSO.

Roof (1989) "Social Housing - what's in a name?", *Roof,* March + April, pp14-37.

Saunders, P. (1984) "Rethinking Local Politics" in Boddy, M. and Fudge, C. (1984).

Saunders, P. (1986) "Reflections on the Dual Politics Thesis: The argument, its origins and its critics" in Godsmith, M. and Villadsen, S. (eds.) (1986).

Seabrook, J. (1984) *The Idea of Neighbourhood: What local politics should be about,* London, Pluto Press.

Scarman, Lord (1982) *The Brixton Disorders April 1981,* London, HMSO.

Short, J.R. (1982) *Housing in Britain - the Post-War experience,* London, Methuen.

Skilton, M. (1988) *A Better Reception: The development of concierge schemes,* London, HMSO.

Smith, M. (1989) (3rd ed.) *Guide to Housing*, London, Housing Centre Trust.

Stewart, J. (1988) *A New Management for Housing Departments,* Luton, Local Government Training Board.

Stewart, M. and Underwood, J. (1982) "Inner Cities: a multi-agency planning and implementation process", in Healy, P., McDougall, G. and Thomas, M.J. (1982)

Stoker, J. (1987)"Pulling in the Private Sector", *Housing,* Sept, pp33,37.

Taylor, T. (1989)"Estate Action - initiative or inertia?", *Roof,* May + June 89, p11.

Waldegrave, W. (mimeo) *Reply Letter to ALA Chairman (Mr Maurice Barnes),* 16.12.1987.

Warman, C. (1986) "A Report From the Cities", *House Builder,* Vol. 45(3), pp68-74.

Whitehead, C.M.E. and Kleinman, M. P. (1986) *Private Rented Housing in the 1980s and 1990s,* Department of Land Economy No. 17, Cambridge, Granta Editions / University of Cambridge.

Woof, B. (1987) "Estate Action", *Housing & Planning Review,* Vol. 42(2) pp10-12.

Young, S. (1982) "Regional Offices of the Department of the Environment: Their roles and influence in the 1970s", in Hogwood and Keating (1982).

Zipfel, T. (1989) *Estate Management Boards: An introduction*, London, Priority Estates Project.

49
50
100

100] - Conclusion = Poorly

255 = Figure 9.1

Figure 3.1

page [illegible]

Table 9.1

100] - Conclusion = Poetry

255 = Figure 9.1
Figure 3.1
page 81

Table 9.1